THE ASIAN SYNOD

Texts and Commentaries

Compiled and Edited by

PETER C. PHAN

Founded in 1970, Orbis Books endeavors to publish works that enlighten the mind, nourish the spirit, and challenge the conscience. The publishing arm of the Maryknoll Fathers & Brothers, Orbis seeks to explore the global dimensions of the Christian faith and mission, to invite dialogue with diverse cultures and religious traditions, and to serve the cause of reconciliation and peace. The books published reflect the views of their authors and do not represent the official position of the Society. To learn more about Maryknoll and Orbis Books, please visit our website at www.maryknoll.org.

Published by Orbis Books, Maryknoll, NY 10545-0308
Manufactured in the United States of America

Grateful acknowledgment is made to the following for permission to reprint previously published material:

East Asian Pastoral Review: Edmund Chia, "Of Fork and Spoon or Fingers and Chopsticks: Interreligious Dialogue in *Ecclesia in Asia,*" 37 (2000): 243–255; Peter C. Phan, "*Ecclesia in Asia:* Challenges for Asian Christianity," 37 (2000): 215–232; Luis Antonio Tagle, "The Challenges of Mission in Asia: A View from the Asian Synod," 35 (1998): 366–378.

Vidyajyoti: Journal of Theological Reflection: Michael Amaladoss, "Expectations from the Synod of Asia," 62 (1998): 144–151; Soosai Arokiasamy, "Synod for Asia: An Ecclesial Event of Communion and Shared Witness of Faith," 62/9 (1998): 666–675; Editorial, "An Ecclesial Event," 63/12 (1999); John Mansford Prior, "Unfinished Encounter: A Note on the Voice and Tone of *Ecclesia in Asia,*" 62/9 (1998): 654–665.

Libreria Editrice Vaticana: Post-Synodal Apostolic Exhortation: *Ecclesia in Asia,* November 9, 1999. Reprinted with permission.

Library of Congress Cataloging-in-Publication Data

Catholic Church. Synod of Asian Bishops (1998 : Rome, Italy)
  The Asian synod : texts and commentaries / compiled and edited by
Peter C. Phan.
    p. cm.
Includes index.
  ISBN 1-57075-429-2
  1. Catholic Church—Asia—Congresses. I. Phan, Peter C., 1943– II.
Title.
  BX1615.A1 C38 1998
  282'.5—dc21

                       2001007765

In gratitude to all the Vietnamese "simple faithful," especially Dong Men Thanh Gia [The Lovers of the Holy Cross], who have humbly and selflessly preserved and nurtured the faith of the Vietnamese Catholic Church since April 30, 1975.

Contents

Part One: The Preparatory Phase

Part Two: The Synod in Action

Preface

A persuasive case can be made that of all the five Special Assemblies of the Synod of Bishops that Pope John Paul II convoked to celebrate the coming of the third millennium of Christianity, the one for Asia (the "Asian Synod") was, theologically speaking, the most exciting.

The issues under discussion, like hand grenades, had to be handled with extreme care lest they blew up in one's face. Theological topics that had been debated among theologians in their recondite journals and books were now brought to the open forum:

- How to proclaim the uniqueness and universality of Jesus Christ as savior in Asia in the presence of the Buddha and other religious founders? More radically, can and should this claim about Jesus still be made?
- What can we say about the Church as the necessary means of salvation in light of other religions which, far from disappearing like darkness before the dazzling light of the Christian faith as past missionaries have confidently predicted, are as vibrant as ever, many of them older and more vigorous than Christianity itself, and continue to nourish billions of Asian souls among whom Christians are but the tiniest minority?
- Why is Jesus, who was born in Asia, still regarded by Asians as a stranger despite more than centuries of intense evangelization?
- Can inculturation, interreligious dialogue, and liberation of the poor and the marginalized be considered intrinsic parts of evangelization? If so, should they replace proclamation?

That these questions are burning issues in current theology can be seen from the recent Declaration of the Congregation of the Doctrine of the Faith, *Dominus Jesus* (August 6, 2000), which has aroused heated reactions among Christians, Catholic as well as non-Catholic, and followers of other religions.

The frankness (what the New Testament calls *parrhesia*) with which many Asian bishops expressed themselves during the synod, even in front of the pope, was alarming to some curial officials who wondered aloud about the legendary meekness of Asians. One bishop from Indonesia calmly reminded the Roman Curia, to its displeasure, that local dioceses are not its branch offices. Several bishops asked, with exasperation, why translations of liturgical texts into Asian languages, which have already been approved by their national episcopal conferences, still have to be approved by Rome whose "experts" know next to nothing about these languages and Asian cultures. Bishops of the Oriental Churches demanded a le-

gitimate autonomy in selecting their own bishops, without interference from the
Roman dicasteries. These expostulations were by no means tantrums from long
pent-up frustration. Rather, they are fundamental to the very survival of Christianity in Asia. Many bishops stated flatly that without a genuine inculturation of the
Christian faith into the Asian cultures—in theology, liturgy, indeed, in every aspect of church life—and without a humble dialogue with other religions and a
committed solidarity with the Asian poor, Christianity will simply have no future
in Asia in the next millennium. Furthermore, for the Asian bishops, these three
tasks of evangelization cannot be effectively carried out without the local
churches enjoying a genuine autonomy—within the *communio catholica.*

To help readers appreciate the impact of the Asian Synod, a highly selected
number of texts is presented here. The order is chronological, and the texts are
given as far as possible in their entirety rather than in short excerpts or summaries.
A few of them were classified *sub secreto* during the synod (and unnecessarily
so). Most of them were written in English, and are reproduced as they are, except
for inconsequential editorial emendations to correct obvious grammatical errors
and stylistic infelicities. A few were in French and Italian (one was even in
Latin!), and these have been translated by the editor.

Besides the official texts of the synod, some essays by Asian theologians that
deal with the synod have also been included to help understand its possible impact. Several of these theologians have pointed out that the voices of the Asian
bishops who spoke at the synod and their concerns are not the same as those of the
Apostolic Exhortation *Ecclesia in Asia* that purports "to share with the Church in
Asia and throughout the world the fruits of the Special Assembly" (no. 4). These
differences are visible when *Ecclesia in Asia* is compared with the Final Statement of the Seventh Assembly of the Federation of Asian Bishops' Conferences,
which was held a few months after the Asian Synod in Bangkok, Thailand. Be that
as it may, it is hoped that the documents here gathered will help readers form an
accurate idea of the challenges facing Asian Christianity in the twenty-first century and of the theologies and pastoral initiatives proposed by the leaders of the
Asian Churches to meet them.

It is my great pleasure to mention here a number of people who have been of
great help to me in composing this book. Unfortunately, the person to whom I
owe the greatest debt will have to remain unnamed. Indeed, that person was willing to help me only under condition of anonymity. Suffice it to say that without
that person I would not have had access to all the synodal documents classified as
sub secreto. To you, my friend, heartfelt thanks! I also thank my graduate assistant, Jonathan Tan, who is an expert in Asian theology in his own right, for his
prompt and efficient help in gathering some materials for this book. To Sue Perry,
editor at Orbis Books, my gratitude for her persistent and gentle encouragement.
To Catherine Costello, my thanks for supervising the production of the volume.
And, finally, thanks are rendered to all the authors whose articles appear in this
volume and whose wisdom and insights are deeply treasured.

If the last three decades of the twentieth century of the Christian era belonged
to Latin America with its liberation theologies, Asia, with its theologies of incul-

turation and interreligious dialogue, seems poised to capture the attention of the Church in the first decades of the twenty-first. The Asian Synod marked the coming of age of the Asian Churches. But it is only a beginning, though a very propitious one. It is hoped that this book, which records its gestation, birth, and growth, will serve as a useful guide to Christians, in Asia as well as in other continents, in their pilgrimage toward the reign of God, which is the only goal of Christian mission.

Peter C. Phan
The Catholic University of America

Abbreviations

Besides the common abbreviations for biblical books, the following abbreviations are used:

AG: *Ad Gentes*

BIMA: Bishops' Institute of Missionary Apostolate

BIRA: Bishops' Institute for Interreligious Affairs

CL: *Christifideles Laici*

CPCO: Conseil des Patriarches Catholiques d'Orient

EA: *Ecclesia in Asia*

EAPR: *East Asian Pastoral Review*

FABC: Federation of Asian Bishops' Conferences

GS: *Gaudium et Spes*

LG: *Lumen Gentium*

NA: *Nostra Aetate*

RM: *Redemptoris Missio*

VJTR: *Vidyajyoti: Journal of Theological Reflection*

Prayer for the Special Assembly
of the Synod of Bishops for Asia

Lord Jesus Christ, Our Savior,
You loved the world so much
that You took upon Yourself all its sin and suffering;
You brought them to the Cross
so as to give eternal life to all humanity,
through the mystery of your death and resurrection.
On the occasion of the Special Assembly of the Synod of Bishops for Asia,
we pray from the depths of our being:
"Come, Lord Jesus! Come, to abide with us
   your people;
Come, to teach us your Gospel of Life; Come, to assist us to continue
your mission of love and service in Asia.
We gather around Mary, your Mother,
to pray that You pour out your life-giving Spirit on us
so that the continent of Asia may experience a New Pentecost.
May each of us, thus inspired and strengthened, work together to build, through
   word and
example, the civilization of love
where charity triumphs over selfishness, peace over war, and unity over division.
We ask You to hear our prayer, Lord Jesus,
You, Who live and reign with the Father and the Holy Spirit,
One God for ever and ever. Amen."

Introduction:
"A Moment of Grace"

Summarizing the Special Assembly of the Synod of Bishops for Asia, the Asian Synod for short, Pope John Paul II described it as "a moment of grace because it was an encounter with the Savior, who continues to be present in his church through the power of the Holy Spirit, experienced in a fraternal dialogue of life, communion and mission."[1] The "encounter with the Savior" is, of course, not the sole reason why the Asian Synod was a grace-filled event, not only for Asian Christianity but also for the universal Church, but it does highlight well the central theme the pope chose for the Asian Synod, namely, "Jesus Christ the Savior and his mission of love and service in Asia."[2]

Synods of Bishops to Celebrate the Great Jubilee of the Year 2000

John Paul II's interest in the Jubilee Year at the end of the second millennium of Christianity has been long-standing and deep. In his very first encyclical, he spoke explicitly of the Great Jubilee of the year 2000, suggesting that the time leading to it be lived as "a new Advent."[3] He even made the task of future historians of his papacy somewhat easier by stating flatly that "preparing the *Year 2000 has become as it were a hermeneutical key of my Pontificate.*"[4] Part of the preparations for the Great Jubilee was the convocation of five continental Special Synods of Bishops: Africa (1994), America (1997), Asia (1998), Oceania (1998), and Europe (1999).[5] The Synod of Bishops is a permanent institution established by Pope Paul VI in 1965 to foster the unity and collaboration of bishops around the world with the Holy See. It meets occasionally, at the pope's convocation, to discuss issues of relevance to the universal Church.[6] The Asian Synod brought together for the first time three groups of churches whose major common denominator is their location in what is known as Asia: the Near and Middle East, the Indian subcontinent, and Central Asia and the Far East.[7] Historically, the churches located in these geographical areas are extremely different among themselves, with diverse ecclesiastical, canonical, theological, and liturgical ("rites") traditions. As well, they face largely dissimilar sociopolitical, cultural, and religious challenges, even though *within* each group of churches there exist enough commonalities to permit a reasonably coherent approach to ecclesial and social issues. On balance, however, bringing together these widely divergent groups of churches in a common synod, while convenient from the organizational point of view, did not permit a full and coherent discussion of the problems each group of churches faces.

1

Procedurally, the synod's preparatory phase consists of three stages. (1) It begins with the selection of the theme in consultation with the Patriarchates, the Bishops' Conferences, the heads of Vatican Offices of the Roman Curia, and the Union of Superiors General. Their suggestions are examined by the General Secretariat of the Synod of Bishops, which makes recommendations to the pope for the final decision on the theme of the synod. (2) Next, the General Secretariat prepares an outline of the synod topic in a document called the *Lineamenta,* which is presented to the pope for approval. The *Lineamenta* [Outline] is then sent to all the bishops for suggestions and comments. A report is prepared by the bishops and sent to the General Secretariat. (3) In light of these reports, the General Secretariat drafts another document called the *Instrumentum Laboris* [Working Document] to be used as a guide for discussion during the synod. After the pope's approval, the document is sent to the participants of the synod.

In the case of the Asian Synod, we were informed by Cardinal Jan Schotte, the General Secretary of the Synod of Bishops, that the topic chosen by the pope "intends to respond to the unique set of circumstances within the Church in Asia as well as to address the actual state of affairs affecting all the peoples and cultures on the Asian continent. In highlighting the centrality of the Person of Christ, His Mission as Mediator and One and Only Savior in God's Eternal Plan of Salvation, the Church in Asia and all Her members will be better prepared to fulfill Christ's Evangelizing Mission of love and service in Asia."[8]

The *Lineamenta,* entitled "Jesus Christ the Savior: Mission of Love and Service in Asia," was sent to the Asian bishops in September 1996 and was composed of a brief introduction and conclusion and six chapters: "Asian Realities," "Evangelization in Asia," "God's Salvific Design in History," "Jesus Christ: God's Good News of Salvation to All," "The Church as Communion," and "The Church's Mission of Love and Service in Asia." After the conclusion, fourteen questions were appended corresponding to the contents of the six chapters.[9] Their function was explained by the General Secretary: "The number and variety of the questions listed in the final section of the document have been deliberately chosen to serve as a guide in structuring the reflections on the topic of the Special Assembly for Asia. These questions, then, and not the *Lineamenta* text, should be the basis of all responses. . . . At the same time, each and every question need not be answered. Depending on individual circumstances, respondents are free to make a choice of those questions which seem relevant."[10] Each local bishop was expected to involve his whole local church in the study of the *Lineamenta,* draft a response to its questions, and send it to his episcopal conference, which would in turn draft an official response of its own and forward it to the General Secretariat no later than August 1, 1997.

While many episcopal conferences sedulously studied the *Lineamenta* and gave detailed responses to its questions in spite of the shortness of time and difficulties in translation,[11] some did not hide their deep disappointment with the *Lineamenta* and the procedure of the synod itself. In particular, the Japanese Episcopal Conference noted that the issues and agenda, as implied in the fourteen questions, betrayed the concerns of the Church in the West, did not take into account the real situation of Asia, and were therefore unhelpful. The Japanese bishops requested more time to study the document, especially the subsequent *Instrumentum Laboris,* before the synod.[12] More importantly, they suggested radical changes in the procedure of the synod itself to allow Asian bishops greater autonomy and freedom in determining the overall direction and agenda of the synod. They also strongly criticized the theology of the *Lineamenta,* in particular its Christology and ecclesiology, as "overly self-complacent and introverted" and inappropriate for the peculiar situation of Asia. The Indonesian bishops questioned the underlying assumptions of the *Lineamenta* regarding evangelization and suggested that the synod's focus should not be on mission but rather on "Asian spirituality," or "Asian religious experience," or "Asian mysticism." The Vietnamese bishops objected to the paternalistic tone of some passages in the *Lineamenta* and its excessive concern for orthodoxy, especially with regard to the uniqueness of Jesus as Savior.

The General Secretariat composed the *Instrumentum Laboris* on the basis of the reports of episcopal conferences and sent it out in February 1998, barely two months before the meeting of the synod in Rome (April 19–May 14, 1998). Clearly, the request for more time to study the *Instrumentum Laboris* was ignored, perhaps in a race to meet the pre-established schedule to complete the continental synods before the magic year 2000.

Space does not permit a detailed comparison, which would be fascinating, between the *Lineamenta* and the *Instrumentum Laboris* to determine whether and to what extent significant changes were made as the result of the suggestions of Asian episcopal conferences. Structurally at least, there were changes in that the *Instrumentum Laboris* has one chapter more than the *Lineamenta:* the latter's first chapter on "Asian Realities" is divided into two in the *Instrumentum Laboris:* "Asian Realities" and "Ecclesial Realities in Asia." There is also a change in the order of two chapters: in the *Lineamenta* the chapter on "God's Salvific Design in History" precedes the chapter on "Jesus Christ: God's Good News of Salvation to All," whereas in the *Instrumentum Laboris* the order is reversed, following the chronological sequence between the economy of the Son and that of the Holy Spirit.[13]

The Asian Synod in Action

The Asian Synod opened on April 19, 1998 with a solemn Mass in St. Peter's Basilica, celebrated by Pope John Paul II. There were 252 participants, comprising two groups: 188 Synod Fathers with full voting rights (67 *"ex officio,"* 96 *"ex electione,"* and 23 *"ex nominatione pontificia"*) and 64 participants with no voting rights (18 experts, 40 auditors, and 6 ecumenical delegates).[14] The president of the synod was John Paul II; the general secretary, Cardinal Jan Schotte; the president's delegates, Cardinals Stephen Kim Sou-Hwan (Korea), Jozef Tomko (Prefect of the Congregation of the Evangelization of Peoples), and Julius Riyadi Darmaatmadja (Indonesia); the general relator, Cardinal Paul Shan Kuo-Hsi (Taiwan); and the special secretary, Archbishop Thomas Menamparampil (India).

Procedurally, the synod was marked by the following important events.[15] First, on April 19, the general relator Cardinal Shan presented a *Relatio ante Disceptationem* outlining the main issues to be discussed by the synod.[16] Second, fourteen general "congregations" (i.e., assemblies) were held from April 20 to April 28, during which 191 eight-minute interventions were made by the participants. Third, on April 28, the general relator Cardinal Shan presented a *Relatio post Disceptationem* purporting to summarize all the interventions and intended as the basis for discussion in the small groups.[17] Fourth, synod participants were divided into eleven small groups according to three languages (English, French, and Italian), known as *circuli minores,* each with an elected moderator and relator. They met thirteen times, from April 29 to May 9, to discuss the *Relatio post Disceptationem* and to prepare the "propositions," that is, formulations of the synod's consensus on important topics under discussion. Fifth, the propositions of all the groups were combined under the guidance of the general relator into a list of fifty-two propositions called the "Integrated List," which was subsequently given to the Synod Fathers for debate and amendments if necessary in six more general congregations, from May 2 to May 8. Sixth, after all the amendments had been examined, the "Final List of Propositions" was drawn up, containing fifty-nine propositions, and voted in the twenty-second general congregation, with either *placet* or *non placet,* each proposition requiring a two-thirds majority of those voting (none received fewer than 140 votes out of 158 Synod Fathers present).[18] Seventh, the "Final Message" (*nuntius*) of the synod was composed under the presidency of Archbishop Oscar V. Cruz (Philippines), affirming the Church's desire to collaborate with all Asians to improve their quality of life, and to share its faith among all, while respecting their religious beliefs and freedom of conscience. It was approved during the twenty-first congregation. The twenty-third and last congregation on May 13 concluded the synod with the closing remarks by Cardinal Julius Riyadi Darmaatmadja, presidential delegate. On the next day, there was a solemn concelebrated Mass with John Paul II in St. Peter's Basilica, followed by a lunch with the pope.

The Asian Synod and *Ecclesia in Asia*

This bloodless chronicle of the Asian Synod cannot, of course, do justice to its spirit, which John Paul II described as "a fraternal dialogue of life, communion and mission." Its joy and exuberance were palpable during the solemn Masses at the opening and conclusion of the synod, a splendid feast of sounds and colors, mirroring the rich cultural, linguistic, liturgical, and artistic variety of the churches represented. At the inauguration Mass, the Gloria was sung in Tagalog, the Gospel was proclaimed in Malayalam according to the Syro-Malabar rite, and the General Intercessions were read in Arabic, Chinese, Filipino, Korean, Tamil, and Vietnamese. The preparation of gifts was accompanied by a Batak *"Tor-tor"* dance performed by a troupe of Indonesian men and women carrying flowers, incense, and candles to an Indonesian hymn *"Bawalah Persembahan"* (Let us bring forth our gifts). At the Great Amen of the Eucharistic Prayer, an Indian dance troupe performed the *"Arati,"* a love dance for the arrival of a spouse. At the concluding Mass, the Gospel Acclamation was sung in Tamil according to the Syro-Malankara rite, while the Gospel was proclaimed in Malayalam according to the Syro-Malabar rite. The General Intercessions were offered in Mandarin, Hindi, Japanese, Malay, Tagalog, and Thai. The Eucharistic gifts were presented by Korean women in their traditional costumes, accompanied by a "*Condo*" dance from Indonesia.

Of course, not all was sweetness and light during the synod. Tensions created by differences of views and experiences, especially between the Roman curia and the diocesan bishops, were inevitable.[19] A dramatic moment occurred when Francis Hadisumarta, bishop of Manokwari-Sorong, Indonesia, speaking on behalf of the Indonesian Bishops' Conference, declared: "The Catholic Church is not a monolithic pyramid. Bishops are not branch secretaries waiting for instructions from Headquarters! We are a communion of local Churches. . . ." He concluded his intervention with some explosive questions: "This vision, where Episcopal Conferences would have the trust and authority to evangelize—in dialogue with the poor, with cultures and with other faith traditions—is both ancient and new. Do we have the imagination to envisage the birth of new Patriarchates, say the Patriarchate of South Asia, of Southeast Asia and of East Asia? . . . Thus, we envisage a radical decentralization of the Latin Rite—devolving into a host of local Rites in Asia. . . ." Apparently, this demand for more autonomy provoked a sharp reaction on the part of Cardinal Jan Schotte, the general secretary: "If glares could kill, he would have died instantly," someone said of the look on the cardinal's face.

Perhaps the fairest summary of the effects of the synod on its participants as well as of the challenges for the Asian churches was given by Cardinal Julius Darmaatmadja (Indonesia) in his "Closing Remarks" (May 13). The cardinal described the synod as a "process of walking together" during which participants had the opportunity to experience the rich variety of the particular churches of Asia and the many forms of ecclesial communion on the local and regional levels: "For almost a month now, we have truly experienced a process of walking together. This synodal experience has allowed us to come to know many particular Churches of Asia with which we had not previously come into contact. We feel spiritually renewed by having been with one another and having sought together ways to make the particular Churches of Asia fully and deeply present as the one Church which desires to serve the many and varied concerns of the Asian people" (no. 4). He went on to say:

> Considering all the challenges in Asia, we feel that the synod theme is quite relevant. "Being Church in Asia" today means "participating in the mission of Christ, the Savior, in rendering his redemptive love and service in Asia," so that Asian men and women can more fully achieve their integral human development, and that "that they may have life, and have it abundantly" (Jn 10:10). . . . In addition to offering hope and new life in Jesus Christ and serving directly people who are needy in so many ways, we must also take part in the task of striving to improve unjust structures, whether in the economic, political, cultural or governmental realms, as

well as of building a new culture of life characterized by love, truth, honesty and justice (no. 6).

The final step of the synod and, in a certain sense, its crowning achievement was the promulgation of John Paul II's Post-Synodal Apostolic Exhortation, *Ecclesia in Asia.*[20] The document was the pope's synthesis and approval of the synod's work, with its contents derived mainly from the pope's past teachings, the synod's various official documents, the interventions of synodal participants, the reports of group discussions, and the synod's final list of propositions. *Ecclesia in Asia* was presented by John Paul II in New Delhi, India, on November 6 to more than one hundred bishops assembled for the occasion.

One measure of the immediate impact of the Asian Synod is the degree to which the fifty-nine propositions, which embodied the consensus of the Synod Fathers, found their way into the papal exhortation. In this regard, it is interesting to note that all but eight of the propositions appeared in *Ecclesia in Asia.*[21] Another gauge, although less easy to employ, is the extent to which the 191 interventions of the synodal participants, as well as their concerns expressed in group discussions, were incorporated into *Ecclesia in Asia.* Even though the full texts of these interventions and the reports of group discussions were *sub secreto,* from their summaries (and especially from a reading of the full texts themselves), it is clear that the Asian bishops were deeply concerned with five issues. These are: dialogue with Asian religions, dialogue with Asian cultures, dialogue with Asian poor, the indispensable role of the laity, and the necessity of legitimate autonomy for the local churches. How well the Apostolic Exhortation "received" these concerns, and especially how it integrated them into the pope's overriding preoccupation with an orthodox Christology and Christian mission in Asia, can only be answered after a careful study of *Ecclesia in Asia.*

But even this criterion cannot measure the true success of the Asian Synod. Its ultimate test cannot but rest with the Asian churches themselves: Will Asian Christians bear effective witness to and put into practice the values repeatedly highlighted by the Asian bishops during the synod, or will the Asian churches continue to do business and let the Roman Curia continue to do business as usual? If the latter, then the Asian Synod would have been a monumental waste of time and energy and, worse, Asian Christians would be guilty of a sinful disobedience to the stirrings of the Holy Spirit. If the former, which we fervently hope that it will be, then the Asian Synod was a "moment of grace" and Christ will become, once again, truly an Asian figure, which he was from the very beginning.

Documents and Commentaries

To facilitate easy access to the documents of the Asian Synod and appreciation of their significance, this volume offers selections of these documents in their chronological order.[22] Most of the selections are publicly available, whereas others were originally classified as *sub secreto.* Space does not unfortunately allow a full publication of the synod's official documents, the 191 interventions of synodal participants, and the reports of group discussions. But it is hoped that the introductions to the selections given here will give readers a comprehensive idea of the working of the synod and its major theological orientations and achievements.

The commentaries are selected for their helpful insights into the Asian Synod and its documents as well as into the context of the Asian Churches. Most of them have been previously published, but some were commissioned specifically for this volume. Their tone, while at times critical, is always respectful and appreciative of the synod. Whatever the theological proclivities of the commentators, their commitment to the Christian faith and their passion for a lasting peace and justice for all the peoples of Asia and for the light of Christ to shine forth on all Asia can hardly be doubted. It is our fervent prayer that all the peoples of Asia, whether Christian or not, "have life, and have it abundantly" (Jn 10:10) through the mission of love and service of Jesus Christ.

Notes

1. *EA* 3.
2. The pope assigned a theme to each of the five continental Special Assemblies of the Synod of Bishops, the one for Asia being: "Jesus Christ the Savior and his mission of love and service in Asia: 'That they may have life, and have it abundantly' (Jn 10:10)." The central theme of the celebration of the new millennium was the Trinity, beginning with Jesus Christ, then the Holy Spirit, and finally, God the Father, with the year 2000 dedicated to the honor of the Trinity. For a study of John Paul II's Trinitarian theology and how it relates to the celebration of the Jubilee Year 2000, see Peter C. Phan, "God in the World: A Trinitarian Triptych," in *The New Catholic Encyclopedia: Jubilee Volume: The Wojtyla Years,* ed. Berard Marthaler (Detroit: The Gale Group, 2001), pp. 33–42.
3. *Redemptor Hominis* (March 4, 1979), no. 1. This theme reappeared many times in John Paul II's subsequent writings, especially in the encyclical *Dominum et Vivificantem* (May 18, 1986), nos. 49–54.
4. *Tertio Millennio Adveniente* (November 10, 1994), 23. Italics in the original.
5. The themes of the other four synods were: Africa: "The Church in Africa and her evangelizing mission towards the year 2000: 'You shall be my witnesses' (Acts 1:8)"; America: "Encounter with the Living Jesus Christ: The way to conversion, communion and solidarity in America"; Europe: "Jesus Christ, alive in his church, source of hope for Europe"; Oceania: "Jesus Christ and the peoples of Oceania: Walking his way, telling his truth, living his life." For brief accounts of these special synods, see *The New Catholic Encyclopedia: Jubilee Year. The Wojtyla Years,* ed. Berard Marthaler (Detroit: The Gale Group, 2001), pp. 165–178.
6. Paul VI established the Synod of Bishops with his *motu proprio Apostolica Sollicitudo* (September 15, 1965). For the nature and working of the Synod of Bishops, see *The Code of Canon Law,* canons 341–348. Up to 2000, there have been twenty synods: ten "ordinary," two "extraordinary," and eight "special."
7. From the Christian perspective, Asia may be divided into three regions: (1) The Near and Middle East, the cradle of Christianity, is the home to several ancient apostolic churches united under the aegis of the *Conseil des Patriarches Catholiques d'Orient* formed in 1991, which meets once a year and comprises seven Catholic patriarchs of the East: the Patriarch of Antioch and all the East for the Maronite Church; the Coptic Catholic Patriarch of Alexandria; the Patriarch of Antioch and all the East, Alexandria and Jerusalem for the Melkite Greek Catholic Church; the Patriarch of Antioch

and all the East for the Syrian Catholic Church; the Patriarch of Babylon for the Chaldean Catholic Church; the Patriarch (*Catholicos*) of Cilicia for the Armenian Catholic Church; and the Latin Patriarch of Jerusalem; (2) The Indian subcontinent is the home to three communities of churches: Latin, as represented by the Conference of Catholic Bishops of India; Syro-Malabar (with a Major Archbishop); and Syro-Malankara (with a Metropolitan Archbishop); and (3) Central Asia and the Far East are the home to many small Catholic churches united under the organization known as the Federation of Asian Bishops' Conferences founded in 1970, which comprises fourteen episcopal conferences as full members (Bangladesh, India, Indonesia, Japan, Korea, Laos-Cambodia, Malaysia-Singapore-Brunei, Myanmar (Burma), Pakistan, Philippines, Sri Lanka, Taiwan, Thailand, and Vietnam; and ten associate members (Hong Kong, Kazakhstan, Kyrgyzstan, Macao, Mongolia, Nepal, Siberia, Tadjikistan, Turkmenistan, and Uzbekistan).

8. Introduction to the *Lineamenta,* second paragraph. For a description of the work of the General Secretariat of the Synod of Bishops in preparation for the Asian Synod (1995–1998), see Cardinal Jan Schotte's eighteen-page report *Relatio Secretarii Generalis,* published by Libreria Editrice Vaticana, 1998.

9. The official English text of the *Lineamenta* may be found in *Origins* 26 (1997), 502–520.

10. Introduction to the *Lineamenta,* sixth paragraph.

11. The longest responses came from the episcopal conferences of Indonesia and the Philippines, each of some twenty-eight single-spaced pages.

12. The Japanese bishops pointed out that it took them three months to have the *Lineamenta* translated into Japanese. They also noted that no Asian country (except India and Philippines) has any of the languages used by the Holy See (Italian, English, French, German, and Spanish) as its native tongue. They asked to have at least six months to study the *Instrumentum Laboris* and simultaneous translations at the synod.

13. The official text of the *Instrumentum Laboris* can be found in *Origins* 27 (1998), 634–652. Besides the introduction and conclusion, the seven chapters are: "Asian Realities," "Ecclesial Realities of Asia," "A Brief Evaluation of Catholic Mission History in Asia," "Jesus Christ: The Good News of Salvation," "God's Salvific Design: The Spirit at Work," "The Church as Communion," "The Church's Mission of Love and Service in Asia."

14. The complete list of participants is available in the *Elenchus Participantium. Synodus Episcoporum. Coetus Specialis Pro Asia,* published by Libreria Editrice Vaticana, 1998.

15. Those interested in the norms and procedures governing the synod as well as its timetable may consult the *Vademecum Synodi,* available in English and French, the two official languages of the synod, from Libreria Editrice Vaticana, 1998.

16. The English text is available from the Libreria Editrice Vaticana, 1998. The thirty-two-page *Relatio ante Disceptationem* comprises three parts: "The Church's Mission in the Context of Asian Realities," "Jesus Christ: The Good News of Salvation," and "The Church and Its Mission." The *Vademecum Synodi* states: "The purpose of the *Relatio ante Disceptationem* is to help the Synod Fathers focus their interventions on the general topic and, under that topic, on points which can be subjected to further study. In view of the conclusions of the assembly, it should be useful to draw briefly the Synod Fathers' attention to some aspects which have already received a more or

less consensus, according to the responses to the *Lineamenta* questions" (Art. 33, f.).
It is essentially a summary of the *Instrumentum Laboris.*

17. The English text, which is said to be *sub secreto,* was published by Libreria Editrice
Vaticana, 1998. The forty-three-page *Relatio* comprises three parts: "God's Offer of
Salvation through Jesus Christ, His Son, and the Holy Spirit in the Context of Asian
Realities," "The Evangelizing Mission of the Church in Asia," and "The Church's
Mission of Love and Service in Asia." A controversy erupted over this *Relatio,* which
was supposed to summarize the interventions but had apparently been completed on
Friday, April 24, before the interventions of Saturday, Monday, and Tuesday were
even delivered. More significantly, this *Relatio* seems to reflect not the concerns expressed in the interventions—inculturation, struggle with the poor for liberation, interreligious dialogue, and the autonomy of the local churches—but those of the Roman curia, especially in the "Practical Questions" appended at the end to be
discussed in small groups (pp. 37–39). For example, Question 2 asks: "How can the
Church deal with some unorthodox trends among some theologians with regard to
the divinity of Jesus and his unique mediation of salvation? How can Jesus be portrayed as more than simply one of the many saviors?" Again, Question 6: "In some
theological circles there is a separation of the mission of Jesus Christ and that of the
Holy Spirit. This dichotomy has led to a one-sided appreciation of the work of the
Holy Spirit in cultures and religions without affirming the need to proclaim Jesus
Christ as the Savior. It might be worthwhile to reflect on this point, based on the concrete experiences of inter-religious dialogue and inculturation." Clearly, the issues of
orthodoxy are central in these questions.

18. Actually there are sixty-one propositions, and not fifty-nine, since two of them contain two parts, each of which was voted on separately. These propositions, gathered
in the *Elenchus Finalis Propositionum,* were *sub secreto.* Although most propositions
were passed overwhelmingly, two propositions elicited a strong minority opposition.
Proposition 43, which speaks about the need of inculturation and states that "local
Churches need the authority and freedom to inculturate by *adapting* it to the local cultures while recognizing the need for dialogue and communion with the Holy See, the
principle of unity in the Church," received fourteen "*non placet*" votes. Proposition
50, which states that "the Oriental Churches are to exercise their autonomy specified
in their Canon Law (C.C.E.O.), in Vatican II documents and in the legitimate customs
of the Oriental Churches," received eleven "*non placet*" votes. In general, there was a
negative response to the demand for more local autonomy and freedom.

19. I have already mentioned the fact that there was heavy criticism of the *Relatio post
Disceptationem* for not incorporating the issues and concerns raised by many of the
191 interventions for group discussions. Theological and pastoral differences were
also discernible among various linguistic groups. For example, the Italian group
strongly emphasized the need to preserve correct doctrines, especially in Christology,
in the process of inculturation. In this respect, it preferred to speak of "interculturation" because it pointed out that Asian cultures need to assimilate the values of Western culture such as rationality (*razionalità*) and legal mode of thinking (*giuridicità*).
It warned against the danger of confusing the minds of people in using "analogies"
between Jesus Christ and other figures present in non-Christian religions. It highlighted the need to pay attention to "some theologians, above all Indian, who have
overemphasized the salvific value of other religions" (*alcuni teologi, soprattutto indi-
ani, che hanno forzato troppo il valore salvifico delle altre religioni*).

On the other hand, the English groups, while sharing the concern for correct teaching, emphasized the pastoral dimension and demanded more local autonomy. Group A stressed the necessity of subsidiarity: "In principle when it is possible and effective the decision making has to be shared in all levels and more trust has to be manifested." Group B: "We strongly suggest that National Episcopal Commissions be given full authority to create Liturgical Commissions that produce and approve translations which the Roman Curia should ratify without much ado." Group C points out the Roman Dicasteries are "the collaborators of the Holy Father and therefore are to be looked upon as regulating, co-ordinating and serving, not controlling agencies." Group D: "In relationships within the local Churches, between the local Churches, between the particular Churches and the universal Church we need trust, the presumption of good will, and legitimate freedom (legitimate autonomy as the principle of subsidiarity). Group H: "The attitude of the Roman Dicasteries in regard to the inculturation of the liturgy is not at all positive. The Latin liturgy is a purely westernized liturgy translated verbatim into the local languages. Even the translations are to be approved by the said Dicasteries, which sounds paradoxical."

20. The English text can be found in the appendix below, pp. 286–340, and in *Origins* 29, 23 (November 18, 1999), 358–384.

21. The eight propositions not referred to in *EA* are: no. 2 (The Challenge of Asia), no. 4 (Ecclesial Realities), no. 9 (Emphasis on God-Experience in Jesus Christ), no. 10 (The Trinitarian Plan of Salvation), no. 26 (The Priesthood), no. 36 (Pastoral Care of Migrants), no. 40 (Proclamation), and no. 46 (Abortion).

22. Many of the synod's documents are available online: http://www.ucanews.com.

Part One

The Preparatory Phase

1

The *Lineamenta*

As noted in the Introduction, in preparation for the synod, the General Secretariat of the Synod of Bishops, under the presidency of Cardinal Jan Schotte, composed an outline of the themes to be discussed at the synod and sent it to all the bishops for suggestions and comments.

In its introduction, the *Lineamenta* explains the genesis and the preparatory phase of the Asian Synod. The purpose of the *Lineamenta* is to "foster a common reflection and prayer" as well as to "generate suggestions and observations" on the theme of the synod, the mission of love and service of Jesus Christ in Asia. To achieve this goal, the document begins by describing the realities of Asia, especially the richness and variety of Asian religions and cultures and the growing sense among the Asian people of "being Asian." It also surveys the many challenges facing Asia, in particular in the areas of socioeconomic development and political ideologies. It goes on to focus on the evangelization of Asia, offering a sketch of the history of mission in Asia, noting a positive feature of the Asian Churches: "One important sign that the local Churches are becoming 'mission-sending' Churches, instead of being exclusively or mostly 'mission-receiving' Churches, is the emergence of new Asian Mission Societies. . . . Today the local Churches in Asia have a number of Asian Missionary Institutes. The Philippines Foreign Mission Society, the St. Thomas Missionary Society and the Heralds of the Good News in India, the Korean Mission Society, and the Thai Mission Society are examples of local Churches becoming 'mission-sending' Churches" (no. 15).

One of the central ideas of the *Lineamenta* is the universality of Jesus as the unique Savior. Jesus is the one and only Savior because the mission of the Spirit, who is present in creation and human history, is to bring everyone to Jesus: "The salvific presence of the Spirit in humanity was to lead all peoples into the full participation of the life of God in Jesus Christ His Son" (no. 20). While appreciative of various Asian Christologies intended to make Jesus relevant to the sociopolitical and religious situation of Asia, the document warns against the danger of partial Christologies, especially those that raised questions about the "uniqueness of Jesus Christ in the history of salvation": "While Asian Christologies must interpret Jesus Christ for Asians, as has been done by others during the twenty centuries of the Church's existence, all Christologies must be measured against the faith of the Apostles, the apostolic Church and the testimony of the New Testament. No sectarian or partial Christology can do justice to the true Jesus Christ of the Gospels. He is more than a social reformer, a political liberator, master of a spirituality, champion of human rights, or savior of the marginalized" (no. 23).

The mission of the Church is described as a continuation of the mission of Jesus and the Holy Spirit, which is "the mission from the Father" whose purpose is "to communicate His divine life to all through the Son in the Spirit" (no. 26). In this sense, "the Church is born of mission and for mission" (no. 26). The document ends by affirming that the path of evangelization in Asia is dialogue; in fact, a threefold dialogue: with other religions, with cultures, and with the poor, though it reminds that "even though dialogue is essential and forms part of every evangelizing activity of the Church, it does not exhaust the whole reality of evangelization, nor is it a substitute mission *ad gentes*, and much less is it to be seen as something in opposition to the proclamation of Jesus Christ" (no. 33).

The *Lineamenta*'s list of questions is given here not only because they highlight what the General Secretariat of the Synod of Bishops for the Special Assembly for Asia considered to be of central importance for the Asian Synod (which some Asian Conferences of Bishops believed to reflect the concerns of the Roman dicasteries rather than those of the Asian Churches), but also because they form the background of the Asian Episcopal Conferences' responses to the *Lineamenta*.

—Ed.

Questions

Chapter I: Asian Realities

1. Describe some of the positive aspects as well as the shortcomings of evangelization in your area in relation to Asian realities, i.e., religious, socioeconomic, political, etc. In light of these realities, what specific areas should receive attention and what specific approaches should be taken by the Church in Her evangelizing mission in Asia?

Chapter II: The Evangelization of Asia

2. Evaluate the state of the Church's missionary activity in Asia and in your area (structures, programs, movements, etc.). Mention specific ways to promote and assist the Church's missionary activity in this regard.

3. What is being done for the formation of the agents of missionary activity, e.g., bishops, clergy, religious, seminarians, laity, missionary institutes, ecclesial movements, etc.? According to your opinion, what should be done in this area?

Chapter III: God's Salvific Design in History

4. What is being done in your area to help members of the Church become better acquainted with the traditions of other religions in Asia? What can the Church learn from Her dialogue with other Asian religions and the knowledge obtained? To what extent can the specific aspects of Asian religions be used and developed in the fulfillment of the Church's mission of bringing salvation to all peoples in Asia?

Chapter IV: Jesus Christ the Savior: God's Good News to All

5. In your area how is the Person of Christ viewed and proposed in the Church's mission of proclaiming Him and His Salvation to the Asian people? Describe ways in which the Church can maintain the centrality of the proclamation of Jesus Christ in very difficult political, social, and cultural situations. In what ways can the Church present Jesus Christ as the one and only Savior as well as the universality of salvation in Him?

Chapter V: The Church as Communion

6. Evaluate in your area the Church's understanding of the need and responsibility of carrying on Christ's mission in the Spirit. How is the work of formation in this regard being fulfilled at various levels of the Church's life? Mention some concrete efforts undertaken by the Church in the mission field in your area and their results. Describe the various elements which should be involved in any future initiatives in this regard.

7. Give an assessment of how Church communion is lived in the local Church in your area. Describe how various Christian Churches give a common witness in their evangelizing activities. How do persons from other religions view these Christian communities? Indicate ways in which Church communities can become more conscious of their unity in Christ and display it more effectively in the Church's evangelizing mission in Asia.

8. What efforts are being made in your area toward fostering greater ecumenical understanding and unity among various Churches and various ecclesial traditions?

9. What is being done by the Church in your area to engage in dialogue with other religions: Hindu-Christian, Buddhist-Christian, Islamic-Christian, Traditional Religion, etc.? What are the different levels at which dialogue is being carried out? What are the concrete results? What should be the concerns of the Church in this area in the future?

Chapter VI: The Church's Mission of Love and Service in Asia

10. Describe the extent of inculturation in the various aspects of the Church's life in your area (e.g., Christian theology, liturgy, spirituality, liturgical art, architecture, etc.) and its effects in relation to the Church's mission. What is the contribution of the efforts at inculturation in your area to the universal Church?

11. How is the social doctrine of the Church being utilized in the Church's evangelizing mission of love and service in Asia (human promotion and development, situations of civil war and ethnic conflicts, refugees, migrants, marginalized peoples, etc.)?

12. What has the Church done in your area to use the means of social communications in the Church's evangelizing mission, especially the press, radio, television, film, video, Internet, etc.? What initiatives need to be taken in the future?

13. How would you describe Marian spirituality and devotion in your area as a means of evangelization and catechesis? In what ways is Our Lady seen and appreciated as the perfect model of Christian discipleship? Give concrete examples of how Marian devotion leads people to a genuine imitation of Jesus Christ.

14. Give any remarks and suggestions on matters related to the synod topic not included in the above series of questions.

2

Responses of the Asian Episcopal Conferences to the *Lineamenta*

Despite shortness of time and numerous difficulties of various sorts, the Asian Bishops' Conferences took the task of responding to the *Lineamenta* very seriously. They organized study sessions and discussion groups to ponder over this preparatory document and provided lengthy and detailed answers to its questions. Besides offering helpful thumbnail sketches of the Asian Churches, these responses highlighted the real concerns confronting Asian Christians, sometimes in contrast to those perceived by the Roman Curia. Again and again, like a mantra, under various guises, the inculturation of the Christian faith into Asia emerged as the central and neuralgic issue: How can Asian Christians present Jesus Christ and the Church with an authentic Asian face? Or, to put it in the words of the Catholic Bishops' Conference of India, how can the Church become "truly Indian and Asian"?

Even from a cursory reading of these responses, it is clear that the uniqueness and universality of Jesus as the Savior was never placed in question. Rather, the burning issue for the Asian Churches, a tiny minority in Asia, is *how* to proclaim this truth about Jesus credibly in the midst of crushing poverty, competing religious systems, and cultural diversity. The unanimous answer to this problem is found to be dialogue: dialogue with the poor, with religions, and with cultures. As the Indian bishops put it, "This dialogal model is the new Asian way of being Church, promoting mutual understanding, harmony and collaboration." The Asian Bishops' reports are surprisingly frank. While humbly recognizing their Churches' strengths, the bishops bluntly highlight their weaknesses, which revolve around the absence of genuine inculturation by means of the triple dialogue mentioned above.

With regard to interreligious dialogue, many Asian episcopal conferences call for not only a respectful dialogue with non-Christians, but also an explicit recognition of the salvific value of non-Christian religions, not as independent from or parallel to Christ, but in relation to him. The Indian bishops affirm: "For hundreds of millions of our fellow human beings, salvation is seen as being channeled to them not in spite of but through and in their various sociocultural and religious traditions. We cannot, therefore, deny a priori a salvific role for these non-Christian religions." The Korean bishops assert: "We have to study and re-evaluate the meaning and role of the great traditional religions in Korea. They too play a part in the salvific economy of God. This understanding is essential for the inculturation of the Gospel." The Filipino bishops urge an exploration "in an open and humble way" of the "'revelatory' nature of the great ancient religions in Asia and its impact on the Church's proclamation of the truth of Jesus." In this connection, the Japanese and the Vietnamese bishops find the

Christology of the *Lineamenta*, with its insistence on the uniqueness and universality of Christ, too defensive and apologetic.

Concerning the dialogue with the poor, the Asian bishops point out that Asia is a continent of massive poverty and systemic oppression and that the Church cannot fulfill its evangelizing mission unless it walks with the poor. The Indian bishops put it starkly: "Clearly India's Christian Community is now being called to an ecclesial conversion: to be a Church of the Poor." In particular, the bishops call for an end to the discrimination against women, both in society and Church.

Regarding the dialogue with cultures, the Asian bishops decry the foreignness of Christianity to Asia and call for a systematic inculturation of the Christian faith in all its aspects, from worship to theology to ministerial formation. The Sri Lankan bishops urge a "divesting of the Western image of the Church in the liturgy, style of life, celebrations, and trying to overcome the present image of a powerful, affluent and domineering institution."

In order to carry out this triple dialogue with Asian peoples successfully, the Asian bishops believe that a certain degree of autonomy and freedom for the local Churches is necessary. They lament a lack of dialogue and even trust between the Asian Churches and Rome. This lack was exemplified, according to some episcopal conferences, in the composition of the *Lineamenta* itself. In the words of the Japanese bishops, "From the way the questions are proposed, one feels that the holding of the Synod is like an occasion for the central office to evaluate the performance of the branch offices. That kind of synod would not be worthwhile for the Church in Asia. The judgment should not be made from a European framework, but must be seen on the spiritual level of the people who live in Asia." Speaking of the goal of the synod, they said, "We do not hope for a synod aiming at discovering how the Asian Church can be propped up by the Western Church, but one where the Bishops of Asia have an honest exchange and learn how they can support and encourage one another."

All in all, the responses of the Asian Episcopal Conferences to the *Lineamenta* evince a remarkable sense of collegiality and maturity. The Asian bishops appreciated the pope's convocation of a special synodal assembly for Asia, but they made it clear that they wanted an *Asian* Synod. As the bishops of the Philippines put it, "Ensure that the synod is truly Asian, with an Asian reflection, with an Asian output, reflecting the Asian perspective of evangelization." It remains to be seen whether this desideratum was fulfilled.

Following are excerpts from the responses of the various conferences of Asian bishops to the *Lineamenta*, which explain well their pastoral concerns and the challenges facing Asian Catholic Christianity.

—Ed.

THE CATHOLIC BISHOPS' CONFERENCE OF INDIA
Becoming Truly Indian and Asian

The Churches in India have a completely indigenous hierarchy. Well over 90 percent of the clergy and religious are Indian. Local languages are used in the liturgy and are media for evangelization. Indian religious traditions are studied in houses of formation (even though sometimes this is done superficially, because this reflection does not include a living encounter with practitioners of the traditions studied academically). Centers of interreligious dialogue and ashrams are promoted. The beginnings of an Indian ecclesial expression of our Christian faith have been made. There are to date separate national professional associations for theology, biblical studies, liturgy, catechetics, moral theology, Church history, and canon law.

But there is a shadow side to this process, which will have to be kept in mind in our remarks about the necessity of being truly inculturated local Churches. Suffice it to say here that we Indians perceive the world as Asians. This unique perception is not an obstacle to evangelization. Rather, it helps for an enriched understanding and practice of mission; potentially it is a great help for collaboration between local Churches and the Church universal. To give but one example of this, we examine the motivation for mission. For Indians, an evangelist is motivated primarily by a deep faith-experience. This is reflected in the Apostles' remark: "We cannot but speak of what we have seen and heard" (Acts 4:20). Faith in the Church's mission is for Asian Christians strongly Trinitarian: it is, first of all, the Father's plan, and its working out can only be by participation in the mission both of the Son and the Spirit (see *AG* 2).

The history of evangelization in India and Asia is witness to the fact that in all matters of religion, what is crucially important is a transforming experience of the divine. Being an overly clerical institution, the Church's ways of thinking, speaking and acting not infrequently hinder her communication and hurt her credibility. For example, she rightly proclaims freedom of conscience and religion, but in matters of grievances within the Church, her public image at times appears harsh and therefore one of counter-witness.

The following statement of the Council regarding the promotion of faith-reflection in new cultural contexts, we believe, has not so far been taken sufficiently into consideration: "It is necessary that in each of the great sociocultural regions, as they are called, theological investigation should be encouraged and the facts and words revealed by God, contained in the sacred Scripture, and explained by the Fathers and Magisterium of the Church, submitted to a new examination in the light of the universal Church. In this way it will be more clearly understood by what means faith can be explained in terms of the philosophy and wisdom of the people, and how their customs, concept of life and social structures can be reconciled with the standard proposed by divine revelation" (*AG* 22).

This, then, we see as a basic reason behind the failure of Christian mission efforts in the East: the spiritual and mystical elements of Asian religions have been practically ignored. In place of understanding, appreciation and promotion of this different yet complementary worldview, we regret to observe that today within the Church there is an atmosphere of fear and distrust. These are destructive of communion and collaboration for mission to be a Church of the Poor. Certainly, some efforts are being made to be with the poor and the destitute in their struggles for a life worthy of human beings. At this time of Jubilee graces, the Church is impelled by the Lord's Spirit to take a much stronger and more prophetic stand on behalf of India's hundreds of millions of poor, irrespective of their religions. At the same time, more and more of the faithful are vocalizing their dissatisfaction with some Church institutions that appear to be more at the service of the rich, powerful and better-off sectors of our country.

Toward Being a Church of the People

A Church of Communion calls for being a participatory Church in which all the baptized are engaged actively and fruitfully in every area of her life and mission. By and large our Asian laity has been very much on the receiving end; it has not yet fully understood its role as a community in a state of mission.

Here we come to the adequate formation of all Christians as the first implied requirement of a participatory Church. John Paul II has stated forcefully that formation is not the privilege of a few laity, but a right and duty of all (see *CL* 63). In theory and public discourse there is a growing consensus on this, but the Churches are far from making it a priority in their annual plans and budgets. Another consensus is that Christian families as domestic Churches need much more pastoral support to help them be formators for mission. India's many priestly and religious vocations are eloquent witnesses of the missionary potential of our families. . . .

Becoming Church through Dialogue

Rather than speaking, as the *Lineamenta* does, of "using" the good elements of Asian religions, we ask: "To what extent can the Church learn from and collaborate with other religions to bring about God's Kingdom and peoples' integral liberation?" This is the language of dialogue, which is understood by members of other religions.

A few other important, preliminary remarks are also in order. In a country and a continent of many living religions, to be religious itself means to be interreligious—that is, to live amicably in dialogue. We see the need to emphasize that authentic dialogue does not seem to be well understood by many Christians. It is, after all, not just a theologian's concern. It is the duty and should be the central care also of the whole Church.

The spirit and practice of dialogue is not restricted to interfaith matters among the Christian-Muslim, Christian-Hindu, Christian-Buddhist and Christian-traditional religions. It very much includes dialogue between the local Church and the universal Church as a Communion of Communions. We believe that much unnecessary embarrassment and pain can be avoided by timely dialogue at this level. For example, about a decade ago, a department of the Vatican issued an Instruction that dealt with methods of prayer and meditation used by Christians who have learnt them from Asian religions. Though no doubt well-intentioned, this Instruction could have been much more effective if only there had been the necessary preliminary consultation among the Churches concerned.

It is an accepted principle that we cannot comprehend a mystery; before it, our attitude needs to be one of reverent acceptance and humble openness. God's dialogue with Asian peoples through their religious experiences is a great mystery. We as Church enter into this mystery by dialogue through sharing and listening to the Spirit in others. Dialogue, then, becomes an experience of God's Kingdom.

This dialogical model is the new Asian way of being Church, promoting mutual understanding, harmony and collaboration. This way of relating to and serving other religions is indicated by a careful reading of the signs of our times. It appears to us as God's will for Christian communities in Asia today. It is a timely answer to Asia's vast and varied problems, which threaten her very life. Among these are religious fundamentalism and communalism, to which unprincipled politicians not infrequently resort.

In sincere dialogue with other cultures and religions, the Churches in Asia have a priceless contribution to make to the life of the communion of Churches and to universal culture around the world. One has only to think of how much the community of nations can learn from Tribal religions and values, starting with their reverence for nature and the environment. We have also learned much from our brothers and sisters of other traditions about growth in prayer life, asceticism and spirituality.

As God's Spirit called the Churches of the East to conversion and mission witness (see Rev 2–3), we too hear this same Spirit bidding us to be truly catholic, open and collaborating with the Word who is actively present in the great religious traditions of Asia today. Confident trust and discernment, not anxiety and over-caution, must regulate our relations with these many brothers and sisters. For together with them we form one community, stemming from the one stock which God created to people the entire earth. We share with them a common destiny and providence. Walking together we are called to travel the same paschal pilgrimage with Christ to the one Father of us all (see Lk 24:13ff, *NA* 1, and *GS* 22).

Jesus Christ, Our Horizon and Our Way

In the mission of collaborating with God's kingdom, Jesus Christ is both our Horizon and our Way. We are sustained by the living memory of his life, death and resurrection. This is God's gift to the Church to share with all peoples in ways that are respectful of their histories. The language of the Church's proclamation must be clear, and at the same time it may not be such that it seems to deny the authentic action of God in other cultures and religions.

A deficiency of our present Christology is that it sometimes uses exclusive language, which deals with only one part of the great mystery of Christ—as though valid for all times and places. For example, we here consider the *Lineamenta*'s phrase, "Jesus Christ . . . the one and only Savior." In union with the Father and the Spirit, Christ is indeed the source and cause of salvation for all peoples; but this fact does not exclude the possibility of God mysteriously employing other cooperating channels, as John Paul II allows so clearly. In speaking of Christ's one universal mediation, he says that "participated forms of mediation of different kinds and degrees are not excluded," so long as they are understood as acquiring meaning and value from Christ's mediation and not seen as parallel or complementary to his (*RM* 5; see also *LG* 62).

This *Lineamenta*'s expression that Jesus Christ is the one and only Savior of humankind is understood in the Indian context, therefore, in a way that takes seriously into account the multicultural and multireligious situations of our country. In the light of the universal salvific will and design of God, so emphatically affirmed in the New Testament witness, the Indian Christological approach seeks to avoid negative and exclusivistic expressions. Christ is the sacrament, the definitive symbol of God's salvation for all humanity. This is what the salvific uniqueness and universality of Christ means in the Indian context. That, however, does not mean there cannot be other symbols, valid in their own ways, which the Christian sees as related to the definitive symbol, Jesus Christ. The implication of all this is that for hundreds of millions of our fellow human beings, salvation is seen as being channeled to them not in spite of but through and in their various sociocultural and religious traditions. We cannot, then, deny a priori a salvific role for these non-Christian religions. In summary, our language strives to be inclusive and holistic as far as possible; and it needs to be of one piece with our lives. The basic, practical lesson for Christian proclamation remains: the word without the deed is empty; and the deed without the word is ambiguous. Jesus' language was always one with his witness as a deed-word proclamation. We, his disciples, however, not only separate the two elements; our practice at times even contradicts our preaching.

There is more than one theology evident in the New Testament. This pluriformity of theology catered to different Churches of varied cultures and life-situations. Christology is never a finished product but always in process, even while admitting the normative characteristics of the liturgical, biblical, patristic and conciliar Christologies. The lived experience of the Christian community, following the indispensable rules and diversities of time, space and cultural conditioning, has an important role in this process. In this context attention is also to be paid to the universalistic and exclusivistic claims to salvific uniqueness by the other religions with whom we live and enter into dialogal contact. In theological methodology, the normative roles of scriptural statements, traditional assertions, the experience of faith communities and the life-context of other God-seekers need further investigation and deepening in the process of developing Christological ideas and expressions over the course of time.

So today the Churches around the world and here in Asia need to create contextualized theologies of our one Faith incarnated into many cultures. A common methodology and faith expression for preaching the Gospel to the Asian people cannot be formulated. Rather, each Asian country should develop by careful discernment its own methodologies according to its pastoral needs. The agents of such contextualized faith expressions are the local Churches themselves under the guidance of "a Magisterium which is predominantly pastoral in character" (John XXIII in his opening speech at Vatican II, Oct. 11, 1962; see also "The Roman Liturgy and Inculturation," *L'Osservatore Romano*, no. 14, April 6, 1994).

In affirming the uniqueness of Christ as the only Son of the Father, sent by him in the Spirit's power, source of salvation for all peoples, we must also pay attention to the fact that this statement is primarily a profession of faith. Being a profession of mature faith, it comes not at the beginning of the faith journey but in the process of that pilgrimage, as the summit and conclusion towards which the one who has been evangelized is led by grace in the Spirit.

At the same time, the Church is bound to give a witness which will be rooted in her memory of Christ. In the risen and exalted Jesus the Church finds the basis for a true, integral vision of reality. For, through him, God's own unitary vision of history is revealed. In him the many are recapitulated into the One, without losing their identity.

Indian Christians as individuals, as families, and as communities need to witness to Christ by lives that are both unambiguously rooted in the Indian soil and modeled upon his paschal self-giving. We believe precisely that it is contemplation that helps us evangelize. Without contemplation we can have no mission. The experience of the death and resurrection of Christ through contemplation leads us to mission; and the paschal mystery challenges us to be radical enough to revolutionize the existing society and its structures in all fields.

The Indian Church's evangelization springs from a twofold ardent love: love of her Spouse and love of her neighbor. By these two loves she discovers Christ in India's religions, cultures and multitudes of the poor. She seeks to unveil his face to others and bravely witness to him, in the hope that they may also recognize and accept him.

THE CATHOLIC BISHOPS' CONFERENCE OF INDONESIA

Challenges to Evangelization

Here are some of the major challenges the Church has to cope with in its mission of evangelization.

Evangelization today is being heavily challenged by the progress of science and technology, by the new mass media culture, by growing materialism and the atmosphere of secularization, which for society at large obscure precious traditional cultural values, conceal the "seeds of the Word," divert people from spiritual values, and disturb their disposition to receive the Gospel.

The encounter of Christian faith with indigenous religious beliefs gives rise to unhealthy syncretism: in young Christian communities traditional religious customs still persist and sometimes create confusion. Sometimes there is dualism: Christian faith and belief in the spirits of ancestors. Religious instruction often is inadequate. Because there is no deep insight and conviction in their faith, many Christians are not ready to meet people of other faiths. Moreover, legalism and a superiority complex within the Church pose obstacles to evangelization. There are not enough well-prepared evangelizers, and they are not well distributed through-

out the country. Efforts at inculturation of Christian faith fall short in many sociocultural fields.

In the present political system, which for the sake of national stability imposes restrictions on propagating religion (except for Muslims), it is difficult to
change from one religion to another. Official recognition of only five religions (Islam, Catholicism, Protestantism, Hinduism, Buddhism) also causes a number of
people to register merely nominally as an adherent of one of the "official" religions in order to find protection, or with other inadequate motivations.

In certain areas in Kalimantan catechetical programs are as much as possible
adapted to the local context. But because of lack of transportation, it is difficult to
make pastoral visits to remote villages. There is not everywhere concerted pastoral planning and close cooperation among parishes. In many parishes very much
depends on the parish priest. Lay participation in planning and activities sometimes is confined to parish councils. Since the area to be covered is very vast, pastoral workers are often too exhausted to think creatively and innovatively. In Irian
Jaya people are very poor and seldom stay in villages; most of the time they roam
the fields. This slows down pastoral care, education and religious instruction in
schools, which quite often lack competent and well-motivated staff members.

Specific Areas Requiring Special Attention

Since in a pluricultural context, evangelization meets with difficulties of inculturation, local beliefs, customs and traditions need to be thoroughly studied for the
purpose of finding appropriate ways for conveying the Christian message. In particular, insight into the teachings of other religions ought to be promoted among
the faithful, particularly among community leaders. It is also to be noted that faith
in the universality of salvation and the positive role of other religions and religious beliefs could give rise to doubts as to the necessity of evangelization.

In agrarian culture, where people depend much on authority in family and society, the presentation of the Gospel message should stress personal independence. It should be a message about a personal God, the God of Love and
Justice.

Asian Religions

The Church in Indonesia has to face the reality of a plurireligious society. Christians live in urban and rural communities together with people of other faiths, who
are bearers of "the seeds of the Word" and try to live up to authentic religious values which lead them to God's Reign. They are our fellow wayfarers to the same
Reign of God, to whom we all have access in the Spirit through Jesus Christ.
Hence, without in any way derogating the mission of preaching Jesus Christ, for
the FABC as well as for us, interreligious dialogue is the primary mode of evangelization.

To us certain parts of the *Lineamenta* sound alarming. The dominant concern
between the lines appears to be: "Too much emphasis on dialogue, so that proclamation is not highlighted enough." Interreligious dialogue is distinct from procla-

mation, but may not be opposed to it, since in dialogue Christians give witness to their faith, and in proclamation Christians respectfully encounter in the hearers of the Word the Truth and Goodness that comes from the God of salvation and leads to him. "Conversion" occurs not only as fruit of proclamation. It is the Spirit of God who alone works "conversion to God" in Jesus Christ through proclamation as well as through interreligious dialogue.

Efforts in Helping Members of the Church Become Better Acquainted with the Traditions of Other Religions

Elements of similarity shared with other religions and religious beliefs are the common "platform" for dialogue. Differences may not be disparaged, but are to be treated respectfully. Therefore, wherever Christians live in diaspora among people of other faiths, they have to know the main traditions and tenets of the religions concerned, and to cooperate with their adherents. Efforts to this effect are being made in some areas through formal as well as non-formal education. Ways are to be found of strengthening Christian faith amid Muslim, Hindu and Buddhist living traditions.

In many places there is no systematic planning for religious encounters and for conducting studies on other religious traditions. But those who are interested in getting to know other religions are to be stimulated to do so. Christians are to develop an open and critical attitude and to maintain communication with people of other religious convictions. Day-to-day dialogue of life, considered a common way of life in most parts of Indonesia, takes place especially in rural areas.

In certain areas there is some interreligious tolerance, but cooperation is still difficult, and dialogue hardly ever takes place. Meetings are held with leaders of other religions to arrive at common efforts in tackling social problems.

On the part of Muslims there are *fatwas* (decrees) which restrict relations between people of different faiths; fundamentalist groups often create tensions; the majority religion tends to impose its values on minority groups, so that these have not the freedom to develop. Not seldom is the atmosphere spoiled by mutual suspicion. Although in some regions Muslims are relatively unassertive, their national *da'wa* (religious expansion) proceeds steadily, apparently backed by international planning and support. The fact that in certain areas Islam is politicized for the sake of national security makes interreligious dialogue a mere formality. Often lay people are better acquainted with Islam.

As regards dialogue with traditional and tribal religions, while these religions can express their religiosity in genuine spiritual traditions and religio-cultural practices, there are Christians whose efforts of "dialogue" betray a tendency to proselytizing, and appear as a way of dispelling the "paganism" and pre-rational animism of indigenous people.

To be ready for dialogue and open for positive values in other religious traditions, Christians need to be clearly conscious of their identity based on their own faith—which in many places is still a goal to be achieved. Ecumenical and interreligious relationships suppose solid formation in Christian faith; this will result in ever-greater self-reliance in dialogue. Diocesan Commissions on Interreligious

Relations are to find ways of promoting good relationships among people of several religions.

It may be helpful to have friendly relations not only with local religious leaders, but also with government officials, because in fact religious activities with some impact on society are subject to state regulations.

What Can the Church Learn from Its Dialogue
with Other Asian Religions?

Since in all religions and traditional religious beliefs the values of God's Reign are found as fruits of the Spirit, to the extent that there is good will they all strive towards the coming of the Kingdom. From them the Church may learn how the quest for the Divine is expressed through a wealth of symbols and has its positive impact on moral behavior in daily life.

Hinduism and Buddhism give some insight on the depth of relations between the human and the Divine. They show how to attain tranquility of mind, how to meditate or contemplate in sensitivity towards the "Mystery." In Buddhism *moksa* is attained when, in peaceful tranquility, harmony and equilibrium with nature, with fellow humans, and with oneself are achieved.

The courage of Muslims who recite their daily prayers in public should inspire Christians to faithfully adhere to their religion and defend their faith. Muslims show a high degree of religious observance and highly respect moral values.

Christians observe how in various religions and religious beliefs cosmic elements are given symbolic roles: water, trees, mountains, sun and moon, the seasons, and how their adherents live closely to nature. They give Christians a good example in seeking solitude for prayer and contemplation.

To What Extent Can Specific Aspects of Asian Religions Be Used
and Developed in the Fulfillment of the Church's Mission
of Bringing Salvation to All Peoples in Asia?

The positive teachings of Buddhism, Hinduism and Islam—containing "seeds of the Word," "Gospel" or "Kingdom values"—can render a valuable contribution to evangelization. Those tenets contain links with the Christian message, for example, their teaching on life hereafter, prepared for by a life of struggle on earth, etc.

Proclamation of Jesus Christ and his Gospel, therefore, has to take full account of whatever good and true is found in other religions, and to proceed according to the Christian principles of authentic inculturation. Sincere Christian dialogue appreciates the values of the Kingdom wherever they are found, and provides room for indigenous Christians to make use of their religious traditions in order to express those values in ways familiar to them. As a matter of fact, often the faithful themselves are not given enough opportunity to form expressions of their faith in Jesus spontaneously and creatively.

In many areas traditional beliefs still strongly influence the people's way of thinking and acting. Native religious values are not to be abolished, but ought to be purified through reflection in dialogue between Christian leaders and leaders of traditional religions. This may result in Christianity being enriched by traditional values, and in a truly inculturated practice of Christian faith.

THE CATHOLIC BISHOPS' CONFERENCE OF JAPAN
The Process of Preparation of the Response

1. Three Months Were Needed for Translation   Upon receipt of the English and French translations of the *Lineamenta* published in Rome on September 3, 1996, we began at once to have it translated into Japanese. This took about three months. Copies of the translation were distributed to each diocese on December 17, 1996. In each diocese, the bishop took the lead in common study sessions and made it the subject of prayer.

2. Discussion at Two Plenary Assemblies   After the bishops of each diocese received the Japanese translation of the *Lineamenta*, they studied them together with the priests of their dioceses for about two months and tried to formulate an answer to the questions of the *Lineamenta*. However, though they had asked their priests for an answer to the questions of the *Lineamenta*, the reaction was that it was not possible to answer those questions. At the discussion at the Extraordinary Plenary Assembly (February 18–21, 1997) on how to prepare the official response, as we shall note below, many opinions were expressed on the questions themselves as well as about requests to be made at the synod itself.

(A) Opinions of the bishops concerning the questions of the *Lineamenta* themselves: Since the questions of the *Lineamenta* were composed in the context of Western Christianity, they are not suitable. Among the questions are some concerning whether the work of evangelization is going well or not, but what is the standard of evaluation? If it is the number of baptisms, etc., it is very dangerous. From the way the questions are proposed, one feels that the holding of the synod is like an occasion for the central office to evaluate the performance of the branch offices. That kind of synod would not be worthwhile for the Church in Asia. The judgment should not be made from a European framework, but must be seen on the spiritual level of the people who live in Asia.

(B) Hopes for the synod: If the synod is to be carried out for the Church in Asia, it must have an approach different from those for other continents. The same approach as [is used] in the West will not be successful. The most important thing is the inculturation of our thinking. As the Holy Father says, our objective must be a "New Evangelization." In other words, a new zeal that is different from that we have had until now, new expressions (and a completely different method of communication), new methods (an approach different from the traditional one). If we are to have a synod for Asia, in order that the method and process may be different from that for a synod for the West or for Africa, the priorities of the Church of Asia must be presented clearly before composing the *Instrumentum Laboris*.

Accordingly, the Japanese Bishops' Conference decided that they would prepare their own questions for the Japanese Church and ask the opinions of the major seminaries, theology faculties, and the various religious congregations.

Four months later, at the Ordinary Plenary Assembly (June 16–21, 1997), they considered more than 325 replies that had been submitted by the bishops themselves, the major seminaries, the theology faculties, religious congregations, individual priests and religious, councils of the laity, etc., and composed the Official Response of the Japanese Church, which is given below.

Requests of the Japanese Church to the Synodal Secretariat

I. Proposals Concerning Methodology

1. Consideration of Asian Countries without a Common Language

Among all the countries of Asia, there is not one that has as its native tongue any of those languages ordinarily used by the Holy See (Italian, English, French, German, Spanish). Countries such as India and Philippines, which have many different languages, use English as a kind of common language. However, among the almost forty nations which are to take part in the Special Assembly for Asia of the Synod of Bishops, they are exceptions. To fail to take this fact into account and to hold the Special Assembly according to the same schedule and methodology as those of Europe and America, etc., is ill advised. It is necessary to provide a period of preparation of at least six months from the date of the publication of the *Instrumentum Laboris* until the synod itself. (We should like to point out that it took three months from the publication of the *Lineamenta* to its translation into Japanese and distribution to the bishops.) The bishops of Japan consider it most important to translate the *Instrumentum Laboris*, study it carefully, and prepare themselves in prayer.

For the same reason we request that, together with determining English and French as the languages to be used at the synod, provision be made for simultaneous translation from English and French to Japanese, and other languages as requested by other episcopal conferences.

2. Use of a Methodology Suited to Asian Spirituality

Unlike Europe and Africa, the differences among the various nations of Asia are so fundamental that a basically different methodology from that used in the synods held up to now is called for. Using the methodology of the West "as is" for the Special Assembly for Asia will not be successful. Some sessions and activities should be included to work toward a united image and a new paradigm to include the varying realities and cultures of Asia, its different mentalities and spiritual traditions.

The issues to be discussed during the synod should be decided right after the bishops have convened. This is to assure that there is ample time for mature deliberation in order to arrive at the final recommendations.

The decision concerning the global direction of the synod should not be made by the Roman Secretariat, but should be left to the bishops from Asia. The choice of the chairpersons of the committees and small groups which are to direct the work of the synod should also be left to the bishops from Asia. They should follow their own sense of the process and the special needs of the assembly.

The bishops taking part in the synod should be permitted to consult and ask for the comments of experts concerning the different matters treated during the sessions. These experts should be persons recommended by the bishops themselves for their knowledge of the Church, the world, and especially the realities of Asia.

3. Use Should Be Made of the Fruits of the Federation of Asian Bishops' Conferences; Focus Should Be Limited from the Beginning For more than twenty-five years, the Federation of Asian Bishops' Conferences (FABC) has been involved with the reality of the Church in our countries and has made important statements. We propose that the fruit of the work of the FABC should be made good use of at the synod. For example, we propose that the practice of having a representative of the Church of each country give a report (which usually takes two weeks) be discontinued, and that a representative of the two blocks, namely, the FABC and the Middle East, first give a report on their history and current problems and thus give focus to the issues to be taken up by the Special Assembly for Asia of the Synod of Bishops. In this way, the very wide-ranging and many-faceted reality of the living Church in Asia will be presented, the main points of the presentation will become clear, and there will be time at the end to make a concrete plan.

4. Dividing into Groups At the synods up to the present, groups were formed according to the languages of the West (Italian, English, French, German, Spanish, etc.). However, we request that for this Special Assembly for Asia the groups be divided not according to language, but according to themes or religious cultures (Islamic Culture, Hindu Culture, Hinayana Buddhist Culture, Mahayana Buddhist Culture, Confucian Culture, etc.).

5. Participation of Various Observers One common anti-evangelical problem among the countries of Asia is discrimination against and oppression of women. In order that we can grasp and judge this reality, we request the participation of women observers well acquainted with this problem. The Major Superiors' Association of Religious Women of Japan is prepared to send a religious woman qualified for this task.

With few exceptions, the Catholic Church in almost all the countries of Asia is [in the] minority. In order to grasp and judge this situation, we request that representatives of the traditional religions and experts in dialogue with other religions be invited to participate as observers.

6. To Revitalize the Catholic Church of Asia The Catholic Church in Asia, at the dawn of the third millennium, has to continue the work of evangelization in the midst of many other religions. Making the most of this fact, we hope that the synod will be one that will encourage the work of evangelization that we are carrying on. The Church in Asia has many tasks and problems, but we hope that, rather than stressing the negative side, this synod will be one that will encourage us to continue our efforts against heavy odds. We do not hope for a synod aiming at discovering how the Asian Church can be propped up by the Western Church, but one where the bishops of Asia can have an honest exchange and learn how they can support and encourage one another. In other words, we wish to participate in the spirit of people really involved with one another, not seeking how "they can have life more abundantly," as if we were speaking of some third persons, but how "we together can have life more abundantly."

7. Focus on Relationship with Other Asian Religions   In Asia, in addition to Christianity and Judaism, there are also Hinduism, Islam, Buddhism, and other great religions. Moreover, there are animistic religions, which believe in the existence of spirits (and popular religions, cosmic religions, etc.), which have a wide influence. A culture that has developed under the influence of these various religions is a fundamentally different reality. Thus, should not the Special General Assembly for Asia consider, not the global connection of Christianity with all the problems of Asia, but the relationship of Christianity with each religion and each culture? Unless we do so, we may end up only with abstract discussions and without anything concrete or useful that the Church of Asia can do for an effective service to the Kingdom of God.

II. Considerations for Composing the *Instrumentum Laboris*

1. Christology   One finds in the *Lineamenta* a certain defensiveness and apologetic attitude. This makes its presentations of certain other theological positions clearly unfair and inadequate. This is especially clear in the section on Christology. This does not help the faith of Asian Christians. What is necessary is an open and spiritual Christology rooted in real life and alert to the problems of modern people.

We should try to discover what kind of Jesus will be a light to the peoples of Asia. In other words, as the Fathers of the early Church did with Graeco-Roman culture, we must make a more profound study of the fundamentals of the religiosity of our peoples, and from this point of view try to discover how Jesus Christ is answering their needs.

Jesus Christ is the Way, the Truth, and the Life, but in Asia, before stressing that Jesus Christ is the Truth, we must search much more deeply into how he is the Way and the Life. If we stress too much that "Jesus Christ is the One and Only Savior," we can have no dialogue, common living, or solidarity with other religions. The Church, learning from the *kenosis* of Jesus Christ, should be humble and open its heart to other religions to deepen its understanding of the Mystery of Christ.

2. Ecclesiology   The image of the Church presented in the *Lineamenta* is not as rich or deep as that of Vatican II. In particular, the images of "the Church as people of God" and "the Church as servant" are not stressed. These two images have special meaning for the Church in Asia, which in order to serve God's kingdom lives in a minority position with and for others. Their absence would be unfortunate for the synod.

The central issues of "Service" and "Dialogue" developed by the FABC are two very important points for the Catholic Church in Asia, which are not sufficiently stressed in the *Lineamenta*.

3. Soteriology   The theme of "Mission of Love and Service" proposed by the Catholic Church in Asia must be one that responds to the real thirst of the people of Asia. That is to say, it must make clear, in a way the people can understand, the content of the salvation that Jesus brings.

Again, in order to proclaim to the people of Asia the universal message of salvation, we must study how to express this message.

4. Missiology   In the *Lineamenta*, without attempting to explain what the term can or should mean, the word "Proclamation" is stressed and used over and over again. Considering the Asian context, not enough attention is given to the necessity of "Dialogue."

In the context of evangelization in Asia, "compassion with the suffering" has been identified time after time at the General Assemblies of the FABC as a most important element. In missionary work among those of other religions, what is more important than convincing words is the attitude of standing by the side of the weak and powerless and showing them compassion. In the *Lineamenta* a great deal is made, as in traditional scholastic theology, of "distinctions" and "differences." However, in the tradition of the Far East, it is characteristic to search for creative harmony rather than distinctions. In the documents published by the FABC over the past twenty-five years, there have been many examples of this "Asian-ness." Isn't it important for the Asian Synod to discuss how we are to accept the truths to be found in Hinduism, Islam, Buddhism, etc., how we are to evaluate them, and how we are to work together?

The questions at the end of the *Lineamenta* ask for an evaluation of our missionary activity. However, when we treat a situation in Asia where it is difficult to increase the number of baptisms, a "success orientation" of "trying for better results" can only discourage the missionary. We need a vision of evangelization that gives joy and a sense of purpose to a Christian living as one of a minority in the midst of many traditional religions. An evaluation based not on the number of baptisms but rather from the point of view of "How faithful have we been to our mission of evangelization?" is necessary.

5. Other Points   The theology on which the *Lineamenta* is based is the theology of the Christian West, and appears to the eyes of non-Christians as overly self-complacent and introverted. Based on this kind of theology, we cannot approach the unsettled Asia of today. In the *Lineamenta* there is a lack of understanding of the Asian culture, especially the Asian culture of today, which is a mixture of traditional Asian culture and an Americanized modern culture. Moreover, it does not appear that we can be satisfied with modern Western theology, either, especially if we consider that we can never say that the redemption of Christ and the work of the Holy Spirit are absent even in non-Christian cultures.

The historical analysis of the Church gives the impression of being centered in India. There is a great lack in the treatment in the *Lineamenta* of the problems of the Churches in the Siberian area of the former Soviet Union, those of the Churches of the Middle and Near East, those presently faced by the Church in China, the difficult situation of the Socialist nations of the Indochinese peninsula, and the pain of separation between the Republic of Korea and the Democratic People's Republic of Korea, etc.

THE CATHOLIC BISHOPS' CONFERENCE OF KOREA

Interreligious Dialogue

1. Activities in Interreligious Dialogue   Shamanism, Confucianism, Buddhism, and Taoism are traditional religions which are very influential on the Korean people. On a personal level efforts for dialogue with these religions are active, but on the official level of the Church, nothing substantial has been done.

2. Perspective for Dialogue and Its Fruit   Confucianism has made an important contribution to the religious life in the area of ethics and morals, and Buddhism has done so in the area of ascetical practice and mystical experience. As a result, there exist friendly sentiments between Catholics and these religions and belief systems. Continued studies, dialogues and collaborations are done at a personal level.

3. Concerns of the Church   We have to study and re-evaluate the meaning and role of the great traditional religions in Korea. They too play a part in the salvific economy of God. This understanding is essential for the inculturation of the Gospel. Ignorance of these religions and their culture, and a sense of superiority and exclusivism in religion should be eradicated.

Inculturation

1. Activities of Inculturation   As far as the inculturation of the Catholic Church in Korea is concerned, this process has been going on for the past two hundred years. The Church was introduced into Korea by Koreans and built by them. The liturgy is celebrated in Korean. As a result, the life of the Church is known to the Korean people. The Pastoral Institute, which is under the auspices of the Catholic Bishops' Conference of Korea, has established the Research Committee for Inculturation. It is aimed at promoting the study of the Korean expression of liturgy, Korean liturgical music, the Korean outlook on God and on human beings, shamanism, and other religions in Korea. Unfortunately, inculturation still remains in its beginning stage. We need to develop a spirituality and Church music that fit the Korean people's religious sentiments. Also, continued studies and efforts in inculturation are needed in the area of architecture. Inculturation should also include vestments and all the liturgical instruments associated with the liturgy. These are still in the European style.

2. Effects of Inculturation on the Church's Mission   Compared with the times when the Korean practice of the veneration of ancestors was forbidden, most Koreans now welcome the changed attitude of the Catholic Church which allows this veneration. This example of inculturation has had a great positive effect on the Church's mission.

3. The Contribution of Inculturation to the World Church   The family structure of the parish formed by clergy, religious, and laity is the fruit of Korean inculturation, and this is a special characteristic of the Church in Korea. We believe the world Church can learn from this model.

Social Teaching

The social teachings of the Church serve as guiding principles for the promotion of human rights, social justice, and the well-being of all in Korea. In spite of their lack of knowledge or interest in these teachings, many clergy, religious, and lay people continue to serve in the name of Christ and in the spirit of the Gospel.

Each diocese has committed itself to social-pastoral care in the light of the Catholic social teachings by establishing various committees for social welfare, justice and peace, labor apostolate, prison apostolate, etc. Charity clinics, orphanages, centers for the handicapped, and homes for the aged are operated in all dioceses. Also, some religious are working at welfare centers that are administered by the local government. All dioceses have a special budget for social-pastoral care.

Presently, the most pressing tasks are aid to North Korea, pastoral care for foreign workers, outreach to youth, and works for social justice by rooting out corruption.

It is not easy to integrate the social teachings of the Church into our daily lives. Implementation will have to be systematic and done in deep faith and commitment.

THE CATHOLIC BISHOPS' CONFERENCE OF LAOS

God's Salvific Plan in the History of Asia

The missionaries have left behind admirable and effective notes, books and directives as well as records of their experiences among the Hmongs (e.g., Father Bertrais, Father Subra, and others) and among the ethnic groups of Boloven (e.g., Father Michel and his school). Finally, Father Zego, Bishop Bayet and Father Coste have left behind books that greatly add to our knowledge of the Laotian customs, rites and beliefs.

In day-to-day contacts, the Christians take part in the great celebrations in the villages, avoiding only what is forbidden by the priests in the practice of the rites such as funeral rites, marriage rites, and the sacrifice of the buffalo among the Lovens and the Brous.

A country of proverbial tolerance, Laos has wise and peaceful children, full of respect for the beliefs of others. Polemics are rare, except sometimes among some older Christians who consider themselves more intelligent and superior because they possess Christ, the Almighty Victor in all things.

On the level of religious leaders, there is dialogue between Catholic priests and Buddhist monks. Venerable Had met with Pope Paul VI. Invitations are extended to Buddhists on the occasion of patronal feasts and ordinations. On the level of villages, gifts are exchanged for the celebration of feasts between villages. Villagers meet each other on these occasions. Thanks to these encounters and dialogue, we have learned to be more tolerant, although we still tend to maintain a polemical spirit: "Defend oneself in order to survive," which is a complex of Christians.

We have a greater sense of the sacred, which manifests itself in symbols that Christians unconsciously tend to distrust. We have more respect for other beliefs. Life among ourselves is more at ease. Opinions about Christians are more favorable and Christians feel less like strangers in the country and are less suspect. In particular, the religious feelings and moral values of other faiths move Christians: compassion, serenity, respect for the monks and the elders. Many more rites and ceremonies should be studied to build up the Christian faith. The rite of offering, the sacrifice of buffalo, sacred dances, local music and songs should be studied more deeply.

Jesus Christ the Savior, the Good News of God for All

In our region the Person of Christ is perceived according to the categories of various beliefs. Among fervent converted Buddhists, Christ is honored as the Messiah expected to come after the Four Great Predecessors, the last being the Buddha, in order to realize the will of God fully and to take care of those that are abandoned or left behind by the other predecessors. He is a divinity who cares most for the poorest, endowed with virtues to defeat demons and evil spirits over whom the other divinities are indifferent or powerless.

For converts from the traditional religions, Jesus Christ is a great Protector among a mass of protectors who takes good care of his protégés, the Christians; who protects his protégés by means of crosses, medals, rosaries, holy water, palms, and blessed coals. These converts evaluate the quality of Jesus the Protector by the beneficial changes to their health, wealth, and reputation, by his triumphs over evil spirits, and by his miracles. The Person of Christ is appreciated more for his power than for his compassion.

For those who are Christian from birth, especially those born in ghetto parishes, the Person of Christ is seen rather as God. He is God, an avatar who comes to accomplish certain feats and to teach the art of overcoming demons and evil spirits. With his cross as standard or sword, he conquers all and arranges everything for the benefit of his protégés.

Those who know and strive to know Jesus Christ as truly man are rare. They repeat the ideas of the catechism without conviction.

What is being proposed to proclaim Jesus Christ in the mission of the Church? Priests and missionaries have exerted a lot of effort, but there are no means to make this proclamation effective. Salvation for Christians and the people is something outside of themselves, something to do with self-interest, with security. Christians have recourse to the practice of the sacraments and rites in order to be assured of salvation, without really knowing the Person of Christ. The new converts, after extensive training courses, always confuse the Person of Christ with the priest who teaches them—his cassock, beard, and his refined behavior or just his kindness.

The Church, and above all our local Church, which has gone through difficult political, ideological, and social entanglements, must center on the Passion of our Lord Jesus Christ, on the mystery of the Cross, which gives birth to wisdom, to true salvation. With the experiences particular to our region, when Christians have well understood the lessons of the mysteries of the Cross thanks to hardships, they will truly discover the identity of Christianity and of Christian life. The drama of humanity reveals itself in the Passion and the Cross.

The Church can show forth Jesus Christ as the One and Only Savior as well as the universality of salvation in him by studying the Gospels and proclaiming him according to the Gospels. Often we repeat the catechism in our proclamation simply by hammering on the ideas or principles about Jesus. Asians, who understand by means of symbols or parables, understand better by reading the Gospels than by the explanations of priests or catechists. One can notice this during pastoral trips.

What is more, rites and ceremonies should be encouraged such as Stations of the Cross and Benediction of the Blessed Sacrament. The life of priests and religious and the prayers for the dead are a good starting point in helping the people understand the Person of Christ. The celebration of the sacraments and the prayers for the dead are meaningful moments to explain the faith. The witness of Christians who do not work on Sundays to go to Mass makes others reflect and leads them to know the Savior Jesus Christ.

THE CATHOLIC BISHOPS' CONFERENCE OF MALAYSIA, SINGAPORE, AND BRUNEI

What is being done in your area to help members of the Church become acquainted with the traditions of other religions in Asia?

1. Participating actively in the Malaysian Consultative Council for Buddhism, Christianity, Hinduism, and Sikhism.

2. At major festivals Christians encounter and learn some of the customs and practices of other religions through the electronic and printed media and social interaction.

3. Prayers of intercession are said in churches for those who celebrate cultural or religious (non-Christian) festivals.

4. In schools Christian staff and students do get acquainted with the traditions of other religions through the formal curriculum and social interaction.

What can the Church learn from her dialogue with other Asian religions and the knowledge obtained?

1. From Muslims, the Church can learn about prayer, fasting and almsgiving.

2. From Hindus, the Church can learn about meditation and contemplation.

3. From Buddhists, the Church can learn about detachment from material goods and respect for life.

4. From Confucianism, the Church can learn about filial piety and respect for elders.

5. From Taoism, the Church can learn about simplicity and humility.

6. From Animists, the Church can learn about reverence and respect for nature and gratitude for harvests.

7. The Church can learn from the rich symbolism and rites existing in their diversity of worship.

8. The Church can, like the Asian religions, learn to be more open, receptive, sensitive, tolerant, and forgiving in the midst of plurality of religions.

To what extent can the specific aspects of Asian religions be used and developed in the fulfillment of the Church's mission of bringing salvation to all peoples in Asia?

1. The Buddhist teaching of love and respect of nature and Islam's emphasis on submitting to Allah's will can be a source of inculturation in presenting the Christian faith and values to the people of Asia.

2. As most Asian values are interlinked with local religious values and customs, it is only proper that the Church acknowledge what is good in them and recognize our Christian values present in them.

3. Integrate some cultural practices and simple rituals from other religions and cultures into our worship.

In your area how is the Person of Christ viewed and proposed in the Church's mission of proclaiming Him and His salvation to the Asian people?

1. Jesus Christ is viewed as a prophet, a holy man, and a great leader.

2. As quite a number of baptized Christians still cling to and observe the practices of their former religions, it appears that their view of Christ is still blurred.

3. Generally, Jesus Christ is taught, both to Christians and catechumens, following the traditional catechism of the Church. Thus, everyone learns much about Jesus Christ and the Christian doctrine.

4. Jesus Christ is proclaimed through our living our faith in love, prayer, service, and sacrifice in the family, working place, neighborhood, Basic Ecclesial Communities zones, and society at large.

5. Through our witnessing and living Christ-like lives, others may view Christ as the only Savior.

6. Through our involvement in social concerns and issues and serving the needs of peoples of different cultures and religions, Jesus Christ is proclaimed concretely as salvation to the Asian people.

Describe ways in which the Church can maintain the centrality of the proclamation of Jesus Christ in very different political, social, and cultural situations.

1. To give genuine witness to Christ, the Church has to proclaim Christ in clear and unambiguous language.

2. The Church must give respect and due recognition to the values of other religions which are compatible with the Christian faith.

3. Encourage Christians to enter into politics and the mass media so as to be influential in forming opinions and policy-making at the highest level of administration. Prior to that they must be well versed in the social teachings of the Church vis-à-vis the promotion of human rights and social justice.

In what ways can the Church present Jesus Christ as the one and only Savior as well as the universality of salvation in Him?

1. By faithfully preaching and teaching the Christian faith with apostolic boldness and without compromise or ambiguity.

2. By dialoguing with other religions in sincerity and openness so that Christ is seen to be the Way, the Truth, and the Life.

3. By faithfully living and witnessing our faith that Christ is the only Savior.

4. By works of reconciliation and peace-making.

5. By recognizing and encouraging the use of various charisms given by the Spirit.

6. By presenting Christ in the context of the people's culture, art, language and value systems.

7. By presenting Christ-centered catechesis and having Spirit-filled liturgies.

8. By proclaiming Jesus Christ through personal experiences and testimonies.

9. By refraining from provoking or ridiculing believers of other faiths while proclaiming Jesus Christ.

THE CATHOLIC BISHOPS' CONFERENCE OF THE PHILIPPINES

Ways of Proclaiming Christ in Difficult Situations

1. The greatest gift that Christians can offer Asia is their faith in Jesus Christ; to give this gift, Christians must become Christ-like, do mission in dialogue and not in any sense of superiority and triumphalism but in true incarnation of Jesus Christ in the cultures of Asia, in mutual enrichment, in human promotion, in the struggle for justice and peace, in the promotion of the Kingdom of God;

2. Present him in the ways the culture understands—inculturation;

3. In Muslim areas, there is no other effective way of proposing Christ as Savior except by really living out a Christian witness of loving, serving, sharing, dialoguing, respecting—to be another Christ;

4. By being faithful to the basic bond of discipleship, actualizing the prophetic character of Christian life and mission;

5. Corporate credibility as a prophetic Church is necessary to authenticate our proclamation of Christ;

6. Proclamation by personal and fearless witnessing to Christ as the Word we preach, as a gentle, compassionate, patient, forgiving person who went about doing good, as Love's unmistakable expression;

7. Humbly and in peace, present the face of the Servant Christ, Christ of the poor, Jesus in his Paschal Mystery—a very much lived reality in Asia; all mission in Asia must be paschal;

8. Focus on Christ as liberator who guides and saves, the peace-maker, above political authority, breaking cultural barriers and traditions, e.g., regarding women;

9. Focus on the Kingdom values that Jesus proclaimed; emphasize his prophetic role in difficult situations;

10. Through homilies, novenas, conferences, religion classes; through mass media;

11. Through interreligious dialogue and prayer fellowship with other religions.

Presenting Jesus Christ as the One and Only Universal Savior

1. Show that Jesus is indeed the Good News not only because he brings us salvation, but because, through our sharing in his mission, we are committed to fight against all injustices that dehumanize millions in Asia;

2. Show that Christ died for all peoples, that he is the fulfillment of all revelations, of all prophecies and laws; he is at the heart of all religions;

3. By emphasizing how Christ fulfills the innermost yearnings of the human heart;

4. By going to the sources, making use of Scriptures, whose milieu had more in common with Asians today than with the Western situation, and present Christ as the universal Savior;

5. By practicing the Beatitudes—which are very close to Asian aspirations; show that the Beatitudes are fulfilled in Jesus;

6. By the personal witnessing of preachers, clergy, religious, catechists, and other pastoral workers;

7. By making Jesus as the model of life, e.g., strongly referring to Jesus and his values in one's own business, political decisions, and in one's solidarity with the poor;

8. Christ as incarnated in each of us, as the center of our lives;

9. By building Christ-centered communities of disciples;

10. By a service of justice, truth, peace, and love; by a spirituality of social transformation;

11. By way of Bible studies centered on Christ, Holy Mass, deep sacramental life, prayer, devotions, novenas, formation, catechesis, mass media.

Suggestions for the Synod

1. Ensure that the synod is truly Asian, with an Asian reflection, with an Asian output, reflecting the Asian perspective of evangelization.

2. Emphasize the FABC thinking that has been maturing for the past twenty-five years, e.g., on inculturation, interreligious dialogue, dialogue with the poor of Asia; or the fact that dialogue is not contrary to [proclamation], but is a mode of proclamation; or that inculturation is not a one-way street but a process of mutual enrichment.

3. There should be some assessment at the synod on the implementation of Vatican II in Asia: e.g., on episcopal collegiality, the local Church, inculturation.

4. A serious attempt should be made at the synod to portray Jesus Christ and the Church in ways that resonate with the Asian aspiration for full life in the midst of socioeconomic, political, and religio-cultural imbalances. On this matter the synod should refer to the Final Statement of the FABC Plenary Assembly in Manila, 1995, and the Final Statement of the FABC International Theological Colloquium in Pattaya, 1994.

5. Jesus proclaimed the Kingdom of God. The Kingdom of God, both a gift and a task, should be used as a perspective of the synod, and this calls not only for personal renewal, but also for prophetic engagement with structures of injustice in Asian societies.

6. The synod should correct or at least clarify what the *Lineamenta* seems to do—to equate the Church and the Kingdom of God. See *Lineamenta*, no. 26 ("Her mission is to be the Kingdom") and especially no. 29 ("The Church is often called the Kingdom of God, that is, the Reign of God").

7. The model of Church as communion should be used. But in the social context of the great majority of Asian peoples, even more use should be made of the model of the Church as servant, a co-pilgrim in the journey to the Kingdom of God where the fullness of life is given as a gift. The depths of the nature of the church as a *"pusillus grex"* in Asia should be explored, albeit with a mission to evangelize.

8. Emphasize the global character of the socioeconomic and political factors that press upon the lives and cultures of Asian peoples:

- The inexorable penetration into Asia—some would say, imposition—of the neoliberal capitalism of the West, dictated by secularism, materialism, and consumerism, which makes God an "unnecessary hypothesis" and leads to religious indifferentism and individualism
- Globalization and survival of the fittest in a free-market world
- The frenetic drive toward industrialization and urbanization which leaves the poor rural peoples of Asia helplessly floundering
- The gradual erosion of Asia's sense of the sacred because of the onset of secular values through science and technology

- The fact or myth of a population explosion in the southern hemisphere
- The destruction of Asia's environment
- The phenomenon of migrant workers

9. Women and youth should be given more extensive treatment.

10. The synod should make some statement about the Church in China.

11. The "revelatory" nature of the great ancient religions in Asia and its impact on the Church's proclamation of the truth of Jesus should be further explored in an open and humble way. While firmly and courageously confessing the truth, any treatment of the uniqueness of Jesus should avoid any triumphalism and superior attitude vis-à-vis the other great religions of Asia.

12. The synod should assess the development of an Asian theology which may or may not follow the thought processes and expressions of Western, and particularly Roman, theology—while surely abiding in dynamic fidelity to the magisterium.

13. For mission, the synod should strike a note of urgency for the need of more liberationist ministries in favor of the greatest majority of Asians, namely, the poor. The implications for the Church of the option for the poor should be explored. How will we actualize this vision of becoming a Church of the Poor?

14. The formation of evangelizers in the Asian context should be treated in depth.

15. The contribution of Asia's heritage of contemplation and spirituality in enriching our faith and spirituality should be highlighted.

16. A more extensive treatment of spirituality for Asia and its agents of evangelization (laity, clergy, religious) should be done by the synod. This should include a development of a spirituality of harmony that is so evident in Asia.

THE CATHOLIC BISHOPS' CONFERENCE OF SRI LANKA

The Church's Evangelizing Mission

The work of evangelization in Sri Lanka, begun by the Portuguese in the sixteenth century, was carried on by the Oratorians led by the great Apostle of Sri Lanka, Blessed Joseph Vaz, during the Dutch persecutions in the seventeenth century, winning back the apostates and bringing many new converts in all parts of the island. This was consolidated by the more recent European missionaries, the Oblates of Mary Immaculate, Sylvestro Benedictines, the Jesuits, and the many women religious congregations that came along with them. The local hierarchy was established in 1893, and today the number of dioceses has grown to eleven, all manned by local bishops and clergy. Assessment of the Post-Independent Period (1948) reveals that there are both achievements and several failures.

I. Achievements

A. Structures:

1. The establishment of national and diocesan commissions for missionary activity.

2. Small groups of religious and laity living in the midst of non-Christians, diffusing the light of faith through witness and service.

3. Missionary associations for children well established in most of the parishes. Several lay theologates that prepare lay leaders for mission.

4. Centers of evangelization organized at national and diocesan shrines, with facilities for convert instruction and counseling.

5. Rise of several national and diocesan institutes: catechetical, biblical; national and diocesan commissions for justice and peace with their centers.

B. Programs:

1. Evangelization through development and witness of social commitment: working for peace, nonviolence, defense of human rights, option for the poor and the oppressed.

2. Seminars at national, diocesan, and parish levels for mission animators, priests, religious, and laity.

3. Elaborate celebration of Mission Sunday, Holy Childhood Day to conscientize the faithful on their missionary vocation received in baptism and to promote missionary vocations.

C. Movements:

1. The laity assuming more and more responsibility in the total mission of the Church. The lead given by the Catholic Charismatic Movement, the healing ministry, Asian Integral Pastoral Approach (AsIPA), Basic Christian Communities (BCC), Marriage Encounter, and other lay apostolate movements launching missionary programs such as Peregrinatio Pro Christo; visiting hospitals, prisons, and refugee camps, etc.

2. Other Bible-based communities diffusing Gospel values and engaging in social action: Christian Family Movement (CFM), Young Christian Workers (YCW), Young Christian Students (YCS), etc.

II. Drawbacks

1. The lack of well-planned and sustained effort for missionary activity by the total Church.

2. The Church becoming introverted, and efforts made to maintain the Church rather than forge ahead.

3. The revival of Buddhism, Hinduism, and Islam and the rise of religious fundamentalism and fanaticism.

4. Restrictions placed by the state on foreign missionaries and their activity in public institutions such as hospitals.

5. The state's takeover of denominational schools in 1962, thus disorganizing the whole Catholic education system, with the consequent decline in religious and moral values; restrictions placed on religious in government schools, their recruitment, training, and promotion, etc.

6. The system of Western-oriented Catholic education leading to discrimination in society, arousing antagonism among the less privileged.

7. Self-complacency of Church ministers and lack of proper motivation in the clergy; misunderstanding of Vatican II's teaching on mission, e.g., the possibility of salvation in other religions, downplaying the role of Christ as the one Redeemer; and lack of appropriation of conciliar teachings in general.

8. The decline in good priestly and religious vocations due to the breakdown of the family, the spread of secularism and hedonism, and the evil effects of present-day mass media.

9. Disunity among various Christian denominations and the accusation of using unethical means of conversion by Christian sects.

III. Specify Ways of Promoting Missionary Activity

1. Missionaries to be made familiar with both vernacular languages (Sinhala and Tamil), especially in areas where both communities are present.

2. Seminarians and religious to learn Asian forms of prayer, meditation and spirituality, monastic and contemplative life, simple style of life in keeping with the majority of our people.

3. Divesting the Church of the Western image in the liturgy, lifestyle, celebrations, and trying to overcome the present image of a powerful, affluent, and domineering institution.

4. Personal contact with people, regular house visitation and praying with the people, and laying hands on the sick, etc.

5. Dialogue with people of other faiths and common action with them in the fields of social action, justice, peace, and human rights.

6. Ongoing formation programs for clergy, religious, and laity at various levels.

7. Promotion of Christ and Word-centered small communities; the decision of the Bishops' Conference to promote AsIPA in all the dioceses.

8. Better and closer cooperation among the various dioceses and Religious congregations.

9. Learning from the experiences of other countries such as Korea.

10. Sharing the resources of the Church in education, culture, etc.

11. A better-organized adult catechumenate at all levels and the establishment of a National Catholic Inquiry Center.

Proclaiming Jesus Christ

1. We live in a multireligious setting in which Jesus Christ is viewed in many different forms: Muslims accept Jesus as a great prophet as he is mentioned in the Koran. Hindus treat him as an avatar, an incarnation of God. Buddhists see him as

a social reformer and a great teacher, and for many others he is a great liberator. Generally speaking, there seems to be an awesome respect for Jesus Christ.

In our non-Christian context, the Church is engaged in a search to discover the images in which the person of Jesus can be presented. The Church bases itself on the biblical witness and makes ample use of its Christological titles and presents Jesus as the Risen Lord and eschatological savior of the world. Reference is made to the compassion of Jesus and the social implications of the Gospel message in the promotion of justice and reconciliation in the service the Church renders to all.

2. At all levels, irrespective of distinctions, Jesus must come across as the source of our inspiration and reconciliation. As the universal source of love, Christ unites and breaks through all differences, while respecting diversity. He is the one who befriends all, calls all people to unselfish love, and to share forgiveness.

Asian Christians believe in the universality of salvation since it is God's will that all people be saved and come to the knowledge of the Truth (2 Tim 2:4). The "uniqueness" of Jesus and of the Church has been a perennial problem and poses its own distinctive difficulties for authentic dialogue. In attempting to resolve it, some have moved from one extreme position to another, viz., from exclusivism with an ecclesiocentric emphasis to pluralism with a theocentric emphasis. Thus, the new challenge to Christology is to speak of the identity of Jesus Christ in the context of the world religions and secular culture. Jesus Christ must be presented as completely fulfilling all human aspirations. He is the model of a completely human person. He lived out the human struggle. He has something specific and "unique" to offer to Asian peoples and has a special message to the poor and the oppressed who are fast becoming a sociocultural group in our country, a by-product of a profit-oriented market economy that is beneficial only to a few. The teachings of Christ can help address the conscience of the rich in favor of the poor.

Our understanding of salvation must be clear. Salvation is not merely an experience of illumination or a feeling of being in union with God. Nor is it merely human or physical liberation. Salvation is what God has done against sin and death in the resurrection of Jesus. He came, lived, and died so that all may find life and the world may be reconciled.

For many people, God and Christ are not the problem. Christ in Sri Lanka came in a foreign garb. Hence, inculturation is becoming part of the missionary mandate for us. All impressions to the contrary must be carefully avoided. We must insist on Christ Jesus as a religious founder who came from Asia, which is such a rich continent in the history of religion.

Thus, there is the necessity of a missionary spirituality of dialogue. In this dialogue we make the author of salvation and grace known, we make others aware of the Christ event, we do not impose things but propose them. Our dialogue will be a two-way street. In this endeavor, we need to cultivate sincere respect for other religions. Hence, for us in Asia, religions are a part of the universal context in which the true identity of Jesus must find new expressions. While we affirm the uniqueness of Christ, we need to move toward a nonthreatening articulation, an articulation that would be more conducive to dialogue in Asia.

THE CATHOLIC BISHOPS' CONFERENCE OF TAIWAN
Inculturation

1. Preliminary Remarks

The Church in Taiwan has been aware of the importance of inculturation since the beginning. However, so far she is still in the searching stage. It is hoped that through the canonization of the Blessed Martyrs of China the process of inculturation will have a new impetus. At present the work of inculturation in Taiwan in various aspects (theology, liturgy, spirituality, etc.) is still limited. There has not been a remarkable contribution to the Church as a whole. Take the example of Hualien. Its population is not numerous. In addition to the ethnic groups of Minnan, Hakka, and the people from other Chinese mainland provinces, there are six tribes of aborigines. Up to fifty years ago, these aborigines did not have their own written language. At present inculturation consists in transcribing their spoken languages into the Chinese script and then translating the Bible and homilies into this script. It is not easy work. Another step is to adopt and adapt their music and dance into the liturgy.

On the other hand, these aborigines now live in a wider environment. In order to communicate with others, they need to learn the Chinese language and culture and possibly a foreign language. In connection with evangelization, it seems to be less consuming of time and energy for them to learn the Chinese language well, obviously without neglecting their own languages.

2. Extent of Inculturation

Liturgy: Except for some liturgical adaptation among the aborigines there has been no notable accomplishment. The funeral liturgy, the rites to commemorate the ancestors on Chingming and Chungyang festivals, and the ceremonies for the Chinese New Year are the most inculturated. They include the use of Chinese incense (joss sticks), Chinese music and hymns, and the offerings of fruits or produce of the local farms. Also prayer papers with the image of the Risen Lord are used instead of paper money and are placed on tombs at the Chingming and Chungyang festivals.

Spirituality: Some efforts have been made to develop a spirituality integrated with the practices of Zen Buddhism.

Religious Art: Chinese art is used for Christmas cards, calendars, and posters. Scrolls with Chinese sayings are hung on doors of houses and churches for the New Year. Some Chinese religious music and hymns are also used.

Architecture: With a few exceptions, church architecture remains predominantly based on the Western model.

Theology: In addition to seminars for this purpose, we can mention the writings of Monsignor Paul Cheng, which are remarkable for their success in tracing similarities or parallels between Chinese classical literature and the Gospels. Also some incipient efforts have been made to promote and develop an Asian feminist theology and spirituality.

Other Aspects: It is quite common in Taiwan to perform some extravagant plays to please the gods. This can be considered as a kind of association of religion with daily life. It is worthwhile to imitate this spirit, not the performance, and to think how to inculturate religious celebrations in this way.

3. Contribution to Inculturation

As has been pointed out above, there has been so far no remarkable contribution in this respect. Nevertheless, efforts to insert good elements of traditional customs into the liturgy or to introduce some Asian practices into Christian spirituality and prayer life have been much appreciated. This has contributed to the conversion of some people to the Catholic Church. However, it is not sufficient to incorporate these elements into the liturgy; the Christian meaning must be added and explained. Superficiality in this regard is to be avoided. Where necessary, rectification must also be made, for example, with regard to superstitions.

Moreover, more efforts have to be made to accomplish what is still missing in the inculturation of theology. For instance, we must adopt terms that can easily be understood by present-day people and use a simple language in the catechism.

Social Doctrine of the Church

The Church has always considered service to the poor and needy a main means of evangelization. This must also be the way of evangelization in Asia. In fact, the success of the early evangelization in Taiwan was due to this way.

Under the auspices of the Catholic Bishops' Conference of Taiwan, the Commission for Social Development (Caritas) and the Commission for Social Justice and Peace have been organized. More personnel are needed to make them more effective. In this regard more coordination is needed to make better use of human and financial resources. . . .

The faithful are to be educated to strengthen their spirit of love and service while doing works of service. They are to be encouraged to study Church social teachings and to put them into practice by means of services to the sick, the elderly, the homeless, foreign workers, prostitutes, abused children, etc.

There is throughout Asia a growing concern for and outreach to migrant workers and, on a somewhat lesser scale, a concern for AIDS education and ministry to people suffering from AIDS. Some efforts are also being made to address issues concerning the role of women in the Church and violence against women, girls, and children throughout Asia, especially the trafficking in women and the prostitution of children. In all of this, the Church's social teachings provide a strong basis and impetus for action on behalf of justice. Consequently, it is essential in Taiwan to promote awareness of the Church's social teachings among Christian grassroots communities and to encourage both individual and group commitment to action.

In Taiwan the voices of the marginalized people such as the aborigines and foreign laborers are being heard. The government has passed new laws to eliminate unjust practices and the exploitation of these people. The Church has set up many centers to help these groups. Masses in English are available for overseas Catholic laborers, and church facilities are made available for their social gatherings, etc. The Church was one of the leaders in setting up educational centers for the intellectually challenged. One group of sisters has set up a university for the elderly. There are also senior citizen centers. Nursing homes run by the Church are also increasing.

Through Marriage Encounter and Engaged Couples Encounter, the sanctity of marriage is advocated and aid is given to couples to strengthen their love and fidelity. A small group of women called the Sprout Group meets regularly to discuss women's issues and act to bring about the elimination of violence against women and children.

Concern for AIDS patients and the promotion of education concerning this disease is being taken up more and more by Church personnel, especially religious sisters. Moreover, the Church's social teachings are penetrating little by little even into the ranks of lawyers and nongovernmental organizations dealing with issues such as the environment, racial discrimination, and human rights.

THE CATHOLIC BISHOPS' CONFERENCE OF THAILAND

Interreligious Dialogue

1. At the national and diocesan levels there are committees for dialogue with other religions. Activities in interfaith relationship include taking part in one another's ceremonies and social action.

2. In schools, Buddhist students are encouraged to participate in their own ceremonies, and monks are invited to explain their religion. Conversely, some government schools and institutions have invited priests to explain the Catholic religion. As a result, Buddhists and Catholics who have joined in those occasions are able to live like brothers and sisters, and former bad feelings are slowly disappearing.

There has been a concern that an immature faith may prevent the formation of Christian identity and will cause religious indifference. Christians run the risk of being assimilated in the end by the environment. In many cases, mixed marriages lead Christians to lose their faith little by little.

Inculturation

1. There are attempts at inculturation, such as

- using the traditional ways of paying respect in the liturgy;
- bringing the Buddhist, Chinese, and Indian philosophies into theological studies;
- in spirituality, there have been adaptations of Buddhist meditation and the practice of temporary religious commitment;

- on the artistic side, churches are built in Thai style, and vestments decorated with Thai designs.

2. Buddhists are still suspicious of our efforts at inculturation. They are afraid that their religion may be absorbed by the Catholic religion. Conversely, there are still a good number of Catholics who cling to the Western ritual, do not want to adapt to Thai ways, and even oppose such efforts.

3. Despite difficulties, attempts at inculturation show that the Church is universal and able to adapt to all traditions, thereby realizing unity through diversity.

THE CATHOLIC BISHOPS' CONFERENCE OF VIETNAM

Catechesis and Pastoral Ministry

Catechesis begins with an initial approach that puts us in contact with people. Past experience has shown how difficult it was for Asians to assimilate the language of Christian doctrine.

Enriched with a spiritual heritage at the highest level, they felt hurt by such expressions as, "There is a unique Savior and it is Jesus Christ," "Baptism is essential to enter heaven," "Evangelization of peoples." These ways of speaking seem to take no account of age-old religious values to which people have grown accustomed since time immemorial. Some of the symbols used in the Catholic liturgy go contrary to Asian ideas (breathing, use of salt in the baptism rite, etc.). The wording of certain dogmas is truly hard and shocking to people accustomed to the idea of the "golden mean" (for example, the infallibility of the pope, the defense of monotheism).

In using this kind of language, some religious and priests propose a way of life which shows them closer to Westerners than to their own compatriots; and since they are better educated than others, their attitude is often that of a self-sufficient people who are very sure of themselves. Churches are normally built in a Western style; some statues, to be sure, have been made along local lines, but there is still nothing specifically Vietnamese about them. In the area of liturgy, apart from some compositions allowed for "experimental" use (Mass texts for the first three days of the Lunar New Year, for the children's feast in mid-Autumn), efforts at inculturation have only touched on the exterior. In certain areas, this "wrapping" takes on inadequate forms: dances for the offering of flowers and multicolored floats in processions evoke the days of the mandarins rather than convey an attitude of deep worship. This style of life and liturgy increases the distance between evangelizers and evangelized, and strengthens the latent impression among the latter that Christianity is an imported religion.

Concerning the lacunae in the means of approach, the situation is more serious: there is an internal contradiction in the evangelizing enterprise itself. On the one hand, the Church seems to be growing rapidly, especially before 1975 and after the opening up of the economy in the late 1980s: there has been an increase of buildings, material purchases of all kinds, churches, monuments, vehicles, top-of-the-line equipment. On the other hand, among agents of evangelization there is a very limited intellectual and doctrinal level, a level of doctrinal formation that leaves much to be desired. This state of affairs is true not only at the level of non-specialized catechists in the parishes (well-meaning people devoted to the apostolate) but also in some seminaries and novitiates. Fortunately, those in charge in this area are aware of the deficiencies: all the responses to the *Lineamenta* have expressed the need to introduce the study of missiology into the formation program.

The Vietnamese Church and the Beatitudes

Grand undertakings such as building institutions and organizing large gatherings of people become suspect and are seen as manifestations of power. They will have to be reduced to the minimum. But for those works that seem elementary, less glamorous—such as helping handicapped children, lepers, and the poor in remote areas where there is no one to help them—appeals will be made to Catholics, especially religious. A self-effacing presence, using the humblest and simplest means, is more easily accepted by all. It is in this way that the Church can return to the poor and make itself closer to them, sharing with them the same human condition. Moreover, the witness of the faithful will make more visible the message and the true face of Jesus Christ, he who became poor among the poor in order to serve them.

Our Perspectives

From the experiences mentioned above, the Church in Vietnam believes it must rethink its ways of evangelizing in Asia. The first reason is that this continent is not a virgin or fallow soil on which any kind of seed can be sown. Rather it is a land of very ancient religions and civilizations when compared to Europe. It is a spiritual font of rich and solid ideas about the universe, humanity, and religion. Its peoples are not without knowledge of God. Quite the opposite, they have a certain experience of his presence and invoke him under different names such as "Sky," "Heaven," "Brahman," etc. Consequently, to "evangelize" in this particular case does not mean to present a God, a Christ, as totally unknown, but, in a certain way—to borrow a Buddhist expression—it is "to make the Light shine more brightly," present but hidden; it is to help people "see the Truth illuminated," which Vatican II recognizes as partially present in other religions, especially those of Asia (cf., *NA* 2).

To put it better, it is to proclaim, in the manner of Christ, to the people that the Word and the Kingdom of God are in their midst, in their very hearts, here and now, and not in Jerusalem or some other place, in another age. In other words, it is from the water of everyday life that we discover the living water (cf. Jn 4:7–26). Since God is the Creator of all things, one should say that, in a sense, the existence of these non-Christian religions is equally part of his Providence.

However, among Asians, the perception of God and the concept of Ultimate Reality are not the same as for Westerners. Asia possesses two principal characteristics of a philosophical and religious nature. First of all, there is a vision of a harmonious synthesis of all Reality that embraces the Ultimate Reality called Sky, Heaven, the Great One, the Brahman, or the Way. This is the *via negativa*, considered as a way to the Real, for it involves a harmonizing vision of the yin and the yang, the internal and the external, the transcendent and the immanent.

Second, not being able to explain what "God" means, one can only affirm that he is not at all like this and scarcely like that, and then to reflect that one must appeal to the heart rather than to reason for an experience of Truth. Western, and especially scholastic, theology is not appropriate for the religions of Asia, because it is too rational. For Asians, one cannot analyze the truth nor explain the mystery. There is a preference for silence over words and not getting entangled in quarrels over words. The word is only the finger pointing to the moon; what matters is the moon and not the finger. That is why Confucius speaks of the "empty" heart (a heart which has been made empty, that is, whole, pure); Lao-Tzu of nonaction (acting as if not acting); and the Buddha of the non-I (*anatta*, that is, not to think of oneself, to consider oneself as nonexisting = self-denial). Is this not the mystery of the *kenosis* of Christ, or something very close to it? And the mystery of the empty tomb, a void, a state of emptiness, but containing a marvelous truth: the Lord Jesus is risen? The empty tomb has become the symbol of the Risen One. In the same sense, the wise men of Asia often say that it is not necessary to speak much when talking of the Real, that it is ineffable in itself. "A way that can be conceived as a way is not a firm (immutable) way" (Lao-Tzu). So the Church of today should accept pluralism in matters of theology. If there is a theological way of thinking and speaking which is proper to the West, there should also be one proper to Asia, at least directed to Asia, and only Asian Christians know how to effect it. The time has come for Asians, after having been formed and enriched by the theological thinking of the West, no longer to be content with repeating and translating it. Jesus is a man from Asia, but his thinking had to detour through the West before coming back to Asia! It is now time for it to be expressed in the language of Asian peoples. More than that of the thinkers of the West, the language of Scripture is effectively closer to that of the sages of the East.

For Asians, "the Way is not far from humanity" (Confucius); Sky, God is not far from humans. That is the reason the mystery of God made human has much in common with the Asian soul. A God full of mercy, a God living among humans, sharing with them the human condition, and taking on the sufferings of humanity: this is very close to the beliefs and hopes of those not accustomed to transcendental heights but very familiar with the figures of bodhisattvas—symbols of compassion—such as the "goddess" Kuan Yin. This is the reason that in Vietnam the Virgin Mary is venerated and invoked not only by Christians but also by non-Christians. For this same reason, a meek and humble Christ (Mt 11:29), a reflection of the mercy of the Father (cf., Lk 6:36)—who wants to gather all into a large regenerated human family, in which all live a relationship of filial piety toward the Father, in the love and harmony of brothers and sisters—attracts the Asian soul more than [does] the feudal image of the Kingdom. The Asian ethic, which stresses the virtues of loyalty, filial piety, and humanity, is very close to the Christian spirit: loyalty toward God, piety toward parents and ancestors, and love toward all. Consequently, we think it is necessary to inaugurate an Asian Christology and theology that is more anthropological and existential.

Together with these disciplines, it is equally necessary to build the Church as a family of God's children more than as a hierarchy endowed with structures and perfectly formulated laws. The Church as a family will integrate better in the Asian society.

Christians will approach their compatriots not as strangers who have come to convince, to overcome, or to treat them as objects of charity but to encounter and share. To share is simultaneously to give and receive. Christ himself did this when he received from humanity his human flesh, which he needed for his nourishment and clothing, his language and culture, etc., so that he could share the love of God with all those from whom he had himself received.

During the Second Vatican Council, one of our bishops made an intervention on this topic in this way: "The Church as the Family of God is an idea very close to man. The presentation of the mystery of the Church in words connected to the family is very familiar and easy for everyone to understand. . . . Presenting the Church as the Family of God helps Christians come back to the Gospel, to the very simple pedagogy of Jesus himself who often made use of family images. In this way, one can understand the Gospel and can more easily penetrate it."

The Church of today does not come to Asia simply to give or to offer whatsoever, not even Jesus Christ. Jesus was from Asia. He was born and lived his life as a human being on this huge continent of the great religions and civilizations of the world. The Church today is equally aware that it is a Church "in the world," and the Churches of Asia, which have their origin in Asia, find themselves among their peers. They continue to receive from the civilizations and religions of Asia values that enrich their own Christian faith, as they share with all the lowly conditions of human living.

That is why the Church in Vietnam thinks of evangelization first as a sharing in life, a life as Jesus himself lived it: a life of love for all, a love which goes to the end (cf., Jn 13:1), so great that he dares to sacrifice his life for those he loves (cf., Jn 5:13). In other words, to evangelize is synonymous with being a witness to Jesus Christ (cf. Lk 24:47–48; Acts 1:8) through a life worthy of being his disciple. And the sign by which the disciple can be recognized is love for one's brothers and sisters (cf., Jn 13:35), a preferential love for the poor, who make up the majority of the Asian continent. It is to these that the Gospel speaks (cf., Lk 4:18), because they are ready to recognize in their difficulties the presence of God in the sign of love. As Georges Bernanos put it, "Only the poor have the secret of hope."

We recall an experience of our Church in its beginnings. In a report dated December 31, 1632, after five years of evangelization, about the Christian community of Thang Long (now Hanoi), Father Gaspar d'Amaral wrote: "The Christians here number more than one thousand. They show such love for each other that those around them, not yet knowing what to call them but having seen how they live, refer to them as 'those who follow the religion of mutual love.'" This was also the experience of the primitive Church in Jerusalem (cf., Acts 2:42–47; 4:32–35).

Desiderata

From our perspective, as mentioned earlier, and in the present circumstances of Asia and Vietnam, we would like to share with other sister Churches our idea of mission and the way in which we would like to see the work of evangelization realized. That is, evangelization is not to try to convince, to make propaganda, still less to conquer, to make at all costs a mass of people enter the Church. It is, on the contrary, to go toward all (cf., Mt 28:19), to be a human person among other human persons (cf., Jn 1:14), as a witness to Jesus Christ, the personified love of the Heavenly Father.

More than ever, the Church in Vietnam today is a seed in the process of falling into the ground, here and there, over the whole field. Few people can discern its abundant harvest, as if we could count and weigh it as we do with ears of corn. But it is precisely these grains that are preparing a new harvest. At the word of God, we are launching our net (cf., Lk 5:5). We have planted the seed, and by night or day, whether we sleep or wake, the wheat sprouts and we have the right to hope (cf., Mk 4:26–27).

Today, the Vietnamese "missioners" are the ordinary lay people, women religious in particular. As in the primitive Church at Jerusalem, here it is the lay people who first carried the Good News out of Jerusalem (cf., Acts 11:19–21). Today, quietly, the laity and the religious, even young people, are giving witness to Christ throughout the whole country. We hope that their efforts and hardships will be recognized and their work encouraged.

To sum up, only a poor Church will be able to adapt itself to a huge mass of poor people. A Church that is humble and small will blend more easily with the poor masses of Asia. A Church without power will more easily approach so many men and women who only ask for the right to live as men and women, to have enough food and clothing, to study and to work. Has not the time come to create new types of Church, such as small communities that are more easily set up in society, especially that of the poor; poorer communities, without ostentatiousness, without obstructions, which instill discomfort and fear in those who wish to approach them; communities that are open rather than closed; communities that are more attentive to the whole of human living—and not just the purely religious—to help improve the physical and material life of the poor, to raise up their cultural level? "Morality comes after sufficient food and clothing," as a Vietnamese saying goes. Of course, the Church has not been sent to solve problems of the social or economic orders, but that is no reason for showing no concern for them. Jesus did not proclaim the Good News only in words; this Good News for him also meant that "the blind see, the lame walk, the lepers are cleansed, the deaf hear, and the dead come to life" (Lk 7:22). Asia is a continent with so many blind, lame, deaf, and lepers who are waiting for the gift of being healed. The Church should share in their sufferings as their "joy and their hope."

3

Theological Evaluation

In his introduction to the *Lineamenta*, Cardinal Jan Schotte, the General Secretary of the Synod of Bishops, invited responses to the document from various groups of the local Church, including seminaries and faculties of theology. Some Asian theologians, many of whom helped draft the responses of their episcopal conferences to the *Lineamenta*, expressed their own assessment of the document and voiced the Asian Churches' hopes and expectations concerning the Asian Synod.[1]

This chapter presents two essays evaluating the theological contribution of the preparatory phase of the Asian Synod. The first, by Michael Amaladoss, evaluates the *Lineamenta* in light of the challenges facing the Catholic Church in Asia. In his view, the Working Document does not embody the vision of the Kingdom of God that will impel the Asian Catholic Church to embark upon the triple dialogue—with the poor, the cultures, and the religions—that the Federation of Asian Bishops' Conferences has been urging. What the Asian Synod must do, according to Amaladoss, is to take seriously the fact of cultural and religious pluralism so pervasive in Asia and "offer concrete strategies to make it a source of richness and creativity rather than of conflict."

The second, by Jonathan Tan, studies in detail the responses to the *Lineamenta* by the episcopal conferences of Indonesia and Japan, arguably the most critical and constructive of all episcopal responses. The essay also highlights two areas in which differences between the *Lineamenta* and the Asian bishops are most visible, namely, Christology and the relationship between proclamation and interreligious dialogue.

—Ed.

Note

1. See, for example, Kuncheria Pathil, "*Lineamenta* for the Asian Synod: Some Observations and Comments," *Jeevadhara: A Journal of Christian Interpretation* XXVII/160 (1997), 249–259; G. Gispert-Saucil, "The *Lineamenta* for the Asian Synod: Presentation and Comment," *VJTR* 61 (1997), 8–15; Chrys McVey, "The Asian Synod: What Is at Stake?" *EAPR* 35/1 (1998), 141–146; and J. Constantine Manalel, "The Jesus Movement and the Asian Renaissance: Some Random Reflections for the Asian Synod," *Jeevadhara: A Journal of Christian Interpretation* XXVII/160 (1997), 133–153.

EXPECTATIONS FROM THE SYNOD OF ASIA[*]
MICHAEL AMALADOSS

The preparations for the Special Assembly of the Bishops with a focus on the Churches in the Asian continent have entered the final stage with the publication of the Working Document or *Instrumentum Laboris*. This document has no other purpose than to outline the topics for discussion at the synod as suggested by the different Churches. The work at the synod itself will start with a presentation by the official Reporter of the Synod and the bishops will be free to take up any topic that interests them for their interventions. The Working Document is only a preparatory tool and does not require any commentary. But it does indicate the points that are of interest to the various Asian Churches as it is prepared with the help of the special commission of bishops that is charged with preparing the synod. It is presented as a synthesis/summary of the responses of the Asian Churches to the *Lineamenta*. We have no means of judging how good a summary it is. But like all summaries it tends to be flat and lacks focus and punch. You think of any topic and you will find a word or a phrase referring to it somewhere in the document. There is no prioritizing. Going through the document, one is likely to miss the forest for the trees. I would like therefore to evoke some points that are our own expectations from the synod as a contribution to its ongoing preparation and celebration. I should further specify that this is an Indian point of view—I am not speaking for the whole of Asia.

A Vision for Asia of the Third Millennium

The Synod for Asia is set in the context of evangelization. Evangelization is the proclamation of the Good News of Jesus Christ. It is the revelation of a vision of a new cosmic-human-divine community as our future, which is God's promise to all peoples and which challenges us to commitment and conversion. It is a community of freedom, fellowship, and justice that mediates God's own unconditional love for us. God will reconcile and unify all things in Christ in a new heaven and a new earth, in which God will be all in all. The human, cultural, and religious riches that God has shared with the peoples of Asia will be integrated in a new cosmic harmony. Economic disparities and social discriminations will disappear. There will be a community of love, mutual service, and peace. The theme of the synod is: *Jesus Christ the Savior and His Mission of Love and Service in Asia: ". . . That They May Have Life, and Have It Abundantly."* The life that is Jesus' gift to Asia brings release to the captives, recovery of sight to the blind, freedom to the oppressed, the favor of the Lord to everyone (cf., Lk 4:18), healing to the sick, food to the hungry, conversion of heart to the sinner, and peace to all people of goodwill. The "Life" that Jesus offers to the peoples of Asia is not merely life after death, but also life before death, life in communion with each other and with God experienced in the breaking of the bread; life that is ever present as hope even

---

[*]Michael Amaladoss, "Expectations from the Synod of Asia," *VJTR* 62 (1998), 144–151.

in the midst of poverty and suffering; life that challenges creativity in the power of the Spirit. This is the Kingdom of God that Jesus proclaimed and that we proclaim again today as the goal of all our strivings. The Church—we Christians—is the symbol and servant of this Kingdom. We have not only to talk about it, but model it in our lives and in our communities. Such a vision and goal will attract, enthuse, and challenge people to creative efforts in the Spirit. Do we live such a vision? Do we propose such a vision to the others? Are we, rather, proposing an individual and other-worldly salvation? Do we have such a comprehensive vision of evangelization or do we just think of a series of tasks like social ministries, interreligious dialogue, inculturation, etc., that lack a unifying and dynamic focus? What is the vision of the Church that animates our reflection and discussions? If we wish the Christians in Asia to be enthusiastic evangelizers in the third millennium, then we have to give them a new vision of the Kingdom of God and a new experience of trying to be a community of that Kingdom here and now in history. If we have such a vision and experience, the different tasks will look after themselves. Let us be honest. How inspiring are we as communities of the Kingdom? Are we more worried about the Church-institution and about planting and enlarging it than about the Kingdom, identifying the Church with the Kingdom in a simplistic way? I do not see such a vision of the Kingdom in the Working Document. I hope that the bishops will evoke it on the floor of the synod: the vision of Jesus giving fullness of life.

A Need for Analysis

Looking around Asia, it is not difficult to list the various problems the people are facing: poverty and injustice, division and discrimination, corruption and exploitation, fundamentalism and communalism, domination and oppression, individualism and consumerism. The list is long and challenging. But we are nowhere near understanding the issues and suggesting adequate remedies if we do not discover the causes and underlying structures through a proper sociocultural analysis.

The year 1998 is five hundred years after Vasco da Gama landed in South India after discovering a new route to India and Asia from Europe. The new route was not for purposes of tourism! Two international seminars in Delhi in January–February explored the themes: *From Colonialism to Globalization: 500 Years after Vasco da Gama* and *Globalization Seen from the Point of View of Its Victims*.[1] The reports of these seminars are found elsewhere . . . , and I need not repeat the points made there. Can we talk of Asia today without thinking of the five hundred years of exploitation that it has undergone at the hands of other peoples? If we speak of international debt today, can we ignore the immense debt that the exploiters owe to the exploited?

Contemporary globalization is lived by the peoples of Asia as a form of economic colonialism. It is supported by open or hidden military might. It is mediated by a monochrome, consumer culture. It gives rise to secularization and an erosion of values. It is dominated by a liberal capitalist system that swears by profits and free markets and indulges in unfair trade practices. It is controlled by multinational companies aided by international institutions like the International

Monetary Fund (IMF), World Bank (WB), and World Trade Organization (WTO). It is helped by corrupt economic and political elite groups in each Asian country. The recent collapse of the flourishing East Asian economies is only the latest example of their vulnerability in the existing international system. Ecological exploitation, economic migration, displacement of peoples, mounting unemployment, sex tourism, destruction of indigenous cultures, fundamentalist religions, etc., are only some of the manifestations of the hidden exploitative structures. We are aware of the global power politics, with economic interests in the background, that [have held] the poor people of West Asia hostage for decades.

Globalization can be positive if it leads to division of labor, sharing and collaboration, facilitating the emergence of a global community. But that is not what is happening. Evangelization in such a situation will be inadequate if it does not address itself to the causes and structures, but limits itself to the effects and then proposes purely spiritual remedies. In today's global situation, the causes of and solutions to some of the problems in Asia actually lie in parts of the world that are identified by Asians as Christian. We could expect that the Synod for Asia offers an occasion to the bishops of the world to become aware, not only of the problems Asia is facing, but also of the responsibility of people elsewhere for these problems so that they can evangelize people in their own areas. Besides pointing to the evils in contemporary Asian society, it will be helpful for the bishops to name the "powers" that are behind it. Since the Church is a global communion of Churches, would the synod look at Asia from a global point of view? The fact that the dominant countries are Christian or post-Christian lays a special burden of responsibility on the Churches in those countries to exercise their prophecy in the name of the Gospel and on behalf of the poor of Asia (and of the world).

Mission with a Focus

The Working Document takes account of the fact that evangelization in Asia has opened out to include a multiplicity of tasks and is no longer limited to what it calls "first evangelization." It refers many times to the description by the FABC of evangelization as a threefold dialogue with the poor, the rich cultures, and the many religions, cosmic and metacosmic, of Asia. I would like to suggest that the bishops must take account of more recent efforts that seek to integrate the many tasks or ways of mission.

The Gospels present the life and preaching of Jesus in the context of an ongoing struggle between God on the one hand and Mammon as the power of money and Satan as the more personal structures of unfreedom on the other. The poor and the oppressed are the victims of the domination of Mammon and Satan, of course through their human representatives. The Kingdom of freedom, fellowship, and justice that Jesus proclaimed is really the contrary of the anti-Kingdom of Mammon and Satan. The conversion to which Jesus calls us is primarily a change of allegiance from the forces of the anti-Kingdom to God. The forces of evil have personal as well as social-structural manifestations. People as well as cultural and religious institutions in which they are involved are affected by the conflicting forces of good (God) and evil (Mammon and Satan). People, cultures, and religions are challenged to conversion and transformation. But they are also called to creative action in building up the new society of the Kingdom.

Promotion of justice and transformation of culture and religion involve each other so that they go hand in hand. But while the Gospel is prophetically against the forces of injustice that make people poor, it engages in a prophetic dialogue with cultures and religions. Just as poverty and oppression are the pointers to the domination by Mammon, promotion of justice and liberation constitute the focus and touchstone of evangelization. The dialogue of the Gospel with cultures and religions is an indispensable aid in the process.

The threefold dialogue of the Gospel with the poor, the cultures, and the religions, of which the FABC speaks, does not therefore represent three separate and parallel activities, but integral dimensions of one complex activity whose focus is promotion of justice and liberation as the signs of the new society of the Kingdom. Helping the poor and the needy is praiseworthy and manifests the love that God has for God's people, especially those who are most in need. But evangelization is not complete if it does not go on to confront the structures and causes that make people poor. Dialogue with cultures and religions is not an academic activity, but becomes evangelically meaningful when there are integral elements or dimensions of an action that is oriented to the realization of the Kingdom—even if the full realization of the Kingdom always remains an eschatological goal and an object of hope.

The core of evangelization therefore is prophetic action, and every other task of the Church is significant only insofar as it contributes to it. Prophecy is not merely critical of the present but it also offers a vision of hope and inspiration to action that seeks to embody that hope. This is the meaning of the saying that the Church is essentially missionary. Will the synod help the Church to discover its missionary dynamism?

An Option for the Poor

In this ongoing struggle between the rich and the poor, the oppressors and the oppressed, the evil and the good, we are called to opt for the poor. It is God's own option as it is manifest in the Bible. This option has a double dimension: being poor and working with and for the poor. It is the teaching, not only of the Gospel, but also of other Asian religions like Hinduism and Buddhism, that one cannot successfully fight against the forces of egoism and greed if one is not oneself egoless, free of attachment. The blessedness of being poor is a challenge to everyone. It is only when we are poor in this sense that we can struggle with and for the poor for liberation from the poverty imposed on them. Opting to be poor and for the poor are two sides of the same coin, two aspects of the same attitude. It is only insofar as one is free from Mammon that one can free others from it.

The Church in Asia has a record of being with the poor. It has engaged in developmental activities of all kinds like education, health, and projects for economic betterment. But can the Church claim to *be* poor? The Church-as-people in Asia is largely poor. But the Church-as-institution is certainly rich, and seems to have, in the eyes of others, inexhaustible sources of income. One sometimes has the impression that the Church hesitates to be prophetic in order to protect its institutions as its sources of income. Can the Church claim to be *for* the poor, fight-ing on their side? One can certainly identify generous individuals or groups here and there or special occasions like the EDSA revolution in the Philippines that overthrew Marcos. But these seem exceptions rather than the rule. Is it significant that the Working Document carefully avoids the word "liberation"? There is one reference to Jesus Christ as "liberator," which discourages such usage. The term "liberation" seems to have been carefully avoided during the Synod for America. I hope the bishops of Asia will not let this happen during the Synod for Asia.

Poverty is not only economic. The spirit of poverty leads to humility. Jesus' *kenosis* is our model. Jesus came as a servant and washed the feet of the disciples. But I have the impression that our preferred image of Jesus in our missionary ac-tion has been that of Christ the King who conquers and dominates. If we recog-nize the presence and action of the Spirit in the other religions and believe that God offers everyone the possibility of being associated with the paschal mystery in ways unknown to us, then our evangelization can be without anxiety and ag-gressiveness. As followers of Jesus the servant, the Church too can be the servant, both of the Gospel that it proclaims and of the world to whom it is proclaimed. The power of God's Word and Spirit does not need the power of money, or of numbers, or of the media, or of the State.

Being an Authentic Local Church

The Church in Asia cannot credibly evangelize if it is not authentically Asian. Un-fortunately, the Church still has a foreign image. The Second Vatican Council spoke of the need for the Church to become a local Church and of the universal Church as a communion of local Churches. It spoke of episcopal collegiality with the pope as the center of ecclesial unity and communion. The need for what came to be later known as inculturation was very much stressed, not only in the field of liturgy, but in all other areas. But all these projects seem still far from realization more than thirty years after the council.

We can speak of the need for the Church to become local at least in three ar-eas: financially, culturally, and in responsibility. The Churches in Asia are still largely dependent on foreign funds. A certain sharing of material goods among Churches is welcome, especially if it goes to help the poor and the needy. Certain special projects may also need special assistance. But I wonder whether the Church cannot slowly become self-sufficient for its basic life and pastoral needs. Should communities of poor Christians have rich ministers, institutions, and su-perstructures of training and administration? What is the witness value of such an institutional setup? How much does such financial dependence affect real free-dom of operation? How can we in Asia learn to be self-dependent and free? Could financial help to the poor come through nonofficial, nonecclesiastical channels so that our freedom for prophetic witness is not compromised?

Everyone in the Church today accepts theoretically the need for the Asian Churches to become culturally Asian. At the same time we know that this is not happening. Becoming Asian does not mean that we adapt or translate perennial structures in a local idiom. We will become Asian when we can respond freely and creatively to the Gospel in our own cultural idiom, giving rise in this way to local theology, liturgy, spirituality, and organizational structures. Do we have this freedom today or do foreign structures still weigh heavily on us, often under the guise of tradition? Even the process of inculturation is centralized. In a continent that boasts of a variety of ritual families, we are told that the unity of the Latin Rite has to be protected, in spite of the provision for "a more radical adaptation" made by the [Second Vatican] Council itself (see *Constitution on the Sacred Liturgy*, 40). This is only indicative of what happens in other areas.

How can a Church emerge as a local Church if it cannot take responsibility for its life and its creative action, for its organization and administration, without detriment, of course, to the communion of Churches and to the role of the pope in this communion? I do not think that we have solved creatively the problem of the just autonomy of the local Churches within the communion of the universal Church. The Synod for Asia could be an occasion to explore such questions.

The International Congress on Mission that met in Manila in 1979 declared that each local Church is responsible for its own mission and co-responsible for the mission of the universal Church. While we are happy that Asians are going out to help other local Churches, we have to ask ourselves whether they are witnessing to an Asian experience of the Christian faith that can enrich the other Churches. This may also be an occasion to discuss the problem of some "international religious congregations" that come to "recruit" candidates in Asia without respecting their cultural identity and for their own questionable goals.

If the Church does not become Asian, it cannot effectively and credibly witness to the Gospel in Asia. It is an irony of history that Christianity, born in Asia, has come back to Asia via Europe as a foreign product. It is a pity that the enthusiasm for becoming an authentic local Church has considerably gone down, especially in official circles, after the first fervor that was there immediately after the [Second Vatican] Council. Recent events make one suspect too whether there are efforts at greater control of incipient manifestations of freedom and creativity.

An Experience and Affirmation of Pluralism

The Asian continent is a living example of pluralism, with its richness as well as tensions: pluralism of races and religions, of cultures and philosophies, of ritual Churches and political systems, of traditions and hopes. All these will be represented at the synod. It can be a rich experience of that pluralism and offer concrete strategies to make it a source of richness and creativity rather than of conflict. Respect for the other, dialogue, and collaboration become the only means of building community and ensuring peace in a situation of pluralism. The South and East Asian religions like Hinduism, Confucianism, and Buddhism have a tradition of tolerance. The synod itself may offer an occasion for a constructive experience of pluralism.

Let us hope that the bishops of Asia, in dialogue with the pope and the bishops of the rest of the world, will rise up to the challenge of reading the signs of the times and of listening to the Spirit active in the many subaltern movements that are emerging all over Asia and discern God's future for this continent in the third millennium. May the Spirit inspire them to prophecy that will inspire and enable the Christians of Asia to become communities that will be symbols and servants of the Kingdom that is God's promise to all peoples.

Note

1. *Colonialism to Globalisation: Five Centuries after Vasco da Gama, Papers Presented at the International Conference held at Indian Social Institute, New Delhi, Feb. 2–6, 1998,* eds. Walter Fernandes and Anupama Dutta (New Delhi: Indian Social Institute, 1999). *Globalization and Its Victims: As Seen by the Victims, Papers Presented at the International Consultation on Globalization from the Perspectives of the Victims of History, held in Delhi, Jan. 18–22, 1998,* ed. Michael Amaladoss (Delhi: Vidya-jyoti/ISPCK, 1999).

THE RESPONSES OF THE INDONESIAN AND JAPANESE BISHOPS TO THE *LINEAMENTA*

JONATHAN Y. TAN

Among the many responses to the *Lineamenta* for the 1998 Special Assembly for Asia of the Synod of Bishops which were issued by the member conferences of the Federation of Asian Bishops' Conferences, the responses of the Indonesian and Japanese bishops stand out from the rest for their frank and critical reflections on the contents of the *Lineamenta*. The significance of these two responses is heightened by the fact that both the Indonesian and Japanese local Churches are little flocks "in an ocean of people who profess other religious faiths or belong to other religious traditions."[1] In the case of the Indonesian local Church, it is a little flock in a country with the world's largest Muslim population, whereas the Japanese local Church is but a tiny entity in an overwhelmingly Buddhist-Confucian milieu. This essay seeks to evaluate the many important issues that were raised in both responses. Part I analyzes the contents of both responses vis-à-vis the *Lineamenta*. Part II examines two important issues that go to the very heart of the perspectives of the Indonesian and Japanese bishops: (1) the emergence of an Asian Christology; and (2) the proclamation vs. dialogue debate.

Part I

The Indonesian Bishops' Response to the *Lineamenta*

The Indonesian bishops preface their response by drawing attention to the teaching of the Second Vatican Council on "particular Churches" (in *AG* 3), and therefore "the necessity of inculturation of Christian faith—the specific responses of Asian Churches should come out clearly as their contribution to the Universal Church as a 'communion of communities'."[2] They emphasize the need for dialogue, and were extremely concerned with the hardline approach of the *Lineamenta*. As they put it: "To us certain parts of the *Lineamenta* sound 'alarming'. The dominant concern between the lines appears to be: 'too much emphasis on dialogue, so that proclamation is not highlighted enough'."[3] For them, a "genuine dialogue of life, in a sincere effort to understand people of other faiths, is a relevant part of true Evangelization, implying concerted endeavor for the common well-being and true unity in a diversity of the entire nation."[4] They decry the approach to evangelization that was taken in the *Lineamenta*, because it failed to reflect adequately the triple dialogue approach of the FABC, that is, dialogue with cultures, religions, and the poor.[5] Instead, they suggest that evangelization has to "take account of cultural and religious pluriformity, and of the many ways people accept the Gospel in a lifelong process."[6]

In the context of a minority religion in an overwhelmingly Muslim nation,[7] the Indonesian bishops took pains to point out that "without in any way derogating the mission of preaching Jesus Christ, as for the FABC, for us too interreligious dialogue is the primary mode of Evangelization."[8] While acknowledging the distinction between dialogue and proclamation, they also emphasize that dialogue is not opposed to proclamation but dialogue is proclamation in the Indonesian context: "in dialogue Christians give witness to their faith, and in proclamation Christians respectfully encounter in the hearers of the Word the Truth and Goodness that comes from the God of Salvation and leads to Him."[9] More importantly, the Indonesian bishops point out that conversion "occurs not only as fruit of proclamation," but it is as much "the spirit of God who alone works 'conversion to God' in Jesus Christ through proclamation as well as through inter-religious dialogue."[10] What is at stake here is the subtle but very important distinction between conversion arising out of a harmonious dialogue on the one hand, and conversion arising out of aggressive proselytism with its negative connotations, and the need to avoid the arrogant triumphalism and instrumentalistic approach of past missionary endeavors. Hence, it is not surprising that the Indonesian bishops find the *Lineamenta* "alarming"—its "dominant concern between the lines appears to be: 'too much emphasis on dialogue, so that proclamation is not highlighted enough'."[11] For the Indonesian bishops, "sincere Christian dialogue appreciates values of the Kingdom wherever they are found and provides room for indigenous Christians to make use of their religious traditions in order to express those values in ways familiar to them."[12]

On the Christological issue—the uniqueness of Jesus Christ for human salvation—which was raised in the *Lineamenta*, the Indonesian bishops highlight the fact that the FABC "makes attempts at an integral and holistic approach to the mystery of Jesus Christ by using 'inclusive language,' so that Christology truly becomes 'Catholic,' i.e., embracing all humans of whatever religious conviction."[13] Not surprisingly, in response to the clarion call in chapter 4 of the *Lineamenta* to proclaim Jesus Christ as the one and only Savior, the Indonesian bishops state thus:

> In pluri-religious societies it is often difficult to directly and explicitly proclaim the central role of Jesus Christ in the economy of salvation. This proclamation must be adapted to concrete life conditions and to the disposition of the hearers. Evangelization ought to start from a "common

ground," i.e., belief in the Supreme being as taught by well-respected spiritual leaders and as explicitly stated among the "Five Principles" (Pancasila).[14]

For the Indonesian bishops, "Jesus does not exclusively belong to Christians, because He is acknowledged and respected by people of other faiths also."[15]

The Indonesian bishops also reject what they perceive as the high ecclesiology of the *Lineamenta*—a somewhat abstract "Ecclesiological pattern 'from above'" in favor of the FABC's ecclesial paradigm of the "Church as 'communion of communities',," which is seen as "a new way of being Church in Asia."[16] Referring to *LG* 8, they stress that the "Church of Christ '*subsistit in Ecclesia Catholica*', and that there is no complete identification between the Church and the Kingdom."[17] They are also critical of the *Lineamenta*'s understanding of inculturation as "an interpretation of faith in context," pointing out that this does not do any justice to the subject.[18] Instead, inculturation should be a way of life, such that "the Christian way of life should be authentic not only in the sense that it is in agreement with the '*Regula Fidei*' but also in the sense that it expresses faith fully within and through the local culture."[19] In this respect, the Indonesian bishops argue that "episcopal conferences need greater freedom of decision making with regard to inculturation," and all efforts at the "continuous and serious study and experimentation by experts not only in liturgy but also in indigenous cultures are required," and such efforts "need to be wholeheartedly supported (and not restricted) by 'Rome'."[20]

In respect to liturgical inculturation, the Indonesian bishops bemoan the fact that:

> many ceremonies have been imported from the West, so that little room is left for a style of community life and of faith communication according to the rhythm of indigenous people. *Clinging too much to the "substantial unity of the Roman liturgy" may end up in rigidity that obstructs proper incarnation of Christian faith.* (emphasis added)[21]

Here, the Indonesian bishops are calling for the development of non-Latin Asian liturgical rites, because mere translations of the *editio typica* of various liturgical texts into the vernacular are not local liturgies—they are and remain Western liturgies.[22] In addition, by calling for greater autonomy in questions of inculturation, the Indonesian bishops are politely telling the Vatican officials that they should have full responsibility in questions concerning inculturation, as well as full authority to produce and approve local liturgical texts and rites. This is because they know the local peoples, languages, and sociocultural contexts of the Indonesian reality. In this regard, the Indonesian bishops also criticize the efforts of the Vatican officials to control the process of inculturation:

> In order to promote the inculturation process the universal Church has to be more open and ready to change its own pattern of thinking, and to allow local Churches the freedom to think and act in response to concrete life situations, guided by the Spirit and led by the local hierarchy. Rigid rules and regulations, in discord with local conditions, will put restric-

tions on the interest in inculturation and will hamper the result of inculturation.[23]

Finally, the Indonesian bishops also challenge the centralization of Church
authority in Rome and called for the establishment of a mechanism "responsible
for exploring the possibility of an East Asian patriarchate, at least endowed with
autonomy comparable to that of the patriarchates in Oriental Churches of the Near
East," so as to "relativize the primacy of the 'Western' Church and enhance
authentic inculturation of Christian faith."[24] Such a demand, although highly radical, is nevertheless rooted in the call of the Second Vatican Council for the Church
to become a local Church, of the universal Church as a universal communion of
local Churches, and of episcopal collegiality with the See of Peter as the center of
ecclesial unity and communion.[25]

The Japanese Bishops' Response to the *Lineamenta*

The response of the Japanese bishops is by far the most radical from the FABC
bishops' conferences. In their response, the Japanese bishops express their dissatisfaction with, and reject completely, the framework of the *Lineamenta* because of
its perceived Eurocentric emphasis and its failure to address the concerns of the
Asian Churches.[26] Instead of replying to the *Lineamenta*, they drew up their own
list of questions and responses in an effort to address the issues which arose in the
context of the Japanese Church.[27] For this purpose, the Japanese bishops suggest
that there are six important considerations in formulating a methodology for the
Asian Synod: (1) a consideration for those Asian countries without a common language, (2) a sensitivity to the rich diversity of Asian cultural and spiritual traditions, (3) a greater use of the fruits of the FABC, (4) the division of discussion
groups by Asian cultural traditions (e.g., Islamic culture, Hindu culture, Confucian culture, etc.) rather than according to European languages, (5) greater participation by women observers and representatives of traditional Asian religions, (6)
an overriding objective of revitalizing the Asian local Churches from within the
Asian milieu.[28]

From a theological perspective, the response of the Japanese bishops also reveals differences between the Japanese bishops and the Vatican officials on issues
of Christology, ecclesiology, and missiology. For example, the Japanese bishops
find a certain "defensiveness" in the *Lineamenta*, especially in the Christology articulated in chapter 4 of the *Lineamenta*:

> If we stress too much that "Jesus Christ is the one and only Savior," we
> can have no dialogue, common living or solidarity with other religions.
> The Church, learning from the *kenosis* of Jesus Christ, should be humble
> and open its heart to other religions to deepen its understanding of the
> mystery of Christ.[29]

In particular, in response to chapter 4 of the *Lineamenta*, the Japanese bishops
criticize the *Lineamenta*'s approach to Christology, and suggested an alternative
approach:

We should try to discover what kind of Jesus will be a "light" to the peoples of Asia. In other words, as the Fathers of the early Church did with Graeco-Roman culture, we must make a more profound study of the fundamentals of the religiosity of our peoples, and from this point of view try to discover how Jesus Christ is answering their needs. Jesus Christ is the Way, the Truth and the Life, *but in Asia, before stressing that Jesus Christ is the truth, we must search much more deeply into how he is the Way and the Life.* (emphasis added)[30]

On the issue of ecclesiology, the Japanese bishops are of the view that the images of the Church in the *Lineamenta* was "not as rich or deep as that of Vatican II, especially of 'the Church as people of God' and 'the Church as servant'."[31] For the Japanese bishops, both of these images are crucial to the self-understanding of the Church in Asia, which "in order to serve God's kingdom, lives in a minority position with and for others."[32] In addition, the "central issues of 'Service' and 'Dialogue' developed by the FABC are two very important points for the Catholic Church in Asia which are not sufficiently stressed in the *Lineamenta*."[33] The Japanese bishops also emphasize the need for collegiality and subsidiarity in all dealings between the Holy See and the local Churches of Asia:

> To take a new look at the connection between the Churches in Asia and the Holy See. That is, to consider a system of establishing relationships not based on "centralization" but on "collegiality." *We ask the Holy See to give more recognition to the rightful autonomy of the Local Churches.* For example, it is strange that approval should have to be obtained from the Holy See even for Japanese translations of liturgical and catechetical texts already approved by the Bishops' Conference. To contribute to the evangelization of the region, to encourage inculturation, to build up real "collegiality" among the Churches in Asia, trust should be shown to the Local Churches and the independence of the Local Churches should be respected in matters concerning administration, etc. (emphasis added)[34]

Responding to the relentless emphasis of the *Lineamenta* on the "proclamation of Christ," the Japanese bishops point out that not enough attention has been given to the necessity of dialogue and an attitude of "compassion with the suffering."[35] They also highlight the need for collaboration and "creative harmony" in any dialogue between the Christian Gospel and other religions in the Japanese context: "In the *Lineamenta* a great deal is made, as in traditional scholastic theology, of 'distinctions' and 'differences.' However, in the tradition of the Far East, it is characteristic to search for creative harmony rather than distinctions."[36] In other words, one's way of daily living may be more effective than preaching abstract intellectual thoughts and beliefs, or as the saying goes: actions speak louder than words. At the same time, the Japanese bishops also criticize the *Lineamenta*'s preoccupation with evaluating the success of any missionary endeavor by the number of baptisms, and propose the following:

> We need a vision of evangelization that gives joy and a sense of purpose to a Christian living as one of a minority in the midst of many traditional

religions. An evaluation based not on the number of baptisms but rather from the point of view of "How faithful have we been to our mission of evangelization?" is necessary.[37]

Finally, the Japanese bishops also propose a list of topics that they would like to see discussed: (1) the development of an Asian theology "based not on a Christ whom we only grasp in our minds, but who speaks to us in our hearts through his living presence and activity," (2) the articulation of "a Christology seen from the cultural ambient of Asia," (3) a "liberation from a Western-style Church and the creation of a new vision" that expresses "the message of universal salvation so that it can be understood by the peoples of Asia," (4) the evaluation of missiological approaches to evangelization in the Asian context, which should acknowledge the "limits felt to the 'Western-type' of missionary activity used up to now," (5) the development of new Asian celebrations and liturgies, (6) the addressing of social, cultural, economic, and political issues in Asia, (7) the renewing of the Asian Churches' solidarity with the poor and marginalized, (8) the effort to "form public sentiment toward respect for human life, respect for human rights, social justice, peace, freedom, solidarity, etc.," and (9) the articulation of an Asian spirituality and inculturation of the Christian Gospel in a spirit of dialogue and harmony with other religions.[38]

Part II: Reflections on the Responses of the Indonesian and Japanese Bishops

The Emergence of an Asian Christology

The theme for the Synod for Asia—"Jesus Christ the Savior: Mission of Love and Service in Asia"—focuses attention on the question of the evangelization of the Christian Gospel in Asia. The *Lineamenta* emphasized the official Vatican position that evangelization has to begin with the proclamation of the person of Jesus Christ and his unique role as the one and only Savior, and that such proclamation is primary whereas dialogue plays merely a secondary role as supporting the evangelistic proclamation. Underlying the approach of the *Lineamenta* is its presupposition that the unity of faith is best safeguarded by the adherence to a high Christological doctrinal formulation with no room for diversity or pluralism. One has to ask what issues were at stake in this strong creedal affirmation, what was being defended by the Vatican officials in their emphasis on the sole mediatorship of Jesus Christ as the only Savior, why this struck a raw nerve with the Indonesian and Japanese bishops, and whether it is possible to reconcile pluralism with the unity of faith. In this regard, a careful reading of both the responses of the Indonesian and Japanese bishops reveals a marked rejection of the triumphalism of an *exclusive Christology from above,* which insists upon the explicit proclamation and acceptance of Christ as the one and only Savior in preference for an *inclusive Christology from below,* which affirms that Christ is constitutive of human salvation even if some people do not acknowledge explicitly his mediatory role.

Underlying the tension between a high and low Christology is the need for attention to temporality, that is, the here and now. This is because doctrinal formulations are not formulated in an abstract or ahistorical vacuum; instead they emerge from within particular socio-cultural-religious contexts and are contextualized in the historicity of human existence, worldviews, and life experiences.[39] It would be simplistic and naive to assume that a particular Christological doctrinal formulation that emerged from an earlier Greco-Roman past could be uprooted and transplanted into the context of the Asian local Churches *merely* in the name of tradition and the need to preserve the unity of faith, because tradition and history can only be apprehended from the present as "tradition-as-reinterpreted-by-the-present," and therefore as a present hermeneutical appropriation of the past.[40] In this respect, the age-old Christological question, "Who do you say I am?," demands an existential response that is contextualized in the here and now.[41] To insist that there is only one possible way of telling the story of Jesus Christ smacks of a reductionistic essentialism as well as decontextualization. What is at stake here is not the identity of Jesus Christ as portrayed in the Christian Gospels, because nobody is disputing Jesus' life, ministry, and death. Rather, what is being pointed out is the oppressive dissonance that arises when the European socioreligious and ecclesial structures, with their emphasis on creeds, codes, and cult, are being imposed upon the Asian context without taking into account the quintessentially Asian inclusivity and pluralism, such that profound experiences with the transcendent reality may be shared by several organized religious groups in varying degrees of formal commitment and fellowship with this transcendent reality.[42] In this regard, the observations of Felix Wilfred give much food for thought:

> [W]e have in Asia the phenomenon of a lot of men and women who are gripped by Jesus, his life and teachings. They are his devotees while they continue to be Hindus, Buddhists, Taoists. What is particularly remarkable is that they can be Hindus, or Buddhists, etc., and devotees of Christ without being syncretistic. Syncretism, they feel, is something which is attributed to them from the outside, while from within, at the level of their consciousness, they experience unity and harmony, and are not assailed by those contradictions and conflicts which may appear to those who look at them from without.[43]

In other words, the Indonesian and Japanese bishops were justified in asking whether it is desirable to look for an overarching and normative construct to define the Christian mystery of human salvation. Could there not be a pluralism in how the Asian Churches appropriate and convey the memory of the one foundational event, the story of Jesus of Nazareth and his crucifixion, within the diverse Asian realities, just as there was a pluralism inherent in early Christianity between the Aramaic-speaking Palestinian Jewish Christian communities, the Greek-speaking Hellenistic Jewish Christian communities, and the Gentile Christian communities? In short, any attempt to interpret and appropriate the Christian Gospel should respect the diversity and pluralism of the Asian world with its many peoples, cultures, and religions, and understand that such diversity and pluralism are not obstacles to the appropriation of the Christian Gospel, and not reduce such diversity and pluralism to a single overarching pronouncement that merely emphasizes triumphalistically the unique redemptive role of Jesus Christ as the one and only Savior.

The Proclamation vs. Dialogue Debate

The Indonesian and Japanese bishops understand evangelization as a complex dialogical encounter between the Christian Gospel, the local Church and its *Sitz-im-Leben* with its rich and diverse myriad of cultures, traditions, religions, and so-cial-ethical conditions. For them, evangelization involves the acknowledgment and acceptance of a fundamental ontological, soteriological, and existential rela-tionship between the Christian Gospel and the myriad of Asian realities. In the process, the Christian Gospel becomes enfleshed in the local Church, contextual-ized in and being fully alive in Asia. Living with other Asian peoples, and becom-ing involved in all the aspects of life, Christians thereby proclaim the nearness of the reign of God in Asia. In emphasizing the need for dialogue, the Indonesian and Japanese bishops are merely reiterating the emphasis of the FABC on dialogue as "an integral part of evangelization" (BIMA II, art. 14),[44] "intrinsic to the very life of the Church," (BIRA I, art. 9),[45] an "essential mode of all evangelization" (*Mes-sage of the 1979 International Congress on Mission*, art. 19),[46] and "a true expres-sion of the Church's evangelizing action" (BIMA II, art. 14).[47] Drawing upon the profound insights of the FABC, this dialogue is a "dialogue of life" that "involves a genuine experience and understanding" and that "demands working, not for them merely (in a paternalistic sense), but with them, to learn from them (for we have much to learn from them!) their real needs and aspirations, as they are enabled to identify and articulate these, and to strive for their fulfillment" (FABC I, art. 20).[48]

In all fairness to the *Lineamenta*, it should be pointed out that the FABC has also explained that dialogue *does not preclude* the need for the proclamation of the Christian Gospel: in fact there could be a moment when "we shall not be timid when God opens the door for us to *proclaim* explicitly the Lord Jesus Christ as the Savior and the answer to the fundamental questions of human existence" (FABC V, art. 4.3; emphasis original).[49] Although the FABC in general, and the Indone-sian and Japanese bishops in particular, do not exclude the explicit verbal procla-mation of the Christian Gospel as mission, however, they also recognize that con-text plays a very important role in determining the best approach to mission. Hence, a distinctively Asian approach of proclamation that is sensitive to the Asian *Sitz-im-Leben* is needed:

> Mission may find its greatest urgency in Asia; it also finds in our conti-
> nent a distinctive mode. We affirm, together with others, that "the procla-
> mation of Jesus Christ is the center and primary element of evangeliza-
> tion" (*Statement of the FABC All-Asia Conference on Evangelization*,
> Suwon, South Korea, August 24–31, 1988).[50] *But the proclamation of Je-*
> *sus Christ in Asia means, first of all, the witness of Christians and of*
> *Christian communities to the values of the Kingdom of God, a proclama-*
> *tion through Christlike deeds.* For Christians in Asia, to proclaim Christ
> means above all to live like him, in the midst of our neighbors of other

faiths and persuasions, and to do his deeds by the power of his grace. *Proclamation through dialogue and deeds—this is the first call to the Churches in Asia.*" (FABC V, art 4.1, emphasis added)[51]

Underlying the call of the Indonesian and Japanese bishops for the Indonesian and Japanese local Churches to engage in a dialogue with the diverse and pluralistic Asian milieu is the question of whether there are soteriological elements in Asian religions and cultures. One notes that the Second Vatican Council had acknowledged the existence of soteriological elements in other religions and cultures[52] which were to be "uncovered,"[53] "set free,"[54] as well as "purified, raised up and perfected"[55] to explain the salvific message of the Christian Gospel to non-European peoples. However, by the 1970s, such an instrumentalization approach to evangelization came to be perceived by many Asian and African Churches to be pejorative, manipulative, paternalistic, and a form of cultural imperialism or theological chauvinism, because it attempted to appropriate, modify, and reorient the religious, philosophical, and cultural traditions of local communities as *ancillae theologiae* to propagate the Christian Gospel without regard to their integrity.[56] In particular, the instrumentalization approach presupposed a universal and unchanging *depositum fidei*. The values and thought forms of a particular community are used, not because they are inherently holy and graced, but as a convenient platform to present the unchanging *depositum fidei*. In this sense, the ontological integrity and the soteriological ethos of the local sociocultural context are not being respected.[57]

It is in view of this historical baggage of evangelization as instrumentalization that the FABC in general, and the Indonesian and Japanese bishops in particular, have chosen the quintessential Asian trait of *dialogue* to undergird their missiological approach in Asia. Therefore, at the heart of an Asian understanding of evangelization lies the *dialogical encounter* between the *local Church* and the Asian context, as exemplified by the triple reality of Asian poverty, cultures, and religions.[58] Therefore, evangelization begins with the *local Church* in *dialogue* with the Asian peoples and their sociocultural realities, because it is only through the "building up of a truly *local Church*" that the Christian Gospel can be "truly incarnated in the minds and lives of the Asian peoples" (FABC I, art. 9).[59] According to the FABC, dialogue "frees the Church from becoming a self-centered community and links it with the people in all areas and dimensions of their lives."[60] This dialogical encounter has also led to the articulation of the nature of the Asian local Churches in dialogical terms: "the Church is *called to be a community of dialogue. This dialogical model is in fact a new way of being Church*" (BIRA IV/12, art. 48; emphasis added).[61]

In order to understand why the Indonesian and Japanese bishops are so insistent on the importance of dialogue in Christian evangelization, one has to see how dialogue allows two different parties, with their different worldviews, to understand each other better and to create harmonious relations between the two parties:

> Dialogue brings to the local Churches in Asia which are in danger of being ghettos an openness to and integration into the mainstream of their

cultures. Christians grow in genuine love for their neighbors of other faiths, and the latter learn to love their Christian neighbors (*International Congress on Mission*, Consensus Paper III, art. 4b).[62]

In this regard, perhaps one of the inherent dangers of proclamation is that it may result in a condescending, triumphalistic, and disrespectful unidirectional *mono-logue* that tramples on the sensitivities of the non-Christians. In addition, procla-mation comes across as being *wordy*, that is, there is an overabundance of words in preaching and proclamation, which aims to prove or emphasize particular truth claims. It has been pointed out that in the Asian mindset, "truth does not impose itself, but rather *attracts* everyone and everything to itself by its beauty, splendour, and fascination"[63]—which is what dialogue is all about.

In other words, proclamation without dialogue runs the risk of aggressive proselytism with its highly negative connotations. Therefore, not only the Asian socioreligious realities may be enriched by Christianity through dialogue, in turn Christianity too may be enriched by the Asian socioreligious realities. Otherwise, a one-way monologue opens Christianity to the charge of instrumentalization, that is, appropriating the soteriological elements in Asian socioreligious realities for Christian use without respecting their integrity within their Asian socioreligious matrix. Corollary to this view is the observation of the Indian theologian, Felix Wilfred:

> Any work of mission which does not recognize what God has been do-ing with a people, with a country and continent and with their history, is simply and purely arrogance vis-à-vis God's own bounteous gifts. . . . Triumphalism and exclusivism of any kind are diametrically opposed to spirituality. They fail to recognize and appreciate the thousand flowers God has let grow, flourish and blossom in the garden of the world; they fail to acknowledge in practice the presence and working of the Spirit in the life and history of peoples.[64]

As for the relationship between dialogue, proclamation, and conversion, the FABC has pointed out, rightfully, that "dialogue and proclamation are comple-mentary. Sincere and authentic dialogue does not have for its objective the conver-sion of the other. For conversion depends solely on God's internal call and the per-son's free decision" (BIRA III, art. 4).[65] Elsewhere, the FABC has reiterated that "dialogue aimed at 'converting' the other to one's own religious faith and tradition is dishonest and unethical; it is not the way of harmony" (BIRA V/3, art. 7). Such an understanding calls to mind the keynote address of the Archbishop Emeritus of Delhi, Angelo Fernandes at BIRA IV/12 in February 1991, in which he pointed out that peoples of other faiths in Asia were not to be regarded as "objects of Christian mission" but rather as "partners in the Asian community, where there must be mutual witness."[66] He explained that the dialogue between the Asian local Churches and the peoples of Asia should be seen as a "manifestation of lived Christianity" with its own integrity, which leads toward the Kingdom of God.[67] Such a dialogue leads to "*receptive pluralism*, that is, the many ways of respond-ing to the promptings of the Holy Spirit must be continually in conversation with one another. A relationship of dynamic tension may open the way for mutual information, inspiration, support and correction" (BIRA IV/3, art. 16).[68]

At the same time, one has also to ask why the Vatican officials are so uncomfortable with dialogue as a mode of evangelization. Perhaps, the underlying presupposition is that proclamation is supposedly *objective* whereas dialogue is *subjective* and therefore is inherently dangerous because it may lead to a relativization of the Christian Gospel.[69] In response, one would do well to heed the advice of Bernard Lonergan that "genuine objectivity is the fruit of subjectivity," that is, "it is attained only by attaining authentic subjectivity."[70] For Lonergan, "genuine objectivity" is not to be found in, nor can it be reduced to, mere doctrinal formulas, but is something that is achieved through religious, moral, and intellectual conversion.[71]

In conclusion, one may observe that all these statements of the FABC, upon which the Indonesian and Japanese bishops drew in their responses to the *Lineamenta*, suggest that in the Asian context, dialogue has a positive connotation of *fostering harmony and solidarity*, rather than the negative connotation of resolving differences. The quintessentially Asian *praxis* of dialogue is the search for common ground in *praxis*, that is, highly situational, contextualized, strategic, concrete, deliberate, and relational activities that are able to reach out across the many barriers and boundaries of beliefs, dogmas, creeds, and so on of the various cultures and religious traditions, to express the Christian mystery of human salvation in a nonconfrontational manner. In short, there can be no purely objective, abstract, and rational interpretation of the Christian mystery of human salvation as part of the universal *missio Dei*. Rather, the essence of this mystery is *relational* and *dialogical*. Hence, a hermeneutical approach that emphasizes doctrinal correctness by focusing on rationality, objectivity, and universality so as to preserve the purity of the Christian Gospel against any attempt at its relativization, syncretism, or eclecticism, whether real or perceived,[72] may not be able to break open the fullness of meanings surrounding the Christian mystery of human salvation, vis-à-vis a hermeneutical approach that is relational in its approach, sensitive to the needs and challenges of the local context, and strives to relate both horizons to understand each other in a dialogical encounter.

Notes

1. FABC Theological Advisory Commission, *Theses on the Local Church: A Theological Reflection in the Asian Context*, FABC Papers No. 60 (Hong Kong: FABC, 1990), 4.
2. *EAPR* 35 (1998), 55 art. 1.0.
3. See *EAPR* 35 (1998), 62 art. 4.0.2.
4. *EAPR* 35 (1998), 56 art. 1.2.6.
5. *EAPR* 35 (1998), 59 art. 2.0.
6. *EAPR* 35 (1998), 58 art. 1.6.1.
7. Catholics number about 2.69 percent of the total population of Indonesia. See *EAPR* 35 (1998), 55 art. 1.2.1.
8. *EAPR* 35 (1998), 62 art. 4.0.1.
9. *EAPR* 35 (1998), 62 art. 4.0.2.

10. Ibid.
11. Ibid.
12. *EAPR* 35 (1998), 64 art. 4.3.2.
13. *EAPR* 35 (1998), 64 art. 5.0.
14. *EAPR* 35 (1998), 64–65 art. 5.1.5.
15. *EAPR* 35 (1998), 67 art. 5.3.4.
16. *EAPR* 35 (1998), 68 art. 7.0.
17. Ibid.
18. *EAPR* 35 (1998), 74 art. 10.1.1.
19. *EAPR* 35 (1998), 74–75 art. 10.1.1.
20. *EAPR* 35 (1998), 77 art. 10.3.3.
21. *EAPR* 35 (1998), 76 art. 10.2.5.
22. It has been pointed out as early as 1969 that "texts translated from another language are clearly not sufficient for the celebration of a fully renewed liturgy. The creation of new texts will be necessary" (Consilium, *Instruction Comme le prévoit: On the Translation of Liturgical Texts for Celebrations with a Congregation*, 25 January 1969, art. 43, in International Commission on English in the Liturgy, *Documents on the Liturgy 1963–1979: Conciliar, Papal and Curial Texts* [Collegeville: Liturgical Press, 1982] 123:880).
23. *EAPR* 35 (1998), 77 art. 10.3.2.
24. *EAPR* 35 (1998), 85 art. 14.6.3.
25. See *LG* 13, 22, 23.
26. *EAPR* 35 (1998), 86.
27. Ibid.
28. *EAPR* 35 (1998), 87–89.
29. *EAPR* 35 (1998), 89.
30. *EAPR* 35 (1998), 89.
31. *EAPR* 35 (1998), 90.
32. Ibid.
33. Ibid.
34. *EAPR* 35 (1998), 94.
35. *EAPR* 35 (1998), 90.
36. Ibid.
37. Ibid.
38. *EAPR* 35 (1998), 91–92.
39. Felix Wilfred, "Inculturation as a Hermeneutical Question," *VJTR* 52 (1988), 423.
40. Wilfred, "Inculturation," 434. As Wilfred explains:

Christianity is not only a fact of history but is *a powerful affirmation of the historicity of human existence, of human beings with their cultures and tradition*, since God has made himself part of history in the person and life of Jesus. The historicity of the event of Jesus does not replace the history of peoples, their cultures and traditions, but rather affirms and values them. (p. 435; emphasis added)

41. Jacob Parappally, "One Jesus—Many Christologies," *VJTR* 61 (1997), 710.
42. Parmananda Divarkar, "The Synod for Asia," *VJTR* 61 (1997), 110.
43. Wilfred, "Inculturation," 429.
44. Gaudencio B. Rosales and C. G. Arévalo (eds.), *For All the Peoples of Asia: Federation of Asian Bishops' Conferences Documents from 1970–1991* (Maryknoll: Orbis, 1992), p. 100.

45. Rosales and Arévalo, p. 111.
46. Rosales and Arévalo, p. 131.
47. Rosales and Arévalo, p. 101.
48. Rosales and Arévalo, p. 15.
49. Rosales and Arévalo, p. 282.
50. The relevant paragraphs state: "While we are aware and sensitive of the fact that evangelization is a complex reality and has many essential aspects, . . . we affirm that there can never be true evangelization without the proclamation of Jesus Christ" (BIMA IV, article 5, in Rosales and Arévalo, p. 292). "The proclamation of Jesus Christ is the center and the primary element of evangelization without which all other elements will lose their cohesion and validity. In the same way, evangelization will gather together the believing community, the Church, through faith and baptism" (BIMA IV, article 6, in Rosales and Arévalo, p. 292).
51. Rosales and Arévalo, pp. 281–282.
52. These soteriological elements are the "seeds of the Word" [*semina Verbi*], which lie hidden in other religious traditions (*AG* 11, in Austin Flannery [ed.], *Vatican Council II: The Conciliar and Post Conciliar Documents,* Vol. I [Collegeville: Liturgical Press, 1984], p. 825). According to the Council Fathers, "[t]he Catholic Church rejects nothing of what is true and holy in these religions. She has a high regard for the manner of life and conduct, the precepts and doctrines which, although differing in many ways from her own teaching, nevertheless often reflect a ray of the truth which enlightens all men" (*NA* 2, in Flannery, p. 739).
53. In this vein, the Council Fathers thought that all Christians "should be familiar with their national and religious traditions and uncover with gladness and respect those seeds of the Word which lie hidden among them" (*AG* 11, in Flannery, p. 16).
54. In the words of the Council Fathers, Christians are called, among other things, "to illuminate these riches with the light of the Gospel, set them free, and bring them once more under the dominion of God the saviour" (*AG* 11, in Flannery, p. 825).
55. For the Council Fathers, "whatever good is found sown in the minds and hearts of men or in the rites and customs of peoples, these not only are preserved from destruction, but are purified, raised up and perfected for the glory of God. . . ." (*LG* 17, in Flannery, pp. 368–369).
56. Cf., Wilfred, "Inculturation," p. 423; Aloysius Pieris, "Western Models of Inculturation: How Far Are They Applicable in Non-Semitic Asia?" *EAPR* 22 (1985), 116–124; Aloysius Pieris, "Asia's Non-Semitic Religions and the Mission of the Local Churches," in T. Dayanandan Francis and F. J. Balasundaram (eds.), *Asian Expressions of Christian Commitment: A Reader in Asian Theology* (Madras: Christian Literature Society, 1992), pp. 35–57.
57. Pieris, "Asia's Non-Semitic Religions," pp. 43–44.
58. FABC I, arts. 12 & 19, in Rosales and Arévalo, pp. 14–15. Cf. Rosales and Arévalo, p. xxv. It is in this sense that the Indian Jesuit theologian, Fr. Michael Amaladoss, points out that becoming a local Church involves more than the mere translation of religious and liturgical texts or the adaptation or accommodation of institutional ecclesial structures in the local idiom. It demands a contextualization of the Christian Gospel in the local idiom such that it "takes responsibility for its life and its creative action, for its organization and administration, without detriment, of course, to the communion of Churches and of the Pope in this communion." In Michael Amaladoss, S.J., "Expectations from the Synod for Asia," *VJTR* 62 (1998), 150.
59. Rosales and Arévalo, p. 14.

60. Rosales and Arévalo, p. xxv.
61. Rosales and Arévalo, p. 332.
62. Rosales and Arévalo, p. 142.
63. Wilfred, "Inculturation," 427.
64. Felix Wilfred, "Fifth Plenary Assembly of FABC: An Interpretation of Its Theological Orientations," *VJTR* 54 (1990), 590.
65. Rosales and Arévalo, p. 120.
66. Angelo Fernandes, "Dialogue in the Context of Asian Realities," *VJTR* 55 (1991), 548.
67. Ibid.
68. Rosales and Arévalo, p. 261.
69. See discussion in arts. 21, 30, 31, 33 of the *Lineamenta*.
70. Bernard Lonergan, *Method in Theology* (Toronto: University of Toronto Press, 1994), p. 292.
71. Ibid.
72. See *Lineamenta*, chapter 6, no. 33. In *Origins* 26 (1997), 516.

4

The *Instrumentum Laboris*

On the basis of the responses of the episcopal conferences to the *Lineamenta*, a team of experts of the synod drafted the *Instrumentum Laboris*, or working document, in Rome on September 30 to October 2, 1997. The working document attempts to incorporate the Asian bishops' shared points of view, contrasting opinions, and suggested themes for further development, as well as to include aspects that have been neglected by the episcopal responses.

The working document, presented in the two official languages of the synod—English and French—purports to develop the overarching theme of the synod, namely, "Jesus Christ, the Savior and his Mission of Love and Service in Asia." Its central focus, however, is not Christology, as its title might suggest, but how the Church must carry out the mission of Jesus in Asia today.

The *Instrumentum Laboris* is composed of an introduction, seven chapters, and a conclusion. Theologically, it represents a significant improvement over the *Lineamenta*. In its introduction, it underlines the importance of the Asian Synod not only for the Church of Asia but also for the Asian peoples:

> The special assembly for Asia is also an important moment for the people of Asia. During the last fifty years many countries in Asia have gained their independence. A modern and more self-confident Asia is emerging with its ancient cultures, philosophies and religious traditions. The twenty-first century and the third millennium will offer new challenges and opportunities to Asian peoples in shaping their own destiny and taking their places on the world scene. The special assembly for Asia, therefore, comes at a crucial moment in the history of the Asian continent. . . . (no. 2)

The document goes on in the first chapter to paint in broad strokes what it calls "Asian realities." It points out that Asia is the home of three-fourths of the world's population as well as the cradle of almost all world religions and religious traditions (e.g., Hinduism, Buddhism, Judaism, Christianity, Islam, Taoism, Confucianism, Zoroastrianism, Jainism, Sikhism, Shintoism, etc.), not to mention what is called today primal or traditional religion. The document acknowledges that "the religions of Asia have molded the lives and cultures of Asian people for several millennia and continue to give meaning and direction for their lives even today" (no. 7).

The document also notes that Asia, despite its considerable economic progress, is still suffering from "a degrading and inhuman poverty" (no. 8), exacerbated by rapid industrialization and urbanization, with attendant social ills such as bonded labor, child labor, prostitution, and forced migration. In many parts of Asia, discrimination is being practiced against Tribals, indigenous peoples, minorities, and a certain social class (the caste system).

Despite these and other forms of social disorders, the working document sounds a note of optimism:

> Everywhere in Asia there is visible a new awareness carrying the Asian people to liberate themselves from the legacy of negative traditions, social evils, and situations associated with the past. The ancient cultures and religions and their collective wisdom form the solid foundation on which to build the Asia of the future. Levels of literacy, education, research and technology are rising daily. Skilled workers, specialists in various sciences, technicians, researchers are on the increase. Democratic institutions are taking firm root in many countries. (no. 10)

With regard to the Church, chapter 2 of the *Instrumentum Laboris* notes first of all its great diversity. Besides the Latin Churches, there are the Churches of Antioch of the Syrians, Antioch of the Greek Melchites, Antioch of the Maronites, the Chaldean Church of Babylonia, the Armenian Church, the Syro-Malabar Church, and the Syro-Malankara Church. In addition to the older Churches, there are newly established Churches, especially in the Central Asian republics such as Tajikistan, Turkmenistan, Uzbekistan, Siberia, and Mongolia. But the most visible fact about Asian Christianity is its minority status in all the countries of Asia, except the Philippines. Another related characteristic of Asian Christianity is its foreignness. The *Instrumentum Laboris* acknowledges candidly: "While the Church is admired for her organizational, administrative, educational, health services, and developmental works, these people often do not see the Church as totally Asian, not simply because much financial support comes from Western countries but also because of her Western character in theology, architecture, art, etc. and her associations with the past history in some sections of Asia" (no. 13).

But also here, against this somewhat bleak background, the document points to several signs of hope in the Churches of Asia, such as a vibrant sacramental and devotional life; the growth of basic Christian communities, charismatic movements and basic human communities; the founding of many missionary societies; the great numbers of priestly and religious vocations; numerous works of charity, social services, health care, and education; and last but not least, the witnesses of many martyrs.

The third chapter of the working document gives an overview of Christian mission in Asia as a way to introduce its central theme, namely, how to carry out the mission of Jesus in Asia today. It takes legitimate pride in the achievements of past missionaries, not only in proclaiming the Gospel, but also in promoting the local cultures with their valuable contributions as outstanding linguists, scholars, historians, poets, and scientists and their work for social development, especially in education and social services. On the other hand, the document also notes the shadow side of past missionary enterprises, in particular their failure to enter into the indigenous cultures, or to use a neologism, inculturation: "Among the causes in the past why the efforts of the Church's missionaries in Asia met with limited success, might there be a lack of proper understanding of Asian religions, their inherent values and strengths, their centuries-old teachings, their inner power of self-renewal as well as a reluctance to adopt methods which were suited to the Asian mentality?" (no. 23).

The next four chapters contain the most important doctrinal and pastoral affirmations of the working document. They deal with Christ, the Holy Spirit, the Church, and the Church's mission respectively. Chapter four speaks of "Jesus Christ: The Good News of Salvation." In its summary of the various responses to the *Lineamenta*, the working document hints at the variety and, at times, conflict of Asian Christologies. While it is admitted that for Asian Christians "the overriding title for Christ among his disciples, associated with his mission to all humanity, is that of Savior and Redeemer" (no. 27), the document acknowledges that there is an intense debate among Asian theologians as to how to present Jesus as the universal and unique Savior, distinct from the founders of Asia's other religions, to the Asian peoples. Different Christological approaches are well represented in the excerpt entitled "Some Perceptions of Christ in Asia" given below. Some Asian Christologies present Jesus, in the Buddhist tradition, as a deeply spiritual, compassionate, and loving person; others see him as a teacher or guru par excellence; still others have no problem with accepting Jesus as God, but as one beside many other divine beings, as in the Hindu tradition. Others suggest that Jesus should be understood in the context of the Asian quest for harmony between heaven and earth, between the divine and the human, between the transcendent and the immanent. Still others propose that a true proclamation of Jesus can be achieved only in the life of discipleship to Christ.

The fifth chapter broadens the Christological focus and unites it with pneumatology. God's plan of salvation in Jesus, the *Instrumentum Laboris* points out, is organically linked with the active presence of the Spirit of God in creation, cultures, and religions: "The Spirit of God touches, purifies and saves not only individuals, but through them, also cultures and religions. Hence they have a salvific role to play . . ." (no. 31). The document goes on to affirm the intrinsic unity between Christ and the Holy Spirit: "Salvific revelation in Christ is not parallel or superfluous to that of the Spirit, but remains its fulfillment and public authentication. Furthermore, whatever the Spirit brings about in human hearts and in the history of peoples, in cultures and religions serves as a preparation for the Gospel and can only be understood in reference to Christ" (no. 31). The excerpt entitled "The Spirit of God at Work in Asia" shows how the Asian bishops see the active presence of the Holy Spirit in Asia, in particular in Asian religions, and therefore urge a truthful, humble, and frank dialogue with them by which both Christianity and these religions are enriched.

The sixth chapter presents the Church as communion and shows how mission is to be realized within this communion ecclesiology. According to this vision of the Church, which is derived from Vatican II, "each particular Church has a vocation of being in communion with each other and the Universal Church. Relations between the local Churches are expressed as an inter-ecclesial communion in which the local Church incorporates elements from the local sociocultural environment, while remaining faithful to the uniqueness and unity of one, holy, catholic and apostolic faith" (no. 37). In as much as the relations among the local Churches must be guided by "the principle of unity of faith, charity, collegiality and subsidiarity," the Asian bishops insist that "more autonomy should be given to the local churches in areas of dialogue, in-

culturation and adaptation" (no. 38). The next excerpt, entitled "Mission of Communion," explains how the division among the various Christian Churches is a grave scandal for Asians and ecumenical unity and collaboration is a sine qua non condition for
an effective realization of the Church's mission of building up unity and bringing
about reconciliation among Asian cultures and religions.

The seventh chapter explores the "Church's Mission of Love, Service" in Asia. It
details the various areas in which this mission is realized, such as proclamation, the
liturgy, biblical preaching, spirituality, the laity, the family, youth, prayer, interreligious
dialogue, human development, and social communication. The last excerpt, entitled
"Bringing Faith to Culture," deals with one of the greatest challenges facing the Catholic Church in Asia, namely, inculturation. This process of bringing the Gospel into cultures and of introducing cultures into the understanding of the Gospel is said to affect
all aspects of Church life and is regarded as the only way to make the Church truly
Asian.

—Ed.

EXCERPTS FROM THE *INSTRUMENTUM LABORIS*

Some Perceptions of Christ in Asia

30. As for the image of Christ among other Asians, many responses point out
that by natural disposition most Asians have a positive outlook toward Christ, seeing him as a deeply spiritual, compassionate, and loving person. Some consider
him a great teacher. A particularly favorite image for Christ among Buddhists is
that of the Sacred Heart.

If some Christians have difficulty in properly understanding the human nature of Christ, most Asians would view him exclusively from this perspective. To
respond sufficiently to this fact, the Church needs to place greater emphasis on
presenting Christ in the wider context of salvation history and the master plan of
God the Creator for the universe, a plan fulfilled in the incarnation and redemption of Christ and still being worked out in Christ, through his Church, in the present moment in time. To achieve this, some insist that a greater attention should be
given to presenting Christ "in Asian garb," that is, using the support of various
philosophical and cultural concepts. Such an approach seems all the more important in the context of the Church's dialogue with other religions, especially Hinduism and Buddhism. The question then is, How can the Church in Asia explain
that Christ is the one and only Savior and unique mediator of salvation distinct
from the founders of Asia's other great religions?[9]

In some cases, followers of various Asian religions are increasingly prepared
to accept Jesus Christ even as God. However, this does not seem to be a reason for
them to accept him as the only Savior. The trend among the followers of these religions, especially the Hindus, is to consider all religions as equally good. For
them, the Hindu gods and Christ are only the different manifestations of the same
God. Even those who believe in Christ as God do not see the necessity to embrace

the Christian religion, much less the Church, despite the fact that the Church and her institutions do much for society in general.

Asian people, both of the classic religions and traditional and cosmic religions, seek to live in harmony between heaven and earth, between the realm of the divine and the human, between the transcendent and the immanent. These apparently contrasting and contradictory realities paradoxically merge into one in many Asian religions. The distance between them is overcome philosophically and liturgically. Christian liturgy expresses it wonderfully when it says: "Would that you rend the heaven and come down" (Is 63:19). Such an encounter between the divine and the human, the absolute transcendent and the finite has definitively taken place in Jesus Christ.

Based on the above situation, many responses state that there is a need to present Jesus in the context of this search by Asian religions and cultures for harmony between apparent paradoxes which confront human existence: between transcendence and immanence, emptiness and fullness, death and life, suffering and joy, the finite and the infinite, poverty and riches, weakness and power, the temporal and the eternal, the historical and the cosmic. In Jesus Christ, the incarnate Word of God, crucified and risen, the above paradoxes find a point of convergence. Some responses to the *Lineamenta* speak of a need for developing a Christology of kenosis, namely, a Christology based on the self-emptying of Christ in the mystery of the incarnation and his glorification in the Paschal Mystery.

However, many responses mention that beyond intellectual arguments true witness to Christ among the Asian people will result when the gap between religion and service is surmounted, in other words, when believers truly become the living signs of the Lord Jesus Christ through the exercise of the spiritual and corporal works of mercy. In this way for the Asian, who sets high priorities on such concepts as community, harmony, peace, and deliverance from evil, the faithful's living of the Christian faith will be a compelling form of witness to Christ. At the same time, the rites of the sacraments, devotions, prayers, etc., also reveal, in their own way, the person of Christ, making his saving message known and providing a powerful invitation to the unbeliever toward participation. In this regard certain responses suggest that greater attention be given to the inculturation of the faith, so as to search for ways among Asian mentalities and cultures—while remaining faithful to the essential content of the faith—to express more clearly and effectively what it means to live in Christ.

The Spirit of God at Work in Asia

32. It was in Asia that God chose to speak to the people of Israel through his chosen servants, the patriarchs and the prophets. And finally he spoke through his Son, Jesus Christ. Today he continues to speak to the peoples of Asia in a variety of ways.

Many responses point out that all which has been said about the salvific presence of the Spirit among peoples is particularly true of the Asian continent, home to most of the great religions of the world. These religions have been in a concrete manner the way to God for a majority of the peoples of Asia and God's way to them. The Spirit of God was at work in the minds and hearts of the ancient sages of the Asian continent. They have left to its peoples the record of their spiritual enlightenment in their sacred books. Their teachings still govern the religious, moral, and social life of many peoples of Asia.

For this reason, other religions in Asia constitute for the Church a positive challenge. They stimulate her both to discover and acknowledge the signs of Christ's presence and the working of the Holy Spirit, as well as to examine more deeply her own identity and bear witness to the fullness of revelation which she has received for the good of all.

This gives rise to the spirit which must enliven dialogue in the context of mission. Those engaged in this dialogue must be consistent with their own religious traditions and convictions, and be open to understanding those of the other party without pretense or close-mindedness, but with truth, humility, and frankness, knowing that dialogue can enrich each side.[21] With other religions there is a giving and a receiving, a listening and a sharing. On the level of human experience and faith, much can be learned from the deep religiosity of people and from their religions.

33. In this regard, responses to the *Lineamenta* recount a variety of situations on the Asian continent. In rare cases some particular Churches mention little or no dialogue activity with other religions. In some of these instances dialogue began with a certain enthusiasm, but subsequently a mistrust and suspicion set in, resulting in difficulties and even hostility. For the most part, however, dialogue with other religions is taking place on the Asian continent with much benefit to all the parties concerned.

At the same time, some responses are eager to point out that dialogue involves more than discussion over belief systems. The task of dialogue involves placing persons in touch with other persons. Fear, mistrust, and suspicion cannot be overcome simply by discussions. The heart cannot be earned simply by words, but it can be conquered by gestures of love. Thus the interreligious dialogue in Asia requires a capacity of love which is great, patient and persevering—a work of the Spirit—before which every Christian may experience many positive aspects as well as shortcomings. In this context, the interreligious dialogue is a human and spiritual pilgrimage in which the witness of Christian conversion is decisive because it gives to the Christian the strength and light to continue the adventure of dialogue and to invite the non-Christian interlocutor to the same process of conversion.

Among the more concrete and programmed initiatives in this field taking place in Asia are the following: courses on Asian religions in seminaries, houses of religious formation, lay formation centers and academic institutions; active involvement in social issues with the followers of other religions where there is a sharing of values; joint charitable programs on behalf of those in need, open and public gestures of mutual respect at special religious periods, etc.

In this movement of the Spirit toward interreligious dialogue, some responses explained a number of difficulties to be considered, e.g., the highly social character of religion, permeating and regulating every aspect of life; a general suspicion of all things Western in some cases, including the Church, etc. These same responses mentioned the above elements can be used as challenges for the Church in presenting her message, using elements from society in the process of inculturation, emphasizing the universality of the Church over Western associations, etc.

At the same time, some responses hasten to mention that dialogue itself can provide the Church with elements which can be beneficial in her program of a new evangelization, in presenting Catholic truth to the Asian mind, e.g., cultural elements, language, thought patterns and rites.

Harmony, for example, is a great value among the Asian people. This intended idea of harmony can find a counterpart in the concept of the kingdom of God in the Bible, where God's justice reigns. To the Asian mentality, harmony is not a matter of simply living in peace, but a creative and dynamic force in relationships. In other words, harmony is not a matter of adding indefinitely to what one already has, but placing one's goods and talents at the service of others so as to make up for what is lacking in another, all in order to reach a perfect proportion. This proportionality is operative primarily in the person in the family, then in society and its institutions, and then in relation to the world. Such an idea of harmony would find resonance in Christ's proclamation of the kingdom of God where he invites reconciliation of the sinner with God, the person with humanity and the whole of creation.

Most responses agree that Catholic truth can be served by a similar borrowing of concepts and ideas which are particularly Asian, all the while remaining faithful to the Catholic faith as presented in sacred Scripture and the Church's tradition.

Many responses point out that contemporary Asia, while clinging to many traditional ways of life and values, is undergoing a very swift and radical transformation.[22] Many value systems and meanings which supported the lives of people in Asia are now threatened and shaken. The Church in Asia is part of this transformation and is bound to its peoples through a common history and destiny:

> We know that in the hearts of our brothers there are these quests today: to find new meanings in their lives and endeavors, to overcome destructive forces and to shape a new integration in our societies, to free themselves from structures which have created new forms of bondage, to foster human dignity and freedom and a more fully human life, to create a more genuine communion among men and nations.[23]

In the Asian peoples' search for meaning to sustain their quest for fullness of life, the Church wants to recognize the presence of the Spirit, who leads them to Jesus Christ, the Way, the Truth and the Life (cf. Jn 14:6). The first plenary assembly of the FABC highlighted this fact in the following words:

> It is our belief that only in and through Christ and his Gospel, and by the outpouring of the Holy Spirit, that these quests can come to realization. For Christ alone, we believe, is for every man "the Way, the Truth and the Life" (Jn 14:6) "who enlightens every man who comes into the world" (Jn 1:9). We believe that it is in him and in his good news that our peoples will finally find the full meaning we all seek, the liberation we

strive after, the brotherhood and peace which is the desire of all our hearts.[24]

At the same time—as a variety of responses mention—Christians in Asia can profit from considering elements shared with the followers of other religions and cultures of Asia, e.g., the centrality of the will of God with Islam; with Hindus, the practice of meditation, contemplation, renunciation of one's will and the spirit of nonviolence; with Buddhists, detachment and compassion; with Confucianism, filial piety and humanitarianism; with Taoists, simplicity and humility; and with traditional religions, reverence and respect for nature. The Church in Asia has much to offer believers of other faiths: the values of reconciliation and peace, obedience to God's will, the sacred dignity of each person, the love and service of neighbor, the Church's social doctrine, human promotion in its many forms, the value of suffering and service which is central to the mystery of Jesus Christ.

The recognition of the presence of the Spirit among all peoples should in no way make anyone blind to the presence of evil and sin in manifold ways. Sin leads to all forms of idolatry of the self, wealth and power. Such idolatry refuses to acknowledge the image of God in self, in one's neighbor, and in the universe. For this reason, humanity stands in need of salvation. The Church believes that this salvation is a free gift offered to all by God in his Son Jesus Christ.

The salvific presence of the Spirit among all people is in the saving plan of God to lead all peoples to a new creation, of which Jesus Christ is "the firstborn and the first fruits of those who have died" (1 Cor 15:20). The "seeds of the word" sown by the Spirit become ripe for eternal life through the word incarnate, Jesus Christ crucified and risen. The universal plan of God for salvation and wholeness of life takes a concrete shape and human form in the incarnation of his Son Jesus Christ. Vatican II had this in mind when it declared:

> The universal plan of God for the salvation of mankind is not carried out solely in a secret manner, as it were, in the minds of men nor by the efforts, even religious, through which they in many ways seek God in an attempt to touch him and find him. . . . Their efforts need to be enlightened and corrected. . . . God decided to enter into the history of mankind in a new and definitive manner by sending his own Son in human flesh.[25]

Notes

9. *GS*, 22.
21. Cf. *RM* 56.
22. Cf. FABC, *Taipei Final Statement*, IV, 4, in Rosales and Arévalo, p. 33.
23. Ibid., II, 6, p. 13.
24. Ibid., II, 7.
25. *AG* 3.

Mission of Communion

39. As the third millennium approaches, the Church in Asia seeks to address the phenomenon of disunity in its many forms and to walk toward greater unity as an expression of her mission of communion. This calls for a sincere examination of

conscience, reconciliation, a renewed commitment to dialogue and expressions of unity.

Responses to the *Lineamenta* sadly point out that Asian societies all too often display the reality of disunity, including tensions between ethnic and religious groups, economic imbalances, conflicts in the political order between the powerful and the powerless, between majority groups and minorities, social distinctions and discrimination, and cultural differences between generations and between people of modern urbanized societies and those of rural societies. In many cases certain groups of people, especially women and children, suffer more than most not only from attitudes of discrimination and oppression, but from various forms of physical and psychological violence. Often these situations within societies simmer unresolved under the surface and occasionally explode into open violence.

The Church too, made up of human persons, is not immune to this reality of disunity. Certain responses note a lack of communion at times between clergy, religious, and lay people. Most admit that the greater the unity in the local Church, the greater will be the unity in other areas and levels of Church life. At the same time some point to the effect of divisions within the Church on those of other religions. The scandal of a divided Christianity is seen by many in Asia as a counterwitness to Jesus Christ. New tensions have also arisen in many parts of Asia by the proliferation and tactics of some evangelical groups. In other places religious movements and sects are creating difficulties.

On the other hand, there are signs of improved relations among certain Churches. Catholic and Orthodox Christians in West Asia often feel a cultural unity among themselves, a sense of sharing important elements of a common ecclesial tradition. The constructive working relationship fostered by many ecclesial structures, including the national episcopal conferences and FABC, offers hope for new ecumenical initiatives in Asia, an outlook which is reflected in the effective collaboration on peace and justice issues in various Asian countries. The Church's participation in other ecumenical initiatives is leading to cooperative pastoral ventures with other Churches in certain parts of Asia. However, the reality remains that much work needs to be done in this area.

The responses to the *Lineamenta* also recount the divided manner in which Christians are sometimes viewed by their neighbors of other religions. For example, Christians are respected and admired for the quality of schools, health care facilities, and social programs for the poor; yet some people suspect the motives of the Church in these activities.

In these various situations of disunity, the ecclesiology of the Church as communion has relevance not only for the internal relationships within the Church; it also underlines the nature of the Church's mission to build communion among all peoples. In the rich diversity of Asian ethnic groups, nations, social classes, cultures, and religions, many responses maintain that the Church is to be a sign and sacrament of the unity desired by God among the peoples of Asia. The struggle to build unity and bring about reconciliation, to promote dialogue with religions and cultures and to break down prejudices and engender trust is to be considered an essential part of the church's evangelizing mission in Asia. This vision of the church as agent of communion in Asia was expressed during the sixth plenary assembly of the FABC. Noting that Christ's mission is essentially one of "nourishing life to its fullness," the bishops affirmed:

> With our Asian sisters and brothers, we will strive to foster communion among Asian peoples who are threatened by glaring economic, social, and political imbalances. With them we will explore ways of utilizing the gifts of our diverse religions, cultures, and languages to achieve a richer and deeper Asian unity. We will build bridges of solidarity and reconciliation with peoples of other faiths and will join hands with everyone in Asia in forming a true community of creation.[34]

Note

34. FABC, *Final Statement* VI, Manila, 1995, "Christian Discipleship in Asia Today: Service to Life," 14, in FABC Papers, 74.

Part Two

The Synod in Action

5

What the Synod Participants Were Saying

The Asian Synod officially opened with the Inaugural Mass concelebrated by Pope John Paul II in St. Peter's Basilica on April 19, 1998, with thirty-four cardinals, six patriarchs, forty-nine archbishops, seventy-eight bishops, and ninety-two priests, at which the pope delivered the opening homily. The pope said that the new evangelization in Asia "calls for respectful attention to 'Asian realities' and healthy discernment in their regard." The synod, he said, "is a providential time of grace for the whole Christian people, and especially for the faithful of Asia, who are called to a fresh missionary outreach. In order that this favorable 'time' may be truly fruitful, the figure of Jesus and his saving mission need to be presented once more in their full light."

At the same time, the Asian churches must listen to what the Spirit is saying to them, "so that they may proclaim Christ in the context of Hinduism, Buddhism, Shintoism, and all those currents of thought and life which were already rooted in Asia before the preaching of the Gospel arrived." He goes on to say that what the Church must proclaim and bear witness to in Asia is "Christ Crucified and Risen, Redeemer of the world."

—Ed.

I. THE *RELATIO ANTE DISCEPTATIONEM*

The synod began its work with a presentation by Cardinal Paul Shan Kuo-Hsi on April 19. As general relator of the Asian Synod, the cardinal had the task of summarizing in a document, known as *Relatio ante Disceptationem*, the main points of the *Intrumentum Laboris* for discussion during the synod. Largely a repetition of the *Instrumentum Laboris*, the *Relatio* helpfully distilled the seven chapters of the working document into three parts: Asian realities as the context of the Church's mission, Jesus Christ as the Good News of Salvation, and the various forms of the Church's mission in Asia.

Three excerpts from the *Relatio* will be given here. The first deals with the task of proclaiming Jesus Christ in images understandable to Asian peoples, the second with a possible Asian Christology, and the third, the Church's mission of love and service in Asia.

—Ed.

The Proclamation of Jesus Christ in Asia

The presentation of Jesus Christ as the Savior of all meets today with many practical, sociological, philosophical, and theological difficulties in the context of other Asian religions, especially Hinduism and Buddhism. Most feel that Jesus must be presented with an "Asian countenance," using Asian philosophical concepts that are available in Asian cultures. This is particularly urgent in proclaiming Jesus Christ to Hindus and Buddhists. But the problem remains of believing in and explaining Jesus Christ as the one and only Savior and unique Mediator of salvation to all peoples.[39]

Some of the followers of the great religions of Asia have no problem in accepting Jesus as a manifestation of the Divine or the Absolute, or as an "enlightened one." But it is difficult for them to see him as the only manifestation of the Divine. Hence, while they do not have any difficulty in believing in Jesus Christ and his teaching, they see no urgency in accepting the Christian faith or entering the Church community through conversion and baptism.[40]

According to the classical, traditional, and cosmic religions of Asia, the Asian people seek to live in harmony between heaven and earth, between the divine and the human, between transcendence and immanence. Both in philosophical reflection and in worship forms, they seek to bridge the apparent contradiction between the two. This could be a point of departure in presenting Jesus Christ to Asian people, since the gap between the divine and the human has been bridged through the Incarnation, death, and glorification of Jesus. In Jesus Christ the infinite and the finite are reconciled and the transcendent has become immanent. In the mystery of Jesus Christ the transcendent, invisible God becomes visible and concretely manifested.[41]

It is within this Asian context that Christians feel the need to present Jesus Christ in a way that is intelligible to the Asian mind. In Jesus Christ, harmony between the apparent paradoxes which confront human existence has been established. It is a harmony between transcendence and immanence, emptiness and fullness, death and life, suffering and joy, the finite and the infinite, poverty and riches, weakness and power, the temporal and the eternal, the historical and the cosmic. In Jesus Christ, the incarnate Word of God, crucified and risen, the above paradoxes find a point of convergence.[42]

In presenting Jesus Christ there is a need to develop a Christology centered on the theme of "kenosis" and "pleroma," namely, a Christology based on the "self-emptying" of Jesus in the mystery of his Incarnation, passion, and death and his being "filled up" in the mystery of the resurrection. It is a Christology based on the Paschal Mystery. This is important in the sociocultural context of Asia. Jesus came to give his life as a ransom for all so that all may have life in its fullness. He emptied himself so that all may be filled with the fullness of life.

A "suffering servant" of the Lord, who shares the pain, poverty, rejection, and exploitation of the Asian peoples and who is able to give them a sense of human dignity, will be appealing to the heart of Asia. In his self-emptying Jesus became the source of life for all. Though he was the eternal Word, Jesus did not cling to his divinity but emptied himself and became like all men in order to give all people his saving grace and a sense of human dignity as children of God. He presented himself as the "Good Samaritan" who cares for the weak, the wounded, and the rejected. He showed himself to be the "Good Shepherd" who lays down his life so that others may live.

The Perception of Jesus Christ in the Missionary Context of Asia

In the missionary context, the Church in Asia has different perceptions of Jesus Christ which place an emphasis on one or another aspect of the Person of Jesus Christ and his relation to salvation. During the past decades, theologians and missionaries have been engaged in expressing the Church's understanding of the Person of Jesus Christ and the salvific value of his passion, death, and resurrection. Such theological and missionary dialogue with the followers of other religions and cultures demands keeping in mind the philosophical and cultural context and religious language of Asia. At the same time, these presentations of Jesus Christ must be in keeping with the faith-tradition of the Church going back to the Apostles.

Such a task is not an easy one. It requires of everyone time and patience. The inculturation of Christology in Asia is an urgent need, but it cannot be done at the expense of the integrity of Christian faith.[43] Integrity of faith, however, does not mean that we cannot present Jesus Christ by initially emphasizing those aspects which are more appealing to Asians and then complementing them with further doctrinal points.

The Church in Asia needs to keep in mind that ultimately it is not doctrinal arguments which will make the Person of Jesus Christ appealing and acceptable to Asian peoples; the witness given by Christians to Jesus Christ will be convincing.[44] Asian Christians must incarnate in themselves the Gospel values which Jesus proclaimed and put on his love and compassion for the poor, the sick, and the lowly. Asian peoples can come to know, love, and accept Jesus Christ as their Lord and Savior only when they recognize him in his disciples in Asia.

Hence the Church in Asia has to put on Jesus Christ and have the same mind and heart which were in Jesus Christ. Having the mind of Jesus Christ, Christians in Asia will seek to understand and respect Asian cultures and religions and recognize the saving presence of the Spirit in their midst and his working among them. Having the heart of Jesus Christ, they will love all peoples, become instruments of reconciliation and channels of love, service, compassion, and goodness.

Notes

39. *Instrumentum Laboris*, no. 30.
40. Cf. ibid.
41. Cf. John Paul II, Encyclical Letter, *Dives in Misericordia* (30 November 1980), 7; *AAS* 72 (1980), 1199–1203.
42. *Instrumentum Laboris*, no. 30.
43. Cf. John Paul II, Apostolic Letter, *Tertio Millennio Adveniente* (10 November 1994), no. 38: "There is an urgent need for a synod on the occasion of the Great Jubilee in order to illustrate and explain more fully the truth that Jesus Christ is the only Media-

tor between God and man and the sole Redeemer of the world, to be clearly distinguished from the founders of other great religions." *AAS* 87 (1995), 30–31.
44. Cf. John Paul II, Encyclical Letter, *Redemptoris Missio* (7 December 1990), 91; *AAS*
83 (1991), 338.

The Church's Mission of Love and Service in Asia

The Service of Dialogue and Inculturation

Today the Church is aware that her evangelizing mission has many dimensions including dialogue, inculturation, and human promotion. The importance of these
elements of evangelization is reflected in all the major documents of the magisterium in recent years.

In the Asian context of a multi-ethnic, multi-religious and multi-cultural situation, dialogue assumes a most important role. In addition, for the first time the
Church is encountering millennia-old religions in a serious manner. Interreligious
dialogue is a respectful and sincere encounter in which the encountering parties
want to know each other, to learn from one another, and to enrich each another.
For the Christian believer, this will also include the desire to communicate the
saving message of Jesus Christ.

The Church in Asia is called upon to enter into a triple dialogue: a dialogue
with the cultures of Asia, a dialogue with the religions of Asia, and a dialogue
with the peoples of Asia, especially the poor, as was stated by the First Plenary
Assembly of the Federation of Asian Episcopal Conferences at Taipei.[64] To carry
on the dialogue with Asia, formation to dialogue is all-important, especially in
formation centers.

Inculturation

Inculturation is another very urgent need in the particular Churches in Asia. While
the Oriental Churches are for the most part well inculturated in the local cultures
of West Asia and South India, the more recently established Churches have a serious need for inculturating the faith in the cultures of Asia and for shedding an appearance of being carbon copies of Churches in Western societies. In this way, the
local Churches in Asia will be able to be better integrated into the cultures of Asia
and shed the mistaken impression of some people that the Church is culturally
foreign to Asia.

Inculturation is the process by which the Christian faith becomes incarnate in
local cultures by assuming, purifying, and ennobling elements of the philosophy,
art, and spirituality of peoples in so far as they are compatible with the values of
the Gospel.[65] Inculturation applies to theology, liturgy, sacred art, spirituality, and
social organization. In order to carry on the process of inculturation, the Church in
Asia needs to study and come to know Asian cultures and to proceed with prudence and due freedom under the guidance of the magisterium. In this way, inculturation becomes a means of evangelization, growth, and mutual enrichment of
the Churches in Asia and the universal Church.

Human Promotion

Christian mission has always been concerned with human promotion from its very beginning. But the context of inhuman poverty in many parts of Asia calls for a special involvement of the Church in human promotion, in promoting the values of the Kingdom of God and in the creation of a just society.

In the first place, the Church must be a prophetic voice for the poor, the oppressed, and the exploited. While the Church in Asia will carry on its vast network of traditional involvement in human promotion through education, healthcare, and works of mercy, new areas are presenting themselves for evangelization, e.g., the promotion of human and legal rights, the struggle against the exploitation of women, children, and minorities, migrants, AIDS, organized prostitution, child abuse, pedophilia, political corruption, and the wanton destruction of natural resources. In her work of evangelization, the Church is also able to enter into collaboration with other groups engaged in human promotion, in attempts toward alleviating or even canceling the international debt or in compensating for collective exploitation, etc.

Notes

64. Cf. Federation of Asian Bishops' Conferences, FABC I, *Final Statement*, *Evangelization in Modern Day Asia*, Taipei, Taiwan, R.O.C., 1974, n. II–V.
65. *RM* (7 December 1990), 52: *AAS* 83 (1991), 299–300.

II. PARTICIPANTS' INTERVENTIONS

After Cardinal Paul Shan Kuo-Hsi's *Relatio ante Disceptationem*, the synod began its work in earnest. Fourteen "congregations" or general assemblies were held on April 19–28, during which 191 eight-minute "interventions" were delivered by the participants. Summaries of these speeches were made available to the public, whereas their full texts were kept by the General Secretariat of the synod.

It is of course impossible to reproduce the full texts of all 191 interventions here, though it would be necessary to study them in detail in order to obtain an accurate picture of the real concerns of the Asian bishops, "live" as it were, before they were filtered through the synod's official subsequent documents. This section presents a cross-section of these speeches, as far as possible in their entirety, rather than their summaries. They are selected for the important problems broached, the imaginative solutions proposed, and the bold vision held out for the Church in Asia. Selections are made not only of speeches by bishops who are members of the FABC but also by those of the Near and Middle East and Central Asia as well as by non-episcopal participants.

Needless to say, not all the interventions represent a "liberal" theology. Unsurprisingly, some curial officials insisted strongly on orthodoxy, especially in Christology, and on the unity of the Church. For example, Cardinal Dario Castrillon, Prefect of the Congregation for the Clergy, asserted that "the Third Millennium will make known in Asia, and in every region thereof, that Jesus of Nazareth is *the Christ*, not 'one' but *the* way, and that there is no salvation except through him." He also made the odd suggestion that the solution of the shortage of priestly vocations can be found only in a "catechesis that is absolutely faithful to the deposit of the faith as this is presented in the Catechism of the Catholic Church." He went on to say that "such publications must be chosen and academic resource centers used as promote that authentic *ecclesiastical spirit,* which can so often appear to be lacking in certain regions. Particular heed should be paid so that "models and theories which have already produced ruinous results here and there are not uncritically transferred to other countries." In the same vein, Cardinal William Baum, Major Penitentiary, affirmed: "There must be no hesitancy on our part as bishops in announcing with apostolic boldness that Jesus Christ is the only Savior, who reconciles us with God His Father." To the printed text he scrawled the following remarks: "The proclamation of the Truth about Christ is always and everywhere, especially in America, an obstacle, a *scandalum.*" As to the unity of the Church, Cardinal Angelo Sodano, the Secretary of State, saw the unity of the Church as identical with the unity with the pope and with his collaborators in the Roman curia and his representatives throughout the world: "If the Lord wanted his Church to be *one* around Peter, the visible principle of unity, it is necessary that the teaching of the pope be always more faithfully followed and that the norms which he promulgates with his pastoral authority be always followed, with a deep filial spirit."[1]

On the other hand, Cardinal Joseph Ratzinger, Prefect of the Congregation of the Doctrine of the Faith, who was expected to hold the conservative line, made a statement surprising for its openness, regarding the issue of Church as institution: "There are real reasons to fear that the Church could take on too many institutions of human law that later become like Saul's armor which weighed on the young David and prevented him from walking (1 Sam 17:39). Institutions taken by themselves can all be well founded, but if they are too numerous, they can immobilize the Church. Hence it is necessary to examine whether certain institutions that were once useful are still of use or rather hinder the growth of the Church."[2]

With regard to the pastoral issues that bishops coming from different parts of Asia and various ecclesiastical traditions brought to the synod, there was of course a great diversity among them as they represented the vastly different faces of the Church in the immense continent of Asia. Nevertheless, on the whole, the Asian bishops did speak with a remarkably consistent voice about the basic needs and tasks of Christianity in Asia. As the FABC has repeatedly insisted, Christian mission in Asia can only be carried out in the form of dialogue in three intimately interrelated areas: with Asian cultures, Asian religions, and Asian poor. Furthermore, to perform this dialogue successfully, the Asian bishops believe that a legitimate autonomy of the local Churches, which is proper to and required by the principle of subsidiarity, is necessary. This autonomy, whereby the local churches can decide, in consultation with the other churches of the same region, what pastoral policies and practices are most effective for their evangelizing mission and for the life of the Christians, without undue control by or interference from the Roman curia, is not opposed to the supreme authority of the bishop of Rome. On the contrary, it promotes the collegiality and communion among the bishop of Rome and the other bishops and thus brings forth the manifold riches of the universal Church.

Another oft-repeated point in the interventions refers to the need of expanding the roles of the laity, especially women, in the life of the Church. The ecclesiological model which the Asian bishops tried to promote is what has been called "participative church," namely, a church in which all members are fundamentally equal in dignity and share responsibility for the whole church, though with different functions and duties.

Most of the interventions were given in English, a few in French and Italian, languages which, though widely used in Asia today, were, in not a long distant past, those of Asia's conquerors and in some places the colonizers' tools to erase the indigenous cultures. There is irony in the fact that Japanese bishop Francis Xavier K. Shimamoto made an eloquent plea for the inculturation of the Christian faith, especially in liturgical matters, and for a greater freedom of the local churches—in Latin![3]

—Ed.

Notes

1. "Se il Signore ha volute che la sua Chiesa fosse *"una"* intorno a Pietro, principio visible di unità, occorrerà che il magistero del Papa sia semper più fedelmente ascoltato e che le norme che egli imparte con il suo governo pastorale siano sempre seguite, con profondo spirito filiale." The cardinal goes on to say that the pope cannot always intervene directly, but at times does so by means of his collaborators in the Roman curia or his representatives throughout the world.

2. "Ci sono motivi reali per temere che la Chiesa possa indossare troppe istituzioni di diritto umano, che diventano poi come la corazza di Saul, che pesava talmente sul giovane Davide, che con questo addosso invano cercava di camminare (1 Sam 17:39). Le single istituzioni possono tutte essere ben fondate, ma se sono troppe rendono immobile la Chiesa. Perciò è semper necessario esaminare se instituzioni che sono state una volta utili servono ancora, o impediscono piutttosto la crescita della Chiesa."

3. "Ad hoc tamen ecclesia localis necessitatem habet gaudendi majore libertate inceptionis et conaminis in elaboratione liturgica, agens enim principalis cuiuslibet inculturationis est ecclesia localis." ET: "For this [liturgical inculturation] however the local church needs to have a greater freedom in initiating and implementing liturgical elaboration, since the principal agent of whatever form of inculturation is the local church."

FORMATION FOR RELIGIOUS IN THE CONTEXT OF ASIAN REALITIES TODAY

ARTURO M. BASTES, S.V.D.
BISHOP OF ROMBLON, PHILIPPINES

Formation for men and women aspirants to the consecrated life should be contextualized in order to enable the religious to respond to the Church's mission in Asia. There are still strong indications that Asian realities have not yet been taken seriously enough in the present practice of the Church's pastoral mission in general and in the formation of religious in particular. There is a need to point out to some areas where shifts and perspectives have to be made so that the Asian Church will truly emerge and consequently the formation of religious will be "Asianized."

I would like to focus on four important areas needing a change of perspective: a shift from the perspective of a Euro-centered Church to an authentically Asian view, a shift in the understanding of history, a shift in the model of the Church, and a shift in the understanding of spirituality.

Shift in the Perspective from a Euro-Centered Church to an Asian Church

The Church's mission in Asia had been approached from the perspective of a Euro-centered Church which was deeply conditioned by the European colonialism of the times. This influence is still clear even in post-colonial times. Formation of religious was or is presently monocultural, which is really Western or European. It is imperative that more recognition be given to the rightful autonomy of the local churches in Asia. Correspondingly, more autonomy should be given to the provinces of religious congregations in the manner of forming members who hail from Asia. Two-thirds of the world's population live in Asia, that is, 3,353 million people of whom only 94.8 million are Catholic. This is rather embarrassing for the Christian mission in Asia after Christianity has been preached for the past two thousand years. However, the opposite is a bit startling in the case of religious vocations. While today religious vocations are rapidly decreasing in Europe and the rest of the Western hemisphere, there is an ever-increasing number of religious vocations in Asia. In fact some religious congregations which originated in Europe are surviving or are even growing a bit because of Asian candidates.

To ensure contextualized formation for religious candidates there should be models of formation that are suited to the mentality of Asians. In some stages of formation, the contextualized models should include real insertion into a particular locality where Asian reality is typically found. Local Asian formators are developing practical methodologies. In contrast, the Western academic model follows the classic pattern of giving inputs by the master/mistress, library research, personal and group study. Admittedly, the academic model is also needed, such as a systematic study of the congregation's constitutions common to all members all over the world. But the academic study must be accompanied by practical methodologies to put the constitutions and the congregation's mission in the light of Asian realities.

A Shift in the Understanding of History

In the dating of history the coming of Jesus Christ is emphasized as the point of reference. But let us also recall that the great world religions, such as Hinduism and Buddhism whose cradle is Asia, antedate Christianity by thousands of years. They have found a home in the hearts of Asians. Christianity itself was born in Asia but it has been alienated from Asia because of the perspective of a Euro-centered Church. The Catholic Bishops' Conference of the Philippines suggests that the Asian Synod must "explore exhaustively in an open and humble way the revelatory nature" of the religions of Asia and their impact on the Church's proclamation of Jesus. Jesus came to preach the Kingdom of God. This is the central theme of his mission. If we too emphasize the theme of the Kingdom in our preaching, I believe that all religions in Asia will be at home in it. For there is much that even the Church can learn from these Asian religions regarding the values of the Kingdom!

Our faith in the mystery of Jesus tells us that history has become the place of encounter between God and the whole creation. This outlook makes the Incarnation of Christ all-inclusive of history, even the periods "before Christ." This truth should make us sensitive to the workings of God's Spirit particularly in the great world religions of Asia.

What are the consequences of this understanding of history for the formation of religious in Asia? Formation communities have to become "sensitive." Those in formation must have a great feeling of respect for other religious traditions, which offer "salvation" even before the coming of Christ. As a Christian, a religious should not feel "superior" to people belonging to these traditions. This humble attitude is to be cultivated during the time of formation. The Asians in formation have to be reminded that they remain Asian even if they join an international congregation.

A Shift in the Model of Church

The Church model is always conditioned by the situation obtaining in every time and clime. When Europe was Christianized, a mind-set arose that considered Europe Christian and the rest of the world non-Christian or pagan. The missionary zeal of the Europeans drove them to bring the God of salvation to the "pagans." Unfortunately, they seemed to identify Christianity with what is European. Today, in light of the Second Vatican Council and of the social teachings of the Church, many local churches in the so-called Third World are striving to shift away from a triumphalistic model of the Church to a Church identified with the social conditions of the people. The model of the Church of the Poor is being adopted by many local Asian churches.

There is massive poverty in Asia. Without a sense of the poor, there can be no genuine following of Jesus in Asia. Hence, candidates for the religious life in Asia should be trained to have both affective and effective commitment to the poor. All religious congregations today emphasize "preferential option for the poor." But the question is: Do they really mean it? The "passing over to the poor" is admittedly one of the most difficult crossings over for a religious congregation.

A Shift in the Understanding of Spirituality

In our traditional Catholic way of looking at spirituality, we associate it with an institutional way of living, either with the religious life or with the ordained ministry. It has been difficult to consider spirituality otherwise than associated with an institution or a religious order. We need to shift our understanding of spirituality from institutionalized spirituality to incarnational spirituality. Indeed, every congregation has its own charism, which somehow determines the "spirituality" of the institute. But more basic to this institutional spirituality is the one rooted in the Incarnation of Christ. There is a dynamic and essential relationship between culture and spirituality in a common humanity. The dynamic name for the image of the Creator in us is the human spirit. In this case the dynamic life of the human spirit is what should be called incarnational spirituality. Three expressions reveal the dynamic life of the human spirit: (1) self-transcendence; (2) drive and search for meaning; (3) gift of self.

There is in each person the capacity for self-transcendence. This is the very heart of every spirituality, both Christian and non-Christian. The search for meaning is what drives us to look for the answers to why we are here on earth. The elusiveness of the modern world in its desire to provide meaning to human existence has shifted its focus of progress from human/spiritual to material development. As the globalization of the free market forces attacking Asia moves into the third millennium, it consolidates itself progressively on a universal scale. The prospects of the third millennium are indeed frightening. For this reason religious men and women of Asia should join forces to fight against consumerism by living a spiritual life that is intelligible to their fellow Asians, to whatever creed and persuasion they belong. But we must bear in mind that while all of us who bear a common human spirit direct ourselves to the ultimate end, we have come to the ultimate end by different names. As Christians we have our own story to tell and our perception of God as part of that story. If we believe that God is the living Lord of history who accompanies his people in weaving their interrelated story, we ask: Would this same God behave in the same way with the peoples of Asia? These different stories led people of Asia to come up with different traditions, cultures, and religions, which conditioned them to perceive the ultimate end differently.

These reflections should lead to the necessity for religious candidates in Asia to seriously study and reflect on the "spirituality" of other Asian religions besides the teachings of Christian scriptures and traditions. The Federation of Asian Bishops' Conferences issued a paper (no. 81) which gives an excellent overview of how the Spirit is at work in various religious-cultural traditions of Asia. A reflection of this sort should be included in the formation of religious candidates of Asia. The presence of the Spirit is found in Hinduism, Buddhism, Taoism, Islam, and even Primal Religion. It is the vocation of Asian religious today to save Asia from the onslaught of materialism coming from global market forces by the wisdom and depth of Asian spirituality with which Asians feel at home. This spirituality is not opposed to the teachings of Christ because it is a true manifestation of God's Spirit working in all peoples.

WOMEN IN THE CHURCH

CRISÓSTOMO A. YALUNG
AUXILIARY BISHOP OF MANILA, PHILIPPINES

In the *Instrumentum Laboris,* there are at least five instances where the word "women" is mentioned with regard to their role as laity and to their pitiful conditions.

a. Nos. 13 and 44 refer to the need for programs of formation for the laity, especially the women (no. 44), since they also desire to take active part in the Church (no. 13).

b. In nos. 20–22, in the context of the missionary backgrounds in the evangelization of Asia, education was seen as an effective tool in the empowerment of women both in the past and in the present. Missionaries in Asia, especially the women religious, have made great contributions in this regard. Through education, there was a raising of new awareness on the dignity of women. This new consciousness led to some social changes.

c. In no. 45, one looks at the factors that deter human promotion, namely, poverty and the consequent exploitation of women and children. . . .

In this presentation I would like to highlight the role that the Church in Asia does and could have in the promotion of awareness and of respect for the dignity of women in Asia. As pastoral director of the Office on Women of the Catholic Bishops' Conference of the Philippines (CBCP), I present these observations as they reflect the Philippine experiences on three levels: on the level of our synodal document, on the level of the Church's pastoral work, and on the level of the Church's task of human promotion.

1. On the Synodal Document

In the *Instrumentum Laboris,* "women" are mentioned with reference to the laity, the youth, and the family. However, it might be proper to have an explicit and separate reference to women as a generic group. While they fall under different categories as members of the Church, a separate reference to them could indicate the Asian Church's deference to their personhood and dignity, and to the distinctive roles they play in the Church and society.

In contemporary Asia, the growing awareness of the dignity and role of women, attested to in various groups and movements, cannot simply be ignored. Their potentials and contributions in helping the Church in her evangelization works need to be explicitly recognized. There may possibly be an apprehension of the feminism in the Western hemisphere which may be reflective of a certain crisis of identity; but the recognition of the "feminine genius" actively present in Asia can help the Church harness more fully the charisms and energies of women.

2. On the Church's Pastoral Ministry

This level can be understood both in the *ad intra* and *ad extra* dimensions. *Ad intra*, we acknowledge the positive steps being taken toward a greater participation of women in the life of the Church. Aside from the presence and proliferation of women religious congregations in the life of the Church in Asia, there is more quality involvement of laywomen in diocesan and parish pastoral councils, in the basic ecclesial ministries and various pastoral ministries. We also affirm the significant roles of women in the field of education—as it begins in the home, continues in the school, is given concrete life in the livelihood programs of the parishes, and is extended in the societal spheres.

We have to take note, however, that while quality education is provided by schools run by the religious, especially the women, the high cost of education (possibly as a means for the school to survive) is likewise prohibitive for competent, deserving, but poor girl students to avail themselves of this tool toward personality development and integral social involvement. Hopefully our synod can address this concern.

On the *ad extra* level, we mention again the missionary roles of women religious in this evangelization task. The presence of the faithful of the Church of Asia in other parts of the world is manifest in the ministries and apostolates done by women religious and lay women missionaries coming from Asia.

A rising phenomenon, though, needs to be recognized. It is true that the labor migration of Asian women due to poverty has caused a crisis in the family. Nonetheless, the presence of Asian labor migrants, especially Catholics from the Philippines, Thailand, Sri Lanka, India, Indonesia, and Malaysia, in other Asian countries or in so-called first- and second-world countries remains a potential tool for evangelization. No doubt, a solid catechesis in the family is the foundation of effective evangelization in the Church as well as elsewhere in the world. The Church in Italy itself bears witness to the growth and the leavening of its ecclesial life with the presence of dedicated foreign worker-apostles. It is however disheartening to note that with their increasing number and the corresponding inconveniences these workers bring, some sister Churches find our Asian sisters and brothers a nuisance. Could this Synod of Bishops from the Churches of Asia urge the sister Churches which host our lay apostles to be more hospitable and sympathetic to the spiritual and human needs of Asian workers? In this way we also bear witness to an effective communion of Churches.

3. On the Level of Human Promotion

The *Instrumentum Laboris* has repeatedly expressed concern over the degradation of women and children and the various forms of their exploitation through drug addiction, prostitution, child labor, pornography, violence against women, and so on. We are happy to note that the Church in Asia, especially in the Philippines, has always boldly spoken out against the violations of the dignity of women. Centers for the protection and promotion of women's dignity have been established by Church groups and/or organized by women religious and nongovernmental organizations.

The CBCP has established the Office on Women with two goals among others: (1) to highlight the evangelization capabilities and the gifts of women in the service of the Church and our society, and (2) to be in the forefront of advocacy on women concerns. At present, aside from the multifarious issues affecting women in the Philippines, there is the recruitment of women and children in the guerrilla warfare of the Moro Islamic Liberation Front (MILF). Recently, the government and the media have brought this fact to national attention. Through the ecumenical pastoral ministry of the Church, something positive toward human promotion could also be done on behalf of those outside the Church. Interreligious dialogue and dialogue for justice and peace can be significant venues for the ministry of the Church in this regard.

The Church in Asia, as an incarnational Church, needs to be the prophetic voice for those who need to be heard in their deep human longings for the divine and to encounter the divine in their human situations.

THE USE OF MASS MEDIA IN EVANGELIZATION

RAMON VILLENA
BISHOP OF BAYOMBONG, PHILIPPINES

For 2,000 years, the Catholic Church has been bringing the word of God to humanity through three institutions: the parish, the school, and charitable institutions.

We set up a parish and we meet the children of God face to face: the parish priest preaches to them from the pulpit on Sunday morning. We set up a school and we put religious Sisters in the classroom, and they teach the children of God face to face, in the classroom. We set up a hospital, or an orphan asylum, or a feeding center, and we minister to the needs of the poor, face to face.

We have done that in Asia, for a long time, and with some success—Xavier in India and Matteo Ricci in China. We have touched Korea, Thailand, Indonesia, Japan. But today, right now, as we speak here in Rome, what impact have we made in Asia? Asia is 2 percent Catholic, at the most. Two out of a hundred! One out of fifty!

And of those 2 percent of Asians who are baptized Catholic, how many go to Mass on Sunday? In the United States and Europe, it is about 10 percent—one out of ten. In Asia, I think, we could raise it a little—to 15 percent or even to 20 percent. But no more than that.

It is true—we are a leaven in the life of Asia. We are yeast. We permeate the whole mass of dough. We have an effect on the cultures in which we live. But we are only 2 percent. And if we continue, using only the methods we have used in the past, it is doubtful that we will remain 2 percent! Rather we will decline!

May I suggest that we should open our eyes to the present; that we should accept the world as it really is, right here, right now; that we should face reality? We are not touching the hearts of the people of Asia!

When our Lord said to his twelve Apostles—eleven, without Judas—"Go, and teach all nations!" he gave them a way to reach the whole known world—the Roman roads. The Apostles went out, over the Roman roads, and changed the face of the earth. In our days, in our new world, God has also given us a way to reach all the children of God—the air waves!

It is true that not too many people come to Mass on Sunday. It is true that not too many children are able to attend Catholic schools. It is true that we do not reach very many in our hospitals, our orphan asylums, our medical missions, our feeding centers. But the air waves are wide open to us! No one owns the air waves. The air waves are the property of the people!

In our day, with the use of light, we can bring the Gospel, vividly, into every home. The Asian who has never learned to read or write can see the birth of God made man, to a virgin, in a stable, in Asia! He can watch the miracles of Christ in Galilee—Lazarus coming forth from the tomb. He can watch the passion and death of Christ on Calvary. He can watch the resurrection and the apparition to Mary Magdalen. We come to the Asian where he is, and how he is—poor, illiterate, hungry for God.

It is true that satellite television does not reach everyone in Asia because large areas do not yet have electricity. And even in areas where there is electricity, television is expensive, out of reach of the poor. But there is no individual in Asia who cannot get a transistor radio! Radio is the saturation medium of Asia.

I would like to use my own country, the Philippines, as an example. Our people are poor. Seventy percent of our people live below the poverty line. Sixty percent of our land does not yet have electricity. But for the squatter, born under a bridge, delivered by a street vendor, whose only way of earning a living is scavenging, his window on the world is the transistor radio. He cannot read. He cannot write. But he can listen. The farmer, plowing in the field, has the transistor radio strapped to the handle of his plow. The housewife, washing the dishes, is praying the rosary with Father Peyton, whose voice comes to her from the transistor radio. Father Peyton is now dead, but he is leading the rosary, every morning, in thousands of homes, in the Philippines!

In Luzon, the northernmost island of the Philippine Archipelago, where I live, we have a primitive people, called the Dumagats. The Dumagats do not wear shoes. They do not wear trousers. They do not wear shirts. They wear G-strings. One afternoon, during our rainy season, a Dumagat warrior was coming down from his home in the mountain to the town, barefoot, through the mud, in the driving rain. But, on this occasion, he was carrying an umbrella! Naked, except for the G-string, and barefoot, but carrying an umbrella! The umbrella was not for him. He was accustomed to living in the rain. The umbrella was for his transistor radio, which he was holding close to his ear!

In my diocese I have a radio station. It is amplitude modulation—AM, because the AM air wave climbs over mountains. It crawls down into valleys, it bounces off of clouds, it reaches all of my people, in a rough, mountainous terrain. Some of them meet a priest, face to face, only once a year, at fiesta time, when the priest comes to their village. But they can hear my voice, in their own native dialect, every day! I have a radio station because it is the only way that I can reach all of the children of God whom God has placed under my care.

I want to have a second radio station—FM, frequency modulation. FM travels in a straight line. It does not climb mountains, or creep down into valleys, or bounce off of clouds. It goes straight out. It does not curve with the earth. It is probably heard very clearly on Mars. But the quality of sound is better. I want AM for quantity, to reach everybody, and FM for quality—quality of sound and quality of audience. Over the FM station, I can talk to the leaders.

In the beginning, I subsidized the radio station. Some questioned me about this. They said, "Should you subsidize radio before you know how many people you are reaching, or what the impact is on them? Should you not have a scientific survey first?" My answer was this: "Every bishop that I know subsidizes parishes. If I have to conduct a survey before I can subsidize my radio station, then I demand that every bishop who subsidizes a parish have a survey on how many people come to Mass on Sunday, and how effective are the sermons of the parish priest."

My surveys are the letters that I receive from my people in the mountains. They listen to me. They understand me. They ask questions. They ask for help. I have contact with the people. That is enough for me.

Present here, in this synod, is His Eminence Jaime Cardinal Sin. He has a radio station. He is the only bishop, on the face of the earth, who called a revolution over radio! He asked the children of God to come out to Edsa—priests, nuns, seminarians, Catholics, Muslims, Protestants, rich men, poor men, beggars, thieves—and they came out! Two million people filled that street for four days, facing a little army, fully equipped, with orders to fire. They dethroned a dictator. They changed the face of the earth. It was a turning point in the history of the world.

Cardinal Sin has been honored with about thirty-seven doctorates, by universities, all over the world, because of what he did. He talked to the people of the Philippines! He led the people—Catholic and non-Catholic, rich and poor, educated and noneducated. How could he do this? Because he had a radio station, and each one of those two million people was listening to him, over radio. He was using mass media to reach the children of God.

I know that in many nations of Asia, right now, the government has seized control of the air waves. The Church is allowed to speak to the people rarely, and at odd times. This is wrong. The government does not own the air waves. The air waves belong to the people!

So my suggestion is that the bishops of Asia make a deliberate, united effort to use the forces of mass media—especially television, and most of all, radio. I think that we should not only be given time to broadcast. I think that, as far as it is humanly possible, we should have our own broadcasting stations, our own transmitters, our own frequencies in radio, our own television channels. Please forgive me for being so passionate about this. I am passionate, because I believe that media is the pulpit of the modern world, and that we must use it.

To summarize what I have said:

1. Our traditional methods of carrying the word of God to people have been the parish, the school, and charitable institutions.
2. These traditional methods are not enough. We must use the modern means that God has given us: the air waves!
3. The medium that reaches all the children of God in Asia, in the most convenient way, at the cheapest price, is radio!
4. As God gave the Roman roads to his twelve Apostles, so he has given the air waves to us. The Catholic Church in Asia should make a deliberate, united effort to use radio, to reach the children of God.
5. The children of God in Asia are not only Catholics. They are Buddhists, Hindus, Muslims, Taoists, Jews—and the millions who do not know what to believe. They are hungry for God. The best way for us to reach them, right here, right now, is radio!

INCULTURATION AS DIALOGUE

FRANCISCO CLAVER, S.J.
BISHOP EMERITUS, APOSTOLIC VICAR OF BANTOE-LAGAWE, PHILIPPINES

From what has been said in the *Instrumentum Laboris* (no. 50), the *Relatio ante Disceptationem* (p. 30) and many interventions so far from the floor, we take it for a simple fact that there is need of a truly inculturated preaching of the Gospel in the Churches of Asia. It is a fact and we don't have to say why it is so. There has been enough blame-setting, and I find it a sterile exercise making judgments from hindsight about our forbears in the faith who were products of their age—as much, I guess, as we are of ours. Knowing what we know now, I think it would be better for us to ask what we can do to correct whatever mistakes were done in the past. That, I believe, is one of the challenges before us today in this synod.

In my intervention today, I would like to focus not so much on what we should be doing, say, in theology or liturgy or catechetics to inculturate the faith, but rather on the approach (and attitude?) we should take as pastors and as Church in general. And it is one that springs from the fact that inculturation, when one comes down to it, is the dialogue we must foster at every level of the Church between people (ourselves and our ordinary faithful) and the Holy Spirit. This is not as farfetched a statement as it seems. Let me explain.

Consider these simple facts: People are the bearers of a culture—culture being their distinctive way of being human. The Holy Spirit is the Giver and Source of Faith, and faith, we know, is a free gift. Hence, if the inculturation process is basically the putting together of faith and culture into an integrated whole, the prime actors in that putting together necessarily are the bearers of culture, that is, the people and the Giver of faith, that is, the Spirit. Not the missionary, not somebody from outside the culture, not primarily bishops, theologians, liturgists, and other experts. The task is the people's—the community's—and the Spirit's.

If the people and the Spirit are then the main actors in the inculturation of the faith, it follows that inculturation is at base nothing more and nothing less than the continuing dialogue between the Spirit and the people, a salvific dialogue in which people directly and constantly have recourse to the Author of faith for light and assistance in their attempts at living the faith fully within their specific cultural milieu.

The way of inculturation is thus most simple: Let them, the people and Spirit, dialogue freely. The formula is indeed simple. But it presents quite a huge problem to us as pastors. I don't think we can stop the Spirit from engaging in that dialogue. But I'm afraid we do put often unnecessary blocks to our people's full participation in it. Back in the early 1980s, the first BILA (Bishops' Institute on the Lay Apostolate) sponsored by the FABC was held in Taiwan and its theme was "trusting and entrusting the laity." The wording of the theme unabashedly said all that was wrong with us at the time: we bishops were not entrusting the laity enough with ministries and responsibilities due them because, if the truth be told, we did not fully trust them. Did you ever stop to think that distrust toward them is also distrust of the Spirit?

Let me give just one example of this lack of trust and it has to do with a simple thing—liturgical language. Why do we have to send vernacular translations of the liturgy to Rome for approval? Or to the bishop of the place, for that matter, if he doesn't speak the language in question? Don't we trust our people enough to speak the language of orthodoxy? But in truth the best judges of the correctness, even theological, of translations and texts are the faithful and clergy of the place where the language is spoken.

The kind of dialogue I am speaking of here is not an invitation to chaos, to private revelations, unbridled charismaticism. But it is to become living communities of faith that are truly discerning and prayerful, involved and active, genuinely participatory and serious about themselves as a Church on mission in the Spirit—such communities as are best exemplified in real BECs (Basic Ecclesial Communities).

I can't help noting here something that we see happening in our BECs: where the faithful fully participate in the life and mission of the Church, as they are encouraged to do in the BECs, they will participate as themselves—as Asians, that is, not as Romans or Westerners—and inculturation, we discover, does take place quite naturally and automatically. Participation by itself is thus another sure and potent formula for inculturation, and the BEC is as good a vehicle as any for bringing it about.

One last thought: we have been speaking in this synod of all sorts of dialogues to engage in—dialogue with the great religious traditions; dialogue with people, the poor especially, women and youth; dialogue with cultures, with ideologies, with modernity. I get the sense, though, that these dialogues are for the most part with partners external to ourselves as Church. If they are that, I am afraid, they will not prosper or succeed as they should unless the kind of internal dialogue that I refer to as "inculturation process" is also taking place: dialogue among ourselves, between top and bottom in the Church, and all of us together as community, in community, with the Holy Spirit. In our experience, it is this dialogue that keeps alive our capacity to be surprised.

I have no specific proposal to make. As I have said, I was going to talk about an approach, an attitude, to inculturation. It is something we can only suggest.

EVANGELIZATION AND CULTURE

LEO JUN IKENAGA, S.J.
ARCHBISHOP OF OSAKA, JAPAN

My topic is evangelization in Asia, especially East Asia, where so many missionaries have preached the Gospel with little result. The faith has never flowered, baptisms are few, and the message of the Gospel has not really sunk into Asian society. Why is this? What can we do about it?

The Conduit of Culture

A Japanese prince, Shoutoku Taishi (574–622), introduced Buddhism from China to Japan. The new religion was well received. Within fifty years Emperor Tennmu had Buddhist temples built throughout the land to pray for peace and prosperity. Half a century was all it took for the Japanese to accept Buddhism as the religion of their land.

With Christianity it was another story. Beginning with Francis Xavier (1549) right down to our own day, it has been a painful struggle to expand but with no great success. Buddhism fitted in easily; Christianity did not. Why? The difference between European and East Asian cultures comes to mind. Before the advent of Buddhism to Japan, the influence of Chinese culture was being felt in Japan, which led to the development of a similar type of culture among the Japanese. So when Buddhism came from China—the senior nation—it was coming through the same conduit of culture and was therefore readily accepted.

What Lies behind Culture?

Pointing to cultural variances does not explain the whole story. In Xavier's day there was a vast difference between the cultures of East Asia and the West. But not so today, when the influence of the West can be seen in many areas: education, political systems, law, technology, not to mention music, drama, fashion, eating habits, housing, and lifestyle. Indeed, Japanese clothing, traditional arts, eating habits, and lifestyle, all have been eroded to a considerable degree by a tidal wave of Western and American culture. In spite of this shift toward a homogeneous culture, Christianity still does not advance. We can therefore assume that there are other factors beside differences in culture that bar the progress of Christianity. In my opinion, the problem is rooted in what lies behind culture, namely, differences in the human heart.

In Christianity clear boundaries are given: God, the universe, the eternity of heaven and hell, sin, punishment, reward, and so forth. When we look at Buddhism we find that many of its Japanese, Indian, and East Asian members are pantheists. They also believe in the transmigration of souls and that we cannot sort good from bad in the actions of a human person. Put in another way, we can say that in the West paternal characteristics are dominant, whereas in Asia, particularly in East Asia, it is the maternal traits that are operative. The fatherly figure divides and selects, the motherly figure unites and embraces all.

The God of Christianity is limitless and possesses both fatherly and motherly elements. However, the Christianity that came from Europe tends to overstress the former. In the East, we need to give greater expression to the feminine aspects of God: the God who permeates the universe, lives in us through faith, receives all people in his embrace, the God of universal love and infinite tenderness, always ready to forgive, the Christ atoning for all the sins of humankind on the cross. If our theology, art, preaching, and evangelization move along these lines then Christianity will take on a gentler, more approachable face for Asian people.

Spreading the Gospel

Let me point out a further difficulty. Traditionally, the steps toward evangelization involved preaching, dogma, and catechism, especially the exposition of the articles of faith. It was with baptism in mind that such instruction was given. But Jesus used other means.˙Truly, the content of dogma and preaching stem from Jesus and his teaching. However, Jesus' mission also involved healing the sick, confronting discrimination in society, helping the poor in practical ways, rejecting Pharisaical religion, and laying blame on those who abuse power. His preaching covered the whole spectrum of human life and society. It was not a mere matter of words; he staked his life on what he said. The Son of God became man and was totally subject to the Father. It follows that the words and actions of Jesus were a perfect expression of the Kingdom of God, and this is what preaching the Gospel is all about.

Asian people, influenced by European and American ways, have learned to take an intellectual and logical approach in announcing truth. But in their hearts, the Asian people place a great importance on the body, on existence, on what is practical, on nonlogical expressions and symbols. From now on, be it in our talks on faith or the evangelization of society, in order to convey firmly the heart of Christianity, we must use Asian ways of expression if our message is to take hold as we respond to the need to proclaim the Kingdom of God.

PASTORAL LIFE IN ASIA AND "THE PRINCIPLE OF GRADUALITY"

BERARD T. OSHIKAWA, OFM CONV.
BISHOP OF NAHA, JAPAN

Pastoral Life in Asia

1. My concern here is mostly pastoral. We do not have to go far to find some of the reasons why Christianity does not grow in Japan. Notwithstanding the frequent exhortations for inculturation and the many related documents, it seems to me that the norms for Christian life, for church discipline, for liturgical expression, and theological orthodoxy continue to be those of the Western Church. And we all know that these norms have developed through long centuries of interaction between the faith of the Mediterranean and, later, North-European and American Churches and their respective cultures.

2. This fact is in itself natural, and good for the West; but when it becomes the operating norm also for the Churches of the East, and, concretely of Japan, then it becomes a very powerful and, unfortunately, very effective block to any pastoral effort to enable for our small, young, and minority Churches a meaningful and realistic process of growth in faith, spirituality, wisdom, and moral life "before God and humankind."

3. In spite of the valiant efforts of both local and foreign agents of the Gospel, the ingrained Westernization of the language of our theology, the rhythm and structure of our liturgies, the programs of our catechesis fail to touch the hearts of those who come searching. The fact that some particularly gifted ministers have had a certain success only underlines the basic problem, where our own human limitations are not helped by the requirements of the present system.

The "Principle of Graduality"

The "principle of graduality" proclaimed and recommended by Pope John Paul II should be a leading principle in the relationship between the Roman curia and the Churches of Asia. I would like to consider this principle from three aspects, which flow from my pastoral experience.

1. Graduality means that we, Asian Christians, take responsibility to grow into Christ and all that it implies for our Christian faith; that we do this out of and through our own cultures in an ongoing rereading and contemplation of the Gospel in the midst of the pains, struggles, and hopes of our societies; that we do this in an Asian religious context where the "Way" is a central and most inspiring image of growth into God's love and wisdom. This means that we make this process of faith a real journey, an experience of growth rather than a mental "Introduction to Christianity," as is often the case.

2. Graduality, on the other hand, also means that the other churches of North and South, and of the so-called West, respect and support these local processes that take place under the guidance and supervision of the bishops of Asia. In a

world that is becoming more and more international and more globally interacting, it is more important than ever to nurture and support the diversity and peculiarities of the different cultures and Churches. Now is the time to learn from our past mistakes and make sure that no imposition of any kind hinders the work of the Holy Spirit in the lives and minds of people who, in the wonderful variety of histories and cultures, look for God with a sincere heart.

3. Graduality also means that the Holy See redefines its role and mediates with prudence, flexibility, trust, and courage a new dialogue of all the Churches in the common pilgrimage to the fullness of Christ. This will mean moving away from a single and uniform abstract norm that stifles genuine spirituality, Asian liturgical expression, earnest Asian theological search, and real growth into maturity in issues involving life and society. It will mean moving to a more spiritual and creative position of working for a new harmony where the gifts of the Spirit to the Churches become the new treasure of the whole Church, into which all others, Christian and non-Christian alike, can be invited to share in the abundance of God's life.

WORLD PEACE AND EVANGELIZATION IN ASIA

STEPHEN FUMIO HAMAO
BISHOP OF YOKOHAMA, JAPAN

When the atomic bombs were dropped on Hiroshima and Nagasaki in August 1945, hundreds of thousands of lives were snuffed out in an instant. A great number of people still suffer from the effects of those bombs. But at the same time, we Japanese well recognize the fact that the dropping of the two atomic bombs and the tragic consequences were the result of military aggression inflicted by Japanese troops. We Japanese are victims of the war but at the same time we were the aggressors also. It is a fact that during World War II the Japanese army trampled on the lives of people on the Korean peninsula, China, the Philippines, and other areas of Asia and the Pacific. The army not only ignored and violated people's human dignity, but killed countless unarmed civilians, including women and children.

In 1995 on the occasion of the fiftieth anniversary of the end of World War II, the bishops of Japan issued a message entitled "Resolution for Peace." In this message, it was stated that during the war the Church in Japan experienced severe hardships because Christianity was considered a foreign religion. Foreign missionaries and Christians alike were considered to be engaged in espionage. The Church suffered from oppression and persecution. At that time Japan was riding the crest of nationalism and was solidly united in marching its armies over the Asian continent and throughout the Pacific area. We must admit that the Church of Japan failed to realize and courageously proclaim how inhuman and out of harmony with Gospel values were the elements of that war. The Church failed in its prophetic role of witnessing to the will of God in protecting human life.

Today we live in a "global village," an interrelated network of nations, cultures, ethnic groups, traditions, and religious families. This is true especially of Asia. Peace cannot be attained unless it cuts across these multicultural, multireligious nations. Peace is a gift, the fruit of a healthy human community. Peace is the final gift, the result of a harmonious and mature integration of fairness, justice, love, truth, liberty, and respect for all. It must include mercy toward the weak and the powerless, tolerance, and a patient waiting for growth. This has been frequently taught in the social doctrine of the Church, for example, in *Pacem in Terris* by Pope John XXIII in 1963, by *Gaudium et Spes* of the Second Vatican Council in 1965, and by *Sollicitudo Rei Socialis* by Pope John Paul II in 1987. In spiritual counseling we say that joy and peace of heart are the sure signs of being in harmony with the will of God. We can say the same about peace in societies and in the world. Peace never occurs in isolation. It is the fruition of a good life for all. For that reason, working for peace is considered to be a highly esteemed spiritual value. Peace is God's greatest blessing to a people. Working for peace should be a central concern of the Church.

True peace will not be attained until we stop considering color, nationality, ideology, culture, and even religion as being the most important elements in evaluating people. Peace will only be attained when we see a brother in every man, a sister in every woman, and a gift of God in every living being in nature. The images of God's "Shalom" that we have in Prophet Isaiah (11:1–10; 65:21–26) are more than eloquent in this respect.

Ecological concerns are also very important elements in the evangelization conducted by the Church. Environmental concerns are not just for the benefit of future generations; all creatures and nature itself are "our brothers and sisters," as St. Francis called them. They are our companions on this earth with which we must strive to live in harmony. This concern for living in harmony with all nature is an important element in procuring peace and is highly valued among Asian peoples. The Church, therefore, should be much more concerned with promoting peace and harmony on all levels of existence, and not concern itself with reasons that would justify war.

An ideal goal to strive for is the complete abolition of all armaments during the twenty-first century, as has been urged in *Pacem in Terris* (no. 112). Perhaps this ideal seems unrealistic and mere fantasy. However, the Christian message is a theology of the Cross and Resurrection, that is, active nonviolence, or resistance without violence. These Gospel values should be attempted on an international scale. I have heard that one or two sovereign states in the world have a constitution similar to that of Japan, in which maintaining a military force and the use of force in self-defense has been abrogated. The existence of such states should give courage to all nations to solve their disputes through peaceful dialogue.

There are very few things to which the Church can dedicate its labors with a more detached and evangelical heart than to the service of peace. It is our earnest desire, and that of the bishops of Japan, that this synod puts peace at the center of our evangelization and mission in Asia today. Our Lord said: "Blessed are the peacemakers, they shall be recognized as children of God."

BAPTISM OF DESIRE

VALERIAN D'SOUZA
BISHOP OF POONA, INDIA

In no. 30, paragraph 3 of the *Instrumentum Laboris* we read of persons of other Asian religions who are prepared to accept Jesus Christ as God but not as the only Savior. They do not see the necessity to embrace Christianity, much less the Church.

I wish to speak of another category of people, not mentioned in no. 30 or in any of the synod documents, who accept Jesus as Lord and the only Savior. People who hear about Jesus and accept him as their savior can be divided roughly into four groups. The first group accepts Jesus and seeks baptism. The second group too accepts Jesus and wishes to be baptized, but because of family, financial, and social constraints, does not ask for baptism. The third group accepts Jesus but does not see any reason to leave its own religion and get baptized. The fourth group has no religion and is content with accepting Christ.

My concern here is with the pain and anguish of the second group. These "believers" would like to be baptized and be members of the Church, but there are practical reasons that restrain them from doing so. Let me describe some of them.

According to the personal law for Hindus, a person leaving Hinduism for another religion loses all rights to heritage. This means being put out onto the streets unless the person has sufficient means. With regard to Muslims, it would mean persecution and even martyrdom unless the person moves away from the neighborhood or even the city. This problem would be common to other countries in Asia as well.

Generally, among Hindus there is animosity toward Christianity and even people close to the Church who work in our schools and institutions and have cordial relations with us. They consider it an anathema if a family member wishes to embrace Christianity. Just before my coming to the synod, a lady approached me. She had been baptized in the Catholic Church before her marriage. Her husband, a non-Catholic, did not want her to be a Catholic. He tore up any religious books she wanted to read and threw religious articles out of the window. So for twenty years she did not go to Church or receive the sacraments. Whenever she stays with her in-laws, sometimes for months, she is not able to go to Church.

Then there is the difficulty of marriage because of this animosity. Converts may not easily find partners in the Catholic community. For girls there is the problem that younger sisters will not be able to marry unless the elder sister, who has been baptized and will not accept the marriage her parents arrange for her, gets married.

It is my personal experience that there are many, if not very many, who belong to this group. Some have approached me for permission to receive Holy Communion. I speak to them about spiritual communion. Some understand this, but as one girl who accepts the teaching of the Church told me, "Bishop, I go to Mass regularly, but the Mass is incomplete unless I receive Jesus in Holy Communion." A priest told me that he had seen a nonbaptized person receive Holy Communion. After Mass he approached the man and politely told him that he was not supposed to receive Holy Communion. The man stamped the ground and said, "But I need Him" and walked away. These persons have accepted Christ and believe in the Church. They definitely have the baptism of desire. We need a deeper theological and pastoral study of this baptism of desire and its relation to the visible Church.

The Church is a communion. The Eucharist is very personal but also has its communitarian side. Spiritual communion may fulfill the personal aspect, but what about the communitarian aspect? People mentioned above belong to Christ but feel that they belong neither to their original religious community nor to the Catholic community. They are caught in suspended animation. On the one hand, we need to understand the genuine difficulties of such people who can be considered *Christbhatas* (devotees of Christ), but on the other hand we need to follow and communicate the right doctrine about Jesus Christ and the Church. This is the dilemma we face. We have to preserve these "believers" in Christ and not to lose them. Pastors have to keep in close contact and fellowship with them. There should be a persevering and appropriate catechesis for them. Perhaps the Church in Asia has to promote this special ministry. The Church in Asia has to discover ways of dealing with these believers in Jesus Christ. It must on the one hand understand their social, cultural, economic, and family difficulties, and on the other hand bring them over to full communion with Christ and his Church. Such people need to be followed up by pastors—as shepherds. They need our care and concern to deal with their problems. They need guidance to understand and appreciate the Church's teaching. A systematic pastoral effort is needed. Perhaps this is a special ministry in the Church that needs to be developed.

INDIGENOUS AND TRIBAL PEOPLES

TELESPHORE P. TOPPO
ARCHBISHOP OF RANCHI, INDIA

This Synod for Asia will want to give a special attention to the indigenous and tribal peoples living in many places all over the continent. There are more than a hundred million of them. They are widespread and scattered, clannish and unorganized. In their own countries they are marginalized, disadvantaged, and neglected people. They were living in their own territories or on their lands before invaders, immigrants, and colonialists pushed them aside, displaced them, and dominated them. They have been either subjugated, enslaved, and exploited or, alternatively, pushed aside into isolation, exclusion, and extinction. They have been victims of injustice, neglect, and starvation, even genocide. There are many hundreds of such groups of people with different languages, customs, and traditions.

The Synod for Asia will want to acknowledge their lively presence, appreciate their culture and heritage, defend their rights, and encourage them to get hold of their own future. The synod should be aware of their openness to the preaching of the Good News and of their generous response to God's call to serve.

These people often practice a traditional religion that includes a deep faith and trust in a supreme and benevolent Spirit. At the same time, they are often possessed by evil spirits that harass them greatly—not unlike what we find in the days of Jesus. No wonder they come to Jesus relatively easily, who sets them free. Though known for their traditionalism, they are remarkably open to change as well. They very skillfully integrate the new with the old. They are very good at inculturation.

The synod, the synodal statements, and the post-synodal document must give ample attention and space to followers of traditional religions, their characteristics, and their openness to the Gospel. They may be disparaged and poor in the world of Asia, but they are likely to be God's chosen instrument to spread the wisdom of Christ and to confound the cleverness of the dominant exploiters. In them the Lord will display his marvelous grace so that with Mary they too may sing their *magnificat*. In God's eyes, they will always remain the first nation, the aboriginal first settlers of the land, the people whom God saved from the teeth of the tiger and from the fangs of the cobra because he destined them to become bearers of Christ.

No one can claim to know all the tribal peoples of Asia. One can be familiar with only a few of them. Though I come from India, I do not at all know the majority of the four-hundred-plus tribes of my country. But being a Tribal myself from Ranchi in the Mid-India Tribal Belt, I do have some experience of the Uraons (Kurukh), Mundas, Kharias, Hos, and Santhals. Like many Tribals elsewhere, they live in "the hill country"—not in the plains from which they had been driven out by the Aryan conquerors. These tribes are quite similar to one another in the practice of their traditional beliefs, though their languages are completely different and mutually unintelligible. Yet they live together peacefully, intermingling with each other in their villages.

The Good News about Jesus first reached them a mere 150 years ago. The miracle of Chotanagpur happened when—just a little over a hundred years ago—Father Constant Lievens, S.J., found that his flock of only fifty-six multiplied in the short period of seven years more than a hundred times, so that by the time of his physical collapse there were close to one hundred thousand of them. He found these Tribals extraordinarily responsive to the Good News of Jesus. A number of local catechists—doubling as teachers too—assisted him in the work of evangelization. He could only marvel when local children—both boys and girls—came forward with evident signs of a vocation to the priestly and religious life. They were Tribals, every one of them. No one had ever heard or seen a thing like this. The Tribals of Ranchi have already provided the Church in India with some twenty bishops and four archbishops, not to mention hundreds of priests and thousands of religious.

I wish to bear witness to the work of the Holy Spirit in this local Church among the tribal groups I know and to urge the Synod Fathers to engage themselves in the support of the indigenous and tribal peoples in Asia. They are the

Church's immediate hope for the third millennium. I would therefore suggest that the Church in Asia turn more and more to the work among the Tribals as these see more and more clearly that their salvation lies in the name of Jesus and of no one else.

Finally, I express the wish that the Holy Father, either in the post-synodal document or in an encyclical, bring together and confirm the ordinary magisterial teaching of the Holy See and of the Episcopate, now at least five hundred years old, concerning the indigenous and tribal peoples around the globe.

LEADERSHIP IN THE CHURCH IN ASIA

GRATIAN MUNDABAN
BISHOP OF BIJNUR OF THE SYRO-MALABARS, INDIA

A Hindu Sadhu once told Abhishiktanandaswamy (the French Benedictine who adopted the Indian religious way of living Christian faith and lived among the Hindu Sadhus): "If you want to touch the hearts of Indians, everyone of you must become a guru." A guru is one who has deep God-experiences. Such a guru does not quote, does not instruct, does not formulate, does not dogmatize, but shares his own personal experiences of God. And this appeals to the Indian/Asian minds and hearts. People in India/Asia look for a *darsan* [teaching] of holy men and women and to listen to what they have to say in the way of sharing. So it is not only the question of presenting Jesus Christ as a guru. It is rather a question of every Christian becoming a guru—deeply rooted in the experience of God.

The early Church was such a community—of disciples of Jesus Christ in whom they experienced the Father. This was possible only because of the power of the Holy Spirit. Jesus himself was a man of the Spirit. The Spirit descended upon him (Lk 3:21–22): Spirit-filled Jesus conquered the forces of evil by the armor of the Word (Lk 4:8–12). Jesus instructed the Apostles: "Stay here in the city until you have been clothed with power from on high" (Lk 24:49; Acts 1:4). The text refers to praying until the coming of the Spirit. Jesus too was praying as the Spirit descended upon him in the river Jordan (Lk 3:22). It is then and only then that Jesus began his mission.

The Spirit-filled and Spirit-led Apostles began their mission with surprisingly great success. Everyday more and more people joined the New Way. The Apostles experiencing the presence of Jesus in the breaking of bread built up communities of the Word and Eucharist. The communities were constantly listening to the teaching of the Apostles, which sustained their conversion of heart and made them turn to one another in fellowship and communion. These communities did not have any worldly power and worldly riches: "Silver and gold have I none, in the name of Jesus I command you to get up and walk" (Acts 3:6). They shared whatever they had. There was no one in need. They cared for the needs of others too. They looked for signs and wonders. They listened to the Spirit who was speaking to everyone. They looked for approval from above for their work. They did not so much formulate or dogmatize. They trusted the Lord and the Spirit. These communities and their lives had a powerful appeal to the people—both the people of Asia and the people of the West. The initial success of the missionary efforts of several early apostolic Churches referred to in *Instrumentum Laboris* was mostly due to this.

Unfortunately, the scenario changed. The communities of the Spirit became institutionalized. When possessions, power, and authority increased, the need to rely on the power of the Spirit decreased. The Holy Spirit became the forgotten person of the Holy Trinity. The humble, poor servant Christ who came "to serve and not to be served" was forced to assume the status of a king of power instead of continuing to be the king of hearts. The Church began to rely on competency and human efficiency—doctrinal as well as juridical. If the Church's power and authority comes only from competency and human efficiency, then we are facing a crisis in our mission. For such a competency, based on knowledge, ideas, administrative skills, and laws will search for legitimacy in the rational, in the human. The power of the Church is the religious, spiritual, power from heaven. When the leaders of the Church are devoid of such a spiritual power, they will take shelter in juridical power.

The Asian soul is drawn by the power coming out of spiritual or religious sources. In the religious ethos of Asia, mere doctrinal, legal, and institutional power does not have any appeal. Further, such an image projected by the Church—powerful, rich, institutional, influential—is looked at as a threat by the indigenous people.

There is an urgent need to change this image. The leadership of the Church has to change the style of functioning, has to become more and more spiritual, free from institutional authoritarianism, and fully at the service of the Gospel and the world. Such a leadership will be able to enable people to experience God and help them translate this experience into fraternal love. This has to be the original contribution of the Gospel to Asia where some religions concentrate on God-experience alone, without making any effort to serve people. The leadership of the Church will have to discern and activate the various charisms of the whole Christian community to build up communities of love and fellowship as did the Apostles. Such a leadership will seek to strengthen the capacity of the people of God to become true faith communities in order to overcome the dichotomy that exists today between faith and life among the Christians. It will help make these communities into powerful evangelizing communities and empower the faithful to face their challenges, present and future, with interior power, power from above, and not with worldly wisdom and efficiency.

When we therefore think of evangelizing Asia, we have to think of a new way of being Church. Following the way of Christ, the Church in Asia has to assume the way of *kenosis*, of self-emptying, of the Cross, of loving and self-giving service. We have to develop a *kenosis* ecclesiology. We have to shed attitudes of power, domination, influence. Such a Church will appeal to the Asian mind. . . .

Let the Synod of Asia be a call to return to the sources, to the spirit and style of the early Church where the Spirit of God reigned. Return to the sources was the call of Vatican II, which has been described as a new Pentecost and which, according to Pope John Paul II, was the first step in the preparation of the Great Jubilee. In the process of return to the sources I would stress two points:

1. Give enough freedom to the particular Churches to grow in their own way, as it happened in the early Church, to develop their own liturgy, theology, spirituality, and even the discipline of the communities in the manner suited and appealing to their people under the guidance of the Holy Spirit, reserving to the Holy See the role of supervising and checking if aberrations take place. Let us trust the Holy Spirit and also trust those who are given the gift of the Spirit.

2. The individual Churches, especially the Oriental Churches, should be given the rightful place and freedom to grow and to evangelize. All the restrictions, if any, that were imposed due to historical development, shall be removed. I am referring here particularly to the restrictions made on the Syro-Malabar Church or the Church of St. Thomas in India. This Church is confined to its *territorium proprium,* that is, a narrow strip of land in the south of India. Because of such restrictions several chances of evangelization are being lost. These individual Churches with their Asian background are in a better position to evangelize Asia.

BEARING WITNESS TO JESUS CHRIST IN AN ARAB-MUSLIM WORLD

ANTOINE AUDO, S.J.
BISHOP OF ALEP OF THE CHALDEANS, SYRIA

To survive and grow as living churches in the Arab and Muslim world, Arab or Oriental Christians need a spiritual vision in their relationship with Islam that is a new way of being sent by Christ to be witnesses of his love.

Islam, religion of the unicity of God (*dîn-al-tawhîd*) and religion of nature (*dîn-al-fitra*), contains a powerful religious consciousness in quest of self-identity, a desire to eliminate whatever is different from its belief. Consequently, if the other is not reducible to the self, it may create disorder for the societies founded on such a vision.

Oriental Christians living in these Muslim societies in the Arab world generally have the status of *dhimmi*: they are in some way protected and are within the law of the Qur'an, and in this sense they are situated in precise boundaries and do not constitute a danger to these societies as long as they stay within these limits.

The context of my reflections is my country Syria, an Arab and Muslim country, where Christians represent 10 percent of the population. I speak as bishop of the Chaldean Church of Syria, where I live and work.

(1) The question that the theme of the synod poses to us may be formulated as follows: How to bear witness to Jesus Christ the Savior and to his mission of live and service in Asia? To answer this question from the perspective of our reality in the Middle East is first of all to accept the fact that we are contained by Islam, that is, we are an integral part of this society, to appropriate the Arab and Muslim culture without reserve, and at the same time to bear witness to the evan-

gelical freedom in the way of approaching this same culture, seeking to desacralize the language of the Qur'an and making it more and more a language of human sciences.

Indeed, Christians of the Arab world should not behave as strangers to the Arab culture either because of the difficulty of the language or because of its archaic or sacred character. A Christian who is able to use Arabic with ease is respected and integrated into the society. Christians, when they say their prayers in Arabic adapted to the society of which they are a part, inspire respect and confidence. The first centuries of Islam as well as the nineteenth and twentieth centuries witness a great number of Arab Christian authors: persons of letters, thinkers, and journalists who have demonstrated originality in their ways of thinking within their own societies.

Embracing the Arabic language without reserve and letting oneself be formed by this culture with its own characteristics do not mean that one becomes their slaves. Arab Christians, who are of Arab culture, must be conscious of their original contribution to this language. For them it is not sufficient to learn Arabic poetry by heart, or to know well the riches of the images in the Qur'an, or to master the finer points of its difficult grammar. The Gospel should help Christians appropriate well this heritage, but at the same time pose the question of otherness and freedom to this culture. In this respect, the Christian is called to engage in the search for the truth, in orienting this society toward justice and peace. In this engagement the Christians feel themselves fully in harmony with the evangelical values and the principles of human rights. They will join forces with Muslims who are concerned with the same values. With them they will enable the Arab world to question itself, on the threshold of the twenty-first century, on modernity and to find answers for Muslim believers.

(2) To develop a spirit of confidence and hope within the Christian communities. In Islam today there is an eschatological tension where an imminent intervention is expected to arise at any moment, and at the same time a fatalism which says that nothing can be done and that everything is the result of the manipulation of the powers that be of this world. Within these societies Christians must bear witness to hope, looking at the future with realism and taking the risk of beginning and beginning again ceaselessly, without yielding to the temptation of fatalism or an imminent eschatology. They must be watchful in a spirit of service that fills with joy the heart of the person dedicated to others, to free themselves from fears, to call for trust in decisions both big and small. It is to be called to mind, without exaggeration, that fundamentalist currents of thought seem to trouble above all the Christian minority. We are challenged to listen to these rumors with confidence and serenity, to inform ourselves about them and to communicate a sense of confidence and not discouragement.

(3) Living in true solidarity. This means not exploiting the poor and the weak and creating around oneself, within the Christian communities, a current of solidarity that will overflow beyond the borders of the Church.

The natural tendency of every human being is to exploit the poor and the weak, especially when there is no law to defend them. We must first of all end the exploitation, but also create solidarity with the "little ones," in the biblical sense of the term. This means to be in solidarity with others by freeing oneself of tribal instincts. The tribe encloses the individual in a limited group where one is protected and defended against others. Christians, by living out solidarity and communion among themselves seriously, create a mind-set that respects the roots of each one in his or her group and call everyone to be in solidarity with all human beings created in God's image.

In appropriating the Arab culture or in an attitude of trust and true solidarity Christians in the Arab world are required to—and they are already doing so—be fully integrated into the society by liberating themselves from fear and marginalization. Within these societies, Christians are called to this difficult task, namely, to bear witness to an attitude of respect for others. The other is not someone that must be reduced to my own vision, the other is not someone I exclude from my field of communication. The Muslim person is someone I accept as different, because I myself, as a Christian, am called to live my freedom as a child of God in Jesus Christ.

THE ORIENTAL CHURCHES OF WESTERN ASIA

CYRILLE SALIM BUSTROS
ARCHBISHOP OF BAALBEK OF GREEK MELKITES, LEBANON

I am referring to paragraph 11 of the *Instrumentum Laboris,* which speaks of the Churches of West Asia and mentions the Churches of Antioch of the Syrians, Antioch of the Greek Melkites, Antioch of the Maronites, the Latin Church of Jerusalem, the Chaldean Church of Babylonia, and the Armenian Church. Of them the document says: "Today most of these churches live among predominantly Jewish or Islamic populations and cultures, serving their faithful who continue the Christian presence in these countries since the first centuries and are witnesses to Jesus Christ among other religions." It further adds: "While these churches are inculturated in Islamic culture and in the Arabic language, and hence well placed for dialogue with Islam, they are also in a region of conflicts and are threatened by religious fundamentalism." In this connection I would like to make three observations.

1. Political and Religious Conflicts

The conflicts to which these churches are exposed are more of the political than religious order. Religious fundamentalism is also of both religious and political orders. Thus the Muslim resistance in Lebanon stems from the Hezbollah Party. This party is also supported by the Shiites of Iran and has as its goal to establish in Lebanon a government with an Islamic constitution as well as to end the Israeli occupation of the south of Lebanon. On the other hand, the liberation of southern Lebanon is also pursued by other Lebanese non-fundamentalist parties. Because

Israel is unconditionally supported by the United States, which is considered a Christian country, Lebanese Christians are often regarded by Muslims as agents of American and Western colonialism. Thus Christian mission toward Muslims is hindered by the unlimited support of the United States for Israel. The solution to the Israeli-Palestinian problem and the liberation of territories occupied by Israel in Syria and Lebanon will be for us Christians of the Middle East a great help in our dialogue and common living with Muslims. Consequently, the Asian Synod should appeal to the great powers to seek a just solution for this problem which has been with us for more than fifty years.

2. The Church's Mission to Muslims

It is composed of two aspects:

(a) "Project the image of a servant Church," as the *Instrumentum Laboris* affirms, and this by means of "works of charity and Christian witness through schools, hospitals and other apostolic works" (no. 11). This aspect continues the Incarnation of the Son of God, as described by paragraph 28 of the *Instrumentum Laboris*. The communities founded by Jesus must, the document says, "follow his example and be characterized by such human qualities as mercy, forgiveness, simplicity, and authenticity of life, brotherly love, and charity in mutual service and sharing of goods, spiritual, and material" (no. 28).

(b) The Church must also work toward changing the mentality of the Muslims and above all of the fundamentalists who aim at establishing the Muslim law (*shari'a*) everywhere. It is in this sense that we must understand Jesus' appeal to the Jews at the beginning of his preaching: "Repent and believe in the Good News." In the face of the Muslim law, just as of the Jewish law before, we must today proclaim, in the footsteps of Jesus, the Gospel of love. This is the central message of our preaching in the midst of the Muslims: God is not a law, God is Love. People are invited to become, not subjects of a law, but children of God, and consequently brothers and sisters to one another. Even if people worship God in different religions, Christianity, in the Gospel of Jesus Christ, challenges them to live in the same family, the family of God. The third millennium will be the millennium of collaboration among religions for solidarity, justice, peace among human beings.

Muslims wait for the salvation that comes at the end of times. It is the Mahdi who will come with Christ to establish a kingdom of justice on earth. The message of Christianity is that salvation has begun in Christ, and that it is a task of every day, realized when people live "as God's children and as brothers and sisters of one heavenly Father" (*Instrumentum Laboris*, no. 28). This is the message that we have to proclaim "in season and out of season," and it is to this message that we are called to convert Muslims as well as followers of other religions. We leave to God the time and moment, which God himself has determined, when we can say to Muslims at baptism in water and the Holy Spirit: "Muhammad, Ali, I baptize you in the name of the Father, the Son, and the Holy Spirit. Amen."

3. Ecumenical Dialogue and Inculturation

In West Asia there are not only Catholics but also three Greek Orthodox patriarchates (Constantinople, Antioch, and Jerusalem), two Armenian Orthodox catholicosates and two patriarchates (Etchmiazzine, Cilicia, Constantinople, and Jerusalem), one Syrian Orthodox patriarchate (Antioch), and one Assyrian patriarchate. The *Instrumentum Laboris* does not explicitly mention these but simply alludes to the "cultural unity" (no. 39) which exists among them: "a sense of sharing important elements of a common ecclesial tradition."

It is upon this common ecclesial tradition that [I] would like to insist and say that the inculturation that is incumbent upon the Churches of East Asia today has already been realized by the churches of West Asia during the first millennium. Were not the divisions that separated the churches of the first millennium and in 1054 due in great part to the inability of the churches to understand the phenomenon of inculturation? The Churches could not accept that the same faith could be expressed in various ways in different traditions: Latin, Greek, Syrian, Armenian. They could not accept that the Church could be administered differently in East and West. Today the solution to the divisions of the churches is to be sought in the acceptance of the diversity of expressions of the same faith and the diversity of ecclesial traditions.

Paragraph 38 of the *Instrumentum Laboris* affirms: "Some responses mentioned that more autonomy should be given to the local churches in areas of dialogue, inculturation, and adaptation. . . ." In the name of the common ecclesial tradition which we have with the Orthodox Churches, I would like to ask that the same autonomy be given to the Catholic Oriental Churches that will be accorded to the Orthodox Churches when the unity between the Orthodox Churches and the Roman Catholic Church is realized. I limit myself to three areas:

(a) Recognize for the synods of the patriarchal churches the right to elect bishops for their own churches independently of the Roman dicasteries. Traditionally, the selection of bishops has been done within each patriarchate. If today the pope nominates bishops for the Catholic Church, he does so as patriarch of the West and not as the primate of the universal Church.

(b) Recognize for the synods of the patriarchal churches the right to create eparchies and to nominate bishops for the faithful of their churches outside the territories of the East, and this independently of the Roman dicasteries.

(c) Recognize for these patriarchal churches the right to have married priests within their eparchies in the West, just as they do so in their eparchies in the East.

These points have to do with inculturation, and by respecting them the Roman Catholic Church will advance the cause of Christian unity to which Pope John Paul II has urgently invited us in his encyclicals *Orientale Lumen, Ut Unum Sint*, and *Tertio Millennio Adveniente.*

On the threshold of the third millennium we are called to accept the diversity of our ecclesial traditions in order to proclaim together our same faith in Christ who came to divinize humanity, so that all people have divine life, "and have it in abundance."

THE CHURCH OF CHINA

JOHN TONG HON
TITULAR BISHOP OF BOSSA AND AUXILIARY BISHOP OF HONG KONG

First of all, I would like to thank the Holy Father for his fatherly concern and love for the Catholics in China. Also I would like to thank His Holiness for extending invitations to two Chinese bishops from mainland China to come to the synod.

My intervention is related to the *Instrumentum Laboris*, nos. 10, 26, and 39. I would like to talk about the power of witness and the need for formation and reconciliation among the Catholics in mainland China. Many brothers have already shared excellent analyses and reflections on the Working Document. So I would like to tell you three real stories which happened in the Church in China.

The first story is about Bishop Matthias Duan Yinming of Wanxian diocese. He is one of the two bishops from mainland China invited by the Holy Father to this synod. The other invitee is his coadjutor, Bishop Joseph Xu Zhixuan. Both have yet to arrive. Bishop Duan is now ninety years old. He made his theology studies in Rome and was ordained a priest in Rome. He was chosen and ordained a bishop by Pope Pius XII on the eve of the Communist regime in China in 1949. In the past fifteen years I visited him four times and still maintain contact with him. I learned that once during the ten years of turmoil of the Cultural Revolution in China, from 1966 to 1976, the Red Guards rushed into his cathedral and took out a statue of Our Lady. They ordered Bishop Duan to break the statue with a hammer. He refused and cried out, "You may take out my head but not my faith." Subsequently he was tortured, imprisoned, and sent to a reform-through-labor farm. Since late 1979, he was allowed to resume religious life under China's open-door policy. He went back to the cathedral and started the diocese again. He is highly respected by Catholics from both the Open Church and the Underground Church, as well as by non-Catholics.

The Church in China has been persecuted for at least thirty years since the 1950s. However, the Catholics in China have sown the seeds of hope with much love and suffering. This may explain why the Catholic population in China jumped from three million in 1949 to at least ten million today. Their life witnesses reflect the truth pointed out by Pope John Paul II in no. 42 of his encyclical *Redemptoris Missio*: "People today put more trust in witnesses than in teachers, in experience than in teaching, and in life and action than in theories."

My second story is about religious vocation. A seminarian in China once told me when and where he heard the call from God. His uncle was a priest. Again, during the Cultural Revolution, his uncle was put on public trial and sentenced to death. The seminarian himself, who was then a small boy, was among the crowd of spectators. He heard the rifles fire and saw the bullets enter into his uncle's heart, followed by a fountain of blood. At once he heard a voice inside him, calling him to priesthood. He told himself, "I must become a priest to continue my uncle's work."

There are many more examples of priest and sister vocations inspired by faith in the difficult times of China. Currently, religious vocations in China are flourishing. By now, there are more than two thousand young priests and four thousand young nuns, but these are insufficient to serve ten million Catholics and to spread the Gospel to many more non-Christians in China.

Originally, the Communist Party, being atheistic, had no place for religion in its ideology. But it was later confronted by the fact that religion exists and cannot be eradicated. The Party had to develop a way to make use of religion to serve the government aims. In recent years, many militant atheists have either died or become interested in China's stability and economic growth. So nowadays, atheism is no longer a dominant ideological factor in the Chinese government's religious policy. What the government is concerned about is whether or not it can control all aspects of society. However, government control is sometimes tightened and sometimes relaxed, and it also depends on the attitudes of local officials toward the Church. All through the years of the Chinese government's control, the gap between the Open and Underground Churches has widened and polarized. Thus the Church in China needs help, particularly in achieving reconciliation between the two sides of the Church.

Fortunately, there is some light shining on the Church in China. Here comes my third story. In a city in central China, I met two bishops. Bishop A is a government-recognized bishop who works in the Open Church, whereas Bishop B is from the Underground Church of the same diocese. Both have been reconciled in stages. With God's help, there often were intermediaries helping with the dialogue. The government does not recognize the Underground Church bishop as a bishop, but allowed him to serve as the spiritual director of the seminary of the Open Church. Last year, before the annual retreat for all the priests in the diocese, the government officials told them that the Underground Church bishop could not preach the retreat. But where there is a will, there is a way. Bishop A preached a short homily, just a few words, then asked: "Are there questions?" Bishop B stood up and asked a long string of questions. After a while, everyone realized if they simply changed those questions to statements, they could hear a well-prepared sermon by Bishop B. The retreatants understood and smiled. Of course, the government officials were not happy but could do nothing about it.

I would like to appeal to all bishops and Catholics from outside China. First, please go and visit the Church in China and meet the Catholics there, prudently and in a balanced way. In so doing, you will show concern to our fellow brothers and sisters in China. Also, listening to their moving testimonies will stimulate and confirm our Catholic faith.

Secondly, I ask all of you to help and support the formation of Chinese seminarians and sisters inside and outside China. Prayers and support such as sending formation materials and books and sharing experiences would help broaden their vision about the universal Church and Church teachings. . . .

THE CHURCH AS COMMUNION
FRANCIS HADISUMARTA, O. CARM.
BISHOP OF MANOKWARI, INDONESIA

I am speaking on behalf of the Indonesian Bishops' Conference. In our response to the *Lineamenta* we referred to the relationship between local Churches at regional and global levels. The Second Vatican Council set forth a vision of the Catholic Church as a communion of Churches (*LG* 23). We are united in a single faith, which is expressed in each and every language and culture. The faith is one, but its expressions are manyfold. As we say in Indonesia: "Bhinneka Tunggal Ika" [unity in diversity]. Catholicity is enriched by the variety of local Churches, each rooted in its local context, each living in contact with the other.

Paul the Collegial Apostle

The Catholic Church is not a monolithic pyramid. Bishops are not branch secretaries waiting for instructions from headquarters! We are a communion of local Churches. Paul is the great apostle of collegiality. Paul tirelessly visited the local Churches, urging, pleading, at times angry or disappointed, at times full of joy and comfort. Paul rarely ordered or instructed; argued yes, commanded no. In Paul's time, decision making was in the hands of the local community with a council of elders (*episcopoi* and *presbyteroi*) at their head.

Synodal Church at Every Level

In our day, ecclesial structures are beginning to reflect this rediscovered conciliar vision. Parishes are living more and more as a communion of Basic Ecclesial Communities, united at the parish level in a council with representatives from each Basic Ecclesial Community and supported by a diversity of ministries. Deaneries and vicariates regularly meet in the council where presbyters and lay people share experience and seek out new ways for evangelization. Dioceses are also a communion of communities, where pastoral and presbyteral councils regularly reformulate the vision and set down guidelines for mission. At the national or regional level, we have episcopal conferences.

Enhancing Episcopal Conferences

Since the Second Vatican Council the role of episcopal conferences in guiding the movement for renewal and mission has been crucial. Episcopal conferences have overseen liturgical translation and adaptation. At present, all this vital work has to go to Rome for approval—to people who do not understand our language! We await encouragement to move from adaptation to inculturation and create new, indigenous rites.

A local Church becomes truly local when its laws are not only in line with the Spirit of the Gospel and ecclesial norms but also with the ethos and the legal tradition of the local people. In many crucial pastoral areas we need to adapt Church law. We need the authority to interpret Church law according to our own cultural ethos, to change and, where necessary, replace it.

There are so many areas where authority should be in the hands of the particular Church, that is, with the episcopal conference. These are, for instance, the selection and appointment of bishops and the education and discipline of the clergy. The ordination of *viri probati* [approved men] has been regularly requested by the Indonesian Episcopal Conference for thirty years. A majority of Indonesian Catholics in most dioceses, including my diocese of Manokwari-Sorong in Irian Jaya, live by the Word rather than by Word and Sacrament. We are becoming "Protestant" by default! Cannot such pastoral concerns be worked out, and decided upon, by the local episcopal conference? Jesus' first words to his Apostles on Easter evening were: "Peace! Be not afraid!" We need to convey the Easter message of hope at the beginning of the new millennium.

Information Rather Than Control

Our Church is Catholic, that is, openly apostolic, transparently pastoral, and universal in its faith. Theology, spirituality, law, and liturgy should be as diverse as our languages and cultures. In the future this should lead to a change in the relationship between the episcopal conference and the various Roman dicasteries. The Roman curia would then become a clearinghouse for information, support, and encouragement rather than a universal decision maker. Like the Apostle Paul, the curia would encourage, urge, and entreat rather than command. The relationship between the local episcopal conference and the Nuncio would similarly change.

Collegiality for the Sake of Mission

I often ask myself: Why is the New Evangelization not taking off as expected? What do we lack? What we need is trust: trust in God and trust in each other. Trust needs to be supported by the necessary authority to make decisions.

In Line with the Ancient Autonomy of the Churches in Asia

This vision, where episcopal conferences would have the trust and authority to evangelize—in dialogue with the poor, with cultures, and with other faith-traditions—is both ancient and new. Do we have the imagination to envisage the birth of new patriarchates, say the Patriarchate of South Asia, of Southeast Asia, and of East Asia? These new patriarchates, conciliar in nature, would support, strengthen, and broaden the work of individual episcopal conferences. As the episcopal conferences, in communion with neighboring conferences in the same (new) patriarchate, move forward in mission, new Catholic Rites would come into existence. Thus, we envisage a radical decentralization of the Latin Rite—devolving into a host of local Rites in Asia, united collegially in faith and trust, listening to each other through appropriate synodal instruments at parish, deanery, vicariate, diocesan, national/regional, continental, and intercontinental levels. Then, almost four decades after the Second Vatican Council, we would truly experience a "great synodal epoch."

CHRISTIANITY AND BUDDHISM

BUNLUEN MANSAP
BISHOP OF UBON RATCHATHANI, THAILAND

I would like to share a few reflections from my own experiences of working with our Buddhist friends to uplift our people, our communities, and our villages in Thailand. Our collaboration in various programs and projects, especially in the promotion of integral human development and justice and peace, has been a process of fostering faith encounters and experiences in "Kingdom Building." These reflections are in reference to nos. 13 and 14 of the *Instrumentum Laboris* that speak about the "Image of the Church in Asia" and "Christian Mission and Asian Religions."

1. I feel inspired by their simplicity of life, their openness, their humane relationships, their unassuming ways in dealing with others. These are values I recognize as values of the Kingdom or values of the Gospel. Could it be said that this is the Good News that the Buddhists can offer us? In our work we try to be witnesses to Christ, but we also realize that our Buddhist friends are evangelizing us by their values. Their compassion for the weak and the poor and their deep respect for nature and all of creation are evident in their attitudes and way of life.

2. On their part, my Buddhist friends admire the Catholic Church for the way we commit ourselves—even though we are still but a tiny minority—to the betterment of society as a whole and of individuals in particular. They appreciate the priority we have given to developing a "Spirituality in Social Action." We enable people to experience the divine, not just in their religious activities, but also in the workings of the Spirit in all aspects of life. Buddhists are touched by the fact that Christians as "religious people" are so concerned about matters that affect their social and economic lives. They see Christians pray in the church but also experience the Christians' love in the villages where they need their presence.

3. The Catholic Church has a considerable influence in the field of education and social action. It is generally recognized that we work for the poor and the underprivileged. The implication is that quantity may not be as important as quality: A few people really committed to their work may do more and be more efficient than a merely passive crowd. Moreover, are we not meant to be the "*pusillus grex*" [the little flock] (Lk 12:32), "the yeast in the dough" (Mt 13:23), and "the salt of the earth" (Mt 5:13)? But it must be recognized that in the field of social justice and human rights the Catholic Church has not done as much as it should have. Perhaps this is due to its "minority complex" or the fear of losing the freedom it still enjoys. At the same time, our Buddhist friends are puzzled by what they see. Our institutions, schools, churches, hospitals are modern, big, effective but they also present the face of a Church that is rich and is often seen as siding with the

rich. Our challenge then is: how are we to make those institutions serve the poor and the poorest among the poor?

4. Sometimes our Buddhist friends seem to be scandalized by our triumphalistic attitude, our absolutism, and our arrogance. They feel that we behave as though we possess the whole truth. They also resent our rigid treatment of human problems with right or wrong solutions, as though everything has to be black or white, whereas the truth is that there might be some shades of gray. In their eyes, in spite of our long presence, the Catholic Church in Thailand still presents itself as foreign and Western in its ways of thinking, its philosophy, its theology, its liturgy, and ways of praying.

It is therefore in this context that we need to ask ourselves: how can we incarnate the Church in Asia? This incarnation seems to call for a deepening of experiences in communion, so that we may be able to witness to the Gospel anew. This can only come about if we realize the importance of forming the laity to act as leaven and salt in the world. Their demand to be true disciples of Jesus in the world of secularism, promoters of simplicity in the world of materialism, and builders of communities in the world of individualism, calls for a new lay spirituality. We need to inject new life into our liturgical services and life of prayer. We need to promote a greater commitment to the process of inculturation in all aspects of our lives as Church. It is only with the freedom of the children of God and not the legalism of the world that we will be able to prepare new missionaries for the New Millennium. To instill fear through threats of punishment is not the way to achieve creativity in the Asian ethos. In the face of new challenges, we need to take new risks and be sensitive to feelings and sentiments of persons. This is our Asian way of making our lives a coherent manifestation of what it means to be disciples of Jesus among people of other faiths.

5. I would propose that we make ours the text of prophet Micah: "What is good has been explained to you, man; that is what Yahweh asks of you: only this, to act justly, to love tenderly, and to walk humbly with your God" (Mic 6:8).

EVANGELIZATION IN VIETNAM

PAUL NGUYEN VAN HOA
BISHOP OF NHA TRANG, VIETNAM

Speaking in the name of the Vietnamese Bishops' Conference, we greet the Asian Synod with joy and hope. We feel that the synod is a powerful moment in which to reflect not only on our concrete tasks of evangelization but also and above all on several theological, Christological, ecclesiological, and missiological problems confronting us. We would like to take advantage of this happy occasion to highlight some that appear to us fundamental. We hope that with your reflection better light will be thrown on them.

We are living in an Asia whose population belongs in overwhelming majority to cultural and non-Christian religious traditions. These traditions had been in existence long before Christ. This fact forces us to pose several problems in different areas.

I. Christological Problems

1. Classical Christological treatises present Christ essentially from the ontological point of view. The main task consists in explaining the exceptional case of the one divine person with two natures.

Contact with Asia invites us to think of Christ under other perspectives, above all from the cosmic and historical ones. Is this Asia which has not yet known Christ already living under his saving influence? If so, how? It seems that in Christology we should reflect more extensively on the presence and place of the Word of God (not only the Word incarnated in Jesus Christ but also the Pre-existent Word) in the life, cultures, and religions of the peoples as the Wisdom of God. Such a Christology will allow us to regard with ease believers of other religions truly as our brothers and sisters, not only because, like ourselves, they come from the same Creator, but also because they are already in a certain way Christians, living under the action of Christ, the Wisdom of God.

2. We live in the midst of followers of other great religions. According to the general worldview of these people, all religions are equally valid, because all religions teach us to do good and avoid evil to reach eternal happiness. All religious founders are teachers of morality. It is difficult to show on the one hand that Christianity is a revealed religion that is based essentially on faith in God's love and not on human morality, and on the other hand that Jesus Christ brings God's definitive revelation to humankind.

3. We Christians affirm with St. Paul that there is but one Mediator between God and humanity, Jesus Christ (1 Tim 2:5). Nevertheless we do not think that this unique role of Christ excludes the collaboration of others in the plan of salvation that God realizes throughout history. If the pagan King Cyrus is called "the messiah of the Lord," the one God holds by the right hand (Is 45:1), what must we say of the founders of the great religions of Asia? It seems to us that an exclusive Christocentrism which characterizes our traditional faith is not able to take into account the positive contributions of these religions to humanity nor does it favor the atmosphere of dialogue among religions.

II. Ecclesiological Problems

Vatican II affirms: "Those can be saved who, without fault on their part, do not know the Gospel of Christ and his Church, but seek God with a sincere heart, and under the influence of grace endeavor to do his will as recognized through the prompting of their conscience" (*Lumen Gentium*, no. 16). This is an important text inviting us to look upon the Church not in its external visible signs but according to its nature as mystery, that is, the church as the people of the redeemed that extends beyond its visible confines. This way of seeing the Church would allow us to perceive the deep link between our Catholic community and believers of other religions. The council presents the Church primarily under the dimension of mystery (see *Lumen Gentium*, chapter 1). However, this dimension does not seem to have been developed in later theological reflection.

III. Missiological Problems

1. Evangelization in Asia seems to us particularly difficult because Asian peoples already possessed high cultures and traditional religions several centuries prior to the coming of missionaries. In this situation it is not easy for us to attract people to enter our Catholic Church. Several reasons prevent them from doing so. One major reason is that they feel bound in conscience to remain faithful to their religions. Men feel they are more obligated than women because they must perform the family cult to their ancestors. They consider this cult as a sacred duty of filial piety. For believers of certain religions such as Islam (in a sense less so for those practicing the cult of ancestors), to become Catholic means betraying their family and even their state. In this context it seems to us necessary to have clear ideas on faith in God, in Christ, in the historical person of Jesus, and on membership in the church.

2. Since an explicit proclamation of Jesus Christ is not always opportune, even forbidden in certain places, we must reflect on certain methods such as interreligious dialogue or collaboration in works of charity, etc. But can dialogue and common activities in the area of charity be already regarded as evangelization, or are they pre-evangelizing activities? What more can we do?

3. Concerning inculturation, how to express faithfully to Asians the data of revelation and the formulations of Christian faith, which up to now have been expressed in European languages, according to European mentalities and cultural traditions? These are questions posed in theology, liturgy, and sacred art. These must be resolved so that Christianity is not regarded as a cultural product imported from the West.

Our contribution here consists more in posing questions than in providing answers. We hope that there will be a closer and more active collaboration among various members of the church, in particular between theologians and pastors, in order to reflect on and carry out the immense task of evangelization in Asia.

INCULTURATION IN THE CONTEXT OF THE VENERATION OF ANCESTORS

STEPHEN NGUYEN NHU THE
TITULAR ARCHBISHOP OF TIPASA OF MAURITANIA AND APOSTOLIC ADMINISTRATOR OF HUE, VIETNAM

We are all persuaded of the importance of inculturation in the work of evangelization. With regard to Vietnam, inculturation must deal with the very serious problem of the cult of ancestors. Nowadays we speak of the "veneration" rather than "cult" of ancestors in order to be more precise theologically. My presentation is an approach to this problem.

1. Veneration of Ancestors in the Vietnamese Culture

All the missionaries and anthropologists who lived in Vietnam, like Léopold Cadière, could easily realize that the cult of spirits (animism) is the principal religion in Vietnam of which the cult of ancestors constitutes the most essential aspect. The other religions or doctrinal teachings such as Confucianism, Taoism, and Buddhism which came from China had to incorporate this essential practice before they could be accepted by the people.

Confucian ethics considers filial piety the foundational virtue of society and the basis of culture. Pious veneration of and services to the parents, living and dead, is a primordial duty. Morality and civilization depend on them.

Taoism prescribes detailed rituals for the funerals of parents and various commemorations such as anniversaries of their deaths. They are the most important duties of children vis-à-vis their parents, especially if they are the first-born. Buddhists also highly esteem this filial piety and consider it the highest practice of Buddhist compassion. Most Vietnamese pray to their ancestors in their family life.

2. Veneration of Ancestors in the Rites Controversy

The historical controversy concerning the Chinese rites, in particular the rites of veneration of ancestors, during the mission to China from the seventeenth to the twentieth centuries is well known. In this controversy, due to misunderstandings of history and culture, several documents have been promulgated against the adoption of the rites of veneration of ancestors into Catholic practice. The Catholic Church in China and Vietnam has suffered much from the consequences of this prohibition. In China the prohibition was not lifted until the publication of *Plane Compertum Est* on December 8, 1939. In Vietnam it was not until 1964 that for the first time the Episcopal Conference of Vietnam was able to authorize the gradual practice of certain forms of veneration of ancestors, setting aside those elements that smack of superstition. Thus it is permitted to have ancestral altars in the family home on which the pictures or inscriptions of the ancestors are displayed and to offer incense and prostrate in front of them.

In spite of all this, Vietnamese Catholics do not willingly adopt these practices which they still consider pagan because of earlier teachings. There is still a deep division among Vietnamese Catholics in this matter. This division is most evident in family life. For instance, on the anniversary of the death of their parents, all the members of the family gather together for the cult, whereas Catholics would not take part in it. Because of this Catholics are regarded as impious children and Catholicism a foreign religion. Needless to say, this is a great obstacle for evangelization.

3. Veneration of Ancestors: A Cultural and Moral Element

In the past the veneration of ancestors was regarded as a form of religion. At first sight the rituals and gestures of this veneration resemble a religious cult. Upon close examination, however, this cult is above all a cultural and moral practice of profound significance for social and familial life (see the instruction *Plane Com-*

pertum Est). Hence, evangelization in Vietnam can make use of this extremely rich cultural element and incorporate it into the doctrine of the communion of saints.

The church in Asia, and especially in Vietnam, must never forget that "it has the duty to announce the Good News in the cultural conditions of the people; that therefore its primordial task is to dialogue continuously, humbly, and lovingly with the cultures and traditions of the people until it is fully incorporated into the people" (see the FABC's declaration in 1974). If this crucial problem is resolved, and if the Church in Asia can give good directions to inculturate this popular tradition, it is hoped that in the future evangelization in this part of the world will make great progress.

This brief presentation is intended only to pose questions for reflection and discussion. Inculturation is not only a process whereby the Gospel is imprinted upon different cultures, as the Catholic rites have penetrated into various family situations, but also a process whereby local customs and cultures are introduced into the life of the Church and find expression in its liturgy and sacramental celebrations. Unfortunately, this has not yet been fully realized in our Churches. What should be done in the future?

6

The Synod in Discussion

Relatio post Disceptationem

Part of the General Relator's responsibilities was to synthesize the 191 interventions into a document entitled *Relatio post Disceptationem*, which would serve as the basis for group discussions. Cardinal Paul Shan Kuo-Shi acknowledged that the document "in no way is a perfect and complete report due to lack of time" and suggested that if some important items had been omitted from the report, they could be brought up in the group discussions.[1] Nevertheless, as previously mentioned, a controversy erupted at the publication of the document, because it had been completed prematurely, before the end of the interventions, presumably due to pressure of time.

More important, it was felt that the document did not reflect faithfully the real concerns of the synodal participants. The sixteen "practical questions" proposed "for deeper reflection and discussion so as to bring the already rich interventions closer to the theme of the synod and to facilitate the formulation of more concrete proposals" seem to express more the concerns of the Roman curia than those of the Asian bishops.

Reports of Group Discussions

With the *Relatio post Disceptationem* as the basis for discussion, the synodal participants were divided into eleven linguistic groups: English (eight groups), French (two groups), and Italian (one group). Each group elected a reporter (*relator*) whose task was to summarize the results of the discussions. Some groups answered each of the sixteen questions proposed; others chose to discuss issues in general.

From the reports, it is clear that there were notable theological divergences among various groups, with English-speaking participants tending to be more "liberal," and Italian-speaking ones more "conservative." The following excerpts from each language group give a sense of the range and substance of their discussions.

—Ed.

Note

1. *Relatio post Disceptationem* (Vatican City: Libreria Editrice Vaticana, 1998), p. 3.

127

REPORT OF GROUP DISCUSSIONS: ENGLISH GROUP A

REMIGIUS PETER
BISHOP OF KUMABAKONAM, INDIA

Before we began the discussion, the group expressed some dissatisfaction with the formulation of the questions in the *Relatio post Disceptationem*. We noted that these questions brought out neither all the concerns of the *Instrumentum Laboris* nor all the interventions of the Synod Fathers.

Part One: Christology and Pneumatology

Belief in Jesus is very much connected with proclamation and bearing witness. Bible stories are found to be the best means for evangelization. Jesus is presented as the most compassionate person, the teacher of truth, the guru, the sansei, the healer, the holy man, the ascetic and spiritual man, the one who shows the way to true life, the one who understands the sufferings of the weak and the downtrodden, and the one who identifies himself with the poor and expresses solidarity with the oppressed. Personal authenticity and life-witnessing are the most appealing methods of presenting Jesus. In fact, lay people have brought more non-Christians to Christ. It was noted that Catholic teachers have been the marvelous tool in bringing people to Christianity, more so than missionaries, especially in Indonesia. Secondary school and college students are also coming to the Church through the influence of these institutions and their staff. RCIA (Rite of Christian Initiation of Adults) is drawing many to experience Christ. Visiting families without distinction of religious affiliations and praying with them and for them in their homes make them realize and experience the power of Jesus.

Non-Christians pray to God the Creator and also to the spirits of their ancestors, who they believe intercede with God for them. However, in times of crisis and calamities, they want to pray to Christ. Contemplative life is very important for bearing witness. However, Christian contemplatives generally remain within cloistered communities and so their witnessing role is minimal, unlike Hindu and Buddhist monks. FABC speaks of dialogue even with individuals and of the need of unity, identity, fellowship, and simplicity to bear witness to Christ in a complex world. There is a widespread belief in evil spirits; people fear them because they believe that evil spirits will punish them for their mistakes. So the image of God as Our Father who loves and forgives is very appealing. The process of maturing into such an understanding of faith should be gradual. It should begin with the more accessible attributes of the person of Jesus, especially as told in the Bible.

Just one or two theologians have come up with some unorthodox opinions regarding Christ, but this is not a general trend in Asia. There was a unanimous view in the group with regard to the divinity of Jesus and his unique mediation of salvation. As John Paul II's encyclical *Redemptoris Missio* (nos. 4, 5, and 6) and the *Catechism of the Catholic Church* state, Christ is the unique savior for all and the only way to God. The official teachings of the Church should be taught in seminaries, and personal views should be conveyed as individual opinions. The teaching of the magisterium is to be safeguarded, and it is the role of the bishop to teach and safeguard the official teaching of the Church. It is true that after the Second Vatican Council theologians have made a lot of reflections and speculations. This needs encouragement, and dialogue with other religions is to be promoted. However, certain grey areas should not be brought to the public media. It should be limited to theological discussion and research in order not to disturb the ordinary people with speculative ideas. Regular dialogue between bishops and theologians is a means for better understanding.

Part Two: The Church's Evangelizing Mission

1. The suffering Church should be supported by activities of solidarity, exchanges of personnel, NGO operations, and information through the radio, the Internet, and the press. However, we understand that there exist constraints in certain countries such as North Korea where people can have access only to one-channel radio (the government channel). More powerful radio sets are confiscated. The group noted that there is no mention in the *Relatio* of the suffering churches in Muslim countries and in North Korea.

2. It is incumbent upon episcopal conferences to give directions on ecumenism and inculturation. It is not appropriate to propose specific directions here at the synod. By baptism, the laity has the right and duty to participate in the evangelizing ministry of the Church. The group enumerated the following requirements for evangelizers: conviction born out of the love of Christ, humility and openness to the truth, discernment, sharing personal experiences, total immersion into the life of the people, empowerment of the people, authentic discipleship to Christ, ethics and morality, and willingness to listen to the people. The laity and youth have proved their ability to meet challenging situations. Instead of telling the laity what to do, we must present them with the real situation and they will find ways and means to meet those challenges. It was observed that in many countries of Asia women and children participate more in the liturgy and the activities of the Church than men, unlike the Muslims. We noted that in rural areas the participation of men is high, perhaps as high as 80 percent. However, when they have to travel long distances, men's participation is less, because of their work. Women are more religious and want to give good examples to their children and other members of the family. . . . Going to church also provides opportunities to socialize. Men participate more when there are opportunities for decision-making. Due to cultural constraints, girls before the marriageable age are not permitted to go to church. . . .

3. Contextualized liturgy and active participation move people more powerfully. It becomes meaningful to them, helps them experience Christ in a better way, and enables them to participate in the liturgy enthusiastically. The liturgy has to manifest unity. The Eucharist is the highest form of unity and the fountain and source of life. Worship of God must be carried out in life and in truth. In Asia, life

means living in poverty and in relation to nature, ecology, and time. Truth means fidelity to values.

Speaking of translation, it was observed that the local churches make use of the services of experts in church matters as well as of experts in the local languages to translate liturgical texts. Many expressed their experience of inordinate delay by the Roman commissions in approving translations.

4. The group related how the Church is perceived in different countries. The Church is seen in places as rich, powerful, well organized, very cautious, with a clear line of authority, acting with responsibility and accountability, having abilities to solve problems, and possessing an admirable integrity. The Church calls for greater sacrifice, austerity, asceticism and high morality. . . . It is known for its services in the fields of education, health, and social action. It has taken the option for the poor. Some say that in India the Church is of the *harijans,* especially in the north. In some places the Church is seen as Western and foreign. In Japan the Church is seen as for the better-off people. In other places, the Church is perceived as so holy and demanding that some people want to receive baptism only when they are old.

5. The terms "universal" and "particular Churches" require more clarification. Collaboration among the Churches has to be strengthened. Though the Church is of hierarchical structure, its functioning must be participatory. Communion recognizes differences and this should lead to solidarity and structural bonds. For example, there should be regional pastoral letters on matters of common concern. In 1931, in his encyclical *Quadragesimo Anno*, Pius XI formulated the principle of subsidiarity, and in 1985, the Synod of Bishops made references to it. This principle in governance has to be put in practice. In principle, when possible and effective, decision-making has to be shared at all levels and there should be greater trust.

Part Three: The Church's Mission of Love and Service

1. The Church has been highly appreciated for its service in the areas of education, health, and social action. More pastoral attention is needed for the migrants. Discrimination based on caste must be denounced.

2. Money-makers and multinational companies have eroded values in the family. Sometimes people are forced to do things against moral principles. Materialism creates more wants rather than needs. There must be lobbies to counter this work of the devil.

Globalization has eroded the cultural values of the local people. Poor countries cannot compete with first-world countries. The local free markets are taken away by the world markets. According to a report of the United Nations, globalization has become a curse for poor countries. The financial crisis in East Asia was caused not only by the mismanagement of local officials but also by the International Monetary Fund and other agencies involved in international business. As a pastoral response, we should appeal that the debts of third-world countries be canceled or lightened.

REPORT OF GROUP DISCUSSIONS: FRENCH GROUP B

EMILE DESTOMBES
TITULAR BISHOP OF ALTAVA AND COADJUTOR BISHOP
OF PHNOM PENH, CAMBODIA

French Discussion Group B was composed of Synodal Fathers coming from very diverse backgrounds, living in very different situations, and confronting extremely varied problems. In the group, some Fathers come from the Middle East, others from the Far East.

The method used was to allow each Father to express himself, give his opinion, and react to the questions, without any attempt at studying all the questions systematically.

Christology

The Logos is incarnated in Jesus. A question was raised: Is it possible that the Logos manifests himself, or even is incarnated, in another being such as Krishna? It is necessary to rethink inculturation starting from Jesus, in interculturality and the reciprocal exchange of cultures.

For some who come from the Middle East, this would be a concession, even a capitulation to other religions such as Islam, in which there are common terms such as Word of God, Spirit of God, Son of Mary who has been chosen from all women. For us Catholics, the Christ is Perfect Man, Perfect God, and these expressions are not found in the *Relatio post Disceptationem*. In Islam the unicity of God is affirmed, but the Trinity is denied. There is no redeeming Incarnation either. On number 15, it is said that all Synodal Fathers have agreed that there must be a new way of presenting Jesus Christ. A Father disagreed, stressing that the expression "Jesus the Enlightened One" should not be used and that to present Jesus as the "fulfilment of myths" is unacceptable. He was equally in disagreement with those Churches that refuse Vatican II's theology according to which salvation is open to all.

Problematic Formulations

Some Fathers were uncomfortable with certain formulations that may offend believers of other religions such as "Jesus, the unique Savior." We must express our faith but without implying that other faiths are worthless. The expression appears too aggressive. Another expression, more humble, must be found. The world waits for witnesses, not preachers. Christ cannot be enclosed in formulations, even though they must be used.

Culture

There is today a globalization of culture, a universal culture which is ever spreading. The issue is not modeling Christ according to culture, "culturalizing" him, but to explain that Christ is important for all of our life. Evangelization cannot be reduced to a cultural question. We must pay attention to cultures but should not enclose ourselves in them since the Spirit is not present in all cultural manifestations. Discernment is required. The Spirit is not present in all historical events but in persons. The Church is universal, but the cultural contexts in which we live are specific. The problem is how to link the universal with the specific, because we are an integral part of this context. That is why we must learn from one another through meeting, listening, and sharing.

How to Transmit the Message?

First of all through witness of life, and not by announcing a theory. It is the gratuitousness of love received and given that must be manifested. The witness of life must also be accompanied by words. The best way to present Christ is to live him. We must discover Christ in any human person since he is identified with her or him: "It is me that you are persecuting." "Whatever you do for the littlest of mine, it is for me that you have done."

The best way to attract people to Christ is the living example of Christians. A saying of Gandhi's was recalled: "I admire Christ, but I am badly impressed with Christians." Witness first, then words, but these must send people back to the One who sent us.

In some cultures Jesus may be presented as the great friend to whom all life secrets can be confided, and with whom everything can be shared. The Christ can be given the names that reflect the cultural situation in which we live: liberator, guru, or others. One Father stressed that the expression "Christ-Guru" could be misunderstood, since a guru is someone exceptional who knows all and decides everything for his disciple, an extraordinary being whom one obeys blindly, whereas Christ shows us love and freedom.

Ecumenism

The issue of ecumenism was discussed. One Father noted that no. 19, which speaks of the Oriental Churches of West Asia, does not reflect what had been said in the general meetings of the synod. First of all, the expression "union of different patriarchates" is unclear. Which patriarchates does it refer to? In the second paragraph of the same number, a doubt is cast on the Oriental Churches themselves. The English version of the text is different and lacks clarity.

Dialogue with the Orthodox in the Oriental Churches of West Asia is met with difficulties which, however, are not dogmatic but psychological. Vatican II has opened a path to dialogue. The Orthodox feel wounded and fear the power of the organization of the Catholic Oriental Churches. These latter may have the complex of the elder brother, like the one in the parable commonly known as the Prodigal Son, with regard to the favors granted by the Catholic Church to the Orthodox. Ecumenism is often one-way: Catholics take the initiative which meets with no response. Moreover, sometimes dialogue seems to be economic, linked with aid coming from Rome. In fact the Catholic Oriental Churches are no longer regarded as the bridge between the Orthodox and Rome. Dialogue is carried out directly between the Pontifical Council for Christian Unity and the Orthodox. The Oriental Churches have the impression that they are regarded as an obstacle to this unity, and not as sister Churches. Sometimes dialogue is seen also as proselytism, like in Russia, where the presence of the Churches united with Rome is regarded as an obstacle for the dialogue with Rome and the Orthodox Church.

Other experiences of ecumenical dialogue in Asia, particularly with Protestants, were also shared. Unity is God's work. Jesus prayed for the unity of his disciples. In dialogue we can know and love one another better, and in praying together, above all during the yearly Week of Christian Unity, ecumenism will make progress.

Creative Ways to Announce the Good News

Are there creative ways of announcing the Good News in the difficult situations of Asia? By promoting human values which are also Gospel values, in the midst of small communities. In Asia, human rights are seen differently than in Europe, but the values of justice and peace can open the way to the message of Jesus.

Number 27 speaks of "persecutions." This word offends the sensibility of China and could be replaced by the word "difficulties."

In the Middle East priests used to visit families in their homes. This practice would permit a discreet but direct announcing of the Gospel. It seems necessary to re-institute this practice, not by priests whose number is diminishing, but by the laity. The Gospel must be announced as an invitation and not an imposition.

Television can be used as a means of evangelization, and programs can be broadcast through satellites. One Father asked why Rome has not yet taken this initiative and launched a worldwide diffusion.

Images of the Church

In Asia the Church is a minority. We have to become aware that God wants us to be where we are and assume our task of evangelization in communion and collaboration with one another.

As far as the image of the Church in comparison with other religions is concerned, the Church appears as an effective organization in the areas of teaching and health and social services, but it is not perceived as a teacher of spirituality in Asia. It also appears as powerful and at times triumphalistic. However, people seem to recognize more and more its concern for the poor, the handicapped, the marginalized, and the excluded.

The Church's act of repentance for its past mistakes and sins is variously interpreted, at times as a gesture in favor of truth, and at times also as a weakness that tarnishes its image.

Liturgy

The problem of liturgy was broached. One Father asked that no. 13 add paraliturgies and popular devotions which are very important in some countries and are sometimes more adapted to the mentality and spirituality of the poor.

We spoke also of some liturgical adaptations which would take into account the culture of the country and local circumstances. But there is not yet liturgical inculturation in the countries of Southeast Asia. One Father proposed that the group take a stance with regard the use of non-Christian sacred texts mentioned in no. 16, and it was agreed that it would be a mistake to introduce non-Christian texts into the liturgy.

Communion in the Church

1. Between the local Church and the universal Church

Some Vietnamese bishops raised the problem of the selection of candidates to the episcopacy whose names have in certain countries to be submitted to the government for approval according to its own criteria. This policy hinders the Church's freedom of choice and often delays the selection of new bishops.

The patriarchs and bishops of the Middle East recalled their difficulties in the nomination of bishops and reiterated their demand for recognition of synodal autonomy. Tensions arise and may be lessened if, as one of these bishops pointed out, the patriarchs begin working together in real collegiality in the midst of the Muslim and Arab population to proclaim the Good News.

2. Among the particular Churches

An exchange of priests among the particular Churches would be a sign and means of communion. The same thing should be said about regular meetings between the bishops and their priests.

3. Communication promotes communion, which is mutual love and trust and whose source is the Holy Spirit.

The Evangelical Character of Action for Social Development in Asia

To acquire a truly evangelical character, works for social development must, as one of the first conditions, be accomplished in an atmosphere of prayer and contemplation. There must be an effort to share the experience of God, a link between prayer life and social life.

In certain socialist countries, the State has the monopoly on works of social development and would not permit any particular group to participate in them. The Church however can concern itself with the formation of the family and offer spiritual companionship to the agents of development.

Sometimes there is the temptation to think that the works established by the Church evangelize automatically. But these educational institutions do not evangelize simply because they are successful. Sometimes they are after prestige and power that have nothing to do with the Gospel.

The Church is not a non-government organization (NGO) whose goal is effectiveness. Rather it must conform itself to Jesus who made himself servant of all out of love. The priority the Church assigns to education and formation is not aimed at making its beneficiaries succeed in life, but rather to make their lives succeed so that they may become in their turn men and women who care for and help their sisters and brothers.

So that the evangelical quality of works of development be fully ecclesial, they must as a whole involve the entire ecclesial community, one way or another. In the Middle East the generosity of Christian volunteering youth is a witness to the society.

How Can Christians in Asia Become Agents of Reconciliation?

The presence of multiracial and international communities of religious men and women shows that it is possible to live joyfully together. The Church should give this witness to the world; it would be an eloquent sign of reconciliation.

Many other examples of service to the poor and the excluded were given. The Church is a servant Church which does not choose its poor, which does not judge or condemn them, but as the Good Samaritan, it comes near to those who suffer and those who are in need and pays with its own person.

REPORT OF GROUP DISCUSSIONS: ITALIAN GROUP

ARMANDO BORTOLASSO, S.D.B.
TITULAR BISHOP OF RAFANEA AND VICAR APOSTOLIC OF ALEP, SYRIA

The Synodal Fathers in the Italian Group noted that in the first part of the *Relatio post Disceptationem* there is the need to speak of, or better to preserve carefully, the mystery of Jesus Christ in the Church. That is, it is necessary to affirm that the church is the sacrament of salvation, as Vatican II has taught. The Fathers noted that no mention has been made of the sacraments, in particular the Eucharist as source and summit of grace and of reconciliation, nor of the proclamation of the Gospel to the peoples of Asia.

If the *Relatio post Disceptationem* speaks of Jesus Christ the Savior and of his mission: "I have come so that they may have life, and have life in abundance," it does not affirm that this life in Jesus Christ is given through the sacraments, especially the Eucharist. The Fathers recalled that the Church is the salt of the earth and that its mission in Asia is to bring Jesus Christ the Savior who is the fullness of truth.

In this connection it was asked how the church should bring salvation to all the peoples of Asia. The Fathers noted that the *Relatio* speaks of temporal salvation, which the church brings through social works, but not of eternal salvation. Let us not therefore forget that Christ came to save the world, giving his life for the salvation of the whole world.

Referring to no. 15 of the *Relatio* the Fathers noted how the person of Jesus Christ is treated, but the tradition of the church, that is, the dogmatic tradition is forgotten or dismissed. In this regard one must not forget the importance that Western thought assigns to reason in the transmission of the faith. In other words, the proclamation of the Gospel cannot occur on the basis of subjectivism or worse, on the irrational level.

Furthermore, the Fathers recalled that inculturation can be a way of evangelization but not the scope of evangelization. It must not be forgotten that in the Gospel there is contained truth in a higher level and fully. Inculturation in Asia must be transformed into interculturation, that is, capable of assimilating the positive values coming from other cultures as well as from Western culture, such as rationality and legal mode of thinking.

With regard to terminology, the Fathers noted that at times the *Relatio* lacks clarity and precision, especially when it speaks of inculturation, Asian spirituality, triumphalism, and interreligious dialogue.

The Fathers of the Italian Group noted that in nos. 48, 49, 50, and 51, the *Relatio* assumes that inculturation in the Church of Asia is clear and comprehensively understood, whereas the concept of inculturation itself still needs further explanation, with particular reference to no. 40 of *Gaudium et Spes* and no. 52 of *Redemptoris Missio*.

In this context, inculturation occupies a fundamental moment in interreligious dialogue, but the Fathers did not agree that non-Christian texts should be used in the liturgy, as no. 16 of the *Relatio* affirms. They therefore asked for a further clarification on the part of the synod.

Furthermore, we must not create confusion in the minds of people by using "analogies" between Jesus and figures of other religions. It seems therefore risky to say, as no. 15 does, that "it is the Person of Jesus Christ that must be presented and not the doctrines about him." Indeed it is not possible to present the Person of Christ without referring to the content of the faith or the doctrinal tradition of the church, even though there is an inexhaustible richness in presenting the Person of Christ to Asian cultures and even though there is not a single way of speaking about the Person of Christ.

However, in carrying out the task of interreligious dialogue and in presenting Christ in a way more attractive to Asian cultures, we should not forget that consecrated persons have the fundamental need of a solid theological formation on Jesus Christ, the only Savior and Mediator, on his mission, and the role of the church for salvation. Hence, there is the need of care for vocations and an initial and permanent formation of candidates that is theologically solid and inculturated, spiritually profound, and rooted in the Gospel and in the teaching of the church.

Coming back to the presentation of the Person of Christ to Asia, of which the *Relatio* speaks, it is necessary to point out that it is only in Christ that one can fully understand the link that unites consecrated persons with Christ the Savior's "mission of love and service in Asia." The form of life of the Word and Christ's total dedication to God the Father and to humanity is, as *Lumen Gentium*, no. 44 affirms, "more faithfully imitated and continually represented in the church" by consecrated life. This life is continued in the world through the total dedication of persons who take upon themselves the following of Christ.

The Synodal Fathers of the Italian Group pointed out how the Lord is blessing the church of Asia with the Cross, that is, with persecution and martyrdom, more than other parts of the universal Church. They therefore reiterated the indispensable value of the theology of the Cross and Resurrection. Situations of suffering and passion of the church that merit special consideration by the synod are occurring in mainland China (the Underground Church), North Korea, Vietnam, and countries of Central Asia. Indeed, in no. 13 of *Salvifici Doloris*, the Holy Father affirms: "Love is also the fullest source of the answer to the question on the meaning of suffering. This answer was given by God to humanity in the Cross of Jesus Christ."

Therefore, God is Love manifested on the Cross, making itself visible in Jesus Christ who has given his life for us. The theology of the Cross and Resurrection is the answer to suffering, persecutions, marginalization, and injustices, which the church in Asia perceives as the sign of Christ's presence.

Jesus Christ could also be presented to Asian youth as Hope and Giver of life who has given his life for others. The Fathers noted that in the interventions during the synod the new commandment of love—including love for the enemy—was mentioned only once, and that it is very important to insert it in the final document for Asia. According to the Fathers, an Asian way of doing theology could be proposed in which in dialogue with Confucianism Jesus Christ is presented as the Elder Brother who leads to the Father and makes up the family of God, in a Confucian and Christian way at the same time. Similarly, in Taoism Jesus Christ could be presented as the Way, and in a communist and atheistic context, as the Liberator who frees people from sin.

The seeds of the Word are also present in Hinduism as contemplation, in Buddhism as compassion, and in Islam as abandonment to God's will.

The Synodal Fathers of the Italian Group would find it risky to speak, as no. 15 of the *Relatio* does, of the presentation of Jesus Christ as "the culmination and fulfillment of the mythologies and folklore of the people of Asia." In this regard, the use of terms such as *Katha* and *Bhaktas* in nos. 11 and 15 of the *Relatio* respectively would not seem justified. The Fathers reiterated that Jesus is not a Teacher or a Guru or a Philosopher but God. Jesus Christ is the Savior: "Only he saves." This affirmation is necessary because in interreligious dialogue, when speaking of Islam, Judaism, and Christianity, there is the risk of presenting them as religions of equal value, creating a confusion for people on the real identity of Jesus Christ.

Furthermore, the Fathers suggested that religious experience of Jesus Christ should be deepened as the way to interreligious dialogue. Attention should be paid to certain theologians, especially Indian, who have exaggerated the salvific value of other religions.

The Fathers pointed out that in the church in Asia one must move from a static dimension of preserving the patrimony of faith to the dynamic dimension of proclaiming the Word of God. That is, there is the need for a New Evangelization in Asia in the third millennium. Because Enlightenment rationalism and postmodern naturalism strike at the heart of the Christian doctrine of salvation, the Church must proclaim the Gospel in Asia with greater force and dynamism.

In this regard the Holy Father has written in his *Crossing the Threshold of Hope*:

What else can the church do? It can show that conviction of sin is not the same as condemnation. The Son of Man has come into the world not in order to condemn it but to save it. Conviction of sin implies creating the conditions for salvation. The first condition for salvation is knowledge of one's own sinfulness, even the inherited sin; the next is confessing it before God who does not wait for anything but this confession in order to save humanity. Save, that is, to embrace and lift up with redeeming love, with a love that is greater than any sin. The parable of the Prodigal Son remains in this regard the unsurpassable example.

In the second part of the *Relatio* it is noted that:

1. The Oriental, Catholic, and Orthodox Churches are all synodal by nature;

2. Communion is expressed in the collegiality among the various Catholic Churches by means of:

a. the assemblies of the hierarchy;
b. the meetings of different patriarchs;
c. and other forms of coordination.

3. Efforts to dialogue with the Orthodox Church should be encouraged since they are of primary importance not only in order to overcome the divisions and to attain the unity wanted by Christ, but also in order to render interreligious dialogue stronger and more effective.

4. The Oriental Catholic Churches should enjoy greater internal autonomy, without detriment to the primacy of the See of Peter. This is done by means of:

a. granting them jurisdiction over their own faithful, not only in the East but also in the diaspora;

b. granting them more autonomy in the election of bishops and in providing clergy to serve their faithful in the diaspora (celibate as well as married clergy).

5. Enabling the Oriental Churches to participate more consistently in composing legislative texts.

6. With regard to charitable works: Recall the tragic situation in which certain Christian communities have found themselves, for example, in Iraq, where not only Christians but the entire population are suffering from the injustices of the embargo.

Furthermore, concerning the laity, the following points should be emphasized:

1. Efforts to form lay associations in various fields of action are important to enable the laity to lend the character of evangelization to works of human promotion.

2. The formation of the laity is important more than ever so that the church may fulfill its mission in Asia. It is the laity who bring the Gospel to the people by living their faith in their everyday life.

3. The proclamation of the Word must be accompanied by witness in all areas of action, in the family, at work, and in political activities.

4. It is therefore urgent to form the laity in the social doctrine of the church.

In the third part of the *Relatio,* four issues are discussed: development, reconciliation, globalization, and the Gospel of Life.

1. Development of the laity so that they may become agents of evangelization. It is clear that bishops and priests are active subjects of such development. The church must be concerned with the problems of work in Asia and with relations with Asian immigrants in other continents.

2. Regarding reconciliation, there is lacking a reflection on the communist ideology. For example, between the two Koreas, there is the need of proposing a national reconciliation that does not sacrifice truth and justice. Then there are enormous problems for the church in China—between the Patriotic Church and the Underground Church—where freedom is to be sought from the communists.

3. The problem of globalization, which makes the poor poorer. The church must take a stand. While the developed countries must collaborate with Asia to solve this problem, the church must, with its evangelizing mission and its social doctrine, promote the dignity of the human person, solidarity, subsidiarity, and the common good of all peoples.

4. The Gospel of Life: it is necessary to have an organization to form the public opinion in the fight for life; to appeal to all Catholics to defend the Gospel of Life; to combat the culture of death with the culture of values, and hence, to defend the human person as a central value. There is a need for initiatives in collaboration with all persons of good will for the Gospel of Life. For example, by collecting signatures, the church in South Korea conducted a campaign against the government's attempt to legalize abortions. More than a million signatures were collected and sent to the parliament, and the government's attempt failed. Followers of other religions have also participated in this collection of signatures.

Finally, the Fathers of the Italian Group, following the example of the evangelization of America, proposed to make Mary the Star and Guide of the New Evangelization of Asia. In Asia, not only Christians have a great devotion to Mary, but also the faithful of other religions see in Mary a model to imitate and a mother close to their hearts. Therefore, *Ad Jesum per Mariam.*

7

The Synod's Propositions

The fifty-nine final "propositions" represent the concrete fruits of the Asian Synod. Most of them were passed overwhelmingly, except numbers 43 and 50. The propositions are a collection of statements ranging from theological principles on Christology, pneumatology, and ecclesiology to specific recommendations on the formation of seminarians and religious, the promotion of the laity, family life (including the practice of Natural Family Planning), and political issues (the debt crisis, aid to North Korea, and the embargo in Iraq).

It has been pointed out that the effectiveness of the Synod of Bishops is substantially reduced by the fact that its recommendations do not have a deliberative but only a consultative force. They are forwarded to the pope for his use in composing his Post-Synodal Apostolic Exhortation. Detailed studies of *Ecclesia in Asia* have shown that the papal document has included all but eight of the propositions (actually not fifty-nine but sixty-one, as two of them contain two parts, each of which was voted on separately).

Of course, the real effectiveness of the Asian Synod can be measured only in years to come, when it will be seen whether the churches in Asia have implemented the recommendations their own bishops have made, or whether these recommendations were simply *pia desiderata*, eloquently expressed on paper, to be passed unanimously again in another synod.

—Ed.

Proposition 1: Introduction

It is with a heart full of joy that we the Synod Fathers thank the Holy Father, Pope John Paul II, for having convoked this first Special Assembly for Asia at this historic moment as we look forward toward the Third Millennium.

With deep faith and hope in Jesus Christ the Savior, we call upon all the particular Churches in Asia to renew their spirit, dedication, and zeal in carrying out the Lord's mission of love and service in Asia. These Churches reach out across the earth's largest continent teeming with peoples who are heirs to ancient cultures, religions, and traditions.

Many have been wounded by the colonial past and poverty. They struggle for economic survival and prosperity, justice, peace, and harmony. They are at the same time threatened by secularism, materialism, and the negative effects of globalization and the ever-increasing challenge of the culture of death. Caught up in this struggle, they are searching for meaning and yearning for happiness and fulfillment in God.

It is this yearning for God that we, as Christians, are called upon to satisfy with the presentation of Jesus Christ as the Good News of God for all. We earnestly plead that the Post-Synodal Apostolic Exhortation focus attention on this yearning and motivate the Church in Asia to announce the answer: Jesus Christ the Savior!

Proposition 2: The Challenge of Asia

In Asia, where about 60 percent of the world's population lives, even after much evangelizing work, only a small minority is Christian and very few know Christ. This fact is a challenge to us, disciples of Jesus Christ, sent to proclaim the Good News to all. With faith and trust in the Risen Lord, we look to the future and commit ourselves to intensifying our communitarian and individual awareness of our missionary vocation to engage in mission.

Proposition 3: An Asian Approach to the Apostolic Exhortation

The Synod wishes that the following Propositions, which the Fathers regard as of great importance, be presented to the Supreme Pontiff, in addition to the documents used in the course of its work, namely, the *Lineamenta*, the *Instrumentum Laboris*, the *Report* of the General Secretary, the *Relatio ante Disceptationem*, the *Relatio post Disceptationem,* and the *Reports* of the *Circuli Minores* and their discussion, and after giving due consideration to the above and related material and information, the Holy Father publish at an opportune time a document on Jesus Christ the Savior and His Mission of Love and Service in Asia: ". . . that they may have life, and have it abundantly" (Jn 10:10).

The Post-Synodal Apostolic Exhortation could have an Asian way of presenting its contents. It could begin with a description of the Asian life situations as presented in the *Instrumentum Laboris* and then move on to discover the "seeds" sown by the Holy Spirit and their fulfillment in Jesus Christ.

The Church's mission of love and service in Asia is conditioned by two factors: her self-understanding as a community of disciples of Jesus Christ and the social, political, religious, cultural, and economic realities of Asia. Hence the local Churches of Asia are called upon to live and witness to their identity as communities of disciples of Jesus Christ, fully aware of the many forces at work in them.

The Churches must be immersed in the diverse, contrasting, and even conflicting realities of Asia. Only such immersion will help the Church to define her mission to the peoples of Asia in an intelligible and acceptable manner. The particular Churches in Asia have to enter into a dialogue with the great religious traditions of Asia such as Hinduism, Buddhism, Taoism, Confucianism, Jainism, Shamanism, Shintoism, Judaism, Zoroastrianism, Islam, Sikhism, as well as with all those who do not adhere to any religion.

Proposition 4: Ecclesial Realities

The ecclesial situation in Asia is as varied as the secular situations. There is a rich variety of Churches by reason of origin, rite, and establishment. The communion of the Church in Asia is a unity in diversity. All these Churches live under different cultural, social, religious, and political contexts with all their related problems, difficulties, restrictions, and even persecution. They are faced with different situations in their life and witness. Opportunities for and methods of evangelization vary from country to country in Asia. Hence no uniform pattern of proclamation, inculturation, or dialogue is applicable to all the Churches in Asia.

Proposition 5: Jesus Christ the Savior of All Peoples

The Church in Asia professes that Jesus Christ, true God and true man, is the one and only Savior and unique mediator of salvation for all peoples. At the center of the Church's life, witness, proclamation of salvation, and service of love to all peoples is Jesus Christ, the Son of God, the Word made flesh, who dwelt among us, was crucified and is risen, and who gave us the Holy Spirit to save us from sin, death, and all forms of evil so that we may have life more abundantly.

It is this faith that prompts her to love and serve all peoples as Jesus did. Jesus Christ is the fullness of the revelation of God and of his love for humankind. In him authentic values of all religious and cultural traditions such as mercy and submission to the will of God, compassion and rectitude, non-violence and righteousness, filial piety, and harmony with creation find their fullness and realization.

Proposition 6: Presentation of Jesus Christ

Evangelization is today a reality that is both rich and dynamic. It has various aspects and elements: witness, dialogue, proclamation, catechesis, conversion, baptism, insertion into the ecclesial community, the implantation of the Church, inculturation, and integral human promotion. Some of these elements proceed together, while some others are successive steps or phases of the entire process of evangelization.

Therefore in proclaiming Jesus Christ to the peoples of Asia, this richness of evangelization should be taken into account: Jesus Christ as the Teacher of Wisdom, the Healer, the Liberator, the Spiritual Guide, the Enlightened One, the Compassionate Friend of the poor, the Good Samaritan, the Good Shepherd, the Obedient One, etc. It must be kept in mind that such initial proclamation will be completed with a fuller catechesis on Jesus Christ as truly God and man.

Proposition 7: Problems in the Presentation of Jesus Christ in Asia

Proclaiming Jesus Christ as the only Savior of all presents some difficulties in the context of Asia's multiplicity of religions, with their belief in mediations of salvation and divine self-manifestation. Such a situation prevailed also in the apostolic times. But Christians nonetheless proclaimed their faith as fully as they had received it.

Encouragement is to be given by this Synod to theologians to pursue their work of developing an inculturated theology that responds to Asian realities. This theologizing is to be carried out with courage, in faithfulness to the Scriptures and to the Church's tradition, in sincere adherence to the Magisterium and with an awareness of pastoral realities.

The Synod proposes that the Church authorities, while overseeing the work of theologians, will also give them the encouragement they need.

Proposition 8: The Joy of Announcing Jesus Christ

The Synod Fathers, hearkening to the words of Pope John Paul II, agree to commit all of the Church's energies to a new evangelization and to the mission *ad gentes* (cf. *RM* 3). We affirm in unequivocal terms that sharing the faith we have in Jesus Christ and offering his Good News is the best service we can make to the teeming millions of Asia. We do it in a "spirit of truth and love" (Eph 4:15) and from the joy of having found a treasure and the desire of sharing it with one and all. We also state that the heart of the Church in Asia will be restless until the whole of Asia finds its rest in the Peace of Christ, the Risen Lord. Many Christian communities in Asia have preserved their faith down the centuries against great odds and have clung to this spiritual heritage with heroic perseverance. For them to share this immense treasure is a matter of great joy and urgency.

The Good News of Jesus Christ can only be proclaimed by those who are taken up and inspired by the love of the Father for his children manifested in the person of Jesus Christ. This proclamation is a mission needing holy men and women who will make the Savior known and loved by their lives. A fire can only be lit by something that is itself on fire. So, too, successful proclamation in Asia of the Good News of salvation can only take place if bishops, priests, religious, and laity are themselves on fire with the love of Christ and burning with zeal to make him known more widely, loved more deeply and followed more closely.

Proposition 9: Emphasis on God-Experience in Jesus Christ

Christian faith, life, and mission have their origin in the revelation of Jesus Christ and experience of God in him, especially in the Paschal Mystery. That experience transformed their lives and the Holy Spirit gave them the power and courage to proclaim Jesus Christ for repentance and forgiveness of sins.

In the Asian context, God-experience is highly valued and those who have it are sought out by religious seekers as their spiritual guides. Hence the important task of every Christian is to deepen his/her experience of God in a daily encounter with him especially in prayer, in the sacraments and in the Word of God, as the source of one's witness and missionary proclamation.

What is specific and unique to the Christian God-experience is that it is a Trinitarian God-experience, which is expressed in the love of neighbor. We must not lose sight of this uniqueness in dialogue and proclamation.

Proposition 10: The Trinitarian Plan of Salvation

It is important that the development of the proclamation of Jesus Christ be situated in God's plan of creation and redemption. Since this plan of salvation is based upon the Christian revelation of the Trinitarian God communicated in Jesus Christ through the Holy Spirit, the development of Christological themes should be situated within the framework of the Trinity.

Proposition 11: The Spirit of God in Creation and History

From the first moment of creation, God's Spirit has been at work and continues to do so in the history of salvation which culminates in Jesus Christ. It is the Holy Spirit who will carry on the work of salvation until the Lord Jesus comes in glory at the end of time. In the same, God's Spirit was at work in the hearts of individuals and societies ("The Spirit of the Lord has filled the world and that which holds all things together knows what is said," Wis 1:7) and continues throughout the ages, to sow the seeds of truth and grace among all peoples, their philosophies, cultures, and religions, as Vatican II affirms in *Ad Gentes* 2, 4, and Pope John Paul II in *Redemptoris Missio* 28.

Proposition 12: The Spirit of God at Work in Asia

It was in Asia that God spoke to his Chosen People through his servants, the patriarchs and the prophets. And finally God spoke through his Son, Jesus Christ, whose incarnation gave a definitive shape and human form to his universal plan of salvation and fullness of life for all.

The earthly ministry of Jesus was fulfilled in the power of the Holy Spirit. The same Spirit has been given to the Church by the Father and the Son at Pentecost to bring to completion Jesus' mission of love and service in Asia.

The Holy Spirit is therefore the prime mover in evangelization in the multicultural and multireligious context of Asia. He is the prime agent also of inculturation, ecumenical and interreligious dialogue and human promotion. He provides his little flock, the Church, with a rich diversity of charisms and ministries to carry out Christ's mission of love and service in Asia.

As good stewards of the mysteries of God, bishops together with the priests, religious, and laity should be alert to what the Spirit is saying to their respective Churches. They must therefore all be Spirit-filled and Spirit-led.

Proposition 13: The Church as Communion

Asia is a continent composed of many peoples and home to the great religions of the world. In this context, the life of the Church as communion assumes greater importance. Founded on the communion of the Trinity, the Church is a community of persons united in the Holy Spirit and in communion among themselves. Therefore the Church is the sign and instrument of communion between God and humanity. Believers of other religions are related to her in varying degrees and ways (cf. *LG* 16).

The Church, by virtue of her catholicity, is a sacrament of unity. She exerts every effort to promote communion within the particular Churches, communion among these Churches themselves, and the communion of these Churches with the Universal Church. The collegiality, lived both within the particular Churches and the Universal Church, is an important way to concretely achieve this universal communion. She fosters ecumenical communion with the brothers and sisters of other Christian confessions and communion of life among peoples of diverse cultures and religions in view of promoting reconciliation, solidarity, harmony, unity, and peace. The Petrine office has a unique ministry in guaranteeing and promoting the unity of the Church.

While acknowledging the service which the Dicasteries of the Roman Curia and the Holy See Diplomatic Corps render to the local Churches, in the spirit of communion and collegiality, we recommend a greater internationalization of the Dicasteries of the Roman Curia and the ranks of the Holy See Diplomatic Corps.

Proposition 14: The Communion of the Local Churches

In order to better express the communion of the local Churches and in view of fostering a better coordination in the work of evangelization, in pastoral commitments and in social services, the Synod Fathers propose prayer for one another, mutual encouragement, a more equitable distribution of priests, a better financial solidarity, cultural and theological exchanges, partnership between dioceses. The Synod supports the efforts of local Churches and encourages these Churches to deepen their communion by increasing regular contacts between their representatives.

Proposition 15: The Diocese as Communion

The diocese is a communion of communities. The Spirit is calling us to live and witness unity within the local Church by becoming a more participatory Church, where bishops, priests, religious, and laity, including youth, through a "dialogue of life and heart," share a common vision of the new way of being Church as a communion of communities.

The Church in Asia will become more alive and efficacious to the extent that the laity and religious will be more actively involved together with their Bishop and parish priests in pastoral planning and even decision making through such participatory structures as Pastoral Councils and Parish Assemblies.

Communion can be lived to the fullest only when every member of the local Church is empowered and given the opportunity to participate in the mission of Christ according to his/her state of life.

Proposition 16: The Parish

In the diocese, the parish continues to be "the ordinary place where the faithful gather to grow in holiness, to participate in the mission of the Church and to live out their ecclesial communion" (Synod of Bishops, *Message to the People of God*, 1987, no. 9).

Pastors are encouraged to devise new and effective ways of shepherding the faithful, so that the faithful will feel that they are part of the parish, the family where each one is important, each one is needed, each one is served and is called to serve and evangelize his/her neighbor.

Pastoral planning together with the lay faithful should be a normal feature in all parishes. This planning should include coordinated formation and renewal programs.

Proposition 17: The Word of God

The Sacred Scriptures or the Word of God in written form, gifted to the Church, have an inherent power to touch the hearts of people, even of other religions. Through the Bible the Holy Spirit reveals God's plan of salvation for humankind. Besides, the Bible has, because of its narrative style, a closeness to Asian spiritual literature and is much sought after.

The present situation of the Church in Asia also requires the frequent use of the Bible. Yet this vital apostolate needs to be further developed.

Hence, we propose that:

- the Bible be more intensively and prayerfully used by and diffused widely among all members of the Church in Asia,
- it be made the basis for all missionary proclamation, catechesis, preaching and methods of spirituality,
- a serious preparation in biblical apostolate be given to all priests, religious, seminarians, and lay Christian leaders,
- every encouragement be given to our Christian families to share the Word of God in small Christian communities as proposed by the Asian Integral Pastoral Approach (AsIPA), and
- theological research on an understanding of the Bible in an Asian context be encouraged.

Proposition 18: Biblical Formation

In the formation of the clergy, religious, and laity a practical course on biblical apostolate with due emphasis on "actualization" (i.e., applying the Bible to life today) ought to be concretely incorporated into the program on diocesan, regional, and national levels. A sound grounding should be given in the Constitution *Dei Verbum* (especially part 6), the biblical encyclicals, and *The Interpretation of the Bible in the Church* (especially chapter 4), for they are the norms for evaluating the validity of the diverse methods of apostolate. Effective seminars (e.g., of the FABC) for bishops and those primarily responsible for biblical apostolate ought to be actively promoted in collaboration with the Catholic Biblical Federation (CBF).

Proposition 19: Spirituality

Study and reflection both of Eastern and Western traditions of the Church on prayer, contemplation, and solitude will lead to a deeper knowledge of our common life in the Word of God and the Holy Spirit. So, too, will a like encounter with peoples of other religions and cultures of Asia. This kind of encounter is itself an act of communion through the Holy Spirit and will enable the Church to discern his presence among them, to learn from them, to live and proclaim the Gospel among them. Christian contemplatives and monks are especially encouraged to engage in such spiritual encounters with monks and devotees of other religions.

The work of justice, charity, and compassion is interrelated with a genuine life of prayer and contemplation, and indeed it is this same spirituality that will be the wellspring of all our evangelizing work.

In order to express more vividly the contemplative dimension of our spirituality, the Church in Asia needs to have a meaningful program of contemplation and solitude.

Proposition 20: Healing Ministry

Following Jesus Christ the model of all evangelization, the particular Churches in Asia should involve themselves in the healing ministry in greater measure. Christian health care workers, especially those caring for the handicapped, need to consider their ministry as a vocation carried out of love for Jesus and their neighbor.

The Synod expresses its appreciation for the great evangelizing witness given by thousands of religious sisters, brothers, doctors, nurses, and other health care workers, especially in the area of terminal illness and spiritual care. The extensive health care system run by the Church in Asia is threatened by economic considerations. These institutions are challenged to find a way to operate without pricing themselves out of the reach of the needy.

The Synod recommends that:

- there should be greater inculturation of the Gospel in Christian facilities so that Christian values and ethics can enter into the heart of Asian health care and transform it from within;
- those involved in the healing ministry should look into traditional methods of healing which have been scientifically proven to be effective as low-cost alternatives to expensive pharmaceuticals;
- Christian health care workers should especially consider the care of the victims of drug addiction, AIDS, etc.

Proposition 21: Education

Education is an integral part of evangelization, not merely a human enterprise. In Asia, education is one of the most visible and extensive ministries of the Church. In many countries, the Catholic education system is known for its administrative efficiency, academic excellence, and community service. Church schools have often provided the only educational opportunities for girls, tribal minorities, rural poor, and less privileged children.

Christian schools still have an important role to play in proclamation, inculturation of the faith, and as opportunities to learn harmonious interreligious life.

Today there is a need to rethink and reorient the apostolate of education. In the first place, it must be oriented more toward the disadvantaged and the marginalized, so that they can be empowered to fulfill their potential as loyal citizens.

The Synod proposes that:

- The great contribution made by Catholic schools to the building up of the Church in Asia be gratefully recognized.
- Our Catholic schools, in spite of financial and other difficulties, be places of integral human formation. They should be open to all, particularly the less privileged, and able to provide alternative programs to formal education; and they should continue to be places where the faith can be freely proposed and received.
- Catholic universities be encouraged to retain a clear Christian identity in addition to pursuing academic excellence in order to provide a Christian leaven in Asian societies.

Catholic institutes for higher education are powerful instruments for the formation of Christian leaders for the Church and society. Well-formed in the social message of Christ, these leaders can make a great contribution towards implanting the values of the Gospel in civil society.

Proposition 22: Human Rights and the Promotion of Justice and Peace

The different sectors of God's people in Asia, namely bishops, priests, religious, and laity, should be more sensitive to the profound challenge that confronts the human family of our continent, so that they may commit themselves to the defense of human rights and the promotion of justice and peace as integral parts of the Church's evangelizing mission. Therefore it is urgent to give a solid formation to all Catholics on the social doctrine of the Church. Consequently, it is necessary to give special attention to it in every place and at every level of Christian education, all seminaries and formation centers included. We Christians in Asia must denounce all forms of corruption and massive misappropriation of public funds by those who hold political power in our countries.

Motivated by the Apostle Paul's exhortation that the love of Christ impels us, we must engage in works of human promotion such as education, health care, apostolate for migrants, indigenous peoples, etc. In Asia where teeming millions are suffering from discrimination, exploitation, poverty, and marginalization, human promotion should engage our special attention. But the evangelizing quality should always be present, since human promotion should have a sign value, i.e., pointing to Christ's mission of love and service toward the fullness of life.

In view of the fact that in many places in Asia, Christians are not allowed to freely practice their faith and proclaim Jesus Christ to others, and even at times basic human rights are denied to the citizens, this Synod pleads for the exercise of freedom of conscience and religion, and for the recognition by all the nations of basic human rights. Noting also that there is a law of death penalty in some countries in Asia and elsewhere, the Synod wishes to speak out and act in defense of life, particularly of those condemned to death.

A thorough knowledge of the social message of Jesus is necessary for an effective evangelization of Asia, which is experiencing situations of poverty and injustice.

Therefore it is proposed that the social teaching of the Church be made responsive and relevant to the realities of Asia.

Proposition 23: Peacemaking

Peace is the fruit of a harmonious and mature integration of justice, love, truth, and liberty. Working for peace should be a central aspect of evangelization. This Synod affirms that the work for peace is integral to our evangelization in Asia.

The Church should be actively involved in international and interreligious efforts for peace, justice, and reconciliation. To achieve social change, active non-violence may be the more Christian response to oppression, disagreements, and injustice, and may be employed in the resolution of conflicts, taking inspiration from the example of Jesus Christ, Lord and Savior.

The culture of death and violence is the consequence of the proliferating use of arms. Weapons of mass destruction, conventional and nuclear, are a wasteful expenditure in national budgets, and exceed the requirements of justifiable self-defense. The use of chemical and biological weapons can never be justified. Vast quantities of land mines now in Asia have maimed and killed hundreds of thousands of innocent people and disturbed the ecology of fertile lands destined for food crops. This Synod asks for a stop to the manufacture, sale and use of such weaponry, and urges that those responsible for the destruction of lives and land should help in the work of restoration.

Proposition 24: Formation of Seminarians

In cooperation with the Congregations for Catholic Education and for the Evangelization of Peoples, the local Church in Asia should adapt seminary formation to the demands of evangelization in the light of Asian realities. This will mean a closer study and implementation of Church documents such as *Pastores Dabo Vobis* and the periodic renewal of the *Ratio Institutionis Sacerdotalis* of Episcopal Conferences. This Synod recommends emphasis on the following:

1. biblical and patristic studies,
2. the study of Christ and the Holy Spirit as central,
3. Asian philosophical and religious traditions,
4. experience of the reality of poverty,
5. building of community,
6. psycho-spiritual formation,
7. use of the *Catechism of the Catholic Church* and of National Catechisms,
8. training for participatory leadership and animation of lay leaders.

Proposition 25: The Formation of Seminary Professors and Staff

We recognize the need of formation of candidates for the priesthood as distinct from that of the academic training of professors in the seminary. The formation of seminarians is not mere intellectual information obtained in lectures from competent professors. Seminarians have to interiorize, integrate, and assimilate the teachings of Christ imparted intellectually and scientifically. Together with the intellectual and spiritual formation of seminarians, care and diligence must be given to their emotional and psycho-sexual formation.

Programs should be developed in Asia to prepare those who will staff and teach in seminaries and theological faculties. After finishing their studies in theology and related subjects, those who are to work in seminaries should follow a one-year training course which focuses on priestly spirituality, experiential knowledge of the elements of Asian spirituality and meditation, tools of guidance and spiritual direction, and the study of priestly formation. They should be led to grow in the awareness of seminary teaching and formation as a true apostolate of the Church.

This could be done by developing programs at the existing institutions or perhaps a central institute in Asia could be set up for this purpose, so that this formation could be carried out in the context of Asian cultural and religious realities.

We appreciate the dedicated ministry of the many priests in Asia. They are a special sacramental presence of Christ, the Head, in the midst of the community. As part of their ongoing formation, we propose that they be given courses on deep mystical theology and spirituality that will prove beneficial to them in their own spiritual life and in their pastoral work. We also propose that there be set up in various parts of dioceses, centers of prayer and reflection where priests could spend some time for their spiritual renewal.

Proposition 26: The Priesthood

The priesthood is instituted within the People of God for the sake of the People of God (*Presbyterorum Ordinis* 2). Priests and their ministry cannot, therefore, be understood apart from the community to which they minister.

For this reason, we urge a serious reflection and review of the relevant documents of the Church, particularly that of *Pastores Dabo Vobis*, to see how and in what innovative ways the priesthood can be authentically and effectively lived for the service and mission of life in Asia.

Proposition 27: Consecrated Life

By their lives of consecration, prayer, and dedicated service, religious are a reminder to all, Christian and non-Christian, of the universal call to holiness, and inspire a self-giving love toward everyone, especially the least of their brothers and sisters. Living in community, they bear witness to the values of Christian fraternity and to the transforming power of the Good News.

In the context of new evangelization, the Synod Fathers call upon the religious for an internal renewal and revitalization of their commitment to proclaim the saving message of Jesus Christ.

Religious are to have an appropriate formation and training which should be Christ-centered and contextualized, faithful to their charisms, with emphasis on personal sanctity and life witness. The spirituality and life style of the religious should be sensitive to the religious heritage of the people with whom they live and whom they serve.

As an integral part of the new drive for evangelization in Asia, the establishment of monastic and contemplative communities should be encouraged. We should also encourage those who wish to witness to a life of consecration in secular institutes.

The whole ecclesial community is responsible for the promotion of religious and missionary vocations and must pray for them. Every diocese should plan a vocation pastoral program. It is strongly suggested that some priests or religious be set aside for full time pastoral work among the young and especially to help them hear and discern the call of God.

Without losing their specific charisms, religious are to integrate themselves, as far as it is possible, into the pastoral plan of the diocese.

Religious orders and congregations have played a major role in the evangelization work of Asia during the past centuries. The Church in Asia is indebted to them and exhorts them to continue the same missionary commitment to peoples of Asia.

Among the many religious men and women, who down the centuries have given committed witness to an authentic consecrated life in Asia, the Synod would like to pay a special tribute to the late Mother Teresa of Calcutta, who was known all over the world for her loving and selfless care of the poorest of the poor.

Proposition 28: Missionary Societies of Apostolic Life and Other Missionary Societies

Missionary institutes of apostolic life and other missionary societies continue to render a great service to the cause of evangelization in Asia as they did in the past. Their contribution is gratefully acknowledged and desired to be continued now and in the future. This will favor a further growth of the missionary institutes of apostolic life, which recently have been founded in several countries in Asia, as the expression of the missionary dimension and responsibility of the Churches in Asia for the evangelization of their own continent and of the whole world.

This Synod recommends the establishment within each local Church of Asia, where such do not exist, of missionary societies of apostolic life, characterized by their commitment exclusively for the mission *ad gentes, ad exteros,* and *ad vitam.*

Proposition 29: Laity and Evangelization

A. In the early Church, the Good News of salvation in Jesus Christ spread to many parts of the world because it was lived and communicated with joy and enthusiasm by lay Christians as they were Spirit-filled and Spirit-led people. The laity are important missionaries of the Gospel to reach out to the millions of the Asian people who otherwise might never be reached by the missionaries from the clergy and consecrated life. Catechists have worked wonders.

The leadership of the Church must continue to discern and activate the various charisms of the whole Christian community, build up true faith communities, empowering them to be powerful evangelizers and enabling the faithful to face the challenges of the modern world with an interior transformation rather than only worldly wisdom and efficiency.

The laity are to be encouraged to assume their proper role in the life and mission of the Church. They are also to be formed for their missionary role, especially in the family and society, in the political sphere, in building up human societies, in nation building. By becoming a leaven in the society in which they live, the lay people can and should eradicate all roots of injustice, inequality, and oppression.

For the Church in Asia to carry out her mission of dialogue, witness and proclamation of the mystery of Christ, and to develop among the laity collaboration and co-responsibility in a spirit of communion and common mission, we should encourage the establishment of lay formation centers at the diocesan or national level where the laity will be formed in accordance with the Post-Synodal Apostolic Exhortation *Christifideles Laici* and where the social teachings of the Church will be taught. Through these lay formation centers, the laity can be formed to respond to the call to transform society, in collaboration with the bishops, clergy, and religious by infusing the "mind of Christ" into the mentality, customs, laws, and structures of society in which they live (cf. *Populorum Progressio* 81; *Gaudium et Spes* 31).

The key to an authentic laity in the life and mission of the Church is a holistic formation, particularly in her missionary dimension and the social teaching of the Church. We strongly recommend this integral formation of the laity as a top priority and that it should be adapted to the particular situations and traditions of Asia. We wish that this formation of the laity be centered on the universal call to holiness and mission, that is, a continuous attention to baptismal consecration, confirmation, and eucharist.

B. Lay renewal movements in the Church are a gift of the Spirit. And we wish to thank God for them as well as express our thanks to them for the great contribution they are making towards the mission of the Church. However, these movements should be properly guided and promoted by pastors so that they can grow into full Christian maturity and be better integrated into the life of the local Church. Proper discernment is to be exercised in order to ascertain the fruit of the Spirit and to avoid excesses and aberrations. These movements are not simply to be tolerated; they should be encouraged and accompanied.

Proposition 30: Basic Ecclesial Communities

Building Basic Ecclesial Communities is a new way of being Church in Asia. BECs provide proper orientation to an overall comprehensive pastoral plan. They provide effective ways of promoting participation in the local Church, especially on the part of the laity.

Basic Ecclesial Communities help Christians to live like the early Christian communities which were believing, praying, loving, and sharing communities. They offer personal insight into the Word of God and its significance for daily living. Through them the Church becomes part of the daily life of the people in the local place. They are a "solid starting point for the new society based on a civilization of love" (*RM* 51). They aim at living the Gospel in an atmosphere of fraternal love and service. Hence they are to be promoted.

Proposition 31: Renewal Movements

Renewal movements, like the charismatic movements, provide opportunities for God-experience, which brings about conversion and fosters communion. They are known to lead the faithful to a personal relationship with God as Father and with Jesus as personal Lord and Savior, to be open to the Holy Spirit's gifts and charisms, to read and share the Word of God, to receive the sacraments frequently, and to lead prayerful and Spirit-filled lives at the service of their neighbors, especially the poor and the marginalized. They should be accompanied and actively encouraged by the pastors of the Church.

Proposition 32: Family

The family in Asia is a very close-knit and solidarity-based reality; therefore, it becomes, though with some negative aspects, the primary place of human formation, mainly in view of the harmony of human relationships. The Christian family, on its part, is a community of mutual love modeled upon the Holy Trinity.

The family as domestic Church is the nucleus of the Basic Ecclesial Community, which is a new way of being Church in Asia. In this age of new evangelization, the family must be the primary and preferential place to live and practice the Christian faith, inserted in and in cooperation with the parish church. Therefore, it is necessary to multiply in the family occasions of prayer and dialogue, of special ceremonies presided by the parents, for particular times and celebrations. Meetings of parents and of whole families should be encouraged, based on geographical residence or on common concerns, for prayer, Bible sharing, exchange of experiences, recreation, etc. So, the Christian family becomes the privileged evangelizer and constitutes both a manifestation and proclamation that God is Love. It is essential that parents inculcate, by word and example, in their children Christian values and attitudes. The Synod recommends that one Sunday of each year be declared World Family Day and celebrated in Christian homes, churches, and in the Universal Church.

To ensure the survival of the family, the Synod stands for the culture of life and registers its protest against the culture of death, such as the worldwide artificial population control programs and linking international aid to artificial population control programs. Attempts by public authorities to promote artificial contraceptive methods should be resisted. The Synod encourages the promotion of Natural Family Planning.

Proposition 33: Pastoral Care of Children

In our concern for the upbuilding of the domestic Church, we must take special pastoral care of children. They are an important part of the family, they are the future of Church and nation. They are agents of evangelization within their own family and within the community. They must hence be fully imbued with faith and a strong missionary outlook as well as the values of the Gospel. They must be given proper education, be recognized as full members of the community and their rights fully respected. They could be introduced to organizations such as the Pontifical Mission Society of the Holy Childhood.

In the Asia of today, we are especially concerned with social evils that touch them directly: child labor, pedophilia, the drug culture—evils which spring from other evils, widespread poverty and wrong concepts and programs of national development, not the least among them. We must face up to these evils, do our best to counteract them in our work of human promotion.

The Church should extend its pastoral care to the youth on the spiritual, intellectual, social, and apostolic levels, so that the youth can feel that they truly form part of the Church. The youth must be spiritually nourished through meaningful liturgy, inspiring homilies, community prayer, discussion, contemplation, and reflection on realities that concern them. To ensure this formation, a full-time youth chaplain/director should be appointed.

At the intellectual level, Catholic schools should form and develop not only the mind but also the emotional and moral character in a framework of Christian values. In addition, the parish should provide them with ongoing formation through Biblical instruction and catechism.

At the social level, the parish should provide greater opportunity for fellowship and communion among the youth by means of organized youth apostolates and youth clubs. It should also empower youth to face social realities by offering them facilities such as career guidance, vocational training, and youth counseling.

The Church should actively encourage the youth to assume their role as agents and co-workers in the Church's mission in her various apostolic works of love and service. We strongly support exchanges of young people between our Churches and our countries: they are peacemakers. The Church should also ensure that youth who are adequately formed and generously committed are involved in the deliberations and decision-making processes of the Church, both at a parochial and diocesan level.

Proposition 34: Youth

Youth who constitute a large section of the Asian population have an important role in the life of the Church and society on the continent. Hence it is essential to ensure that they are formed and empowered to discern and fulfill this role.

Proposition 35: Women

The foundation of the dignity of women is found in the design of God for humanity created in God's image as male and female. The complementary nature of men and women is part of Catholic teaching. Women make an indispensable contribution to the model of life open to the mystery of love (Pope John Paul II's *Letter to Women*).

Receptivity is embodied in women's very person and finds expression in "openness" and "waiting in anticipation."

Though the awakening of women's consciousness to their dignity and rights is one of the most significant signs of the times, the poverty and exploitation of women remains a serious problem throughout Asia. Discrimination and violence against women is often in the home, workplace, and legal system. Thus, female illiteracy is much greater than that of males. The abortion of females greatly exceeds that of males. Women are treated as commodities in prostitution, tourism, entertainment industries, etc.

The Church is called to stand against all forms of discrimination and injustice against women and encourage the participation of women in the life and mission of the Church.

1. The Church in Asia should take up Human Rights activities for women in each country in Asia.
2. The Church should institute new ministries for women in order to recognize their skills and abilities and service in health, education, peacemaking, and preparing the faithful for sacraments.
3. The study and promotion of "women as collaborators" should be an integral component in the formation of priests and religious.

Their unique feminine contributions have often been undervalued or ignored and this has resulted in a spiritual impoverishment of humanity (cf. Pope John Paul II's *Letter to Women*). The Church in Asia can witness to Christ, the promoter of women's true dignity, and become a credible sign of women's dignity and freedom by taking a firm stand against forms of discrimination and injustice committed against women and by encouraging active and responsible participation of women as equal partners with men in the Church's life and mission. For this, women should be given opportunities to study theology and related subjects. The presence of women in the Church's mission of love and service contributes greatly to bring the compassionate Jesus, healer and reconciler, to Asian people, especially the poor and marginalized. Dialogue between Christian women and those of other religions can be an important factor for building justice and harmony in society.

All this calls for a change of attitude in our understanding of the role of men and women in the family, in the Church, and in society. The recovery of the feminine dimension will come about through a change in the self-awareness of men and women. Such a shift would have profound effects upon Asian societies.

Proposition 36: Pastoral Care of Migrants

Our times have witnessed an unprecedented flow of peoples in Asia as refugees, asylum seekers, migrants, and guest workers. Migrants in the new circumstances find themselves culturally estranged, linguistically inadequate, economically exploited, and friendless in a strange place. Often they suffer from loneliness and nostalgia. Migrants need the support and care of the Church, without which they can tend to become indifferent, irreligious, or be misled by sects and new religious movements. Bishops who have migrant workers in their territory have to show special concern and solicitude for their spiritual care. The pastoral care of migrants from Oriental Churches in Asia is a special problem. They need to receive pastoral care according to their own ecclesial traditions. The Second Vatican Council and the subsequent Magisterium have given sufficient guidelines in this matter. Bishops should see that migrants from Oriental Churches receive pastoral care from their own clergy. This Synod makes an earnest plea that this pastoral need of the Oriental faithful of Asia be met without delay, paying due attention to the local situations.

Migrant faithful, deep rooted in their faith, are sometimes good evangelizers and heralds of the Gospel, and this is another reason for proper pastoral care for them. Migrants are not only the objects of pastoral care but also agents of evangelization in their new surroundings through witness, deed, and word.

The host dioceses need to know the cultural, social, political, economic, and religious factors that have formed migrants. The host dioceses need missionary priests and catechists from the migrants' country of origin, who can help the migrants be integrated into the host culture and local Churches without their being assimilated and losing their cultural and Christian heritage.

Proposition 37: Pastoral Care of Tourists

Asia receives numerous tourists. Tourism is an excellent occasion for facilitating the encounter among peoples and the sharing of their cultural richness.

The tourism industry also has negative aspects. Tourism is too often used for purely hedonistic ends, and also for the sexual exploitation of children.

The Synod urges the Churches of Asia to include in their pastoral plans the question of tourism.

Proposition 38: Indigenous/Tribal Peoples

In almost every country of Asia there are large indigenous/tribal populations in various stages of economic growth. Their social, educational, and health needs demand special attention from the Church.

At the Synod, it was repeatedly affirmed that as a group, indigenous/tribal people are attracted by the person of Jesus Christ and by the Church as a community characterized by loving and caring ministry, carried out in the name and after the example of Jesus. The Church has served them well in the past. This Synod expresses its gratitude and appreciation to all in this ministry and prays for its intensification. The local Churches in Asia should respond positively to the indigenous/tribal peoples who are open to the proclamation of the Gospel. In many countries, indigenous/tribal people are becoming evangelizers to others, for which we thank God.

Given the importance of the role and place of indigenous/tribal peoples in the Church today, pastoral efforts should be initiated at whatever level of Church life is possible, to attend to their concerns, the questions of justice that affect their lives, Traditional Religion and its values, ways of empowering indigenous/tribal peoples to achieve their liberation, and the role of indigenous/tribal peoples as evangelizers.

Proposition 39: Option for the Marginalized

In her maternal solicitude, the Church has always championed the cause of the oppressed and the marginalized, and appealed to the nations to respect their dignity and uphold their fundamental human rights. In South Asia, the number of such persons (such as the Dalits in India) runs into millions, a sizeable percentage of whom are discriminated against solely on the basis of their religion, namely Christianity.

This Synod proposes that the Church advocate amendments to the Constitutions of the countries concerned so as to remove such discrimination and promote respect for the human dignity of all persons irrespective of the faith they profess, and undertake developmental activities which will provide opportunities for their integral growth and empower them to take their rightful place in society.

Proposition 40: Proclamation

Following the mandate by the Risen Lord (cf. Mt 28:18–20) and the examples of the Apostles (cf. Acts), the Church in Asia wants to share the Good News of the Gospel by announcing the riches of Christ to all people of goodwill. "How can they believe in him if they never heard of him? And how will they hear of him unless there is a preacher for them?" (Rom 10:14). Proclamation "reveals and gives access to the mystery hidden for ages and made known in Christ, the mystery which lies at the heart of the Church's mission and life, as the hinge on which all evangelization turns" (*RM* 44).

Proclamation has manifold forms: the teaching of prayers by a mother to her own child; catechism as simple talk on what a Christian is and believes; explication of the Christian kerygma and answers on the main questions of life and of death; offering the Gospel message in an appropriate form; presenting the Word of God, which has an intrinsic mysterious power and response to an expectation even if an unconscious one; well-prepared biblical or cultural meetings, discussions, and homilies, etc.

By proclamation, the Church addresses people with full respect for their freedom. The Church proposes, she imposes nothing, she respects individuals and culture, and she honors the sanctuary of conscience (*RM* 39).

Proposition 41: Interreligious Dialogue

A. Following the Second Vatican Council, this Synod expresses the desire of the Catholic Church to meet other believers. This is particularly important in Asia, home to many world religions. Interreligious relations are best developed in a context of openness to other believers, willingness to listen, and the desire to respect and understand others in their differences. For all this, love of others is indispensable. This should result in collaboration, harmony and mutual enrichment.

For effective dialogue, it is important to understand the religious tradition, cultural heritage, and socio-economic-political background. To deal with one dimension of a person and to ignore the other aspects is to blind oneself to the reality of that person in whom the three dimensions are joined as one. The threefold dialogue is one integral movement of the Christian's evangelizing mission.

Interreligious dialogue requires of Christians that they be credible witnesses of Christ, who was meek and humble of heart. Christians who meet other believers are to note that it is important that such Christians retain a clear Christian identity. Interreligious courtesy does not demand that we hide or put under doubt that we are followers of Christ. Only Christians who are deeply immersed in the mystery of Christ and who are happy in their faith community can without undue risk and with hope of positive fruit engage in interreligious dialogue.

B. We ask the Pontifical Council for Interreligious Dialogue to make a "directory" for interreligious dialogue, with special attention for Islam.

Proposition 42: Ecumenism

Jesus Christ desired that his Church be one. He prayed, and does not cease to pray, for the visible unity of his disciples, so that the world may believe that the Father sent him (cf. Jn 17:21). Following the example of her divine Head, the Catholic Church desires this unity, which she definitely considers a gift and work of the Holy Spirit, the Spirit of communion and of unity. She prays and works untiringly, above all as the third millennium approaches (*Tertio Millennio Adveniente* 34), for its realization. But she painfully notes that the scandal of a divided Christianity is a great obstacle for evangelization in Asia.

The Synod proposes that:

1. The Episcopal Conferences in Asia invite other Churches to enter into a process of prayer and consultation to explore possibilities of new ecumenical structures and associations to promote Christian unity.
2. The Week of Prayer for Christian Unity be meaningfully celebrated.
3. Ecumenical centers of prayer and dialogue be encouraged in Asia.
4. Adequate formation for ecumenical dialogue be included in the seminaries, houses of formation, and educational institutions.
5. The Oriental Churches be encouraged to assume the dialogue of love with their Orthodox sister Churches.

Proposition 43: Inculturation

The work of rooting the Gospel in the different cultures of Asia requires much thought and discernment, particularly in societies where the secular culture and Traditional Religion are so intimately intertwined. Suitable, creative, and dynamic ways and approaches must be found for promoting inculturation in the fields of theology, the liturgy, the formation of priests and religious, catechism, spirituality, popular religiosity, etc. There is need for specialized persons both in theology and the human sciences to help in this process.

This Synod is very concerned with the inculturated proclamation of the faith and encourages continuing theological investigation both by theologians in particular and by each local Church at large. Such theologizing is to be carried out with courage, in faithfulness to the Scriptures and to the Church's tradition, in communion with the Magisterium and in full awareness of pastoral realities.

The liturgy is a main instrument for evangelization. In the Oriental Churches, it saved the faith and it was successfully inculturated. It must touch the heart and be meaningful to people of the local Church. For many Asian Catholics, the official liturgy is often experienced as alien and does not touch their hearts. This points to the need for inculturating the liturgy in such a way that the liturgy becomes more meaningful and nourishing for people in the setting of their own cultures (cf. *Evangelii Nuntiandi* 48).

Consequently, local Churches need the authority and freedom to inculturate the liturgy by adapting it to the local cultures while recognizing the need for dialogue and communion with the Holy See, the principle of unity in the Church.

The Synod requests the Congregation for Divine Worship and the Discipline of the Sacraments to grant Episcopal and Regional Bishops' Conferences the authority or competence to approve translations of liturgical texts in the vernacular which are to be ultimately forwarded to the said Dicastery.

It must be recognized that the inculturation of the liturgy, though necessary, is a delicate task which cannot and may not compromise the essentials of liturgy and of the Christian faith.

Proposition 44: Human Promotion and Evangelization

Human promotion is a constitutive dimension of the preaching of the Gospel. This has particular relevance in Asia where some of the poorest nations on the face of the globe are found and where more than 50 percent of the population suffer under deprivation, poverty, and exploitation.

The Church's preferential love for the poor and her duty to raise her prophetic voice demand that she actively support and participate in the struggle of the poor for justice and better humane conditions. On the question of population, very much linked with human promotion, we, the Synod Fathers, wish to state that it is not merely a demographic or economic problem but especially a moral one.

The Synod Fathers call on all Catholics everywhere to adopt a lifestyle consonant with Gospel teachings so that their lives may better respond to the

Church's mission and that the Church may become a Church of the poor and for the poor.

Proposition 45: Social Communications

Recommendations for a more effective presentation of the message of Christ and his Church in the communications media include:

- an active communications and public relations office in each diocese;
- formation of priests, seminarians, religious, and Catholic lay professionals in this field and media education programs in Catholic schools and parishes;
- ecumenical and interreligious cooperation in seeking access of religion and religious values to the media and guaranteeing respect for moral values in the media;
- the development of pastoral plans on communications on the episcopal conference and diocesan levels, in accordance with the Pastoral Instruction *Aetatis Novae*;
- education of Catholics and others on the judicious use of the media; and
- the use of alternative media, especially the Asian indigenous means of social communication.

Radio Veritas Asia, which is the only continental radio station for the Church in Asia, is to be commended for almost thirty years of service and should be further supported through contributions of appropriate language programming, personnel, and financial help from episcopal conferences and dioceses in Asia. The assistance of missionary aid agencies to Radio Veritas Asia is gratefully acknowledged and their continued support to this continent-wide evangelization effort is sincerely requested.

Catholic publications and news agencies can be effective instruments of information and continuing religious education and formation, and—especially in places in Asia in which Christians form a minority—they can be an important means of sustaining and reinforcing a sense of Catholic identity and of articulating Catholic moral principles.

Proposition 46: Abortion

The Church's preferential love for the poor and her duty to raise her prophetic voice demand that she actively support and participate in the struggle of the poor for justice and better humane conditions. On the question of population very much linked with human promotion, we, the Synod Fathers, affirm the teachings of *Evangelium Vitae* and call upon the Church in Asia to defend human life in all its stages from conception to natural death, especially of infants who are imperiled by the possibility of abortion.

The Synod recommends that, every year, March 25, the feast of the Incarnation of Our Lord, be observed as World Pro-Life Day, when, besides hailing with gratitude God's precious gift of life, prayers for atonement will be offered for those who have resorted to, or who have been innocent victims of, the hideous crime of abortion.

Proposition 47: Ecology

Various man-made and natural disasters have brought to the fore our responsibility to safeguard the integrity of our natural resources. Our Christian vision of stewardship toward creation can provide all people with an adequate response to ecological problems. In the race for development, in which many Asian nations have entered, the Christian vision provides that "development is for people, and not people for development." Thus, in all forms of technological progress, human dignity must be the first consideration.

Furthermore, we must think of leaving future generations with a sustainable environment. This Synod, concerned with the fullness of life, calls on policymakers, entrepreneurs, and all other persons who harness the earth's resources to be responsible stewards of the earth.

Proposition 48: The Debt Crisis

International debt has caused much suffering to the developing countries. Weaker economies have been pressured to limit the subsidies of life's essentials—food, health, education, etc.—in order to service their debts to international monetary agencies and banks. A substantial percentage of the GNP is spent at the cost of social obligations to service their debts to international financial agencies and banks. While aware of the technical complexities of this matter, we believe that this issue tests the capacity of peoples, governments, and societies to value the human person and lives of millions over and above considerations of financial or material advantage.

In the spirit of the Third Millennium Jubilee (cf. Lev 25:8–12) of the Savior's coming as Lord with the mission of love for all, this Special Assembly for Asia appreciates the concern of His Holiness John Paul II on the matter (cf. *Centesimus Annus* 35) and ask all national conferences of bishops, particularly those of the wealthier nations and economies, to encourage the international monetary agencies and banks to renegotiate the debts of the poor and developing countries even to the extent of cancellation.

At the same time, this Synod emphasizes the need for developing a sense of national responsibility in the debtor countries and the importance of transparency, sound economic planning, and good governance, as well as fighting against corruption.

Proposition 49: Globalization

While the phenomenon of globalization has many positive effects, it also has a negative impact on the poor of Asia. The 1997 Human Development Report of the United Nations Development Program observes that the process of globalization tends to push poor countries and poor people to the periphery. Many nations are increasingly being trapped under foreign debt and are becoming bonded to multinational bodies. This is more so when the negative effects of globalization make countries victims of the market forces.

Moreover, through social communications and the information highway which facilitate the process of globalization, a new emerging global materialistic, secularist, and consumerist culture is rapidly causing the erosion of traditional cultural and family values in Asia.

Therefore, we commit ourselves to follow up the call of the Holy Father for "globalization without marginalization" (*World Day of Peace Message*, January 1, 1998). In view of the Great Jubilee of the Year 2000, we urge the Holy See to facilitate concrete solidarity between the particular Churches in the First and Third Worlds in order to provide ethical and juridical norms for the world's free markets and tools of social communication. Together we need to strongly press these norms on governments, financial and trade institutions such as the World Bank, International Monetary Fund, World Trade Organization, and multinational corporations.

Proposition 50: The Oriental Churches

The Oriental Churches have maintained from apostolic times a precious spiritual and theological patrimony. They have a synodal tradition which gives them freedom to elect their own bishops. This tradition deserves to be respected.

Vatican II gave orientations in order that these Churches take care of their faithful, even outside of their own territories.

The Oriental Churches also acquired a precious experience of inculturation and of interreligious dialogue, especially with Islam, experience that can be useful to other Asian Churches.

The Oriental Churches are directly and vitally concerned about any ecumenical dialogue with the Orthodox Churches. They ask to take part actively in it at all levels.

The Oriental Churches are to exercise their autonomy specified in their Canon Law (CCEO), in Vatican II documents and in the legitimate customs of the Oriental Churches. So, all their legitimate freedom in disciplinary and liturgical matters is to be preserved.

Further, we appeal to international communities like the United Nations Organization to work toward full freedom for all peoples to profess and practice their religion.

Proposition 51: Particular Churches in Difficult Circumstances

With deep respect and fraternal solicitude, the Synod Fathers express their solidarity with particular Churches which are experiencing intense trials in the practice of their faith. They encourage them to unite their sufferings with the crucified and risen Lord Jesus. In this connection, the Synod Fathers appeal to the bishops' conferences to set up an office to render assistance and guidance to these Churches. They also respectfully request the Holy See to use its good offices through diplomatic relations for the same purpose.

Proposition 52: The Church in China

The Synod Fathers declare their admiration for the heroic witness, unshaken perseverance, and steady growth of the Catholic Church in China, achieved in spite of harsh persecutions both in centuries past and in more recent times. With intense concern and fraternal solidarity, and with great eagerness, they look for the day when their Chinese Catholic brothers and sisters will be permitted to exercise their religion in full freedom, and to enjoy full communion with the See of Peter, an integral part of their Catholic religion.

The Synod Fathers have a further eager hope to witness the canonization of the blessed Chinese martyrs. Their heroic constancy in suffering, their unshakable perseverance in faith in Jesus Christ the Savior and in loyalty to his Vicar on earth, give great examples and encouragement to our Chinese Catholic brothers and sisters to endure their difficult situation and to keep up the work of evangelization.

The Synod Fathers yearn to promote reconciliation, harmony, communion, and unity in China, both in its society at large and also within the Church in China. They staunchly believe that this reconciliation, harmony, communion and unity, far from diminishing the personal commitment of Chinese Catholics to the building up of their great nation, will give them courage to join in greater efforts for the promotion of the Chinese people.

Proposition 53: North Korea

In a spirit of fraternal compassion and common solicitude, the Synod Fathers express their special solidarity with the Church in South Korea in their efforts to give assistance to the people of North Korea who are deprived of minimal means of survival, and to bring reconciliation among two countries of one people, one language, and one cultural heritage.

We express to them our solidarity, urging support and aid from other countries of the world.

Proposition 54: Asian Saints and Martyrs

The Church in Asia has been blessed by many Saints and Martyrs, witnesses of fidelity in God and love for neighbor. They have been a source of spiritual richness and a great means of evangelization. They also have a "marked ecumenical character" (*Tertio Millennio Adveniente* 37). Therefore, it is desirable to institute a day dedicated to the commemoration of all the saints and martyrs of the Churches in Asia.

Proposition 55: Embargo in Iraq

For more than eight years, the Iraqi people have suffered from the consequences of the embargo in which the poor are the ones who primarily suffer as well as young children, many of whom have died because of the lack of medicine. Both family and society are deeply affected by this situation. The Synod Fathers express their gratitude to His Holiness Pope John Paul II for all the efforts which he has made, at different times, to put an end to the suffering of the Iraqi people and to declare his solidarity with these people and the Church in Iraq, and ask for the lifting of the embargo on Iraq, calling upon God to enlighten the consciences of those who have the power to work to bring about a world founded on peace and justice.

Proposition 56: Churches in New Areas

The particular Churches in Asia are aware of the new possibilities opened for the Gospel message in countries that have gained their independence recently, such as Siberia (Russia), Mongolia, Kazakhstan, Uzbekistan, Kyrgyzstan, Tadjikistan, and Turkmenistan. We want to offer them our moral, spiritual, and material support and that of personnel in the very difficult task of sharing the love of God revealed in Jesus Christ with the peoples of these countries. We accompany them with our prayers and share their hope, joys and sufferings.

Proposition 57: Jerusalem

Jerusalem is a holy city for the three monotheistic religions: Judaism, Christianity, and Islam. It is the heart of Christianity, because it is the city where the redemptive acts, the death and the resurrection of our Lord Jesus Christ, took place. In it the Holy Spirit came upon the Apostles and from there they brought the Gospel to the whole world. Therefore, in the beginning, the Church of Jerusalem was called the Mother Church.

Today the Church in Jerusalem is involved in a process of reconciliation among the two peoples and the three religions present in the Holy City. Jerusalem, the city of reconciliation of men with God and among themselves, is today a city of conflict, death, and hatred. On the peace and stability in Jerusalem depends the survival of Christians in it. The peace of the region and of the world depends also on the peace of Jerusalem.

Therefore, this Synod calls upon all the Churches to show their solidarity with the Church in Jerusalem, to share her sorrows, to pray and to act with her for the realization of peace, justice, and reconciliation among all. This solidarity of the Churches will profit not only the Church and Christians alone, but also all the inhabitants of the Holy City—Jews, Christians, Muslims—and the peace of the world.

Proposition 58: A Word of Gratitude

The Asian local Churches are deeply grateful to all the Popes who have taken initiatives to facilitate and guide the work of evangelization in Asia, the Congregation for the Evangelization of Peoples, the other Dicasteries of the Roman Curia, and the Pontifical Mission Aid Societies who have supported the Churches in Asia.

They want to express in a very special way their gratitude to all the missionaries, men and women, religious and lay, foreign and local, who brought the message of Jesus Christ and the gift of faith.

A special word of gratitude again must be expressed to all the Churches who have sent and still send their missionaries to Asia and national agencies that have supported the work of evangelization, works of charity, health care, and human promotion. We are happy that today some of these Churches are receiving in turn missionaries from Asia. Thus we rejoice in the mutual sharing of generosity between the old and the new Churches.

We, the Fathers of the Special Synod for Asia, conscious of the important role which the Pontifical Mission Societies offer to the Church in educating and creating a missionary consciousness and love for the missions among the faithful, as well as of their role of undertaking an effective collection of funds to subsidize all the missions, each according to its needs, and of fostering vocations *"ad gentes"* in both the older and younger Churches, request that all these societies be established in every particular Church in every country, for promoting an organic pastoral solidarity in favor of the mission "to the ends of the earth."

Proposition 59: The Blessed Virgin Mary

Wherever the disciples of Jesus went they carried with them not only the Good News of Jesus Christ, but also their memory of the Mother of Jesus as we see in the Gospels and in the whole history of evangelization. This is true of Asia too. Thus Mary forms part of Catholic evangelization.

Mary is truly the Mother of all evangelizers. Asian Christians have great love and affection for Mary and revere her as their own mother and the Mother of Christ. Throughout Asia there are hundreds of Marian sanctuaries and shrines where not only the Catholic faithful flock together, but also believers of other religions, too. Mary is indeed where people of all faiths can meet.

Mary is the example of perfect discipleship, of total commitment to the mystery of salvation in Jesus Christ, and of evangelization. With her total dedication and collaboration in the work of salvation carried out by Jesus, Mary shines forth as the Mother of all disciples and evangelizers.

We invoke Mary, finally, as the Mother of the Church in Asia, to help us in fulfilling her Son's and our mission of love and service to Asian peoples according to the salvific plan of the Father through the power of the Holy Spirit.

8

Message of the Synod of Bishops for Asia

The Message of the Special Assembly of the Synod of Bishops for Asia was approved on May 12, 1998, at the Twenty-First General Congregation of the Special Assembly of the Synod of Bishops for Asia.

—Ed.

Dearly Beloved Sisters and Brothers in Christ:

1. Called by the Holy Father Pope John Paul II, on the eve of the Third Millennium, we the Fathers of the Special Assembly for Asia of the Synod of Bishops, together with the Fraternal Delegates and other Invitees, met in Rome from 19th April to 14th May, 1998. United with you all, our hearts are filled with profound gratitude to God the Father. He loved the world so much that he sent his only Son Jesus our Savior, so that all may have life and have it abundantly (cf. Jn 10:10).

A Time of Grace

2. Our coming together, for the first time, from all parts of Asia, made this Synod a unique experience and a foundational event upon which our particular Churches could build. From the very start, we gathered round the Holy Father to offer the Eucharistic Sacrifice near the tomb of St. Peter. We prayed and sang in the different languages of Asia. We invoked the martyrs and saints of our people, and we worshiped the Lord with gestures taken from our own cultures. We listened to the Apostle John sharing with us the revelation he received: "Listen to what the Spirit says to the churches . . ." Rev 3:6) of Asia. "Write what you see in a book and send it to the seven Churches . . ." (Rev 1:11).

This Synod brought together participants from all over Asia as well as representatives from other continents. We thank God for the profound sense of communion we have felt in Christ, for the sincere sharing of pastoral concerns and for the deep solidarity we have experienced. The presence of delegates from countries such as Myanmar, Vietnam, Laos, and Cambodia, as well as from Central Asia, Mongolia, and Siberia was a special reason for us to thank God. Previously, persons from these places had difficulties participating in such assemblies. We were sad that the two Bishops, who were expected to bring us the voice of the Church in Mainland China, could not be with us, but we prayed for them and benefited by their prayers.

All the testimonies of the great work done by the thousands of missionaries in Asia from the time of the Apostles down to our times evoked in us a deep sense of gratitude. We are thankful for all the help received from the various mission agencies, especially the Pontifical Mission Societies and other Church organizations, which generously assisted the Church in Asia.

We are grateful to God for the inspiration and heroic example we have of many missionaries and Asian martyrs. We also thank the Lord for our sisters and brothers who today carry on the Church's mission in challenging circumstances in different countries. Their trials were recalled on various occasions during the Synod.

Greeting the Peoples of Asia

3. We respectfully greet all our sisters and brothers in Asia who have put their confidence in other religious traditions. We gladly acknowledge the spiritual values of the great religions of Asia such as Hinduism, Buddhism, Judaism, Islam. We esteem the ethical values in the customs and practices found in the teachings of the great philosophers of Asia, which promote natural virtues and pious devotion to ancestors. We also respect the beliefs and religious practices of indigenous/tribal people, whose reverence for all creation manifests their closeness to the Creator.

Together with all Asian peoples, we wish to grow in sharing our richness and in having mutual respect for our differences. We resolve to work together to improve the quality of life of our people. We consider our faith as our greatest treasure and would like to share it with all, fully respecting their religious beliefs and their freedom.

Listening to the Spirit

4. We prayed together and listened every day to the one among us who had been chosen to comment on the Word of God for us. The interventions in the plenary assembly, the group discussions, and the peaceful and orderly dynamics of the entire Synod, made us experience day after day that the Spirit of the Lord was by our side. He made us aware of our shortcomings and failings because of which we may be poor witnesses of Christ's saving love. We ourselves need to be evangelized while we strive to evangelize others. We wish to so live, that by seeing us, others may catch a glimpse of the marvelous riches that God has bestowed on us in his Son Jesus.

It is the Holy Spirit who helps us to understand what vision of the Church in Asia we should have as we stand on the threshold of the Third Millennium. The presence among us of representatives of particular Churches who were persecuted in the past and of those now facing increasing intolerance, has added to our understanding of the situation of Christians living in difficult circumstances.

The Fraternal Delegates from other Christian Churches rekindled in us the longing for unity of all Christians which Our Lord desired and prayed for. This reminded us of the urgent need to foster ecumenism. The contributions of special guests and representatives from the laity, religious, and apostolic associations have sharpened in us our awareness of our pastoral ministry beyond our traditional and institutional concerns.

Mission of the Church

5. The Church was entrusted by the Risen Lord with the task of proclaiming the Good News of God's Kingdom in the power of the Holy Spirit. It takes as its model the early Christians who "devoted themselves to the apostles' teaching and fellowship, to the breaking of bread, and the prayers" (Acts 2:42).

Our understanding of mission is that all may have life and have it abundantly (cf. Jn 10:10). Having its source in the Blessed Trinity, this life is communicated to us by Jesus, the Son of God, sent to save all humankind from sin, evil, and death, and bring us to the dignity and unity to which we are called by God.

The Word of God should have central place in our lives and should nourish us spiritually. The Bible is not an ordinary book, but rather the living voice of the living God who calls us every day to carry out his plan for our lives and our world. We are happy to note that thanks to good Bible translations available in local languages, people have access to "the Words of Eternal Life" (Jn 6:68).

All Christians have the duty to proclaim Christ. The urge to do this springs from the joy of having found a treasure and the desire of sharing it. In Jesus Christ, the unknown and inaccessible God fully reveals and communicates himself. The living Father sent Jesus, who draws his life from him (cf. Jn 6:57). This is the life Jesus has come to share with us. It is the source of all life and lasts forever.

Many creative ways, in consonance with Asian cultures, were suggested to present Jesus to our sisters and brothers. We acknowledge the wonderful service being rendered by those who bring the Good News to Asians who have not heard about Jesus Christ. We believe that the presentation of Jesus as the personification of God's love and forgiveness has great relevance for Asia.

We are all aware that the liturgy has a key role in evangelization. It is an event where people may touch God and experience him as the One who takes the initiative to meet them. This evokes our response in adoration, contemplation, and silence. For this, however, the liturgy must be participatory. The gestures should convey that something solemn and holy is happening. Even though we felt the urgent need to take more and more into account the local cultures in our liturgical celebrations, we note with joy that practically everywhere in Asia the liturgy is held in the language of the people.

Above all, it calls for a deep missionary spirituality, rooted in Christ, with special emphasis on compassion and harmony, detachment and self-emptying, solidarity with the poor and the suffering, and respect for the integrity of creation. The witness of monastic and contemplative communities is particularly called for to reveal the authentic countenance of Jesus; likewise, the life and work of consecrated men and women.

For this purpose, we need formation programs to train priests and religious who are men and women of God devoted to prayer and living deep spiritual lives and who are able to guide and accompany others on their road to God. Christians in Asia need to have zealous pastors and spiritual guides, and not simply efficient administrators. The personal example of formators has a crucial role to play in the formation process.

We highlighted the importance of inculturation so that "the Church becomes a more intelligible sign of what she is and a more effective instrument of mission" (*RM* 52). In the Asian context of a multi-ethnic, multi-religious and multi-cultural situation, interreligious dialogue has clearly become a necessity. In our times, the Church is making major efforts to encounter the millennia-old religions in a serious manner. Interreligious dialogue is a respectful and sincere meeting in which the encountering parties want to know each other, to learn from one another, to enrich each other and to love one another, as Christians and Muslims are trying to do in Lebanon, where their mutual relationship augurs well for the future. For the Christian believer, this will include the desire of sharing the saving message of Christ. The Church in Asia is called upon to enter a triple dialogue: a dialogue with the cultures of Asia, a dialogue with the religions of Asia, and a dialogue with the peoples of Asia, especially the poor. To carry on such a dialogue, formation for dialogue is all-important, especially in our formation centers.

We acknowledge the wonderful service in the field of education rendered by priests, brothers, sisters, and the lay people in Asia. We commit ourselves to promote Gospel values and foster Asian cultures and traditions, such as hospitality, simplicity, respect for sacred persons, places, and things. The curriculum must foster critical thinking, equipping our students with the skill of analyzing the various forces at work in society and to discern situations when people are exploited. We must pay greater attention to non-formal education. From time to time, we must evaluate our education system, its contents, its methodology, the benefit to its recipients, the relationships engendered, the values inculcated, and the impact on society.

A pastoral plan for social communications should be made in all dioceses so as to include a public relations office. Due attention should be paid to media education, the constructive use of the media, such as press and publications, television, radio, and the Internet. The media is rightly called the modern Areopagus, and it is here, as in other fields, that the Church can play a prophetic role and, wherever necessary, become the voice of the voiceless.

Entrusted by God the Creator to be stewards of his creation, we must have a respect for mother earth and the life systems which nourish us. We should do all in our power to prevent the degradation of the environment, which is the consequence of unbridled greed among other causes. If not, the result will be the pollution of land, rivers, and air and the cutting down of forests. We must work for ecologically sustainable development, particularly in the agricultural sector.

The laity has an important role to play in the mission of the Church. Many signs indicate that the Spirit is empowering them for an even greater role in the coming millennium which could be called the Age of the Laity. Some signs are: their commitment to evangelization, their involvement in ecclesial life, and their active and enthusiastic participation in small Christian communities. Renewal programs, catechesis, and Catholic educational institutions have a decisive role to play in forming our laity to be missionaries. To equip them for the transformation of the socio-cultural and politico-economic structures of society, we must impart to them a thorough knowledge of the social and ethical teachings of the Church.

The family is the most endangered institution in Asia. Population control tends to discriminate against the girl child in some countries and targets the poor of the Third World. Traditional family values are being overturned and replaced by egotism, hedonism, materialism, and greed. Direct assaults on life are made by contraception, sterilization, and abortion. We must save the family, which, because it welcomes and protects human beings, is the basic cell of society and the Church. If the family is destroyed, society is destroyed. The family is the domestic Church located at the core of the Christian community. The home is the first school. Parents are the first teachers. The first textbook for the child is the relationships within the family, between parents themselves and with their children and with other families.

One of the significant signs of the times is the awakening of women's consciousness of their dignity and equality with men. The Church in Asia, to be a credible sign of the respect and freedom of women, must give witness to Christ as the promoter of the true dignity of women. This can be done by encouraging active participation of women as equally responsible for Christ's mission of love and service.

Youth are the hope of Asia and of the Church. The need of the hour is that the Church gives youth the formation they need to face the challenges of our fast changing society and our quite uncertain future. By taking proper care of the millions of young people in Asia, we fill their hearts with hope and enable them to be evangelizers. We recognize with gratitude and wish to harness the evangelizing power of youth already at work in the shaping of a better future for the Church and society.

Special attention must be paid to migrant workers. Millions of them leave their families to earn their livelihood in other countries. Pastoral care for them in their own ecclesial tradition is most necessary. If they are Christians, a proper formation will enable them to be evangelizers in their host countries.

Another group of people that should cause us concern are the refugees. There are millions of them in Asia who have left their countries and are in great need of all kinds of assistance.

Appeals for Justice and Peace

6. We could not help but feel deeply concerned when hearing of the hardships people have to undergo in several countries of Asia on account of recurring violence, internal strife, tensions and wars between countries.

There is also the problem of Jerusalem, the heart of Christendom, a holy city for the three monotheistic religions: Judaism, Christianity, and Islam. We appeal to all concerned to do everything within their power to preserve the unique and sacred character of this Holy City.

When considering the suffering of the people of Iraq, especially women and children, we strongly urge that steps be taken to lift the embargo against that country.

Elsewhere in Asia, people are suffering under political regimes that pay no heed to their legitimate claims for more freedom and greater respect for their basic rights. Others are struggling to regain sovereignty or greater autonomy.

We need to create a greater awareness of the dangers of the development and expansion of the armaments industry. These trends serve to suppress the people's demand for justice and democracy.

While there are beneficial effects of globalization, we are concerned about its harmful effects. We call on the particular Churches of the First World to be in solidarity with the poor in Asia and to be their advocates with their own governments and with world economic institutions such as the World Bank, the International Monetary Fund, and the World Trade Organization so as to bring about what Pope John Paul II called in this year's World Day of Peace Message: "Globalization without marginalization. Globalization in solidarity."

We strongly recommend that during the Jubilee Year 2000, the Third World debt be re-negotiated and its crushing burden alleviated.

Reasons for Hope

7. Our greatest reason for hope is Jesus Christ who said: "Take heart, it is I; have no fear" (Mt 14:27) and "I have overcome the world" (Jn 16:33).

Another reason for hope is the religiosity of our people who have great resilience even in the most difficult situations.

In the midst of these peoples—who are obviously called to play a more and more important role in the evolution of humankind—the Church is already present. Barring the special case of the Philippines, Christians are everywhere a minority and in some cases, a tiny minority. Nevertheless, particular Churches in Asia are very much alive and some of them manifest an extraordinary dynamism.

Practically everywhere, we see a high number of vocations to the priesthood and religious life, but we are equally happy to see that in many countries of Asia a high number of lay people are fully conscious of their Christian responsibilities. They take part in the activity of the Church in many ways. Moreover, among them, some are very much conscious of their obligation to be authentic witnesses of Christ and to contribute to the progress of God's kingdom.

Wherever the Church has taken root, she renders highly appreciated services to the people. Though it may happen that some institutions are not truly at the service of the poorest, we are happy to note that more and more efforts are being made to ensure that the Church's institutions are truly helping the most needy. At the same time, we are happy to see that some do not hesitate to get out of institutions to share the life of the most oppressed and to struggle with them to defend their rights.

So let us be confident. The Spirit of the Lord is obviously at work in Asia, and the Church is quite active in this continent. With Christ, we have already defeated death; with him, we have already risen.

Without being self-complacent about our past achievements we should pre-serve our fervor of spirit as Pope Paul VI said, "Let us preserve the delightful and comforting joy of evangelizing even when it is in tears that we must sow. May it mean for us . . . an interior enthusiasm that nobody and nothing can quench . . . and may the world of our time which is searching sometimes with anguish, some-times with hope, be enabled to receive the Good News, not from evangelizers who are dejected, discouraged, impatient or anxious, but from ministers of the Gospel whose lives glow with fervor, who first received the joy of Christ, and who are willing to risk their lives so that the kingdom may be proclaimed and the Church established in the midst of the world" (*Evangelii Nuntiandi,* 80).

In this message, we refer only to a few issues raised during the Synod. Many other matters were discussed which will be taken up in the various propositions to be presented to the Holy Father and eventually to be incorporated in the Post-Synodal Apostolic Exhortation which we await.

Concluding Prayer

8. As we began the Synod so we conclude it with the same Eucharistic Sacri-fice, wherein through the words of consecration the bread and wine become the Body and Blood of Christ, and where the assembly is transformed into "one Body and one Spirit" in Christ. This encounter with Jesus must now continue in a greater measure all over Asia. This is the work of the Holy Spirit who is always the One at our side to help us. We turn to Mary in whose body Christ was formed by the Holy Spirit. We pray that she may intercede for us so that, like Jesus her di-vine Son, the Church may become ever more a Servant Church to continue its mission of love and service to the people of Asia, so that "they may have life and have it abundantly" (Jn 10:10).

9

Ecclesia in Asia: An Ecclesial Event[*]

Perhaps the best reflection on the significance of John Paul II's visit to New Delhi, India, where on November 6, 1999, he presented his post-synodal Apostolic Exhortation *Ecclesia in Asia,* as well as on the Asian reception of the document itself, is given by the editorial in *Vidyajyoti* (vol. 63/12 [1999]), which is included here as an introduction to the papal exhortation.

—Ed.

An Ecclesial Event

What happened in Delhi in early November was not merely the conclusion of the Special Assembly of the Synod of Bishops for Asia, but a rich moment in the life of the Church in the continent. For a few hours the capital city of India, illumined with the lights of Diwali, became the Catholic capital of Asia. The events at the Cathedral, at the Jawaharlal Nehru Stadium and at the elegant Vigyan Bhavan, official venue of many national and international conventions, must be seen as one whole and as the symbolic expression of the life of the Church in Asia. The event holds many lessons for us, some of which we will mention here, others will be perceived by other participants and observers. They all call for reflection.

The first obvious lesson of the days before, during, and after the visit of the pope, is that we live in a world where our presence is noticed. Never, probably, had there been so much reporting in the press, positive or negative, about the Christian activity and presence in the country, both in the past and in the present, as during these weeks. The centuries of ghetto Christian life are over. What we do, what we say, and even what we think in our beliefs, is done, said, and professed publicly. This means that our expressions need to be understandable to the larger public that interprets words by the meaning they have in the media. We cannot respond to misinterpretations of our intentions by appealing to hidden theological meanings if our words suggest different meanings to people. What we say in our theological discourse must be understandable, even if not acceptable to everybody. Words like conversion, evangelization, proclamation, mission, are often heard with different nuances than those they have in our internal forum. We need to reformulate our expressions. Not that we want to camouflage our faith, are ashamed of Jesus Christ. But the way we articulate our beliefs must convey the Christian message of Good News, an announcement of the universal and self-sacrificing love of God.

---

[*]Editorial, "An Ecclesial Event," *VJTR* 63/12 (1999).

Another lesson we learned from the Delhi event is that we live in history. Our history is with us, for joy and proclamation, or for sorrow and repentance. This is natural and in many ways to be welcome. Not only our personal, but also our missionary past is with us, and we cannot afford to ignore it or be too selective in what we want to remember and what to forget. The history of the Christian community affects the way in which its present words and deeds are judged. This history itself needs redemption, and in the Catholic tradition forgiveness involves confession.

The event of Delhi had a pastoral core: as the conclusion of the Synod, it showed the Church of Asia acquiring a new consciousness of its call to serve at the beginning of the third millennium. This consciousness pervaded the deliberations of the Synod and found a papal expression in the Post-Synodal Apostolic Exhortation *Ecclesia in Asia*. We hope eventually to pay a more detailed attention to this important document which has been called, not without a certain exaggeration, the Magna Carta for the Church in Asia in the third millennium. The Exhortation is not a Conciliar Constitution like *Gaudium et Spes*, nor a Conciliar Decree like *Ad Gentes*, not even a doctrinal Papal Encyclical. It is what its title says, an Apostolic Exhortation, which offers guidelines from the Supreme Pastor of the Church for the practical involvement of the community in this vast continent. The pope presented the Exhortation as the fruit of a collegial deliberation of the Synod. This it clearly is, but he has made the themes of the bishops, Asian or Roman, his own, and added to them his insights and reflections. There is symbolic meaning in his will to sign it in Asia, perhaps the first ever document signed in our continent by the Bishop of Rome. The Exhortation was received with love and gratitude.

It is necessarily phrased in general terms: a document meant for the whole of Asia, from Siberia to East Timor, from Japan to Palestine, cannot but use general terminology and draw from the millennial faith of the Church. Each country, each cultural group, needs to make a re-reading of the document and apply it to its specific social and historical context. As the pope said in *Fides et ratio*, his letter on the relationship between faith and reason, "In India particularly, it is the duty of Christians now to draw from this rich heritage the elements compatible with their faith, in order to enrich Christian thought." The pope naturally makes no apology for being rooted in the Church's faith, as some comments in the media have pointed out. Like every good, this faith is self-diffusive and the pope encourages us to share the memory of Jesus with all. We all need this encouragement in times when the Christian witness is often misrepresented in its intentions, its methods and its effects—whether in good or bad faith.

The teaching of the pope in the Exhortation acquired new tones in his personal address to the bishops gathered in the Cathedral of Delhi. . . . He clearly felt at home in what he called the "blessed soil of Asia" (Hindus often call India *punyahhumi*), "cradle of great religious traditions and ancient civilizations," and he is moved by its "ceaseless passion for the Absolute." If he spoke of the Lord's command to preach the Gospel he sees this as a consequence of our faith in Jesus Christ calling *us* to conversion. This witness, he knows, means often a Calvary, the way of the cross, the way of the martyrs, as it has been for many Asians in history. It is a witness to love, a love whose fruit is justice. "It is surely the work of the Holy Spirit that Asian Christians are turning more and more to the defense of human dignity and the pursuit of justice." In obedience to the Lord's command of love we "expend immense energies in practical charity and in human promotion and liberation." "Let no one fear the Church!," he reassured his larger audience outside the Cathedral.

The pope encouraged the Church to engage in a "dialogue of salvation," and told us what is the specific Christian contribution to this dialogue: *"The word which we must speak is the word of the cross of Jesus Christ."* The pope thus called the Asian Church to a spirituality of kenosis, at the same time inviting all Asians "to contemplate *the figure of the crucified Jesus"* [all italics in Vatican printed text].

No human word in history is a final word. The word is always pronounced and heard in dialogue, and the dialogue continues as long as the human pilgrimage continues. The Church is always in "syn-odos"—walking together. As the Word of the Gospel is heard and given new expression in every era and cultural situation, so also the papal teaching is read in each specific context that gives it more concrete shape. Theologians speak of a re-reading of the Church's doctrinal documents in every generation. A fortiori this applies to pastoral documents. We experienced firsthand this activity of re-reading in the Delhi event: Cardinal Darmaatmadja, President Delegate of the Synod and Archbishop of Jakarta, gave the first response to the Apostolic Exhortation of the pope. He spoke the language of the concrete Asian experience, and one could feel at once how his words found deep resonance with the listeners in the Cathedral. He said that Christ is already present in the reality of Asia, and spoke of service, liberation, love, dialogue, within which the Christian announcement of Jesus Christ is made. The teaching was the same: the stresses, the context, the language were different. . . .

If the session in the Cathedral was the final "working session" of the Synod, the Nehru Stadium became the next day the Cathedral where the Asian community celebrated with its Supreme Pastor the Light of Christ and the proclamation of the Synod, and gave thanks to God for this privileged moment of Asian ecclesiology which was the Synod. There the pope encouraged specially the laity of Asia (many lay representatives came and received personal copies of *Ecclesia in Asia*) to fight for justice and for a right order of society. The mission, as it touched the laity, was clearly a mission of transforming society. The homily and other addresses at the stadium also deserve a close study.

Perhaps we could venture to say that the climax of the Delhi event was beyond the Cathedral and beyond the sacred liturgy. It was when the Church, in the person of the pope and many other followers, laity, religious, priests, and bishops, met with representatives of other religions at New Delhi's "Vigyan Bhavan" or "Hall of Wisdom." This was living dialogue wherein each participant gave witness to the strength and inspiration she or he received from their respective faiths. Such personal testimonies were received gratefully. Here we communicated with the heart, as was clear in the loud applause and cheers of the participants when the

Sankaracharya Madhavananda Saraswati and the pope joined hands and raised them together for the whole community to see. It was, it is true, a symbolic meeting. What they did is more important than what they said. One could say that there was relatively little content in the dialogue. At present, symbolic gestures of this type, reminiscent of the Assisi meeting, are very important, for they have a great symbolic power and speak better than apologetic words.

The message of the pope? Simply that God is love, quoting from 1 John 4:16–20, and that dialogue is an activity of love and that we must avoid all temptation to choose paths of isolation, division, and conflict. He did not name Jesus Christ, but Asia listened eagerly to the pope's word and received it with joy. This was an announcement of Good News that sets a pattern for the mission of the Church in Asia. Here, at least for a moment, the false opposition between dialogue and proclamation was bridged. . . .

It would be wrong, we think, to take only one element of the Delhi event and see it as the only result of the Synod. The whole Synod, the rich witnessing and sharing that took place in Rome and its meaningful conclusion in Delhi, is its own message, and each element must be taken in total context. The assimilation of the Synod by the Asian Church remains the task ahead.

Part Three

The Future of Asian Christianity

10

Looking into the Future

The Asian Synod, and especially Pope John Paul II's Post-Synodal Apostolic Exhortation, have prompted many Asian theologians to reflect not only on the synod and the papal document, but also more broadly on the future of Christianity in Asia itself.

Soosai Arokiasamy reflects on the Asian Synod as "an ecclesial event" with long-term consequences for Asian Christianity, especially with regard to the development of a "language of faith" based on the lived experience of Christian faith in Asia. This language will be elaborated as a result of a close collaboration between Asian theologians and bishops, in the midst of basic ecclesial and human communities, as happily evidenced in the FABC.

James H. Kroeger goes to the very heart of the Asian Synod by considering the Church's evangelization mission in Asia. With helpful statistics on Asia and on the Asian Catholic Church he expounds the theology of mission in *Ecclesia in Asia*, and shows that the Asian churches are not simply mission-receiving but have become mission-sending with six missionary societies.

Luis Antonio Tagle, an "expert" at the Asian Synod, details the challenges of mission in Asia in light of four lessons of the synod: learning from Jesus as a missionary, "contemporalization" of Jesus' mission in Asia, emphasis on Jesus as the focus of evangelization, and attention to some specific areas of mission for the church (proclamation, communion, dialogue, peace-making, and formation).

In a searching essay, Michael Amaladoss presents a vision of mission in Asia, different from that of *Ecclesia in Asia*, based on the experience of lived faith in India, especially on the fact that the vast majority of Asian people have access to salvation in and through their own religions. The focus of the church's mission, in his view, is prophecy, challenging people to transformation, in service to the Kingdom of God.

John Mansford Prior offers a fascinating study of the Apostolic Exhortation, contrasting its "voice" and doctrinal emphasis with the concerns of the Asian bishops expressed in their interventions and examines the teaching of *Ecclesia in Asia* in three areas: interreligious dialogue, solidarity with the poor, and inculturation.

Peter C. Phan places the Asian Synod in the context of Asia and highlights the need to develop the "Asianness" of Christianity. What is required is not simply transplanting Christianity into Asia but, as the FABC has repeatedly emphasized, finding a "new way of being Church" in Asia in terms of ecclesial *communio,* collegial participation, dialogue, and prophecy.

Vu Kim Chinh analyzes the theology of inculturation as developed in the official documents of the synod, in particular the *Lineamenta* and the *Instrumentum Laboris*, and in the Apostolic Exhortation. He concludes by showing how this process of inculturation as "a new pedagogy" can be applied to Christianity in Vietnam.

Finally, Edmund Chia argues that the disputed question at the Asian Synod as well as in *Ecclesia in Asia* is not the *who* or the *why* of mission, but the *how* of mission. Using culinary metaphors, Chia points out that in theology as well as in cooking, just as there are Western foods (spaghetti and cheese) there are Western modes of theologizing about Christ and Church (represented by *Ecclesia in Asia*); and just as there are Asian foods (rice and curry), there are Asian ways of doing theology (represented by the speeches of the Asian bishops). He concludes by highlighting the significant differences between *Ecclesia in Asia* and the Final Statement of the Seventh FABC Assembly in 1999. Chia ends on a hopeful note: with John Paul II leading the way in interreligious dialogue, it is possible that one day both spaghetti and rice, cheese and curry can be eaten together, all by the same person!

11

Synod for Asia: An Ecclesial Event of Communion and Shared Witness of Faith[*]

SOOSAI AROKIASAMY

The special Synodal Assembly for Asia was an ecclesial event not precisely because it was held in the Vatican in the presence of the pope, or because of the external paraphernalia that mark events in the Vatican, but primarily because it was an experience of communion of faith and sharing of witness of the local churches of Asia in their diversity and complexity, a witness deeply sensitive and responsive to the contextual realities of the continent. The synodal communion was also a witness to the discipleship of the Church in Asia, lived sometimes in difficult circumstances of deprivation, persecution, and struggle—a discipleship involving a commitment to a mission of love and humble service. The synod testified to genuine efforts in learning and promoting solidarity with the poor and dialogue of life with people of other faiths. The rich variety of shared witness manifested the different paths of mission of the local churches of Asia, fruit of their discernment of the Lord's will, done in maturity of faith marked by openness, freshness, and zeal.

Many interventions spoke of sharing faith with people of other religions, which could be perceived as a dialogical proclamation by a personal and collective witness marked by respect for the dignity and freedom of our brothers and sisters and for God's work in them, without obsessions about numbers or the size of the Christian communities. Asian Christian witness to faith and its sharing in dialogue and service of all, especially the poor, are not verbal proclamations but witness-deed proclamations within which a sharing of the experience of God in Christ and God's redemptive love embracing all humankind also takes place. Creeds and doctrine are important, but sharing the Good News concerns primarily God's encounter with humankind, above all in Jesus, the Son, the Word of God made flesh, whose witness is continued in various ways by the Spirit. The pastors of the Church in Asia and the Christian communities, secure, confident, and courageous in their faith, are concerned about how the Church can become truly a Church in Asia and of Asia, and live a discipleship of witness and service to fellow Asians. Rooted in the Asian soil and its spiritual traditions, the Church learns

---

[*]Soosai Arokiasamy, "Synod for Asia: An Ecclesial Event of Communion and Shared Witness of Faith," *VJTR* 62/9 (1998), 666–675.

the Asian way of being Christian and Church, and the Asian way of sharing faith and service. The Synodal Assembly bore abundant witness to this.

A question can be asked: did the leaders of the Church in the West, especially in Rome, listen to these experiences of the specific quality of Asian witness and learn from this communion of faith and the ways of the Spirit during the Synod? I presume they did. If not, they missed an opportunity of grace.

In this connection, I would like to make a comment on listening. Listening is a spirituality, an exercise and experience of faith. Without self-kenosis, one cannot listen or be open to the mystery of the other, or to the surprising ways of the Spirit, which blows where it wills, as seen in the marvelous variety of witness shared during the synod. One could see there the emerging features of Asian Christianity and a fruitful cross-fertilization of ideas. We may ask if there is a general culture of listening in the Church. Listening takes places within a relationship. It creates communion and strengthens it. It is an ecclesial act. A Church called in its mission to be a Church in dialogue should grow in genuine and intense listening and discerning. As the fruit of his listening the pope praised the Lord for the marvelous gifts of God to the Church in Asia (cf. his homily in the concluding Mass). Many would have expected such expressions in the interventions of some of the curial members of the synod. All those who lived this listening during the synod are definitely the better for it. I heard some bishops say: let us bless the Lord for the marvelous ways he works among peoples and in the local churches of Asia.

In this listening experience, the pastors and others felt affirmed, encouraged, built up, and confirmed by each other. Confirming the brethren as a charism belongs to the whole Church, but especially to the See of Peter. The Church in Asia looks forward to a formal expression of this aspect of the Petrine charism in the forthcoming Apostolic Exhortation.

Emphasis on God Experience

In the synod, there was a specifically Asian emphasis, namely the emphasis on God-experience. In our Christian discipleship, the experience of God is the first authenticating criterion of our Christian faith. A number of bishops emphasized this feature of Asian religiousness and a fortiori of Asian Christianity. Cardinal Darmaamatdja referred to this emphasis in the concluding speech of the synod.

In India we call it *anubhava*. This emphasis is precious to the spiritual tradition of Asian religions, to which we belong. Because we are heirs to this tradition, the God-experience should mark Christian witness and discipleship. Sometimes one was irked by the lack of comprehension of this mark of Asian religions and their spirituality on the part of some delegates of the synod, who were intellectually saddled with an over-conceptual approach to faith and over-suspicious of modernism, etc. In the synod, the interventions were indeed sharings of faith, experiences of the local churches of Asia. The presumption was that the listening was intense. Among the Asian delegates, there was spontaneous understanding and affirmation of this emphasis because they come from this tradition. Some of the interventions, especially from Vatican dicasteries, though not all, made me wonder if the speakers understood this emphasis or appreciated it. If not, it was for them a synod of missed opportunities.

Language of Faith

In this connection I would say that the Church in Asia is in the process of developing a language of faith based on the lived experience of and reflection on Christian life. It has new emphases and new foci of interest and is attuned to the religious and spiritual idiom of the peoples of Asia. Christians learn from fellow Asians in the daily dialogue of life and special encounters, all part of the life of the Church. Some, though limited, expression of this language of faith was heard in the synod.

The sources of the emerging language of faith are the Church's solidarity with the poor; the dialogue with religions and cultures, which also involves a counter-culture of prophecy against the forces of death; the dialogue with the religiosity of the peoples and the common struggles for a just, participatory, harmonious, and peaceful society. From such experiences, people spontaneously encounter Jesus as Guru, as Reconciler, as Healer, as Liberator, the Enlightened One, the Compassionate One, Friend of the poor, etc. In this way, they meet God and experience God's redemptive love revealed in Christ. The above perceptions of Jesus denote spontaneous appropriations of his person and message, not strategic adaptations made by experts for public communication. This language of faith reflects the inherited faith tradition, but it also embodies more meaningfully the appropriated faith of believers rooted in the humanity and religiosity of Asian peoples.

There was a strong sense of appreciation of this and mutual learning among the sister Churches. We presume it was also valued by the participants from the Vatican dicasteries. We recognize more and more that in one communion of faith, there is plurality and variety of experiences with a corresponding language. This is not a mere cultural adaptation but a fruit of the Spirit active in the Church in Asia.

The Synodal Process

Concerning the interventions, the synodal structure needs basic change and not just peripheral improvements with more computers, etc. An ecclesial event needs a dynamic that reflects and embodies the very beautiful ecclesiology often stated in fine phrases only.

Hence a comment on the dynamic regarding the interventions of the participants: when there are more than two hundred participants, management of time for the interventions is necessary. Without abandoning this managerial exigency, there is need to look at the nature of the interventions, their value and meaning for the participants and for the synod and beyond the synod. The interventions were indeed sharing of experiences, and testimonies of the local churches, of their struggles, agonies, and concerns, their questions, their hopes, above all their faith. They did create a milieu for discerning, supportive, searching, and confirming interactions. An ecclesial event of communion and shared witness, which the synod (etymologically, a "journey together") is, falls short of its meaning and dignity if there is not some measure of interaction in the long first part of the synod. It is also necessary that the full texts of the sharings are made available at least to the participants. Synod after synod, participants express frustration about the first part. If we are serious about discernment and communion as essential to the synodal event, we must find a way out to fill this lacuna—for that matter, also many other lacunae and limitations of the synod.

Littleness of the Church in Asia

I mentioned earlier that there was no compulsive anxiety about the numerical increase of Christians in Asia. There was no doubt that the Church in Asia should grow, and it should become strong in the quality of discipleship and witness. In this connection, the synod and the pope mentioned the minority status of the Church. There was need to reflect theologically on the Church as a "little flock."

From the Gospel perspective, the "little flock" that the Church is (3 percent in Asia) seems to be in line with and challenged by the Gospel image of the leaven in the dough. The Christian discipleship of the Asian Church, in servanthood and as a kenosis, that rejects all trappings of power and triumphalism, lives its witness and mission of love in a true evangelical sense if it becomes a transforming leaven within Asian society. The presence of the Kingdom as a leaven in the dough is a challenge to the faith life of the Church everywhere. Similarly, to be the salt of the earth, to be a city built on a mountain or a lamp lit and put on a lampstand are the Gospel expressions of the mission entrusted to the disciples, the Church, by Christ. I did not find sufficient theological thinking and articulation of this perspective and understanding of the mission in the synod. We look forward to some development and articulation of this perspective in the Apostolic Exhortation. The local churches themselves have the task to develop this mission perspective of the Gospel of Jesus. It would be wrong to think of this perspective as a pragmatic adaptation or accommodation to the situation.

Theology and Theologians in the Synod

About the role of theology and theologians in Asia, the bishops in the synod recognized their contribution and their ministry within the ecclesial communion of faith. In the case of the FABC, theologians from different countries of Asia have made remarkable contributions to its life. Some of them have become bishops and continue to contribute as bishop-theologians to the growth of Asian theology at the service of the Church's mission. The theological thinking of FABC has grown over the years by reading the signs of the times, interpreting the Spirit's work in the contextual realities of Asia, articulating a theological vision for being Church in Asia, and fixing pastoral priorities of mission. This was done in the General Assemblies and through the various institutes and workshops organized by the different offices of the federation. The theological thinking of the FABC entered substantially in the deliberations of the synod, to a greater extent than expected.

Unfortunately, as some participants remarked, the synod did not have among its experts the best Asian theologians. The Synodal Secretariate, with its bureaucratic curial structure and approach, failed to enlist the services of some of a number theologians who have made remarkable contributions to the local churches of Asia. The Synod for Asia deserved better. I hope this failure will not be repeated. Some have suggested that the local churches or episcopal conferences should appoint the theologians of the synod.

We need to remember that even a pastorally oriented synod needs to be theologically supported. A pastoral vision and its priorities need sound theological support rooted in the substance of our faith. Theology is involved in our giving reason and account of our hope. Cardinal Darmaatmadja, one of the presidents of the synod, referred to theology and the need for good theologians in the concluding speech. He said, "For reliability, renewal and development of the Church we need good theologians to do careful and creative theological reflection" (*L'Osservatore Romano*, June 17, 1998, p. 11). In case of disagreement, he suggests rightly the way of dialogue, "dialogue in a spirit of love and mutual trust is necessary so that differences do not result in divisions but rather become a path to growth and renewal" (ibid.).

The participants of the synod spoke of the encouragement to be given to theologians to develop an inculturated theology responsive to Asian realities and to theologize with courage faithfulness to the Word of God, the living tradition of the Church, a sincere fidelity to the magisterium and sensitivity to pastoral situations. This requires that theological positions are sound in doctrine. Sometimes one is irked by the loaded negative phrase "overseeing the work of theologians" by Church authorities. It seems to be an expression of compulsive anxiety. If theology is done in cooperation and dialogue with the pastors of the Church, and as a *diakonia* sensitive and responsive to the pastoral realities, the emphasis would be on a living theology that really responds to the realities of the continent for the mission of the Church, a demand that pastors and the whole Church can make on theology and the theologians. In the work of FABC, there has been a marvelous cooperation between theologians and bishops. Such is the case in many bishops' conferences. Differences and conflicts are sorted out in a spirit of dialogue and cooperation without the weight of juridical "overseeing" structures. If the Church is a *communio*, a *koinonia* sent on *diakonia*, we need facilities for dialogue and an ethos of trust rather than juridical structures of "overseeing and monitoring," which evoke suspicion and prejudice.

In Asia, and for that matter in the whole Church, theology is becoming a work of bishops and men and women theologians, not only priests and religious but also lay. Anyone who teaches faith, be it a bishop, a priest, a religious, or a lay person, man or woman, is giving a reason and an account of the hope we have. It means he or she theologizes in a basic sense of explaining and communicating the meaningfulness of our faith. I would say that a bishop or a pastor in a parish or any Christian who does not theologize in this sense will not teach the faith properly. This of course presupposes the primary way of communicating faith through the witness of life and action. One wholesome feature of theology in Asia is that it is not an abstract theology unrelated to the contextual realities. It is a theology of a Church in dialogue and in mission. In the thinking of the FABC, the Church fulfils its mission in the triple dialogue with the poor, cultures, and religions. This triple dialogue experience is the *locus theologicus* in Asia. Such an approach was recognized in the synod.

In the synod, the predominant perception and understanding of theology was that it is a ministry in the Church, and it is a work done in cooperation and dialogue with the pastors, to respond to the demands of the mission. There was also the other perception on the part of a few, including some members of Roman dicasteries, that the work of theologians needs careful watching and overseeing. We wonder what gestalt of theology this supposes! Is theology primarily something that needs monitoring and overseeing, or is it something that needs promoting and strengthening in the Church's life and mission as a work of *koinonia* and *diakonia*?

The Kingdom and Theology

The perspective of the Kingdom figures in the *Lineamenta*, the *Instrumentum Laboris* and the *Message* of the synod. In Asian theology, in the FABC, in India, the theology of the Kingdom receives prominence in so far as it is the central message of Jesus as given in the Synoptic Gospels. It helps toward a broader understanding of the mission of the Church as the mission of Christ. It helps to expand the areas of mission in fresh and creative ways. The Kingdom, announced and inaugurated in the person and ministry of Jesus, becomes the focus of the mission of the Church. The Church is a sign, a sacrament and servant of the Kingdom, and thus continues the mission of Christ. I am told that in the propositions there is hardly or no reference at all to the Kingdom. My hope is that in the Apostolic Exhortation the Kingdom will be a central perspective and focus. The Kingdom is not an invention of theologians or a theology of the Church. It is the central message and in a sense the theology of Jesus in the Gospels. The mission Christ entrusted to the Church is to announce the Kingdom, the creative, liberative, and redemptive love of God embracing all humankind and creation.

Being Church in Asia

The participants in the synod spoke again and again of the identity of the Church in Asia in terms of its being rooted in the Asian soil and of its having an Asian face. The Church has to be the "burning bush" for the Asian peoples, their religions, cultures, struggles, their history. Being Church in Asia goes beyond adaptation and translation and inculturation. As a community of disciples, the Church shares in the joys, pains, agonies, and hopes of its brothers and sisters in the continent. The Church is an insider and a participant in the contextual realities of Asia.

Such a Church is spontaneously present in all critical situations of the people's lives, especially when the rights of the poor and powerless are violated or threatened. It opts for a presence of solidarity with those who suffer. In some situations, the Church itself is part of the excluded and violated people. This presence supposes that Christian discipleship is lived in servanthood, in a kenosis and self-sacrificing love shorn of all triumphalism, and in the triple dialogue with the poor, cultures, and religions. In this way the Church learns to be itself, a Church in Asia and a Church of Asia. Its very identity becomes its witness and mission to serve and love, to build, to reconcile, to work for peace and harmony, to promote and strengthen a dialogue of life with people of other faiths, to live its solidarity with the poor. In this process, the Church becomes not only a Church with the poor and for the poor but also a Church of the poor.

Basic Ecclesial and Basic Human Communities

In the synod, building basic ecclesial communities was often stressed. There was little mention of building basic human communities. But one important apostolic purpose of basic ecclesial communities is to build, serve, and strengthen basic human communities. To be Church in Asia, we must join others—all our brothers and sisters of other faiths and people of good will—in basic human communities. I was happy that in his concluding address Cardinal Darmaatmadja mentioned the work of building basic human communities. We do it together with the followers of other faiths and help build a "religious culture," a "culture of love," and a "culture of life," all of which is opposed to religious indifference, the culture of competition and violence, and the culture of death (cf. *L'Osservatore Romano*, June 17, 1998, p. 11). Building basic human communities is a demand of the Church's mission and an authentic sign of being Church in Asia.

In many Asian countries, the churches are doing this work, a ministry worthy of their mission. In and through this, proclamation also takes place. In India, we want to build a secular, democratic, participatory, and peaceful society and work for communal harmony, all of which is a work of building basic human communities of justice, peace, harmony, solidarity.

Globalization

Cardinal Julius Darmaatmadja, in his final summing up of the synod, speaks of the economies. He states that they have not fulfilled their promise. They have multiplied inequalities to the benefit of a small proportion of the population leaving many in poverty, and pushed to the margins of society—tribals, refugees, migrants, displaced persons.

The cardinal speaks of the invasion of a new culture as a result of the globalization of the world economy—we would call it a homogenized culture. Called to live, witness, and work in the triple dialogue with cultures, religions, and the poor, the Church faces a particular challenge in the invasive homogenizing culture linked to globalization. It is promoted by the modern media marked by "materialist, consumerist, and hedonist attitudes, fierce competitiveness, greed, and selfishness." In its prophetic role, the Church has to be a counterculture on behalf of which it affirms the manifold cultures of the Asian peoples, their identities as peoples, and the values these cultures embody, such as hospitality, sharing community, harmony, peace with nature, etc. Globalization is a complex phenomenon.

Clearly the synod could not go into it in a deeper way; but the perspective in which it was mentioned was very inadequate. No attention was given to the systemic nature of globalization and to its massive negative impact on the poor and the Third World countries themselves.

12

The Asian Churches' Awakening to Mission

JAMES H. KROEGER

"This is a time of grace when the Church in Asia is called to a fresh missionary outreach" was the enthusiastic headline for a newspaper article reporting the opening of the Asian Synod in Rome in April 1998.[1] As Pope John Paul II noted in his homily at the synod's inaugural Eucharist, the continental synods formed an integral part of the "launch of the new evangelization for the new millennium."[2] The pope asserted that for Asia "the new evangelization calls for respectful attention to 'Asian realities' and healthy discernment in their regard." The pontiff set forth the synod's vision and agenda: "Ours is the task of writing new chapters of Christian witness in every part of the world and in Asia."[3]

The Post-Synodal Apostolic Exhortation *Ecclesia in Asia* (*EA*) notes that the month-long, multifaceted synod was "a moment of special grace" (no. 3) and "an ardent affirmation of faith in Jesus Christ the Savior" (no. 4). As the local Churches of Asia gathered in Rome, "the Synod Fathers sought to discern the principal areas of mission for the Church in Asia as she crosses the threshold of the new millennium" (no. 18). What are the most significant signposts for mission to be gleaned from *EA*? How does *EA* "discern the Spirit's word to the Churches in Asia" (no. 51)?

Asian Realities

As noted earlier, the pope's homily at the inaugural Eucharist of the synod called for "respectful attention to 'Asian realities' and a healthy discernment in their regard." *EA* devotes its entire first chapter to an exploration of the concrete situation of contemporary Asia—its religious, cultural, economic, social, political, and historical realities (nos. 5–9). This inductive approach, characteristic of current Asian theological reflection, mirrors the method and experience of the Federation of Asian Bishops' Conferences. The Asian Church accepts that "a critical awareness of the diverse and complex realities of Asia is essential if the People of God on the continent are to respond to God's will for them in the new evangelization" (no. 5).

As *EA* notes, "Asia is the earth's largest continent and is home to nearly two-thirds of the world's population"; its many peoples are "heirs to ancient cultures, religions, and traditions." One is amazed "at the sheer size of Asia's population and at the intricate mosaic of its many cultures, languages, beliefs, and traditions."

Asia is "the cradle of the world's major religions" and "the birthplace of many . . . spiritual traditions" (no. 6). Economically, socially, and politically, "situations on the Asian continent are very diverse, defying any simple classification" (no. 7). *EA* highlights various concrete pastoral concerns: rapid change, migration, nuclear power, tourism, population growth, poverty, women, and a host of additional challenges.

This world of Asia is a diverse, rich, complex, challenging field of mission. Inserted within Asia's life-realities, the local Churches of Asia have but one ambition: "to continue his [Christ's] mission of service and love, so that all Asians 'may have life and have it abundantly'" (no. 50). Thanks to the theological-pastoral insights of the Second Vatican Council and its "new understanding of mission," the Church has "the framework of a new commitment" for mission in the Asian context (no. 9).

Theological Foundations

Three chapters of *EA*, focusing on Jesus and the Spirit, describe a type of "doctrinal" orientation to the Church's Asian mission. *EA* builds upon the Trinitarian foundations of mission found in Vatican II: all mission "is revealed only within the communion of life and action of the Trinity" (no. 12).

The mission and saving action of Jesus "has its origin in the communion of the Godhead" (no. 12). The Holy Spirit "is an absolutely vital part of the mystery of Jesus and of the salvation which he brings" (no. 15). In a word, *EA* asserts that Christology is necessarily integrated with pneumatology as well as Trinitarian faith. It is the "uniqueness of Christ which gives him an absolute and universal significance" (no. 14); one cannot "separate the activity of the Holy Spirit from that of Jesus the Savior" (no. 16). Jesus and the Spirit are only adequately comprehended with the "Trinity's plan of salvation" (no. 15); there are no two parallel economies of salvation.

The thematic of "gift" is a creative optic frequently found in these theological chapters of *EA*. Jesus the Savior is a gift to Asia; this faith-gift is to be both appropriated and proclaimed. "The Church's faith in Jesus is a gift received and a gift to be shared; it is the greatest gift which the Church can offer to Asia" (no. 10). "Only if the People of God recognize the gift that is theirs in Christ will they be able to communicate that gift to others through proclamation and dialogue" (no. 31; cf. no. 20). The Church in Asia must ask itself a probing question: how do we "share with our Asian brothers and sisters what we treasure as the gift containing all gifts, namely, the Good News of Jesus Christ?" (no. 19).

Proclaiming the Christian faith-gift meets unique challenges, particularly in the "multi-ethnic, multi-religious, and multi-cultural situation of Asia" (no. 21). Asia has its indigenous religions, soteriologies, and savior figures (cf. nos. 14, 19–20). This reality demands a humble, dialogical stance on the part of the Church: "Proclamation is prompted not by sectarian impulse nor the spirit of proselytism nor any sense of superiority" (no. 20; cf. nos. 4, 31, 46). And yet, this genuine respect and reverence for the Church's dialogue partners "does not eliminate the need for the explicit proclamation of the Gospel in its fullness" (no. 20;

cf. no. 31). By its very identity the Church is "a community aflame with mission-ary zeal to make Jesus known, loved and followed" (no. 19).

Affirming the relevance of Jesus for Asia (nos. 1, 9, 10, 18, 50) demands a particular approach to proclamation. The Church "needs to follow a pedagogy which will introduce people step by step to the full appreciation of the mystery." It should employ "narrative methods akin to Asian cultural forms" and follow "an evocative pedagogy, using stories, parables, and symbols so characteristic of Asian methodology in teaching." In a word, the Church must "evangelize in a way that appeals to the sensibilities of Asian peoples" (no. 20). Engaging Asian peo-ples, their cultures and religions (i.e., FABC's triple dialogue) demands genuine commitment to inculturation (nos. 20–23) and interreligious dialogue (nos. 29–31).

A Missionary Community

The longest section of *EA* (nos. 24–49) focuses on the Church and its mission in the vast Asian continent. Four main themes are dealt with: Church as Communion for Mission (nos. 24–28), Dialogue (nos. 29–31), Human Promotion (nos. 32–41), and Agents of Evangelization (nos. 42–49). *EA* presents a vision as well as concrete approaches for mission; these emerge from a particular faith-stance: "The question is not whether the Church has something essential to say to the men and women of our time, but how she can say it clearly and convincingly" (no. 29). *EA* recognizes "the pressing need of the local Churches in Asia to present the mystery of Christ to their peoples according to their cultural patterns and ways of thinking" (no. 20).

"Communion Ecclesiology" finds strong expression in *EA*. The Church is a "privileged place of encounter" between God and people; its first purpose is "to be the sacrament of the inner union of the human person with God." It is also "the sacrament of the unity of the human race." This means that "communion and mis-sion are inseparably connected [and] they interpenetrate and mutually imply each other." Communion is "both the source and fruit of mission." In short, "commun-ion gives rise to mission and mission is accomplished in communion" (no. 24).

The Church in Asia promotes internal communion and participation on many levels: with the Successor of Peter, among various sister local Churches, dioceses, basic ecclesial communities ("a positive feature of the Church's evangelizing ac-tivity"), renewal movements, the Catholic Eastern Churches, other Christian Churches (cf. nos. 25–27). Internal communion emanates outward toward other groups throughout Asia: the variety of peoples, cultures, and religions with whom the Church shares life (no. 25), Churches and peoples in Mainland China, North Korea, and the ex-Soviet territories of Asia (no. 28). Regional and continental as-sociations of bishops that are organized to foster communion (e.g., the FABC) are recognized and praised (no. 26), even though their profound insights are never di-rectly quoted.

An inherent demand of "communion ecclesiology" is dialogue. This "desire for dialogue . . . is not simply a strategy for peaceful coexistence among peoples; it is an essential part of the Church's mission, . . . a veritable vocation for the

Church" (no. 29). A particularly helpful section is devoted to interreligious dialogue (no. 31), seen as "a part of the Church's evangelizing mission, an expression of the mission *ad gentes*."

The advent of the new millennium offers the Church "a great opportunity for interreligious dialogue and for meetings with the leaders of the great world religions." Following the lead of *Nostra Aetate*, "the Magna Carta of interreligious dialogue for our times," the Church in Asia is called to a double fidelity: to affirm its "belief that the fullness of salvation comes from Christ alone" and to gladly acknowledge "whatever is true and holy in the religious traditions of Buddhism, Hinduism, and Islam as a reflection of that Truth which enlightens all people." Interreligious dialogue seeks "mutual advancement . . . [and] the elimination of prejudice, intolerance, and misunderstandings" (no. 31).

Dialogue demands will only increase with passing years. Persons must be formed to have "a mature and convinced Christian faith," which qualifies them "to engage in genuine interreligious dialogue." They need to be "deeply immersed in the mystery of Christ . . . [and] happy in their faith community." The call to dialogue requires the Church in Asia "to provide suitable models of interreligious dialogue." In dialogue it is imperative "to revitalize prayer and contemplation" and to give witness to "the great Christian traditions of asceticism and mysticism" (no. 31).

The entire sixth chapter treats human promotion and Church social teaching. Striving to build a "civilization of love," the Church views all human development not only as a "technical or economic question; it is fundamentally a human and moral question" (no. 32). An integral, holistic approach to evangelization is employed, encompassing the areas of human dignity (no. 33), preferential love of the poor (no. 34), health care (no. 36), education (no. 37), peacemaking (no. 38), globalization (no. 39), foreign debt (no. 40), and the environment (no. 41). In these diverse fields, the Church resists "the culture of death" in accord with its vision of "the Gospel of Life" (no. 35).

Agents of Evangelization

Chapter VII, entitled "Witnesses to the Gospel," focuses on the Church's missionary identity in Asia. The Church strives to be a credible witness, because "people today put more trust in witnesses than in teachers, in experience than in teaching, and in life and action than in theories." In the Asian context, "people are more persuaded by holiness of life than by intellectual argument" (no. 42). *EA* asserts that it is a "genuinely religious person [who] readily wins respect and a following in Asia" (no. 23).

Gospel witness in Asia needs holy men and women who themselves are "on fire with the love of Christ and burning with zeal to make him known more widely, loved more deeply, and followed more closely." Why? "A fire can only be lit by something that is itself on fire"; Christian witnessing demands "a true missionary spirituality of prayer and contemplation" (no. 23). Asian peoples, especially the youth, manifest a "deep thirst for spiritual values" (no. 6). In a word, living Christian mission in Asia incorporates—in fact, demands—"contemplative action and active contemplation" (no. 23).

EA addresses a variety of gospel witnesses: pastors (no. 43), religious and missionaries (no. 44), theologians (no. 22), laity (no. 45), families (no. 46), young people (no. 47), and those whose apostolate is social communications, "the Areopagus of the modern age" (no. 48). Striking insights are often presented: "People in Asia need to see the clergy not just as charity workers and institutional administrators but as men whose minds and hearts are set on the deep things of the Spirit" (no. 43). "The Synod Fathers were most concerned that the Church should be a participatory Church in which no one feels excluded, and they judged the wider participation of women in the life and mission of the church in Asia to be an especially pressing need" (no. 45).

Asia's Missionaries

The role of missionaries, past and present, is often highlighted in the Apostolic Exhortation. Words of encouragement and gratitude are frequent (nos. 20, 42, 44, 50). The synod participants took advantage of the occasion "to express in a very special way their gratitude to all the missionaries, men and women, religious and lay, foreign and local, who brought the message of Jesus Christ and the gift of faith" (no. 20).

Mission is never completed or fully realized; it demands continuous revitalization. Thus, while recognizing the initiatives and accomplishments already achieved, the pope declares: "I cannot fail to urge the Church in Asia to send forth missionaries, even though she herself needs laborers in the vineyard"; missionaries are encouraged "not to waver in their missionary commitment . . . [and] to renew their zeal to proclaim the saving truth of Christ" (no. 44). *EA* calls upon "the great host of Asian martyrs, old and new . . ., to teach the Church in Asia what it means to bear witness" (no. 49).

The role of Asia's local Churches in mission is elaborated and highlighted. Recalling that Vatican II "taught clearly that the entire Church is missionary and that the work of evangelization is the duty of the whole People of God" (no. 42), *EA* rejoices that "in several Asian countries, missionary institutes of apostolic life have recently been founded in recognition of the Church's missionary character and of the responsibility of the particular Churches in Asia to preach the Gospel to the whole world" (no. 44).

John Paul II then reiterates the strong affirmation of the synod (Proposition 28), which recommends "the establishment within each local Church of Asia, where such do not exist, of missionary societies of apostolic life, characterized by their special commitment to the mission *ad gentes, ad exteros,* and *ad vitam*" (no. 44). Such a concrete initiative for evangelization "is sure to bear abundant fruit not only in the Churches which receive the missionaries but also in the Churches which send them" (no. 44).

Asia already has six such indigenous missionary societies of apostolic life; they exist in India, Korea, the Philippines, and Thailand. All founded in the wake of Vatican II, these Asian-born missionary communities are The Mission Society of the Philippines (1965); Missionary Society of Saint Thomas the Apostle [India] (1968); Catholic Foreign Mission Society of Korea (1975); Missionary Society of the Heralds of Good News [India] (1984); Mission Society of Thailand (1990); Lorenzo Ruiz Mission Society [Philippines] (1997).[4]

Unique Challenges to Mission in Asia

Ecclesia in Asia is an important signpost for the Asian Church's missionary pilgrimage in the new century. The Asian Synod had surfaced crucial mission questions facing local Churches in Asia. *EA* reflects several of these pastoral-missionary concerns.

The question of Jesus' "Asianness" surfaced in various discussions: "Jesus is often perceived as foreign to Asia. It is paradoxical that most Asians tend to regard Jesus—born on Asian soil—as a Western rather than an Asian figure" (no. 20). "It is indeed a mystery why the Savior of the world, born in Asia, has until now remained largely unknown to the people of the continent" (no. 2). To address and overcome this reality, the Church must open itself to "new and surprising ways in which the face of Jesus might be presented in Asia" (no. 20). How can Jesus be effectively proclaimed—bearing an "Asian face"?

The subject of mission and *religious freedom* arises, because in various places in Asia "Christians are not allowed to practice their faith freely" (no. 8); "explicit proclamation is forbidden and religious freedom is denied or systematically restricted" (no. 23). Christians are forced "to live their faith in the midst of restrictions or even the total denial of freedom" (no. 28). Governments are enjoined to "guarantee religious freedom for all their citizens" (no. 28), assure "immunity from coercion" (no. 23) in religious matters, and recognize "the right to freedom of conscience and religion and the other basic human rights" (no. 34).

A comparison between *EA*'s statements on mission and the reflections of Asian bishops on the same theme reveals many similarities—and some divergences (e.g., the role of dialogue and the explicit proclamation within evangelization). Since 1974 in its document "Evangelization in Modern Day Asia," the FABC has promoted the local Church's triple dialogue with Asia's peoples, cultures, and religions. This vision is found in *EA* (cf. nos. 1, 15, 18, 20, 21, 24), although with some nuanced differences. Again, the FABC pastoral priorities enunciated over the years, particularly the focus on the family, women and the girl child, youth, ecology, and the displaced (cf. FABC VI:15) are also highlighted by *EA* (nos. 34, 37, 41, 46, 47, etc.). The FABC itself is mentioned (nos. 2, 3, 26, 31), though none of its fine work is directly quoted or even noted in the copious endnotes.

The missionary theme of *inculturation* received much attention during the synod, and certain particular areas were identified as requiring concentrated focus, such as "theological reflection, liturgy, the formation of priests and religious, catechesis, and spirituality" (no. 21). Central to inculturating the faith is the biblical word, the message of salvation, the sacred text. Sacred Scripture is proposed as "the basis for all missionary proclamation, catechesis, preaching, and styles of spirituality" (no. 22). As to the criteria for authentic inculturation, *EA* notes, "The test of true inculturation is whether people become more committed to their Christian faith because they perceive it more clearly with the eyes of their own culture" (no. 22).

The Christian virtue of *compassion* appears repeatedly in *EA* (e.g., nos. 11, 12, 14, 20, 45, 51). The Apostolic Exhortation is correct in expressing the Church's mission in terms of this appealing focus. Presenting Jesus as "the Compassionate Friend of the Poor" (no. 20) will find a resonance and reception among Asians. In the Church's mission of love and service, women evangelizers contribute greatly "to bringing the compassionate Jesus, the healer and reconciler, to Asian people, especially the poor and marginalized" (no. 45). In Jesus, the God-Man who saves, "Divine compassion had never been so immediately accessible" (no. 11).

As the missionary Church in Asia enters the new millennium, it faces some very demanding challenges. *EA* highlights some important apostolates: women (nos. 7, 34, 45), youth (nos. 6, 47), nuclear power (nos. 7, 38), peacemaking and reconciliation (no. 38), globalization (no. 39), foreign debt (no. 40), and the environment (no. 41). The authenticity of the Church's "mission of service and love" (no. 50) will indeed be tested: will it produce "a great harvest of faith . . . in this vast and vital continent" (no. 1) of Asia?

Ecclesia in Asia concludes, as it begins, on a clear note of optimism and gratitude: "Blessed be God for the peoples of Asia, so rich in their diversity yet one in their yearning for peace and fullness of life" (no. 50). With committed faith, "the Church in Asia joyfully makes her pilgrim way into the Third Millennium" (no. 50). "Mary, model of all disciples and bright Star of Evangelization . . ., look tenderly upon the Church of your Son planted on Asian soil. . . . O Mary, Mother of the New Creation and Mother of Asia, pray for us, your children, now and always!" (no. 51).

In this mood of gratitude and optimism, the local Churches of Asia accept the Holy Father's gift: *Ecclesia in Asia.* Its contents are a mixture of the old and the new (cf. Mt 13:52), a blending of missiology "from below" and "from above," a summation of Asian reflection and insights of the Vatican II era, a presentation of the mission agenda for Asia's faith-communities, a program for evangelization in the new millennium.

All in all, *EA* is a much appreciated gift. Its treasures need opening in the coming years and decades; its dream for the Church—God's holy people—beckons implementation; its theme—abundant life in Jesus the Savior—requires contemplative action. Jesus' Asian disciples joyfully affirm that the Holy Spirit who moved upon Asia in times past, "moves now among Asian Christians, strengthening the witness of their faith among the peoples, cultures, and religions of the continent" (no. 18).

Contemplating God's salvific deeds and wonders during the Easter Vigil liturgy, the Universal Church proclaims in the *Exultet*: "Rejoice, O Mother Church!" In similar fashion, the local Churches in Asia proclaim God's marvels in their midst; they joyfully affirm the Asian Synod event as a "celebratory remembering of the Asian roots of Christianity" (no. 4). They pray that the proclamation and subsequent internalization of *Ecclesia in Asia* will confirm the Church in its servant mission to bring Christ's love and abundant life (Jn 10:10) to Asia and her peoples. They invoke the renewing, transforming action of the Holy Spirit, "the prime agent of evangelization" (no. 17), to accompany them in becoming authentic witnesses. *Veni, Creator Spiritus*!

Appendix: Introducing Six Asian *Ad Gentes* Missionary Societies

The indigenous missionary initiatives of Asia's local Churches received a very encouraging endorsement both during the Asian Synod and in *EA*. This positive— even enthusiastic—recognition of the contribution to *ad gentes* mission that has been made by Asian-born missionary institutes is cause for rejoicing, particularly among the Asian mission societies themselves.

On the synod floor during the Ninth General Congregation (April 24, 1998), the FABC Assistant Secretary General, Father Edward Malone, M.M., spoke of mission realities in Asia and the praiseworthy contributions of many international institutes of men and women. Then he added, "I wish to highlight a unique and essential form of missionary response—missionary society of apostolic life" (MSAL). Malone noted that six such societies of men have emerged in Asia.

Malone pointed out that these groups have a mission charism that is "*ad gentes, ad exteros,* and *ad vitam*." Specifically, *ad gentes* because they address those who have not yet heard the salvific and liberating Good News of Jesus Christ; *ad exteros* in so far as they work among people outside their own cultural-language group and nation; and *ad vitam* because they make a life-long commitment to this unique form of missionary witness. All are focused on "apostolic" life; they do not pronounce "religious" vows, though they bind themselves permanently (*ad vitam*) for the *ad gentes* and *ad exteros* mission.

"The number of societies of apostolic life which are working in Asia is large," Malone continued. "Now it is Asia's turn to give, to be a continent of missionary hope." The gift that such societies are makes them "bridges of communion" and brings many benefits: "Asians evangelizing Asians; the emergence of missionary local Churches; the strengthening of bonds of communion among the Churches of Asia and of communion and filial oneness with the See of Peter."[5]

The most direct and concrete mission initiative taken by the synod came in Proposition 28: "This synod recommends the establishment within each local Church of Asia, where such do not exist, of missionary societies of apostolic life, characterized by their commitment exclusively for the mission *ad gentes, ad exteros,* and *ad vitam*." Pope John Paul II took special note of the synod discussion and recommendation; he incorporated this theme into his "Message for World Mission Sunday," celebrated on October 18, 1998.[6]

Ecclesia in Asia builds directly upon the contribution of several voices and mission recommendations expressed in the synod hall.[7] *EA* examines the role of

the "consecrated life and missionary societies" in the missionary activity of the
Church; the final key paragraph reads as follows:

> In the context of the communion of the universal Church, I cannot fail to
> urge the Church of Asia to send forth missionaries, even though she her-
> self needs laborers in the vineyard. I am glad to see that in several Asian
> countries missionary institutes of apostolic life have recently been
> founded in recognition of the Church's missionary character and of the
> responsibility of the particular Churches in Asia to preach the Gospel to
> the whole world. The Synod Fathers recommended "the establishment
> within each local Church of Asia, where such do not exist, of missionary
> societies of apostolic life, characterized by their special commitment to
> the mission *ad gentes, ad exteros,* and *ad vitam.*" Such an initiative is
> sure to bear abundant fruit not only in the Churches which receive the
> missionaries but also in the Churches which send them. (no. 44)

Below is a short synopsis of the history, charisms, statistics, membership, and apostolic works of each of Asia's missionary societies.

The Mission Society of the Philippines

Although the formal establishment of the Mission Society of the Philippines
(MSP) dates back to the mid-1960s, the seeds of its foundation are found in the
four hundred years of interaction between the Filipinos and Christianity (1565–
1965). History identifies 1565 as the beginning of the effective colonization and
systematic evangelization of the Philippine Islands. Since then the country has
had a long history of receiving missionaries from various parts of the world.

Early MSP Beginnings

The seed of faith needs to sprout and grow. The strong interest in mission among
the local hierarchy led them to state on Pentecost Sunday: "We decided to set
aside the present year of 1959 as Mission Year in the Philippines." The bishops
desired a mission awakening and hoped that "it be said of the Filipino nation . . .
that they gave freely what they freely received, and that they took their full share
in the work of bringing the joy and peace, the justice and mercy of Christ to the
peoples of Asia."

Five years later, in 1964, during the Filipino bishops' annual meeting, Bishop
Epifanio Surban pursued the idea of having a Philippine Mission Center as a response to the local Church's missionary task. In addition, Bishop Surban proposed the establishment of a Philippine Foreign Mission Society composed of
Filipino diocesan priests. The proposal was enthusiastically and unanimously accepted. Bishop Surban was chosen to be the first National Director of the enterprise; he was requested to concretize his proposal.

The Filipino hierarchy saw that the fourth centenary of the evangelization of
the Philippines (1565–1965) was a golden opportunity to launch a new evangeli-

zation and to form an indigenous mission society. Their January 29, 1965, pastoral statement, which formally began the project, declared:

> Desirous to fulfill our divine commission "to preach the Gospel to every creature," we, the Catholic Hierarchy of the Philippines, herewith declare our firm determination to share the light of faith with our . . . neighbors. It is our conviction that we as a Christian Nation have reached a mature stage in our four centuries of development and that we are prepared to assume the responsibility of such maturity. We, therefore, proclaim officially our intention to undertake a national effort to orient our people to the Missions. To achieve this and to express in the concrete our gratitude to God for the gift of our Faith we will organize the Foreign Mission Society of the Philippines.

Initial MSP Growth

A handful of mission-minded Filipino diocesan priests volunteered to be pioneer members of the newly established society. Although there have been numerous growth pains and uncertainties, the society has continued. It has experienced its own "dark moments of history" and shared "a lack of sense of direction [that] nearly caused a dissolution." Several bishops have continued their strong support of MSP; notable among them are Archbishop Gaudencio Rosales and Jaime Cardinal Sin. It has been often affirmed: "God is not yet through with MSP—He has only begun."

The official or statutory name of the society is Mission Society of the Philippines (MSP), but it is often popularly referred to as "Fil-Mission." As a mission community, it has passed several tests of growth. From a handful of volunteer members, its number has slowly increased. It averages about four ordinations each year and in 2000 has sixty-five permanent members.

Over the decades, the majority membership has changed from volunteer diocesan priests (at its early beginnings) to "true, blue-blooded MSP" members (priests who entered as seminarians and received a solid MSP-designed missionary formation). MSP continues to welcome diocesan priests as associates in mission. The society defines its charism in these words: "In love and gratitude to the Father, ours is a joyful missionary spirit flowing from deep union with Christ through Mary and in the power of the Holy Spirit, willing to spend and be spent in sharing His Gospel to all."

Current Status

From its beginnings, MSP has desired pontifical status. Rome requested the MSP to begin on the local level. Jaime Cardinal L. Sin approved the society's statutes on January 29, 1988, giving juridical personality to MSP as a Society of Apostolic Life of Diocesan Right, and established it as such by virtue of the Decree of Establishment on April 25, 1989. Membership in the MSP is open to natural-born Filipinos; the society also welcomes Filipino diocesan priests as associate members to serve in foreign mission.

MSP considers its mission apostolate in *de jure* and *de facto* mission territories as its foremost duty and privilege. Although MSP was established with a strong interest in Asia, the movement of the Spirit has also led MSP to work in Oceania and the Pacific Region. Presently, MSP missionaries are working in Taiwan, Hong Kong, Thailand, South Korea, Japan, Papua New Guinea, Solomon Islands, and New Zealand.

Mission Preferences

MSP seeks to choose locations for mission that reflect its statutory mission commitment. This is an option for (1) the incarnation of the Church among non-Christian believers through evangelization; (2) supportive evangelical service in favor of young churches until they attain ecclesial maturity; and, (3) auxiliary apostolic ministry for the renewal of churches rendered unable to catechize their own people until they achieve ministerial self-reliance.

Looking forward in mission in Asia has enabled MSP to focus on five areas, namely (1) working for the cause of justice and peace; (2) upholding the sacredness of life, human dignity, and the integrity of creation; (3) promoting interreligious dialogue; (4) engaging in inculturation; and, (5) proclaiming the gospel. These are not new issues, but they will continue to be the path of mission for MSP in the next millennium.

MSP views its primary commitment as mission *ad gentes*. It affirms its mission "to proclaim the Gospel to all peoples even those beyond our present care." There are standing invitations from Pakistan, Kenya, Tanzania, West Indies, Samoa, and Uganda. The desire to expand is strong; however, there is a shortage of personnel. The society quickly adds, "This should not discourage us to go on and carry out our mission commitment."

The Missionary Society of St. Thomas the Apostle

The Missionary Society of Saint Thomas the Apostle (MST) in India is an indigenous missionary institute of the Syro-Malabar Archiepiscopal Church. It was founded on February 22, 1968, by Mar Sebastian Vayalil, the first bishop of the diocese of Palai, India. As a society of apostolic life, it has the sole purpose of "mission *ad gentes*" in territories and among peoples in which the Church has not yet taken root.

Early History

With the reorganization of the Syro-Malabar Church in 1923 under native bishops, there was a tremendous religious renewal and missionary awakening in this apostolic Church. After the independence of India in 1947, there was an increase of missionary vocations. About 60 percent of the vocations that aided mission in India at this juncture originated from the Syro-Malabar Church. This response came quite spontaneously.

All the missionaries carried on their apostolate in the tradition of the *sui juris* church where they labored. This predicament urged Mar Sebastian Vayalil to embark upon a historic endeavor to begin a new missionary society. It would carry out missionary activity under its own banner and in a manner consistent with the heritage of the Syro-Malabar Church. In 1960 Vayalil sought the permission of the Holy See to found a missionary society. He received a positive response from the Holy See in 1963, and by 1964 he submitted a draft constitution. He conscientiously kept Popes John XXIII and Paul VI, as well as relevant Congregations of the Roman Curia, informed of his progress. Vayalil actively sought and received their guidance and encouragement.

Foundation of MST

On the advice of the Holy See, the proposed society began as a Pious Union of Diocesan Clergy in 1965. Pope Paul VI congratulated Vayalil during his *ad limina* visit in 1966 and assured him of his patronage for the society.

In 1967 the Holy See approved the statutes of the nascent society and authorized Bishop Vayalil to promulgate them and erect a pious union of diocesan clergy as the Missionary Society of St. Thomas the Apostle. The formal foundation of MST came on February 22, 1968, at Melampara, near Bharananganam. It was witnessed by Mar Sebastian Vayalil, Maximilian Cardinal de Fürstenberg (Prefect of the Congregation for the Oriental Churches), Joseph Caprio (Apostolic Pro-Nuncio to India), prelates of the Syro-Malabar Church, and a large number of clergy, religious, and laity.

During this foundation ceremony Cardinal Fürstenberg blessed and laid the foundation stone for the Central House and Minor Seminary complex of the society. Thus, the long cherished dream of Mar Sebastian Vayalil and the diocesan clergy of the Saint Thomas Christians became a reality.

MST Today

The society, which started functioning in 1968 with eighteen diocesan priests, has grown into a major missionary movement. In 2000 MST had 227 priest-members, 161 students-seminarians, 3 formation centers, and 3 mission regions.

On the occasion of the silver jubilee of the society in 1993 the Syro-Malabar bishops again owned the society through a joint pastoral letter; they exhorted the faithful to extend support to its missionary activities. On July 3, 1997, the revised constitutions of the society were approved by the Church, and the society was recognized as a "Society of Apostolic Life of Major Archiepiscopal Right" in accordance with the Code of Canon Law for the Oriental Churches, no. 572 (corresponding to "Pontifical Right" in the Roman Church).

Mission Regions of MST

The *ad gentes* mission activities of MST are found in the less Christianized regions of India and beyond. The first mission region entrusted to MST was the Apostolic Exarchate of Ujjain. Geographically, Ujjain is located in the state of Madhjapradesh in central India. The population is 90 percent Hindu, 8 percent

Muslim, and 2 percent Jains, Buddhists, and Christians. Responsive to the current socioeconomic and educational realities in the area, health care, charitable works, social development projects, and education are employed as the means of missionary contact. Mar Sebastian Vadakel, consecrated in 1998, serves as the second bishop of Ujjain.

In 1978 MST received the Mandya mission district, located in Karnataka in Kerala. Hindus make up 90 percent of the population, with Muslims as the second largest religious community. Agriculture is the main occupation of the people. A wide variety of development efforts are undertaken by MST, at times in collaboration with the government. There are also outreach services extended to slum dwellers and prisoners.

The largest MST mission territory is the Sangli Mission; it was entrusted to the MST in 1990. Education, health care programs, and AIDS awareness projects are sources of contact with the people. In 1995 MST took up the challenge of evangelization in Leh-Ladakh, known as the "Roof of the World"; it is a very challenging area for missionary activity. Three valiant MST missionaries serve in this area.

Mission *ad gentes* is the main criterion for MST in accepting mission works and regions. Following this principle, MST will accept missionary apostolates both inside and outside of India. It is noteworthy that over 60 percent of the missionaries in India are from the Syro-Malabar Archiepiscopal Church. MST has recently extended the scope of its work to the care of migrants; this is seen as an entry-point for *ad gentes* mission.

MST is grateful to God for the growth and positive impact of its society; it has been rendering dedicated service in difficult and even unwelcoming situations. MST believes it can contribute much to Asian countries; it is eager to cooperate with other Asian missionary institutes. The society has this fervent prayer: "May the Holy Spirit inspire and quicken us to live and propagate the message of Christ in the whole of Asia. Let the future be a millennium of Christ and the Church for Asia."

Catholic Foreign Mission Society of Korea

The Catholic Church in Korea began with a group of educated Koreans who studied Christian literature they obtained from Peking in 1777. Yi Sung Hun was baptized in Peking in 1783; upon his return to Seoul he soon converted many of his influential friends. So successful was the apostolate of these first converts that when James Chu, a Chinese priest, secretly entered Korea in 1794, he found four thousand Catholics, none of whom had ever seen a priest. By 1801, when Father Chu and three hundred other Christians were put to death for their faith, the Church had grown to ten thousand.

From the early beginnings, when Koreans accepted the gospel on their own, thanks to the inspiration of the Korean martyrs and the labors of countless missionaries, the Korean Church has grown steadily. The local Church also became

conscious of the need to move from being a receiving Church to becoming a sharing Church, which would contribute to the growth of a world Church.

Brief History

The Catholic Foreign Mission Society of Korea (KMS) traces its origins to late
1974 when a Korean preparation committee was established to explore the possible formation of a mission society. It was the dedicated efforts of Bishop John
Choi Jae-Sun that ultimately led to the establishment of the society by the Korean
Bishops' Conference on February 26, 1975.

A formation house was opened in early 1976. The first KMS priest was ordained in 1981. The initial sending ceremony was held on November 18, 1981,
and the first KMS missionary was sent to Papua New Guinea.

Other significant dates in KMS's history include the following: March 25,
1986, marked the first Oath Ceremony of the society for both temporary and final
commitment; February 12, 1988, saw the beginning of the Spiritual Formation
Year; April 5, 1990, was the first KMS sending ceremony for mission to the
Hshin-Chu Diocese in Taiwan; on January 7, 1992, the society began its Overseas
Training Program for seminarians; on December 19, 1996, the first KMS missionary was sent to Hong Kong and China.

Mission Vision

KMS has expressed its identity and spirit in several inspiring texts:

> The founding of this Society is a symbol of appreciation for the great
> grace which God has given to the Korean Church and our sense of re-
> sponsibility that the Church has for the evangelization of all peoples. Our
> Society is a sign of a mature Korean Church. We especially have a con-
> cern for the world Church, so we desire to devote ourselves to a life of
> mission service for all people. The Society wishes to respond to the
> needs of the Church especially the Asian Church and the intentions of
> the Congregation for the Evangelization of Peoples. Our preference is to
> bring the Gospel message to countries where the Gospel has not been
> proclaimed or evangelization has not yet been fully realized. . . .
>
> Taking the command of Jesus Christ, we desire to devote ourselves
> to the call of mission until the end of time all over the world. The goal of
> mission which we pursue is to gather into one the scattered children of
> God (Jn 11:52) and to advance the time when all people will worship the
> Father in spirit and truth (Jn 4:23). . . .
>
> Our Society desires to entrust its members to the care of our Blessed
> Mother, to model ourselves on the evangelical spirit of the Korean mar-
> tyrs who witnessed to Jesus even unto their death, and to devote our-
> selves to the work of evangelization for all people through the example
> of the Korean martyrs. We practice a life of prayer, service, and poverty,
> in order to be a witness to Jesus Christ, imitating the Apostle St. Paul as a
> model missionary. . . .

If charity is truly the spirit that animates the Korean Foreign Mission Society, the result will be unity. There can be no serious progress without unity. There can be no true unity, but only division, without charity. Charity will safeguard unity, and unity will safeguard all of us in fulfilling the divine purpose for which God created the Korean Foreign Mission Society. Only men of charity can be missioners. Only charity can be the spirit of our Society.

Current Statistics

In 2000 KMS had a total of sixty-six members of whom twenty-four priests and two deacons were in permanent oath. There are six major seminarians, seven spiritual formation year candidates, and twenty-seven temporary oath seminarians.

Geographically and apostolically, the twenty-four priest members are distributed in eight locations with a variety of commitments. Five members are located in the Seoul Center House; they serve as the leadership-administration of the society. Three missioners are assigned to the Suwon Formation House and one serves the Choam Catholic Church.

KMS members are in six countries outside of Korea. Four missioners are in Madang, Papua New Guinea; two labor in Hshin Chu, Taiwan; one is in language study in Hong Kong; Beijing is home for two members in language study; Auckland, New Zealand is the assignment for another missioner. Finally, four KMS priests are in renewal courses at the East Asian Pastoral Institute in Manila as they prepare for overseas mission placements.

In recent years KMS has opted to give much emphasis to both initial and continuing formation for mission. Its vision is expressed as follows:

Being based on the spirit of the Korean martyrs and the spirituality of our founder, which is poverty, gratitude, and charity, the purpose of our Foreign Mission Society is the training of members of the Society to realize a humble life style and to devise solidarity and development of a community in imitation of Christ. All are trained for mission by developing their intellectual abilities, good character, and intense spiritual life. . . .

In order to follow the spirituality of Preaching the Message of the 103 Korean martyrs, our Society's patrons, especially the first Korean priest and missionary, St. Andrew Kim, members are urged to read the biographies and study the lives of the martyrs and make pilgrimages to the martyrs' shrines every year.

Future Challenges

The year 2000 marked the Silver Jubilee of the Catholic Foreign Mission Society of Korea. In a renewed spirit of commitment to *ad gentes* mission in the new millennium, KMS enunciated four focused priorities:

(1) In response to the needs of the Church, especially the Asian Church, and the intention of the Congregation for the Evangelization of Peoples, the Korean

Foreign Mission Society plans to open new missions in Cambodia, Mongolia, Central and South Asia.

(2) The Korean Foreign Mission Society intends to cooperate with other mission societies and mission organizations in developing areas of mutual concern.

(3) The Korean Foreign Mission Society hopes to establish an Asian Mission Research Institute and a Center for Missionary Education.

(4) The Korean Foreign Mission Society will encourage the Church in Korea to be more mission-minded and open to proclaim the gospel to other areas in Asia by accepting diocesan priests through temporary membership.

Mission in the third millennium continues to inspire the missionary outreach of the local Church in Korea through its indigenous mission society.

Missionary Society of Heralds of Good News

The Missionary Society of Heralds of Good News is a Clerical Society of Apostolic Life of Pontifical Right. This society of priests was founded by Father Jose Kaimlett on October 14, 1984, in the Diocese of Eluru, India. The objective of the Heralds (HGN) is "training and supplying zealous, dedicated, hardworking, and saintly priests wherever there is need, especially due to shortage of local vocations in the Universal Church." Mary, Queen of Apostles, and Saint Joseph the Worker are the society's patrons.

Historical Overview

Father Jose Kaimlett, the HGN founder, was keenly aware of the shortage of priestly vocations all over the world. He believed that a clerical missionary society of apostolic life could be of great help to the needs of the Universal Church.

In December 1976 the Holy See decided to create the Diocese of Eluru with the territory carved out of the Diocese of Vijayawada. Father Kaimlett was requested to manage the separation and serve as the administrator of the new diocese. Later Bishop John Mulagada became the first ordinary of Eluru. Father Kaimlett went to study canon law in Rome. His journeys abroad brought him face to face with the priest shortage in many parts of the world, particularly in Western countries.

Father Kaimlett continued to dream of a male missionary institute. When he returned to serve the Diocese of Eluru, he received enthusiastic encouragement from Bishop Mulagada to pursue his vision. As a preliminary step he gathered like-minded persons together. Three priests and two seminarians expressed their willingness to join the apostolic endeavor.

On October 14, 1984, Bishop Mulagada placed his seal of approval on the Basic Constitution of the Institute. Less than four months later, on February 2, 1985, the pioneer members (the founder, three priests, and two seminarians) made their permanent commitment to the institute.

Additional dates of historical significance for the HGN are: May 5, 1991, Erection of the Missionary Institute of Heralds of Good News as a Clerical Missionary Society of Apostolic Life of Diocesan Right; November 2, 1994, Inauguration of the First Province of HGN, the South Indian Province; and May 5, 1999, HGN raised to the Pontifical Right by Pope John Paul II.

Current Situation

HGN Society has made rapid progress both in the area of personnel and on the level of apostolic activities. In fifteen years (1984–1999) its membership has increased to 109 permanently incorporated members, about half of whom work in India, the others labor abroad. The society has 607 seminarians at different levels of formation. All members are expected to contribute actively in vocation promotion activities.

Currently, HGN has nineteen houses (fifteen in India; four abroad), seven seminaries (two major; five minor), five schools, four service institutions, and two leprosy rehabilitation centers. The Heralds serve in twelve dioceses in India and in sixteen abroad (South Africa, Tanzania, Kenya, Uganda, Papua New Guinea, Italy, and the United States). The two major commitments of the society are in seminaries and social centers. Father Kaimlett also founded a female institute in 1992, known as the Sisters of Good News; they currently have seventy-five sisters serving in India and Italy.

Criteria for Placements

The Heralds admit that they have been blessed with numerous vocations: "We, as a responsible part of Mother Church, would like to make use of this divine providence for the benefit of the Universal Church."

The only criterion used in the selection of areas of work is "the need and earnestness of the request we receive from the local ordinaries." However, the society also insists that the local Churches that benefit from their services should underwrite—depending on their resources—some of the formation and retirement expenses of the missionaries.

The Future of HGN Mission in Asia

As an indigenous Asian mission society, HGN sees that "at the approach of the third millennium the Church in Asia is called to renew its understanding of evangelization, which, in fact, has acquired a greater urgency than in the past." HGN affirms that evangelization "consists of a complex reality and as such has many essential elements: witnessing to the Gospel, working for the values of the kingdom, struggle for human liberation and promotion, dialogue, the mutual sharing of God experience. . . ."

Members of the HGN note that "one of the priorities of the Church in Asia is the witness of life. . . . The first Christians preached the Gospel by the testimony of their lives. . . . There is no mission without adequate witnessing. Christian mission in Asia is a call for individual and community witnessing in *being* Christ-like as well as *doing* deeds which are Christ-like."

What does it mean to serve in mission in Asia? "The mission of the Church in Asia becomes more meaningful and effective when she identifies herself with suffering humanity. Hundreds of millions of people still live in inhuman poverty. Jesus' concern towards the hungry and the needy and His compassion and love for them must be a guiding principle for all of us. One should not forget that solidarity with the poor, involvement in their struggle for justice, reawakening the consciousness of the society to the needs of the poor, and works of charity are all means of expressing integral salvation, which God offers to humanity in Jesus Christ."

As an Asian missionary community, HGN asserts, "In this context of Asian realities the Church is carrying out its mission of salvation. Although the Church in Asia is numerically a small flock, she is called forth to transform every Asian reality through its mission of love and service."

Missionary Society of Thailand

The Missionary Society of Thailand traces its beginnings to its first priestly ordinations in the early 1990s. The society uses the initials MET from the French language, *Missions Etrangères de Thailande* in imitation of the Paris Foreign Mission Society (MEP—*Missions Etrangères de Paris*) that has labored for centuries in this part of Asia.

Historical Overview

In March 1987, the Superior of the Paris Foreign Mission Society in Thailand addressed a letter to the Thai Bishops' Conference suggesting the formation of a missionary group of Thai priests. They were to work with the Hill Tribe peoples in northern Thailand. The idea was already present in the mind of some bishops. The Thai Church needed such an initiative; there was a great demand among the Hill Tribe peoples themselves. The vision was favorably received by the bishops.

In 1989 Bishop Banchong Aribarg, the bishop's conference delegate for this missionary initiative, gathered all those directly concerned with the project. Of those present, an MEP missionary was to initiate something in the Major Seminary; a PIME (Pontifico Istituto Missioni Estere) priest was to contact religious congregations and laity.

At this time, four seminarians volunteered to become members of the society; some sisters and laypersons were also ready to join. One seminarian underwent some specific missionary formation. He was ordained on Pentecost 1990, and during the ceremony he received his mission cross from the Cardinal Archbishop of Bangkok. In January 1991 another ordination-missioning ceremony took place in Udorn diocese. MET sources attest: "We hold that these ordinations mark the foundation of the Missionary Society of Thailand."

These two pioneer members of MET continue to work among the Hmongs in northern Thailand. Additional missionary formation sessions were conducted in 1992, and when Cambodia reopened, MET sent a priest, two sisters, and a laywoman to work there.

MET began functioning without any definite constitution or structure in its early years. The project was under Bishop Banchong of the bishops' conference.

In 1995, the first provisional constitution was approved for three years. In 1996, the bishops appointed Jean Dantonel, MEP, as the first superior of MET. The constitutions were reviewed and again approved for three years by the bishops' conference. Bishop Banchong has retired and is replaced by Bishop Chamniern Sanitsukniran of Nakornsawan.

Current Statistics

MET is less than a decade old. Other than the superior, the society counts only three priests as full members. Six religious women from three congregations are associate members; five laypersons are with the MET. In 1999, a young priest was preparing to join MET; another seminarian had the consent of his bishop to join the society at his ordination in two years.

Among the members, two priests and two sisters work with the Hmongs in Northern Thailand; they have served this mission for eight years. Another priest, four sisters, and a laywoman work with the local Church in Cambodia. Two laywomen are at the PIME Center in Northern Thailand. Finally, two additional female lay catechists are in the northeast area of Thailand.

Much of the society's apostolate is missionary-pastoral work among the minorities in Thailand. All missioners have had to learn new languages; they collaborate with the local bishop for the formation of Christians and catechumens. Those laboring in Cambodia serve the needs of the local Church in education and catechesis.

Rationale of MET Apostolate

The MET constitution states that the society aims "to announce the Gospel to those who do not know Christ yet, both in Thailand and out of Thailand. . . . Our main aim is not so much to work *ad exteros* but rather to go *ad gentes*." There is a clear reason for this. The number of Thai Catholics has not increased for the last fifty years; in fact, it has decreased both in percentage and in absolute figures.

There is an urgent need to enkindle the missionary spirit within the Church in Thailand, inspiring priests and Christian communities to reach out to those who do not yet know Christ and the gospel. In addition, there are many areas within Thailand itself that demand of missioners a real change of culture, style of life, and language. For Thais from central Thailand to go and work in the north demands a true missionary transformation. Even within the central plain of Thailand, there are many groups not touched by the Church—the poor, people living in slums. This can be a direct area for missionary work.

In Thailand's neighboring countries, the number of priests and missionaries remains small and insufficient. A clear example is Cambodia. MET also looks with hope to the day when Laos will open its doors.

Mission in the Third Millennium

Although MET is small and it is difficult to present clear perspectives for the third millennium, one point remains true: MET needs to promote a distinct opening of the Christian communities toward people who do not know Jesus Christ. This is an important objective for MET within the Church in Thailand. Laypeople will certainly play an important role in this opening to Thai society.

A mission society must work to help prepare local seminarians and priests for greater involvement in the evangelizing mission of the Church. Priests can do much for *ad gentes* mission—if they are made aware of the possibilities and urgency of missionary work.

MET continues to see the needs of its neighboring countries, Laos and Cambodia. Because the Thai language and culture are very close to the Laotian language and way of life, MET is in a good position to help the Church in Laos, whenever a concrete opportunity becomes available. Cambodia, too, is still in need of more priests. MET sees these two countries as the priorities of its *ad exteros* mission work.

It has been noted that the third millennium may be the "Millennium of Asia." Consequently, an important dimension of mission will focus on the encounter with the religions and cultures of Asia. Very little has been realized in these areas. As an Asian missionary society, MET (along with other Asian societies) is in an advantageous position to foster this intercultural and interreligious dialogue.

Lorenzo Ruiz Mission Society

The Lorenzo Ruiz Mission Society (LRMS) is a Clerical Society of Apostolic Life of Diocesan Right with its ecclesiastical seat in the Archdiocese of Manila. The LRMS draws its inspiration from Saint Lorenzo, the first Filipino saint who was of mixed Filipino and Chinese descent. He was martyred in Japan where he went as a lay catechist with Spanish Dominican friars in the 1600s.

Historical Synopsis

In 1949, during civil disturbances in China, the Saint Joseph Regional Seminary, which was under Jesuit administration, was transferred to Manila. In the ensuing years about sixty Chinese seminarians were ordained in the Philippines. They went on to found fourteen Filipino-Chinese parishes and eighteen Filipino-Chinese schools.

To facilitate the continuation of these apostolates and to recruit and train younger clergy, Jaime Cardinal L. Sin of Manila established the Lorenzo Mission Institute (LMI) on June 6, 1987. LMI is a Filipino-Chinese diocesan seminary and trains missionary priests for the Chinese Apostolate in the Philippines. The first priest to be ordained in Bacolod was Esteban Lo on October 16, 1991; the next priest was Jose Vidamor Yu who was ordained in Davao on January 17, 1993.

Pope John Paul II visited the LMI seminary during his stay in the Philippines for World Youth Day in January 1995. He instructed Cardinal Sin to "maintain and preserve the said seminary at all cost." The pope also requested that the institute not only prepare priests for the Chinese Apostolate in the Philippines, but also for mission in China.

It is within this context that LRMS was formed. On January 14, 1997, on the occasion of the tenth anniversary of LMI's establishment, Jaime Cardinal Sin created by special decree the Lorenzo Ruiz Mission Society (LRMS) and approved its constitution. LMI continues as the formation house of LRMS.

Current Situation

At the dawn of the new millennium, LRMS has thirteen ordained priests, ten students of theology, fifteen students of philosophy, and one special-English student. Members committed to LRMS are: perpetual (thirteen), temporary (seven), novices in their Spiritual Formation Year (five).

Two LRMS priests are in Changchun City, Northeast China, studying the Chinese language in a university setting. One is completing a doctorate in theology in Rome, and another will soon depart for Rome for studies in spiritual theology. The remaining LRMS priests are engaged in pastoral ministry in the Philippines.

LRMS is "intrinsically and eminently missionary in spirit and finality." Continued discernment is needed for a young mission society to shape its mission commitments. For the present moment LRMS members "will help the Chinese Apostolate in the Philippines, with the evangelization of China in their vision, by living a simplicity of life, giving some special attention to the poor in their pastoral ministry."

LMI provides a unique and essential service for priests and seminarians from China. LMI has become a kind of coordination center for Chinese Church personnel who come to the Philippines for pastoral exposure, renewal courses, or theological studies. In recent years such assistance has been afforded to seven Chinese priests, two deacons, three Jesuit scholastics, and six seminarians. In addition, three seminarians have come from Taiwan.

Successes and Challenges

LRMS has experienced some initial success in the recruitment of personnel. As noted earlier, thirteen men have been ordained. In addition, there are seven temporary members and five novices. Recruitment remains a priority for LRMS.

A distinct challenge emerges from the realities of the Church in China today. It is a divided Church, split between the so-called Patriotic Catholic Church and the clandestine or underground Church. The government-sponsored Patriotic Church must abide by the religious policies of Communist China; it must be self-supporting and self-propagating, and must sever all relationships with the pope concerning the election and ordination of bishops. Although the underground Church professes fidelity to the Bishop of Rome, it is illegal and has no right of existence in China.

In addition, due to the deficiency of theological and pastoral formation of the clergy in China in both churches, constant conflicts occur between these two churches. Often, these conflicts have no importance for faith and morals. Unfortunately, there is frequent misunderstanding, and hatred has even found its way into Church life. There is an urgent need to initiate a movement of reconciliation based on a better understanding of faith and the Christian spirit.

Mission Placements

Presently, China remains closed to missionary activity. There is the possibility of sending priests to China as teachers or students; their activities are very limited. Recognizing these constraints, LRMS continues to concentrate on the Filipino-Chinese apostolate in the Philippines.

LRMS began work for Filipino-Chinese many years ago. Currently, there are fourteen parishes and schools. These are often staffed by Chinese priests and re-tired missionaries. These activities meet people's real needs; it is also hoped that they may be a source of vocations.

The mission of LRMS focuses on preparing personnel for the foreign mis-sionary field. The society does not exclude the possibility of assisting overseas Chinese if personnel are available. In addition, there is a commitment to help the seminary formation of the local clergy of China as soon as China is open to mis-sionary activity.

Mission in Asia in the Third Millennium

It is foreseen that, over the next twenty to thirty years, China will become more open, and this will permit more mission endeavors. Current Chinese leadership, trained in Communist Russia and the former Soviet Union, will give way to a younger generation. This transition will occur as thousands of young Chinese who have studied in Canada, the United States, and other countries come into leadership positions.

This new generation is fully aware that the communist system will not work. Once they achieve higher positions in the government, they may improve or even modify the communist system into one that is socialist, like many former commu-nist leaders of Eastern Europe.

The LRMS leadership foresees a great need of missionaries in Asia in the third millennium. For LRMS, the next decade will witness the first General Chap-ter of its own priest-members with perpetual commitment. This chapter will be an important milestone toward self-governance and stability for LRMS as an inde-pendent missionary society of apostolic life.[8]

As the third millennium dawns, it is appropriate to recall John Paul II's per-sistent focus on the continent of "Asia, towards which the Church's mission *ad gentes* ought to be chiefly directed."[9] The emergence, growth, and continued vi-tality of Asia's own missionary societies are a special blessing for all peoples in Asia. Under the lead of the "befriending Spirit,"[10] Asia will emerge as a continent of missionary hope in the third millennium.

Notes

1. *L'Osservatore Romano*, English edition, April 22, 1998, p. 1.
2. Ibid.
3. Ibid.
4. On these six indigenous mission societies, see the appendix to this essay.
5. *L'Osservatore Romano,* English Edition, May 13, 1998, p. 14.
6. *Fides,* May 31, 1998, p. 380.
7. Important synod interventions that focused on specifically missionary themes were made by: Franco Cagnasso, PIME; Francisco Claver, SJ; Joseph Fernando (Sri Lanka); Edward Malone, MM; Raymond Rossignol, MEP; Petrus Turang (Indonesia); and Charles Schleck, CSC.
8. The story of evangelization in Asia is rich and multifaceted. No doubt, much more could be written about these Asian-born missionary societies. In this connection, the reader's attention is directed to a colloquium held in Thailand in April 1997, organized by the Office of Evangelization of the Federation of Asian Bishops' Conferences. It brought together representatives of the Asian missionary societies as well as personnel from several other such missionary societies that serve in Asia. The proceedings and papers of this colloquium have been issued as *FABC Papers 88* (FABC Secretariat, 16 Caine Road, Hong Kong); these documents and additional materials have been published in the book: James Kroeger, *Asia-Church in Mission* (Manila: Claretian Publications, 1999).

   A second colloquium of the Asian Missionary Societies of Apostolic Life organization (AMSAL) was held in the Philippines in August 1999. Its theme focused on the *ad gentes* mission in Asia in the third millennium. Superiors and representatives of all AMSAL members were present. Representatives of other Asian local Churches that have no indigenous mission societies were invited to participate in the colloquium. The proceedings and papers of this colloquium will be issued as *FABC Papers 89* (FABC Secretariat, 16 Caine Road, Hong Kong).
9. *RM* 37. See also nos. 55 and 91.
10. *GS* 3.

13

The Challenges of Mission in Asia:
A View from the Asian Synod[*]
LUIS ANTONIO TAGLE

I would like to thank all of you and the organizers of this assembly for the opportunity to reflect once again, with a group of people committed to mission—especially here in Asia, on the significance of the recently concluded Special Assembly of the Synod of Bishops for Asia.

It was a great joy for me to have been invited as one of the so-called "experts" to help in the work of the General Secretariat. Thus, I was given an insight into the workings of the synod, and I was able to do some work behind the scenes. When the Post-Synodal Council was set up, I was surprised that I was asked to go back to Rome to assist in the council's tasks. The main work of the council was to give proposals to the Holy Father for the Apostolic Exhortation, which he will promulgate here in Asia.

The topic given me for this presentation is "The Challenges of Mission in Asia: A View from the Asian Synod." I will try my best to address this topic and give some sort of introduction to the synod and its theme. The theme of the synod itself already gives us some indications regarding the challenges of mission in Asia. I will address some specific challenges or areas of mission as pointed out by the whole synodal event and by the coming Post-Synodal Exhortation of the Holy Father.

The Nature of the Synod

First, I will begin with a description of the synod's nature. The day before the formal opening of the Synod of Bishops, the so-called "experts" were called into a meeting by Cardinal Schotte, CICM, the secretary-general of the synod. One of the reminders that he gave us was this: "I am reminding all of you (most of you are theologians) that this is a Synod of Bishops. This is not a Synod of Theologians, and you must be clear about that. This is not your synod. It is not your ideas that must dominate the synod. You are supposed to help. In other words, this is a Synod of Pastors." From that very identity of the synod, as a Synod of Pastors, we could already expect that the gathering would be dominated by pastoral concerns.

[*]Luis Antonio Tagle, "The Challenges of Mission in Asia: A View from the Asian Synod," *EAPR* 35 (1998), 366–378.

This fact was verified even in the small group discussions. When an item that sounded too theological or academic arose, the reaction of many bishops would be, "We'll leave that to the theologians to discuss." Then, they would focus on what are more pastoral and more missionary concerns. I noticed that pastoral and missionary were not distinguished in the synod. So, I will be using the words missionary and pastoral almost interchangeably.

The concern I saw in the synod was focused on the state of the Churches. Where do the Churches stand in Asia right now, in these many worlds of Asia? The bishops were there in order to assess and to discern the status of our local Churches. In the context of the rich sharing about the state of the Churches, the challenges of mission naturally surfaced.

I will treasure in my heart the many stories that accompanied the interventions of the bishops. No intervention was purely academic; they were always set in context of stories of concrete men and women, concrete Catholics, concrete experiences of local Churches and Catholics. The challenges of mission I discerned were embedded in those stories of life and struggle, of persecution and difficulties, all encountered in living out the faith in different contexts of Asia. That is the first thing that defined this synod as truly a missionary-oriented synod. It was a Synod of Bishops, of pastors, whose concern was how to promote the mission of the local Churches in the particular context of Asia.

The second element concerns the very theme of the synod. It was chosen by the Holy Father upon consultation with the Pre-Synodal Council. The various Episcopal Conferences sent representatives to form a Pre-Synodal Council, and they suggested to the Holy Father possible themes of the synod. Eventually, the Holy Father chose the theme "Jesus Christ the Savior and His Mission of Love and Service in Asia: '. . . That They May Have Life, and Have It Abundantly'" (Jn 10: 10). The theme has a rather long formulation and is also quite comprehensive.

Like the themes of other continental synods (the African Synod, the Synod for America, and the Synod for Lebanon), this also focused on mission and evangelization. The theme of the Asian Synod explicitly mentioned the mission of Jesus Christ. This theme was not chosen in an arbitrary fashion. Much reflection went into it, and I think it is important to pick up some of the nuances. I believe that the nuances of the theme and the history of choosing the theme already indicate some of the challenges of mission in Asia.

Allow me to highlight a few important points. First, the theme reminds us that it is Jesus Christ who is the Missioner *par excellence*. Jesus Christ is the Missionary; he is the One sent by the Father. I think the theme wants to stress this. Mission is his mission; Jesus is the Missioner. A second nuance was very much in the mind of the Holy Father in choosing the theme: this Missioner Jesus Christ is also the Savior. He is the One Savior, the Only Savior, the Only Mediator between humanity and God. So, mission, his mission, the mission of Jesus Christ, the One sent by the Father, is the mission of fulfilling the saving plan of the Father. It is a mission of salvation. That is why Jesus as Savior was included.

I was told that there were many formulations before this final wording. It started as Jesus Christ as the Only Savior, Jesus Christ as the One Savior, Jesus as the Unique Savior. Then they dropped all the qualifications and just said: Jesus Christ, *the Savior*. The Holy Father stressed that portion: *Jesus Christ in his mission as Savior*.

The third element is that the description of the saving mission of Jesus is phrased concretely in the theme in terms of *love, service,* and *abundance of life*. Three categories define the mission of Jesus Christ. It is a mission of love. It is a mission of service. It is also meant to bestow life, to share life with the people of Asia. This mission of the Savior is to be incarnated, as it were, or is to be prolonged in time specifically in Asia. The focus of the synod: how to incarnate this mission of Love, Service, and Life in the concrete reality of Asia.

In the experience of the synod, the interventions did not always focus on the theme. The bishops were free to talk about topics of their choice. That is why it was a difficult task for the secretaries. We were in the secretariat and twice a day we had to summarize all the interventions. It was quite difficult because one had to read between the lines. What are the bishops really saying? How are the interventions related to the theme? The connections were not always obvious and not always explicit. It was part of the work of the secretariat not to read too much, but also to try to unpack some of the hidden wealth found in the interventions.

As a gathering of pastors, the synod was meant to address missionary concerns and missionary challenges in Asia. At the same time, the theme chosen by the Holy Father wanted all to reflect on mission within a particular framework: the Christological dimensions, Jesus as the Missioner, the mission of Jesus as salvific, and all this as concretely experienced in a mission of love, service, and life incarnated in the Asia of today. . . .

The Challenges of Mission in Asia

I have four specific points. The first challenge that I see based on the theme of the synod is quite significant: the Churches in Asia are being invited to a humble, discerning stance regarding mission. At the close of the millennium, the missionary fervor that the Holy Father and all the bishops in the synod wanted to see in Asia is one rooted in the faith conviction that it is Jesus' mission in the Spirit that must be at work in Asia. It is Jesus' mission, not ours—it is Jesus' way of fulfilling the Father's salvific plan. It is Jesus' way of concretizing love, service, life-giving love and service. This is the norm for mission—it is Jesus' way. This is one thing that was mentioned over and over: as we face the third millennium, the Churches in Asia must go back to the manner in which Jesus fulfilled his mission!

The first challenge, I think, coming from the synod is the basic challenge of learning again from Jesus. We need to allow ourselves to be taught by Jesus, to behold Jesus as the missioner and to be converted. We must undergo this conversion to his ways, to his missionary ways. This first point that I raise is closely connected to missionary spirituality. The synod stressed that it is his mission. It is not ours; it is his mission. This liberates us a lot.

For discussion during the synod, we were divided into different small groups. I remember the first three sessions of the small group to which I was assigned. The atmosphere of the sharing was, "This is a problem; that is a problem. How do we address problems?" After the third or fourth sharing and after all the debates, we became more realistic and the atmosphere changed.

One bishop said in our small group, "You know, we are pretending as though we are the ones who will save Asia and we cannot even agree on one particular question like the inculturation of liturgy. So how could we be the saviors here in Asia? Maybe the first thing that we can do as people interested in really promoting the mission of Church here in Asia is to be humble and admit that it is not our mission. It is primarily Jesus' mission. How do we learn from him?" That liberated our small group. Imagine the weight that our shoulders would have to carry believing that we are the saviors. How freeing it was to realize that we just have to learn from the One who was sent by the Father! I think this is one challenge of mission in Asia: to behold Jesus again. The more contemplative side of mission is to behold him in order to learn from him the ways of mission.

The second challenge worth mentioning is this. While it is true that it is Jesus and his mission that are still present, we in the Churches in Asia are being asked to prolong, to make visible, to put flesh unto this mission of Jesus in the contemporary realities of Asia. I do not know whether it is an acceptable or accepted term: this task demands some sort of "contemporalization" of the mission of Jesus Christ within Asian realities. I think the Churches in Asia are being invited to facilitate some sort of encounter, intersection, or meeting between the mission of Jesus which is ever present in the Spirit and the life realities of Asia. That is what the Churches in Asia are asked to do. They are not to substitute for the mission of Jesus, because the mission of Jesus is very much present in the Spirit. The challenge is to facilitate the encounter of the Spirit-filled mission of Jesus with the realities of Asia; in that intersection the mission of Jesus takes on flesh, takes on a form that is contemporary for the people of Asia.

This challenge was expressed in the synod in different ways. Let me indicate two ways in which this concern for the challenges of a mission surfaced. The first thing that was striking to me was that in the synod there was a constant call for the Churches in Asia to take seriously and earnestly what Asia truly is. This means to take seriously the different worlds of Asia, because we realized there is not "one Asia." Asia is not a uniform reality. This was a constant appeal in the synod: "Take the different worlds of Asia seriously and not only in a nostalgic fashion."

You must have seen photographs of the opening and the closing mass of the synod; they were very colorful. The different parts of the Eucharist were assigned to different Churches. The Gospel was proclaimed, I think, in the Syro-Malabar tradition, and the Alleluia was done in the Syro-Malankara tradition. The presentation of the gifts was done by Indonesians with the dance of three steps forward and four steps backward. The procession seemed to reach the Holy Father after thirty minutes. All very colorful! During the Consecration, women from India with flowers and candles were dancing. At the end, all were quite happy that all the different colors, languages, and melodies of Asia were celebrated in that Eucharist.

One bishop told me, "But you do not see Indian women dancing that way in contemporary India. You do not see Indonesian women dressed that way in contemporary Indonesia." He said, "Why is it that whenever we want to recognize the worlds of Asia we do it in a nostalgic fashion? Why can we not face the contemporary world of Asia?" He asked, "In the Philippines do your women still wear those special dresses?" I said, "No. It is just for programs." He said, "That is it! We are transforming the synod into a cultural program."

I was surprised, but it got me to thinking. When one says, "Be true to the worlds of Asia," it means more than just a nostalgic thing in terms of costume and colors. Are we facing the contemporary worlds of Asia affected by this globalization of cultures and values that has been changing the cultural and the human landscape? What is Asian now? I thought it was a good reminder. When we talk of the worlds of Asia and the cultures of Asia, it is not just a nostalgic view of cultures; the Church must confront the fast-changing, dynamically changing cultures that define the worlds of Asia today.

Why is this true? Because it is in and through these Asian realities that the saving mission of Jesus must be incarnated. So, it is not just for curiosity. We need to know the reality in which the so-called drama is to be played out. The world of Asia is not just a stage. It is a constitutive part of the incarnation of the mission of Jesus right now. Today's Asia must be taken into consideration. In and through contemporary Asian realities, the saving mission of Jesus will become more alive in Asia. This means attentiveness to the worlds of Asia.

The second thing that I discerned in terms of this appeal to be alert to the realities of Asia is this. I noticed in the synod a deep sense of a celebration of the "*Asianess*" of the Christian faith. I think the Holy Father was also behind this push. The Holy Father seldom talked and in fact did not intervene during the synod's deliberations. He had the opening homily and the closing homily. Everyday he would have some remarks or short jokes to begin the session.

I remember one morning (I do not know whether he was joking, but it had some punch to it) he said, "Jesus was born in Asia." I saw the bishops were very happy to be reminded that Jesus was born in Asia. Then the pope added, "Oh! In that part of Asia that looked out to Europe." So, he was born on Asian soil but in that part of Asia that is open to the universal. He wanted to maintain the two dimensions. I noticed especially in the small group and in the Post-Synodal Council that there was this push to celebrate the "*Asianess*" of Christianity.

Jesus was born on Asian soil. He had within him the cultural traditions of Asian people. That is why even in the way the Gospels were written and in the images employed, the methodology was very Asian in approach. The Church and the Christian movement, Christianity itself, all have Asian roots. That is what the Synod of Bishops wanted to bring to our attention as part of our missionary challenge. Can we celebrate the Asian aspect of the Christian faith? It was almost a refrain during the synod that Christianity in Asia is still looked upon as something alien. So, there is a need to recover the compatibility of the Christian faith with the Asian mentality, with the Asian cultures. In fact, the recovery of the Asian character of the saving gospel is part of the missionary challenge of the synod.

Additional Reflections

Let me go to the third point. There was an awareness in the synod that the unique contribution of Christians in Asia is our faith in Jesus Christ. We can collaborate with all other peoples of Asia in the quest for life, in the quest for justice, in the promotion of human dignity and all of those things. But the synod also stressed the fact that what is unique to the Christian Churches is Jesus Christ. Nobody can share Jesus Christ the way we can. If there is anything that we can say to the people who are asking deep questions about life, our answer as Christians is Jesus and all that he stands for. That is our contribution.

In some quarters and small groups there was a reaction to some tendencies within theological and missiological circles to first bracket the faith element. One bishop from India depicted it this way; he said, "Many theologians and many missionaries will first somehow pretend that they are not Christians. They will bracket that fact in order to relate with others just on the human level. They say, 'We share a common humanity, so let the Christian element enter later on'." This bishop also said, "But the non-Christians are surprised that we are not mentioning Jesus, because if they know that you are a Christian, they expect you to talk about Jesus. So, why are you postponing that? Why are Christians hiding this fact while others are expecting it from you?" The discussion also went into pedagogy and methodology. The agreement and the consensus at the end of that session was, "Yes, we do not have to hide the truth that it is Jesus whom we are bringing to people. It is Jesus that we are proclaiming. In fact, that is our main contribution."

Now, this Christological focus is not as neat as it sounds. There are many complicated missionary and theological-pastoral issues connected with the proclamation of Jesus. One very important question raised in the synod was: How do we understand Jesus as the only Savior in the face of the many religions and soteriologies in Asia? That remains an issue. Another thing that surfaced was the meaning of salvation. We say that Jesus came to bring salvation, but what is the meaning of salvation? How do you present it in a way that will make sense to the quest of Asian people for fuller life? What about the connection between Jesus and the Holy Spirit? Many bishops said that some people, in order to avoid talking about Jesus, just appeal to the Holy Spirit. But where you find the Spirit, there you find Jesus Christ. So, is there a need to mention Jesus Christ? In the synod, there was a big push, especially from the bishops of India, to clarify the relationships between the mission of Jesus and the mission of the Spirit. They also asked more practical questions of how to present Jesus in ways appealing and understandable to Asians.

In addition, this question is not just in the area of theology, but also in terms of Church, her structures and policies. Why? People will get to know the values of Jesus Christ through our policies, through our structures, through our ways of relating with one another in our communities. In fact, I remember one bishop even proposing that we in Asia should reflect on how the papal ministry should be conducted in a way that is in keeping with Asian mentalities. How do you rethink the Petrine ministry in terms of Asian mentalities? This is not easy.

In the small group where I belonged there was a suggestion: "Maybe we should present Jesus as a guru." Then, a bishop from China said, "People from China will not understand guru. What is guru? We will have to say: 'The Enlightened One. Jesus is the Enlightened One'." In short, we must take images that are close to Asian mentalities and experiences and use them for the presentation of Jesus. That is my third point: the Christological focus and challenge of the synod.

Specific Mission Challenges

Finally, the fourth area is more numerous and includes some specific areas of mission for the Church. In what areas of life in Asia did the synod feel we should enter and bring the saving mission of Jesus? How do we incarnate the saving mission of Jesus? Here I identify five major areas, which will probably appear in the Post-Synodal Exhortation, because these are some key areas raised by the bishops during the synod.

The first specific item is the proclamation of Jesus. This has been the standing critique coming from the Vatican with regard to the documents from Asian bishops. They assert: We Asians are very weak in the proclamation of Jesus. Many of them fear that we are substituting dialogue for explicit proclamation of Jesus. So in the synod this was affirmed vigorously: the need for explicit proclamation of Jesus. Of course, you know how the Asian bishops did it. They affirmed it, but then you look at the text of their interventions. What do the bishops of Asia understand by proclamation of Jesus? The first obvious thing is proclamation through the Word of God. In fact, some bishops were even proposing that biblical scholars in Asia start finding ways of doing exegesis in an Asian manner. Can Asian ways of interpreting texts evolve? They would be scientific but also attuned to the mentalities of Asian people.

Another bishop said, "The proclamation of Jesus must move through a contemplative life and an exchange among people (Catholics, Christians, non-Christians) in the area of contemplation." There was a strong reaction to the intervention of one bishop who said, "Why is it that in Asia, when people are looking for quality in education, in health care, social services, they instinctively go to Catholic institutions, Catholic hospitals, the Catholic Caritas and all of those things? But, when they are looking for spiritual guidance, they go to Buddhists, they go to Hindus."

Catholics in Asia are not known for their spiritual wisdom. So the synod emphasized that the proclamation of the Word should be accompanied by a contemplative life. We have a long and rich contemplative tradition that can be part of the proclamation of Jesus. One bishop asserted that we have not maximized the contemplative tradition of the Church for missionary dialogue and the proclamation of Jesus. There is also proclamation through witness of life.

In short, the proclamation of Jesus was given prominence in the synod, in the Post-Synodal Council's meetings, and in the recommendations to the Holy Father. The different Vatican offices and congregations were quite pleased. They are assured that the people in Asia believe in the proclamation of Jesus. They are really worried about that, I do not know why, but they are worried.

The second aspect or specific area of mission for the Church is communion. *Communio* in the Church is a way of mission; communion is a way of missionary witness. The missionary proclamation is about Jesus, especially in Asia where there is always a search for harmony, harmony within human relationships and harmony with the cosmos. Therefore, if communities, especially Christian communities, could be witnesses to the possibility of communion, then we would be already proclaiming Jesus. The challenge is something *ad intra*, within the Church. The Church works for communion within itself as part of its missionary task. It is not simply an inward-looking thing; we settle our internal affairs so that we live in communion among ourselves. For the synod, communion is for mission. So, communion in the BECs, communion in the parishes, communion in dioceses, and communion in the Universal Church is not just for smooth relationships within the Church so that Christians will be in harmony with one another. It is part of our missionary proclamation. Missionary proclamation in Asia, where harmony is given primary value, includes a particular calling here, in terms of communion. The communion with Churches in difficult situations is envisioned. The Holy Father mentioned many times that when he wakes up in the morning, the first thing that he prays for is the Church in China. This intention also includes North Korea, but we are not even sure whether there is a Christian presence there. We have no news. Communion with people in difficult situations was a frequent synod theme.

I was particularly moved by the interventions of the different bishops and administrators of the newly liberated republics in Central Asia, e.g., Kazakhstan and Kyrgyzstan. The Archbishop of Iraq, a Chaldean, is the only bishop for the whole of Iraq, for all the Chaldeans. He has only sixty priests for the whole country. He asked me, "How many priests are there in your diocese?" I said, "We are close to eighty." He said, "Look at that; that is only one diocese, and we have the whole country with only sixty. Send some of them to us." I said, "Yes, we will send." I said yes, but I do not know whom to send!

Then he said another thing, "Please help us reflect on the mystery of the disappearance of the primitive Churches. Many of these Churches were even founded by the Apostles. But it is a mystery to us. Why does the Lord allow these Churches to disappear?" Then he said, "Are we not to be true to our vocation in Asia? Are we not being called, really, to be the little flock? Should we really work towards increasing numbers of Christians? Or, is it our calling in Asia to disappear?" This is a very difficult missionary question.

I was surprised that when he talked about the mystery of the disappearance of the primitive Churches, he said, "Should we go against the calling? Is it a calling? Can we really be called to remain a little flock? Should I not be faithful to that? Is it part of the missionary challenge of the Church in Asia not to increase, but maybe even to disappear? And when that moment comes, not to resist it?" I told him, "Bishop, I am not prepared to answer. That is a difficult question."

The third specific area is dialogue. This is not new to us anymore. For the past twenty-seven years or so, the basic intuition of the FABC is that the mode of mission for Asia, the mode of evangelization for Asia, is dialogue. What is new is that this was elevated to the universal level during the synod; I believe it has been sanctioned. I believe the mission of dialogue will be part of the Apostolic Exhortation. So, although there is nothing new, we are very happy that what some used to fear, dialogue, will now even be proposed. Of course, we will wait, because at this time we do not have the final Apostolic Exhortation.

Another specific area for mission focuses on peace-making. It was Bishop Hamao from Japan who really pushed for this, as one of the areas where Jesus' mission of love, service, and life should be intensified in Asia. I thought it was good that it came from him; his intervention was almost like a public confession. He went back to World War II; he recalled some of the unjust things that were done by the Japanese forces during that time. He said that the Church in Japan did not raise its voice against all those inhumanities. He also said that we really have to commit ourselves to the promotion of peace. It was a wonderful occasion. I felt some sort of healing, forgiveness, and reconciliation.

Finally, another specific area of mission for Asia is developing, forming, and preparing agents for mission, agents of the Gospel of Life. Here the basic intuition of the FABC was again affirmed. Of course, the Holy Spirit is the principal agent of mission, but in Asia it is the local Churches that are really the missionary agents—not individuals but local Churches. All the different sectors that comprise the local Church are to be animated for mission. There was even a suggestion that tourists and overseas workers could be tapped for evangelizing work. All sectors means people who work in social communication, women, families, the youth, laity, religious, communities of apostolic life, and different pastors.

Conclusion

As you see, some of these things are not new. We are already aware of these different areas. We should not take these areas in isolation from what we have already mentioned regarding the mission of Jesus Christ, regarding the Asian realities and the awareness that our unique contribution to mission in Asia is our faith in Jesus Christ. I cannot go through all the synod details here. I am not even sure how the Holy Father will discuss these elements in the Apostolic Exhortation.

I have a concluding remark. The fruits of the synod will be shared with us in November here in Asia. Before the opening of the Church's celebrations of the great jubilee of redemption, I think it is appropriate that the fruits and theme of the synod will be shared with all of us here in Asia. The focus will be on Jesus the Redeemer. So, the Church in Asia will face the new millennium with her eyes focused on Jesus the Redeemer, Jesus the Only Savior.

I think the post-synodal reflection will alert us to the fact that Jesus is not only the message to be proclaimed in our missionary work. Jesus is the Missioner who should not be replaced. He will remain the Missionary here in Asia. So, he is both the Message and the Agent. He is the Message to be proclaimed; he is the Missioner that must do the work. I think one fundamental challenge for the Churches of Asia is to take that seriously. If Jesus is not the Message, if Jesus is not both the Message and the Missioner for us, then we might be betraying his being the Savior. For him to be the Only Savior means he is not only the Message but also the one who will do his Mission.

Ours is a modest contribution. We are not substituting for Jesus. We are not substituting for his Spirit. We have to be more of a discerning Church, waiting for the Lord to indicate to us where we will cast our nets. But, he must direct the catch, because he is the one who is Missioner. I do not always know how to translate that into concrete areas of mission. However, I think underneath all of these areas of mission which the Holy Father will propose to us for scrutiny in his Apostolic Exhortation, there is a fundamental challenge. We are to become more spiritual. We must adjust our missionary perspective: Jesus is the Missioner, and we are just participating in his mission.

14

Mission In Asia: A Reflection on *Ecclesia in Asia*

MICHAEL AMALADOSS

In his Post-Synodal Apostolic Exhortation *Ecclesia in Asia* directed to the Christians of Asia, John Paul II recalls how the "Synod Fathers courageously called all Christ's disciples in Asia to a new *commitment to mission*" and "bore witness to the character, spiritual fire, and zeal which will assuredly make Asia the land of a bountiful harvest in the coming millennium" (*EA* 4). This encourages the pope to suggest that "just as in the first millennium the Cross was planted on the soil of Europe, and in the second on that of the Americas and Africa, we can pray that in the Third Christian Millennium *a great harvest of faith* will be reaped in this vast continent" (*EA* 1).[1] That is why John Paul II calls the people of God in Asia "to recognize the gift that is theirs in Christ" and "to communicate that gift to others through *proclamation* and *dialogue*" (*EA* 31).

There is no doubt whatever that a call to mission is the basic theme of the document *Ecclesia in Asia* and that the goal of this mission is to increase the number of Christians in Asia. The Hindus in India were quick to pick this up. An Indian English daily, *The Indian Express*, expressed in its editorial (Nov. 9, 1999) its disappointment that conversion still "remains the cardinal objective of the Church." Other Hindus, writing in that and in other papers, agreed with this assessment.[2] An Indian commentator has suggested that "the point about 'a great harvest of faith' in Asia does not represent the thrust" of the pope's document, whereas "a stress on the 'mission of making Jesus Christ better known to all'" (*EA* 2) would have been more acceptable to Indians and Asians.[3] But he seems to ignore that in the very next paragraph John Paul II goes on to specify that "Christ is the one Mediator between God and man and the sole Redeemer of the world, to be clearly distinguished from the founders of other great religions" (*EA* 2). This "face" of Christ will not certainly be acceptable to the other believers in India and Asia!

Mission in *Ecclesia in Asia*

Let me look at the document rapidly to see how John Paul II understand, this mission. The thrust and goal of mission may be seen more clearly if we understand the vision of history that provides its context. The pope offers this in the very beginning of the document. God reveals and fulfills his saving purpose through the patriarchs starting with Abraham, then through Moses and the chosen people, and finally through his Son, Jesus Christ. Palestine, in which Jesus was born, lived, died, and rose again, becomes a land of promise and hope for all humankind. "And from this land, through the preaching of the Gospel in the power of the Holy Spirit, the Church went forth to make 'disciples of all nations' (Mt 28:19)" (*EA* 1). So there is a narrowing down from creation to Palestine and then an opening out to embrace the whole universe.

Evoking the mission of the Apostles, the pope says, "Following the Lord's command, the Apostles preached the word and founded Churches" (*EA* 9). I may recall here that "founding churches" or *plantatio ecclesiae* has been a traditional goal of mission. Speaking of a "new understanding of mission" after the Second Vatican Council, John Paul II enumerates "the universality of God's plan of salvation, the missionary nature of the Church and the responsibility of everyone in the Church for this task" and goes on to evoke "the new possibilities for the proclamation of the Gospel" in Siberia and in Central Asia (*EA* 9). In Asia the Church finds itself "among people who display an intense yearning for God," which "can only be fully satisfied by Jesus Christ, the Good News of God for all the nations" (*EA* 9). John Paul II can therefore go on to affirm: "Contemplating Jesus in his human nature, the peoples of Asia find their deepest questions answered, their hopes fulfilled, their dignity uplifted, and their despair conquered" (*EA* 14). One can see here a paradigm of preparation-fulfillment.

The pope acknowledges that the Spirit is present and active in everyone. But the Spirit's action is meant to be fulfilled by Jesus.

> The Church is convinced that deep within the people, cultures and religions of Asia there is a thirst for "living water" (cf. Jn 4:10–15), a thirst which the Spirit himself has created and which Jesus the Savior alone can fully satisfy. The Church looks to the Holy Spirit to continue to prepare the peoples of Asia for the saving dialogue with the Savior of all. Led by the Spirit in her mission of service and love, the Church can offer an encounter between Jesus Christ and the peoples of Asia as they search for the fullness of life. In that encounter alone is to be found the living water which springs up to eternal life, namely, the knowledge of the one true God and Jesus Christ whom he has sent (cf. Jn 17:3). (*EA* 18)

Such an encounter, of course, has been mysteriously prepared already because the pope recalls that Jesus himself is present in every human being to show them how to be fully human. He refers to a text of the Second Vatican Council which says that "by his incarnation, he, the Son of God, in a certain way united himself with each individual."[4]

The Church is therefore called to be "a genuine sign and instrument of the Spirit's action in the complex realities of Asia" and discern its call "to witness to Jesus the Savior in new and effective ways" (*EA* 18).

Having clarified and clearly stated what he sees as the goal of mission, the pope goes on to discern the principal areas of mission. The most important of these is the "the explicit proclamation of Jesus as Lord" (*EA* 53). While recognizing the "rich array of cultures and religions in Asia," the pope points out that "neither respect and esteem for these religions nor the complexity of the questions raised are an invitation to the Church to withhold from these non-Christians the proclamation of Jesus Christ" (*EA* 20). It may be that the proclamation of Jesus as the only Savior "is fraught with philosophical, cultural, and theological difficulties, especially in light of the beliefs of Asia's great religions, deeply intertwined with cultural values and specific world views" (*EA* 20). In this context, the experience of St. Paul who dialogued "with the philosophical, cultural, and religious values of his listeners" is evoked. But this leads the pope to stress the need to share with everyone the riches of the Greco-Roman culture in which the first Ecumenical Councils tried to formulate their faith (*EA* 20).

Dialogue is "an essential part of the Church's mission because it has its origin in the Father's loving dialogue of salvation with humanity through the Son in the power of the Holy Spirit" (*EA* 29).

> Interreligious dialogue is more than a way of fostering mutual knowledge and enrichment; it is a part of the Church's evangelizing mission, an expression of the mission *ad gentes*. Christians bring to interreligious dialogue the firm belief that the fullness of salvation comes from Christ alone and that the Church community to which they belong is the *ordinary means* of salvation. (*EA* 31)

Dialogue is therefore the way in which mission as proclamation has to be carried on.

Though there is an occasional reference to the "mission of service and love" (*EA* 50), the real goal of mission is made clear when, concluding the document, the pope asks Mary to pray "that through the Church's love and service all the peoples of Asia may come to know your Son Jesus Christ, the only Savior of the world" (*EA* 51).

The document does begin with quite an elaborate analysis of the economic, socio-political, cultural, and religious conditions and problems of Asia (*EA* 5–9). Correspondingly, there is also an elaborate list of activities in which missionaries can engage in their efforts to lead people to the "abundant life" that Jesus Christ brings (*EA* 50). There is hardly any work the missionaries do that is not mentioned, appreciated, and encouraged. Every missionary can therefore find a text that supports his or her work. But I am concentrating here on the framework in which all these diverse activities are set and which gives them a special orientation and focus. Before I go on to reflect on this general framework or vision of mission, it may be helpful to summarize it.

The goal of mission is to save people. This salvation is available ordinarily to those who have faith in Jesus Christ and are members of the Church. Jesus saved us in and through his paschal mystery two thousand years ago, and he has sent us into the world to share this good news and salvation with others. The others, in whom also the Spirit of God is present and working, are yearning and waiting for this salvation. To fulfill this yearning and lead them to the fullness of salvation is the aim of mission. One can achieve this goal through various means such as proclamation, dialogue, witness, and loving service. Of these, proclamation is primary and the other activities are ordained to it.

Another Paradigm

This is a coherent vision, quite consistent in itself, given its starting point and context. It is also traditional. I do not wish to contest or to argue with this vision. But I would like to place by its side another paradigm that has been emerging in Asia in recent years from the context of its experience. In the emergence of a new paradigm, a new element or experience makes us not throw away any of the existing elements, but relate them in a new way, perhaps with new emphases. It claims to give a better account of current experience and a more adequate answer to its questions. This means that people who have not shared the new experience may have difficulty in seeing the relevance of the new paradigm. This new paradigm has been spelled out briefly by a group of Indian theologians meeting in Pune, in March 2000.

> According to the new paradigm, creation itself is a self-communication of God, who is reaching out to all peoples through the Word and the Spirit in various ways, at various times, and through the different religions. This ongoing divine-human encounter is salvific. However, God's plan is not merely to save individual souls, but to gather together all things in heaven and on earth. God is working out this plan in history through various sages and prophets. Jesus, the Word incarnate, has a specific role in this history of salvation. But Jesus' mission is at the service of God's mission. It does not replace it. Taking a kenotic form, it collaborates with other divine self-manifestations in other religions as God's mission is moving towards its eschatological fulfillment. As disciples of Jesus, we must witness to the Abba and to his Kingdom of freedom and fellowship, love, and justice. The "preparation-fulfillment" framework that links Judaism and Christianity cannot be projected on to other religions.[5]

For us in India, therefore, one of the primary tasks of mission is to be agents of an ongoing universal reconciliation. In this task the Church is not alone in the world but can find allies rather than enemies among the followers of other religious traditions and persons of good will.

Let me now try to spell out the experiences and developments that are at the origin of this paradigm and some of its principal elements. I do not have the space here to evoke the whole development of the contemporary theology of mission in Asia. I shall limit myself to a few pointers, both experiential and theological. *Experientially*, there has been a growing realization in Asia that the vast majority of its people have access to salvation in and through their own religions. The Church experiences its mission as an element of God's own, which is both broader and deeper. Finally, mission has many integral dimensions: the dialogue of the gospel with the poor, the cultures, and the religions of Asia. *Theologically*, the Kingdom of God is seen as the goal of mission. In pursuing this goal, the Church sees its own role as the symbol and servant of the Kingdom, with the other religions as its collaborators and allies in a common struggle against the enemies of the Kingdom, namely Satan and Mammon. The focus of mission then becomes prophecy, challenging people to transformation.

Religions as Ways of Salvation

There is a widespread conviction today among theologians and even bishops in Asia that the members of other religions are saved, not only in spite of, but in and through, their religions. Nearly three-fifths of the world's population live in Asia and nearly 98 percent of them do not believe in Christ as their savior. But they are very religious people. The Second Vatican Council said that salvation is made available to every human being, but in ways unknown to us.[6] A number of Asian theologians believe that it is in and through their religions that God reaches out to them.[7] Previously Karl Rahner had said that if people belonging to other religions are saved, then this happens through human, symbolic, and social mediations within the various religions.[8] This a priori argument has been confirmed a posteriori by the bishops of Asia, who "accept them [the other religions] as significant and positive elements in the economy of God's design of salvation" and "acknowledge that God has drawn our peoples to himself through them."[9] This conviction is reaffirmed and defended by most Asian theologians. Most theologians affirm that this salvation is mediated by Jesus Christ, though there is an ongoing discussion about how Christ saves and how his action is mediated to members of other religions.[10] There are many theories of redemption, but there seems to be a consensus emerging that Christ saves precisely in so far as he is divine.[11] But this mediation by Christ does not require an explicit faith in Jesus and a membership in the Church as a visible community that he founded. They feel supported by the recent affirmation of John Paul II that the Spirit is present and active in other religions.[12] His repeated assertion that the Church is the ordinary way of salvation seems to acknowledge, at least implicitly, other religions as *extraordinary* ways.

   The acceptance of all religions as ways of salvation makes people belonging to them co-pilgrims with us in our journey toward ultimate fulfillment. One is also less aggressive and anxious in mission. Older missionaries believed that people who were not baptized were going to hell. But our reasons for mission have to be something more than and different from saving people who would otherwise be lost forever. The goal of mission should be different from merely making others explicitly aware of what is happening to them without their conscious knowledge.

Mission of God

The second factor of experience is the realization that mission is primarily God's activity. The activity of the Church is at the service of God's action in the world. The Second Vatican Council, looking for a theological foundation for mission, found it precisely in the mission of the Son and of the Spirit. It said, "The Church on earth is by its very nature missionary since, according to the plan of the Father, it has its origin in the mission of the Son and the Holy Spirit."[13] The relationship between the mission of the Church and the mission of God can be seen in two ways. On the one hand, we can reduce the mission of God to the mission of the Church: God's mission is concretized today in the mission of Christ and of the Church. On the other hand, the mission of God can be seen as including and legitimating the mission of the Church without being reduced to it. David Bosch speaks of it in the following way.

> In the new image mission is not primarily an activity of the church, but an attribute of God. God is a missionary God. "It is not the church that has a mission of salvation to fulfil in the world; it is the mission of the Son and the Spirit through the Father that includes the church." Mission is thereby seen as a movement from God to the world; the church is viewed as an instrument for that mission. There is church because there is mission, not vice versa. To participate in mission is to participate in the movement of God's love toward people, since God is a fountain of sending love.[14]

The final phrase of Bosch echoes the Second Vatican Council, which speaks of the divine plan that "flows from 'fountain-like love,' the love of God the Father."[15] The vision of mission as an action of God brings in a Trinitarian dimension. It highlights the actions of the Father and of the Spirit without subordinating them to the action of Jesus and of the Church. The mystery of Christ however is seen as a hidden presence everywhere and at all times. Reflection on mission focuses no longer on soteriology and ecclesiology but on the Trinity and creation. The whole of history becomes a history of salvation and the secular becomes sacred. The universal salvific will of God is highlighted.[16] Asian theologians pick up this language in their reflection on interreligious dialogue.

> The unique and definitive action of the Father to save all peoples who have him as their origin and goal is leading all of us to a unity. Christ in whom God is reconciling all things to himself is urging the Church to be the servant of this communion. The universal presence and action of the Spirit is calling everyone to the realization of the oneness of the Kingdom. As a response to this mystery, dialogue is a process of growing into the fullness of divine life. It is a participation in the quest of all peoples for the full realization of the Truth. It is love for people which seeks communion in the Trinity.[17]

We can compare this with the traditional ecclesiocentric language of mission.

Mission's Integral Dimensions

The Federation of Asian Bishops' Conferences, meeting for its first general assembly in 1974, spoke of evangelization as a threefold dialogue with the cultures, the religions and the poor of Asia.[18] Together they constitute the Church's task of proclaiming the gospel. Looking at these activities as integral dimensions of evangelization is different from looking at them as merely pre-evangelization or indirect evangelization. John Paul II calls them "the paths of mission."[19] Further reflection has led the Asian theologians to point to their twofold integrality with evangelization. The three dialogues mutually involve each other in such a way that we cannot do adequately any one of them without doing also the others. Second, the threefold dialogue with the poor, the cultures, and the religions coalesce around the building of the Kingdom of God as a community of freedom and fellowship, justice, and love.[20] Mission is a call to conversion and prophetic action in the ongoing struggle with the powers of evil, namely Satan and Mammon.[21] Such an approach avoids instrumentalizing inculturation, interreligious dialogue, and liberation as means of mission, which is identified with the proclamation of the gospel leading to baptism and membership in the Church.

People who are involved in dialogue with the poor, cultures, and religions have the experience that they are witnessing to the gospel and contributing to the transformation of these realities in the context of the Kingdom of God. They see this as evangelization. In Asia people are rooted in their great and developed religions. They are open to be challenged by Jesus and be converted to his values in personal and social life. But they do not see the need to join the Church as a social institution, both because it still remains "foreign" culturally and socio-politically and because joining it leads to needless social disruption. In such a context, spreading the "values of the Gospel" is seen as a meaningful goal of mission, even if one always hopes that the people will become members of the community of the disciples of Jesus.

Starting with this threefold experience, theologians in Asia have been rethinking the goal and character of mission as well as the role of the Church in it. In doing this they are moving away from or qualifying traditional formulations. Let us now briefly look at this development.

Kingdom as the Goal of Mission

The traditional goal of mission has been *plantatio ecclesiae*—the establishment of the Church as a visible community. The Church, though it is also a human, hierarchical institution, is seen primarily as a "mediator" of salvation through faith and the sacraments, Baptism in particular. Even when God's action is recognized outside the Church it is seen as leading people to the Church. God's action may be seen as belonging to the economy of creation, which is contrasted to the action of Jesus and the Church, which belongs to the economy of redemption. This distinction between the economies of creation and redemption however breaks down when other religions too are seen as ways of salvation. It is always God who saves, not the religions. But all religions are seen to mediate or facilitate God's saving action.

When the Church's mission is set in the context of God's mission, the obvious tendency is to subordinate the Church to God. The Kingdom of God is the sphere of God's action. Therefore it is seen as the goal of God's mission. The

Church is sent into the world, not to build itself up in opposition to the Kingdom, but to be at the service of building up the Kingdom. The Church then is seen as the symbol and servant of the Kingdom.

The relationship between the Church and the Kingdom has been problematic in recent years. John Paul II devoted a whole chapter to it in his encyclical *Redemptoris Missio*.[22] There are three ways of looking at the Kingdom in contemporary theological discourse.[23] Traditionally, one simply identified the Church with the Kingdom in history. The second way is more nuanced: it distinguishes the Church from the Kingdom, seeing it as the Kingdom's beginnings and first fruits. The Kingdom then becomes the future of the Church. The Church grows through history into the Kingdom, which is eschatological, not to say other-worldly. A third way of looking at the Kingdom is to see it as a human community of justice and fellowship, and freedom that we have to build up here and now in history. This has been the stress of liberation theology, at least in its early years. Asian theologians see the Kingdom simply as the sphere of the presence and action of God. It embraces the whole universe and the whole of human history. It is both historical and eschatological. It is in the process of being built up by human beings. It includes also the other religions, even if the Church has a special relationship to it. As a human community of freedom and fellowship, justice, and love, we can even say that its primary focus is not religious but "secular." Speaking of growth of the Church, one is not talking of the development of any particular religion(s). Even people who do not belong to any religion, but who are of good will, contribute to the building up of the Kingdom and are its members.[24]

Church: Symbol and Servant of the Kingdom

The Church is sent into the world to be the symbol and servant of the Kingdom. The phrase "symbol and servant" translates into contemporary language the traditional word "sacrament," which is further spelled out as "sign and instrument." In the words of the Second Vatican Council, "The Church, in Christ, is in the nature of sacrament—a sign and instrument, that is of communion with God and of unity among all men."[25] We can say therefore that the Church is the "sacrament" of God's Kingdom. Sacraments are not exclusive means of grace. Nor is the Church an exclusive "sacrament" of the Kingdom, simply because God—Father, Son and Spirit—continues to act also outside the Church, through other religions and even through people of no religion.

The Church as symbol must make visible and realize in itself as a human community the various aspects of the Kingdom. The efficiency of its service depends on the authenticity of its symbolic character. As the servant, the Church must seek to realize the Kingdom, not only in itself, but also in the wider human community, by promoting the values of the Kingdom. Precisely in order to serve the Kingdom in every time, place, and culture, the Church seeks to be present everywhere, raising up viable communities where it is not present and strengthening them where it is already present. The goal of the Church's mission also includes therefore the building up of the Church as the symbol and servant of the Kingdom. In proclaiming Jesus and his good news, the Church also invites and welcomes people who feel called to become disciples of Christ and to join the community of the Church in it mission.

The goal of the Church's mission can then be reformulated as the building up of the Kingdom of God and of the Church as its symbol and servant. As subordinate to the mission of God, the Church has to discern God's presence and action in the world and collaborate with it, not claiming to be its exclusive representative.

Some refuse to accept the limits imposed on the institutional Church in this manner by claiming that the Church is a mystery. The Church is indeed a mystery in so far as it is a sacrament of divine presence and action. But it is not helpful to use this concept to extend the Church's invisible borders. We are speaking of the Church in history in its relationship to other religions. It is therefore helpful to speak about it as a visible human community.

Mission as Prophecy

The Church's service to the Kingdom is in history, historical. It has to get involved in the ongoing struggle between God and Mammon and witness to the good news of Jesus. As a community of the disciples of Christ, it has to bring to bear the special perspectives of the life and teaching of Jesus on the historical situation. The way of Jesus was one of humility and love, self-giving, and sacrifice even unto death, option for the poor and struggle with them for justice, challenging the rich and the powerful to conversion, and building up a group of people who could be models of a new human community. God became incarnate in Jesus, not to promote a purely other-worldly salvation. Although Jesus has not promised a this-worldly heaven either, he does want his disciples to struggle for justice, to serve the poor and the oppressed, and to spread the message of love and peace here and now.

In the process of building up the Kingdom, though the Church will be struggling against the forces of evil in its various forms, it will find in the members of other religions and in all people of good will allies rather than enemies. While the values of the Kingdom are the same, it is possible that the Church has developed some of them in particular ways given its human, historical, and cultural conditionings, whereas the others have developed those and other values in different ways. A pluralism and perhaps even a mutual enrichment through dialogue is possible. The Church however always tries to throw the light of Jesus on everything that it encounters. This task in view of the Kingdom can be seen as prophecy.[26] Prophecy is a call to conversion. But this conversion can be a turning to God without a change of religious community.[27] One of the reasons for this is the fact that joining another religious community is not merely a religious act, but also a sociopolitical act in many parts of the world. At least in Asia we are becoming increasingly aware that announcing Jesus Christ is not the same as announcing the Church.

Mission as Universal Reconciliation

It is now easy to see how Asian experience and reflection lead to a new way of looking at mission. I think that the difference between the two paradigms comes down to the point from which we look at God's world. We can look at it through the single eye of the story of Jewish people as narrated to us in the Bible or we can perceive it through *two eyes*, the second one being the rich stories of God's self-manifestation to other peoples across the world and through human history. One does not have to choose between the two eyes but through both of them can achieve a more complete and balanced vision.[28]

Looking through both eyes will make us realize that mission is not characterized by exclusivity and conflict, but collaboration and dialogue. The Kingdom, which is the goal of mission, is seen in the New Testament as universal reconciliation. Speaking of the plan of God, Paul speaks of God's intention "to gather up all things in him, things in heaven and things on earth" (Eph 1:10); "to reconcile to himself all things, whether on earth or in heaven" (Col 1:20) so that finally God "will be all in all" (1 Cor 12:28). This unification is certainly achieved by God in Christ through the Spirit (Rom 8:19–23).

Does this mean that whole world will become Church, visibly and institutionally, or rather will it be a multireligious, multicultural assembly? Even if the whole world were to become Church some day, which seems unlikely, as even the "Christian" world is becoming de-Christianized, there would still be billions and billions of people who have reached the Kingdom through history without any visible or conscious link to the Church. On the other hand, because universal reconciliation is God's plan for the world, the Church is called to work toward such unification, not presenting itself, but the Kingdom of God as the focus of this unity. This unity is meant to be achieved, not in some abstract, mysterious way, but in a visible manner through dialogue and collaboration. It is a historical process to which God's plan and its mission commits the Church. This is the reason the Church is called and sent to go everywhere in the world to be actively at the service of the divine plan of unification. Salvation itself should be seen, not as the rescuing of individual souls from hell, but as the historical-eschatological project of building up the Kingdom of God as a communion of all human beings and of the whole universe.

Priorities in Mission in Asia

If we look at leading people to the Church through proclamation as the goal of mission, then every other activity becomes a means toward or an expression of this one activity. John Paul II does give a long list of tasks for the Church in Asia. But if the focus of mission is the Kingdom then we can say that, when the Asian Bishops spoke of mission as a threefold dialogue with the poor, the rich cultures, and the great religions of Asia, they were spelling out both a method, namely dialogue, and priority areas for such dialogue. While all people of good will in Asia will agree that the promotion of justice and the transformation of culture are necessary,[29] religions seem to be becoming sources of increasing conflict all across Asia. That is why interreligious dialogue that helps to free religions from becoming the political tools of communalist and fundamentalist forces and to encourage collaboration among religions to promote peace and harmony among all peoples seems a priority for mission in Asia.[30]

Responding to John Paul II as he promulgated *Ecclesia in Asia* in Delhi, Cardinal Julius Darmaatmadja, Archbishop of Jakarta, Indonesia, said, "Yes, it is true that there is no authentic evangelization without announcing Jesus Christ, Savior of the whole human race. But for Asia, there will be no complete evangelization unless there is dialogue with other religions and cultures."[31]

The full impact of this statement can be grasped if we recall that earlier in the same address the cardinal had said, "We can learn also from the world, precisely because we are faithful to Jesus; that is, we can find Jesus present in the world. He has always been present and working in the world, including the world of Asia."[32] The Church may be new and even unwelcome in many parts of Asia, but not Jesus Christ.

The cardinal also pointed out the need to "continue our search for a fuller way for the Church to be rooted in Asia and to grow more in Asian appearance . . . deeper and deeper rooted in our own cultures and in our deepest inner aspirations as peoples of Asia."[33] *Ecclesia in Asia* makes much about Jesus being an Asian. But we have to confess that neither the Jesus presented to Asia nor the Church doing the presenting seems very Asian today.

Building up an authentic local Church that is involved in promoting the fullness of life in continuing dialogue with the cultures and religions of Asia seems to be the priority for mission in Asia.[34] If the post-Christian societies of the West are any indication, having more Christians in Asia may not be the best solution to promoting God's Kingdom there. A small but authentic and committed Christian community may be more important than a mass of nominal and alienated Christians.

Conclusion

The day after signing *Ecclesia in Asia,* John Paul II spoke to a group of leaders of other religions in Delhi, India:

> It is a sign of hope that the religions of the world are becoming more aware of their shared responsibility for the well-being of the human family. This is a crucial part of the globalization of solidarity which must come if the future of the world is to be secure. . . . Religious leaders in particular have the duty to do everything possible to ensure that religion is what God intends it to be, a source of goodness, respect, harmony, and peace! . . . Dialogue is never an attempt to impose our own views upon others, since such dialogue would become a form of spiritual and cultural domination. This does not mean that we abandon our own convictions. What it means is that, holding firmly to what we believe, we listen respectfully to others, seeking to discern all that is good and holy, all that favors peace and cooperation.[35]

If our proclamation of Jesus and his good news is done in such a context, it will be welcomed everywhere in Asia. As a matter of fact, John Paul II does mention that Asian bishops at the synod evoked various images of Jesus that will be welcome in Asia: "the Teacher of Wisdom, the Healer, the Liberator, the Spiritual Guide, the Enlightened One, the Compassionate Friend of the Poor," etc. (*EA* 20). But the image that seems to animate the traditional vision of mission is that of Jesus the conquering king.[36] Much stress is laid on the need to present Jesus as the only and universal Savior. But, in mission one proclaims and witnesses to the good news of Jesus' life, actions (miracles and ways of relating and behaving) and teaching. One does not reduce this good news to a catechism or a creed. One does not proclaim a dogma or theological conclusion regarding "ontological notions" (*EA* 20) concerning Jesus.[37] These are the things that need inculturation in Asia. This is certainly one reason "Jesus is often perceived as foreign to Asia" (*EA* 20). As a matter of fact, starting with the mission paradigm proposed by the Asian Churches, we can develop an Asian way of proclaiming Jesus, inspired more by the wisdom and prophetic tradition of the Bible than by the dogmatic tradition of the Church.[38]

The mission of the disciples of Jesus in Asia is more urgent than ever. The forces of globalization and modernization are widening the gap between the rich and the poor. The subaltern peoples like the Dalits and the Tribals are rising up, demanding justice and asserting their identity. The traditional cultures are crying for transformation as people move into the twenty-first century. In a quest for freedom and participation, even religions are getting politicized. In such a situation, the message of Jesus for peace with justice, love, and reconciliation is very much needed. But in proclaiming the good news of Jesus, the Church is called to follow him who emptied himself and took the form of a servant. It needs to be freeing and serving, humble and loving, listening and learning, dialoguing and collaborating. Opting for the poor, it will still have to build communities in solidarity. It has to be contemplative, experiencing the presence and action of God in people and reading the signs of the times, before discerning its own course of action. It has to incarnate itself in every culture, big and small, rediscovering its identity-in-difference. It will not identify itself with God or Jesus, but learn to be at their service. While learning from others, it will boldly and clearly assert its identity and specificity, avoiding an easy irenicism and accepting and welcoming pluralism. Respecting others and respecting the action of the Spirit in them, it will search for harmony so that, in Christ and through the Spirit, God may be all in all.[39]

Notes

1. John Paul II often quotes his own previous documents. The references to these can be found in *EA*. They show however that the pope is rather consistent in his teaching.
2. For brief quotations and references, see J. Saldanha, "Conversion in *Ecclesia in Asia*," *Mission Today* 2 (2000), 174–175.
3. Ibid., 178–179.
4. *GS* 22, quoted in *EA* 13.
5. "A Vision of Mission for the New Millennium" (Conclusions of the Ishvani-Kendra Research Seminar, Mar. 9–12, 2000), *Mission Today* 2 (2000), 253–254.

6. *GS* 22.
7. See Jose Kuttianimattathil, *Practice and Theology of Interreligious Dialogue* (Bangalore: Christu Jyoti Publications, 1995), pp. 326–349. See also Jacques Dupuis, *Towards a Christian Theology of Religious Pluralism* (Maryknoll: Orbis, 1997).
8. Cf. Karl Rahner, "On the Importance of the Non-Christian Religions for Salvation," *Theological Investigations*, vol. 18 (London: Darton, Longman and Todd, 1984), pp. 288–295.
9. Gaudencio Rosales and C. G. Arévalo (Eds.), *For All the Peoples of Asia*, Vol. I (Manila: Claretian Publications, 1997), p. 14.
10. Cf. Errol D'Lima and Max Gansalves (Eds.), *What Does Jesus Christ Mean?* (Bangalore: Indian Theological Association, 1999).
11. Michael Amaladoss, "Jésus Christ, le seul Sauveur, et la mission," *Spiritus* 41 (2000), 148–157, 163.
12. John Paul II, *RM* 28.
13. *AG* 2.
14. David Bosch, *Transforming Mission* (Maryknoll: Orbis, 1991), p. 390. The quotation within the quotation if from Jürgen Moltmann, *The Church in the Power of the Spirit: A Contribution to Messianic Ecclesiology* (London: SCM Press, 1977), p. 64.
15. Cf. *AG* 2.
16. Cf. *GS* 22.
17. *Theses on Interreligious Dialogue* (FABC Papers 48, 1987), p. 8.
18. Rosales and Arévalo, pp. 14–16.
19. Cf. *RM* 41–60.
20. See M. Amaladoss, "Integral Evangelization," *VJTR* 61 (1997), 223–232.
21. Cf. Joseph Mattam and Sebastian Kim (Eds.), *Mission and Conversion: A Reappraisal* (Mumbai: St. Paul's, 1996).
22. See chapter 2.
23. Cf. M. Amaladoss, "Le Royaume, but de la Mission," *Spiritus* 36 (1995), 291–304, and Jacques Dupuis, "Pour le Règne de Dieu: quelle Église? Quelle mission?"*Spiritus* 41 (2000), 227–240.
24. M. Amaladoss, *Making All Things New* (Maryknoll: Orbis, 1990), pp. 103–120.
25. *LG* 1.
26. See M. Amaladoss, "Mission as Prophecy" in James A. Scherer and Stephen B. Bevans (Eds.), *New Directions in Mission and Evangelization* 2 (Maryknoll: Orbis, 1994), pp. 64–72.
27. Cf. M. Amaladoss, "The Kingdom, Mission and Conversion" in *Mission and Conversion: A Reappraisal* (note 21), pp. 31–51.
28. Cf. John A. T. Robinson, *Truth Is Two-Eyed* (London: SCM, 1979).
29. See M. Amaladoss, *Living in Freedom: Liberation Theologies from Asia* (Maryknoll: Orbis, 1997).
30. Cf. "Asian Christian Perspectives on Harmony," in Franz-Josef Eilers (Ed.), *For All the Peoples of Asia*, vol. 2 (Manila: Claretian, 1997), pp. 229–298.
31. Cardinal Julius Darmaatmadj, "A New Way of Being Church in Asia," *VJTR* 63 (1999), 891.
32. Ibid., 888.
33. Ibid., 888.
34. See M. Amaladoss, *Beyond Inculturation* (Delhi: Vidyajyoti Educational Welfare Society/ISPCK, 1998).
35. See the text in *VJTR* 63 (1999), 885–886.

36. See M. Amaladoss, "Images of Christ and Orientations in Mission: A Historical Overview," *VJTR* 61 (1997), 732–741.
37. Cf. Josef Neuner, "Proclaiming Jesus Christ: Reflections on *Ecclesia in Asia*," *VJTR* 64 (2000), 536–543.
38. M. Amaladoss, "The Asian Face of the Good News," *Mission Today* 2 (2000), 166–172.
39. Cf. *RM* 28.

15

Unfinished Encounter: A Note on the Voice and Tone of *Ecclesia in Asia*[*]

JOHN MANSFORD PRIOR

This papal exhortation is an encouraging word to the diaspora Churches of Asia. Something of the vibrant atmosphere of the 1998 synod and the living faith of Asian Christians is caught in *Ecclesia in Asia*'s positive tone.

This note is limited to comments starting with the sources referred to in the footnotes of *Ecclesia in Asia*. In this way, I hope to determine the character and tone of the document, and so discover how to interpret its voice contextually.

Sources Used by *Ecclesia in Asia*

There are 240 footnotes in *Ecclesia in Asia*. Some 145 of them, or 60.4 percent, refer to documents from the Synod for Asia. The remainder refer to Roman sources, except for a single reference to Augustine and another to John Chrysostom.[1] John Paul II quotes himself 68 times (28.3 percent of the footnotes). The only other popes directly referred to are Paul VI (five times) and Leo XIII (once).[2] Other Roman documents include the Roman Missal (twice), the *Catechism of the Catholic Church* (twice) and the Congregation for the Doctrine of the Faith (primary reference once, footnote 166). The only council referred to directly is Vatican II (fifteen footnotes, or 6.2 percent of the total). Conciliar teaching has receded into the background, whereas contemporary papal teaching is very much in the fore (30.8 percent of the total).

The Special Assembly for Asia is the dominant source, taking up 60.4 percent of all primary references. The *Lineamenta* is referred to three times, the *Instrumentum Laboris* twice, the *Nuntius* once, the *Relatio ante Disceptationem* seven times, the *Relatio post Disceptationem* thirteen times and the *Propositiones* some 119 times or almost half (49.6 percent) of all the footnotes. The synodical documents cited were all drawn up by committees appointed by the Vatican. While the *Lineamenta, Instrumentum Laboris,* and *Nuntius* have been circulated in ecclesial circles, the major source—the *Elenchus Finalis Propositionum*—is *sub secreto*. Only participating bishops received a copy, which they duly voted on, recommen-

[*]John Mansford Prior, "Unfinished Encounter: A Note on the Voice and Tone of *Ecclesia in Asia*," *VJTR* 62/9 (1998), 654–665.

dation by recommendation. The booklet was then handed back to the Synodical Secretariat. Nobody outside Rome has a way of checking this source.

This secrecy seems quite unnecessary. These innocuous propositions were accepted by the bishops with virtual unanimity.[3] Most could have been written thirty years ago. Their language is consensual, sensitive topics having already been removed. What needed to be kept secret was the disparity between the draft proposals from the bishops' groups and the resultant recommendations. Thus, proposals from the working groups on the need to reform the Roman Curia, to democratize and decentralize the Latin Rite and to allow much greater scope to the local Churches to forge ahead with deep inculturation find no space in the *Elenchus Finalis Propositionum*. To hear the bishops' voices, we must return to their interventions during the first days of the synod. This is not easy to do. Participating bishops received only a brief summary of the interventions, not the complete texts. The complete texts of the interventions, like the recommendations, are the property of the Synodical Secretariat.

In *Ecclesia in Asia* there is not a single direct reference to any intervention by an individual bishop, nor to interventions by bishops in the name of their conferences. There are no direct references to regional episcopal bodies such as the Federation of Asian Bishops' Conferences (FABC) or the Council of Oriental Catholic Patriarchs (CPCO).[4] In the introduction FABC Assemblies and Seminars are viewed as contributing "to preparing the synod and making possible an atmosphere of intense ecclesial and fraternal communion. . . . These other assemblies of Asia's bishops served providentially as remote preparation for the Synod Assembly" (*EA* 3; see also 26). I am not sure this Rome-centrism is acceptable in much of Asia.

The Voice of *Ecclesia in Asia*

The pope describes the Synod for Asia as "an encounter-in-dialogue of the Bishops and Successor of Peter, entrusted with the task of strengthening his brothers" (*EA* 8). The Apostolic Exhortation forms half of this encounter. It is a papal document, the pope's response to the voice of the Asian bishops toward the end of his pontificate. As such it is an important document. For the voice of the Asian bishops we have to look elsewhere.

Unfortunately, not many will have heard the voice of the bishops to which the pope is rejoining. Few Episcopal Conferences have published the intervention of their delegates.[5] In order to understand *Ecclesia in Asia* as an important part of "an encounter in dialogue between the Bishops and the Successor of Peter," we would need to read the interventions of the Asian bishops to discover whether *Ecclesia in Asia* responds to the key issues outlined by the bishops, or to key issues as seen by Rome. The Apostolic Exhortation is one side of the synodical encounter. Reading *Ecclesia in Asia* is a little like hearing one end of a telephone conversation. It is certainly worth listening to, but so too is the voice at the other end of the line! Only when these two voices are brought together can we have an "encounter-in-dialogue." Such an ongoing encounter is vital and should help to shape the future of Asia's diaspora communities of faith in the twenty-first century.

Thus, it is important not to read *Ecclesia in Asia* in isolation, but as part of an on-going conversation.

The Voices of Asia

To discover whether *Ecclesia in Asia* is speaking in the same language and about the same concerns as the Asian bishops, we need to turn to their 191 interventions delivered during the first seven days of the synod. Twenty-three of these were on interfaith dialogue, eighteen on the Local Church as a Communion of Communities (a participative, collegial Church), sixteen interventions concerned inculturation, and another eleven, the option of the Church to accompany the poor and marginalized. Ten more dwelt on the challenge of economic globalization. Another ten took up questions of Asian spirituality and God-experience; seven were on youth; and another seven on the Church in China. Six interventions focused on the ancient Apostolic Churches of the Middle East, five took up the question of women, five more the laity, four on schools, four on ecumenism, four on indigenous peoples, four more on family life.

Most of these interventions (76.3 percent to be exact) can be clustered around four main topics.

1. Right at the top comes the dialogue between the Asian Churches and other faith traditions (22.5 percent of the total).
2. At a very close second comes the need for the Church to become authentically Asian through an ongoing dialogue with living cultures (21.4 percent of the total).
3. In third place comes the need for the Churches to learn to dialogue with the poor (17.2 percent of the total).
4. And, in fourth place, the bishops acknowledge that the Asian Church is a church of the laity (15.2 percent of the total).

These are the key issues that have engaged the FABC over the past thirty years. Are they also the key issues of *Ecclesia in Asia*?

Rome's Concerns

Virtually every paragraph in the exhortation rings with phrases like, "preaching . . . the saving Death and Resurrection, of Jesus Christ must be your absolute priority" (*EA* 2); "proclaim with vigor in word and deed that Jesus Christ is the Savior" (9); "Jesus is the greatest gift which the Church can offer to Asia" (10); "The disciples of Christ in Asia must . . . be unstinting in their efforts to fulfil the mission . . . the love of Jesus the Savior" (50). For the pope, the key issue is the direct proclamation of Jesus Christ to those who are not yet committed to him. To this end, the Asian Church needs to hold firmly to a correct formulation of faith in Jesus Christ as Savior. An explicit, complete proclamation of Christ must be the overriding concern of the Asian Churches.

Looking again at the 191 interventions, and remembering the informal conversations during synodal coffee breaks, I can say with absolute certainty that not a single Asian bishop would disagree with the who of mission, with the subject of proclamation. The faith we live is Christic, the ongoing practice of the Asian Churches is a faithful following of the Incarnate Word; on this the integrity of our mission is founded. The key issue that the bishops grapple with is the *how* of mission.

Episcopal Authenticity and Roman Orthodoxy

A central thread running through the synodal interventions is that Jesus Christ is made known primarily through authentic witness by believers who are transparent in their experience of God.[6] The centrality of Christ is made manifest through building up a truly local Church—rooted in local cultures while open to social change, in dialogue with the great Asian religions and the cosmic religions of indigenous peoples, above all by becoming a Church of the poor and marginalized. Many Asian bishops do not separate proclamation from dialogue; in Asia we proclaim in and through dialogue. Dialogue is the best and, often enough, the only viable means of proclamation dialogue of life and action, of hopes and ideals, of faith and convictions.

In *Ecclesia in Asia* I hear an articulate expression, in European theology, of who Christ is. In the bishops' interventions I meet with pastoral overseers struggling to live as *alter Christus*, often in difficult situations. In the Apostolic Exhortation and the synodal interventions we listen to two different voices coming from two different worlds. The voice of Asia is vibrant with life authentically lived in all its vitality, color and spontaneity. The rhythm of Rome beats to a doctrine correctly intoned and broadcast in its entirety. From their interventions, the Asian bishops are aware that the ecclesial situation in Asia is as varied as is the world in which they live. There is a rich variety of Asian Churches by reason of origin, rite, and establishment.

As was explicitly stated in the *Instrumentum Laboris*, there are "Churches of Antioch of the Syrians, Antioch of the Greek Melkites and Antioch of the Maronites, as well as the Latin Church of Jerusalem. There are also the Chaldean Church of Babylonia and the Armenian Church . . . Apostolic Churches, coming from the Syrian tradition, i.e., the Syro-Malabar Church and the Syro-Malankara Church."[7] The communion of Asian Churches is *"bhinneka tunggal ika"*[8]—a unity in diversity.

All these Churches live under different cultural, social, religious, and political contexts with all their related problems, difficulties, restrictions, and even persecution. They are faced with very different situations in their life and witness. Opportunities for, and methods of, evangelization vary from country to country. Hence no uniform pattern of proclamation-in-dialogue, solidarity with the poor, or inculturation is applicable to all the Churches in Asia. Interestingly enough, recommendation no. 4, which acknowledges the pluriform nature of the Asian

Churches, was one of eight recommendations nowhere referred to in *Ecclesia in Asia*.[9]

The Primacy of Witness

More than this, in complex and difficult ethnic, religious, economic, and political situations, evangelization is not so much a question of baptizing (Church growth) as of day-to-day witnessing to the authentic love and hope in Jesus the Christ (leaven, salt, light). A mission spirituality of witness consists of an interplay between contemplation and action.

Missionary witness needs to be hard-headed, tough-minded, pragmatic. Holiness is found in doing what there is to be done (*age quod agis*). While God-experience and authentic witness get their due mention in the Apostolic Exhortation (cf. 23), they do not form the pivotal prism through which to view the holistic mission of the Church, as was the case in many of the bishops' interventions. However, the justice dimension of authentic spirituality (recommendation no. 19) is quoted in the exhortation. Nevertheless, in general, the key for the pope is doctrinal (the *who* and *what* of mission), whereas for the bishops it is pastoral-practical (the *how* and *when*).

Truly Asian, Authentically Christian

Whereas the pope sees the crux of the matter as doctrinal (Christocentrism), the bishops' interventions saw their problem as not with Jesus the Christ—who is widely accepted and loved by Asians—but the presence of a foreign Church burdened by a colonial past. As many Asians have put it over the years, "Jesus of the Gospels—yes; your Western Church—no!" *Ecclesia in Asia* finds it strange that Jesus the Asian has become a foreigner in Asia (*EA* 20).

Apart from the indigenous Churches in the Near East and Kerala, most remaining Churches are the result of colonial expansion and missionary outreach working hand-in-hand. Whatever the nuances, however great the social contribution of the mission Churches in the past, however heroic the sacrifices of cross-cultural missioners over the centuries, the fact remains in stark clarity: the Latin Churches of Asia are a foreign presence. They are alien in the official dress of their leaders; alien in their rituals (despite use of mother tongue); alien in their formation of cultic and community leaders in foreign thought patterns in seminaries whose professors are foreign-educated; alien in their large, often rich, institutions among people who are generally poor; above all, alien in that Christians have had to uproot themselves from their own cultural identity in order to claim a "hybrid" Christian one.

This is a major issue for most Asian bishops. However, *Ecclesia in Asia* mentions it in passing in a single sentence as though the problem were over: ". . . the Church in many places was still considered as foreign to Asia, and indeed was often associated in people's minds with the colonial powers" (9).

These are fundamentally different readings of history and therefore of the present situation. For the bishops, the way forward in mission is a radical renewal of the Church that it become authentically Asian proclaiming the Jesus of the

Gospels, above all through life-witness in a radical service to the poor and in shining examples of God-experience, that is, orthopraxis in all its gospel radicality. This comes out clearly in the work of the FABC over the past thirty years and is vindicated by the many synodical interventions.

Ecclesia in Asia is surely right in placing Christ rather than, say, the Church, whether Latin or Oriental, at the center. This is not to separate Christ from his body, the Church, but rather to accept the Church as sign, sacrament, and instrument of Christ's saving presence. The eternal, incarnate, redemptive, cosmic presence of Christ can neither be confined to, nor controlled by the Church. The central problem is neither Christ nor his acceptance/rejection by his fellow Asians. The key missiological problem is rather the Western Church's alien tone and idiom inherited from colonial times. Meanwhile, the Oriental Churches of the Near East and South India have too easily allowed themselves to become encapsulated within certain social strata of local culture. On the *who* of mission, both the Apostolic Exhortation and the bishops' interventions are in agreement, although the languages are clearly different. As for the *how* of mission, we need time, patience, and perseverance in order to move away from insulated, devotional ghettos and re-invent ourselves as dynamic *diaspora* living out a dialogue of life and action.

Which Model for Inter-Faith Dialogue?

Papal doctrine is important. The theology of religions in *Ecclesia in Asia* follows the fulfillment theory. Three examples from many:

1. "The religious values [world religions] teach, await their fulfillment in Jesus Christ" (*EA* 6).
2. ". . . as the incarnate Word who lived, died, and rose from the dead, Jesus Christ is now proclaimed as the fulfillment of all creation, of all history, and of all human yearning for fullness of life" (14).
3. ". . . the Incarnate Wisdom of God whose grace brings to fruition the 'seeds' of divine Wisdom already present in the lives, religions, and peoples of Asia" (20).

This theology is good in that it preserves intact the Christological formulations of past centuries. It has become inadequate in the face of the experience of heart-to-heart interfaith dialogue.

Here we should note that throughout the synod bishop after bishop gave great encouragement to their theologians to discover and formulate Asian theologies. Paragraph 22 quotes recommendation no. 7, which, despite its caution, remains a positive encouragement to Asian theologians. The quote reads, ". . . this theologizing is to be carried out with courage, in faithfulness to the Scriptures and to the Church's Tradition, in sincere adherence to the Magisterium and with an awareness of pastoral realities." The fulfillment theory must not become the only normative formulation possible. Asian theologians need to continue working on the question from their deep involvement in interfaith struggles for justice and in considered reflection upon that involvement.[10]

Solidarity and Compassion with the Poor

There is a large measure of agreement between Rome and Asia on the Church's compassionate solidarity with the marginalized. The emphasis of the bishops' interventions on social engagement is found throughout *Ecclesia in Asia* and in its continual underscoring the importance of living out Christian Social Doctrine (cf. 7 and especially chapter VI, 32–41). The Gospel of Life is a splendid holistic treatment (35). Perhaps that is why the rather strident recommendation on abortion (no. 46) is not referred to. My only regret is that this fine paragraph is separated from the section on peacemaking (38)—also a fine treatment of the theme.[11]

One tragedy in the North American Church is that those working for preserving life in the womb and those working for peace among nations are divided into two quite separate camps. However, the Gospel of Life is a "seamless robe"; work for unborn children and the ending of war as a way of "solving" intercommunal and international problems belong together. In Asia, the issue is absolutely vital, for many of our countries have long become militarized and our cultural values brutalized.

The Apostolic Exhortation seems to identify Christian Social Doctrine with Petrine Social Doctrine. As important and dynamic as the social encyclicals have been over the past century, it remains true that social engagement "at the coal face" is producing rich seams of social doctrine also. This is clear in both the documents of the FABC and those of various Asian Episcopal Conferences. I feel that neither the episcopal interventions during the synod nor *Ecclesia in Asia* itself has made an adequate analysis of economic and political globalization with all its social, ethical, and humanitarian consequences. Perhaps the FABC Office for Human Development can help us to coalesce all this committed involvement and considerable reflection into a common focus.

Which Model for Inculturation?

Time and again, *Ecclesia in Asia* interprets inculturation as a matter of translation and presentation (e.g., *EA* 20–22). Asia is the "external context," whereas Rome asserts a "normative" and "universal" theology. Some might see this translation model as almost "colonial"—the integration of elements of "satellite" cultures into a dominantly Roman frame! However, for Asian theologians, present currents and future trends in society are not simply context; rather they provide material, questions, and significant existential answers for discerning the provident way of God. The *logoi spermatikoi*, in an attentive reading of the signs of the times, are part of the revealing Word of the Eternally Provident God and Father of Jesus the Nazarene.

The Asian Churches are struggling not only to affirm but also to rediscover and regain the cultural identities of their peoples. They are engaged in an intercultural process. From the interventions on inculturation, it is clear that for many bishops inculturation has hardly begun.[12] The Western Church tradition has yet to be reinterpreted and creatively given new expressions. Not appropriation but encounter, not absorption but colloquy, not translation from a European model but the freedom to allow a slow, gradual "natural" growth of new embodiments of the incarnate and crucified Word. These new embodiments create new theologies, new ethics, new community arrangements, new worship. They also transform local cultures from within as yeast, as light, as New Life. The gospel challenges each and every culture—even while it is itself always expressed within certain cultures—Hebrew, Greek, Roman, European, Asian. In mission, priority needs to be given to the evangelization of cultures. That is, a fundamental, deep-structured dialogue with indigenous thought patterns in the context of rapid sociocultural changes.

Constrictive pastoral directives do not heed the mystery of the incarnation. *Christus heri, hodie, semper* (Heb 13:8) is present in a multiplicity of ministries (*plura et diversa*) in the one Body of Christ with many diverse functions. Inculturation is hampered by each and every form of prescribed conformity. An authentic dialogue between Word and culture is at the heart of true inculturation.

Asia and the See of Peter

The need for a culture of dialogue within the Communion of Catholic Churches has never been greater. Any tension between the universal and the particular is overcome through interpretation and dialogue—a dialogue between theory and reality in cross-cultural communication. We need to develop an open particularity in a communion of local Churches, not ethnic congregations encapsulated in local ebbs and tides.

Ecclesia in Asia identifies the Universal Church with Rome, that is, with the Petrine ministry and its Roman Curia (e.g., nos. 26 and 43). They, and their Western theology and discipline, are the norm. This ideology underpins the ever-increasing—and utterly untraditional—centralization of the Roman Rite which has accelerated rather alarmingly over the past twenty years. Asia has been seeking freedom to proclaim the Gospel in Asian ways, whereas Rome seems to be responding with ever closer control! The many concrete recommendations by the bishops for redistributing power in the Church are totally absent from the exhortation—even the simple suggestion that Rome need not insist on approving liturgical translations in languages they do not know![13]

A personal note. The many sharp criticisms of the Roman Curia and Roman centralism made on the synod floor should not necessarily be interpreted as the wish of every bishop to build up a democratic, participative Communion of Churches. Experience shows that, often enough, greater local autonomy is nothing but an opportunity to work in a more "local" way, whether that be neo-feudal, overtly ethnic, or whatever. Greater autonomy from Rome is certainly going to be on the agenda of the next General Council. However, we should be aware that for some bishops it might simply mean a chance to build up a local power base. At least, this is what has been happening in many religious congregations.[14] Maybe, that is what has also happened in some of the Oriental Rite Churches over the years. Therefore, in the words of the FABC, we need a "new way of being Church"[15] that is not simply a passing down of the powers and rights of the Roman Curia to the local bishop or to the local Synod of Bishops. We should not replace Roman centralization with local encapsulization.

Recommendation no. 13, entitled "The Church as Communion," welcomes the Petrine office and its ministry in guaranteeing and promoting the unity of the Church. In this recommendation, the many proposals on the need for a root-and-branch reform of the Roman Curia have been reduced to a single recommendation for a greater internationalization of the Roman dicasteries. Even this remnant is missing from *Ecclesia in Asia*. The Apostolic Exhortation does, however, have an oblique reference to the bishops' dissatisfaction with curia interference: "An essential feature of this service [of the curia] is the respect and sensitivity which these close co-workers of the Successor of Peter show towards the legitimate diversity of the local Churches and the variety of cultures and peoples with which they are in contact" (no. 25).

Toward a New Ecumenical Council

Ecclesia in Asia gives us the voice of Rome; in FABC and the synodical interventions we hear voices from Asia. In the pope's words, these two voices need to be brought into an "encounter-in-dialogue." However, neither the mechanisms of the Episcopal Synod nor its methodology made for a true encounter-in-dialogue between East and West. A synod has no decision-making powers. Even the few modest proposals that were allowed into the recommendations have not been included in the Apostolic Exhortation. A more universal and authoritative instrument is necessary, able to confront issues freely in the full exercise of episcopal collegiality.

At the Synod for Oceania, held six months after the Synod for Asia, Michael Curran, Superior General of the Missionari del Sacro Cuore di Gesù (MSC), called for a culture of dialogue in the Church. He said, "There is a fairly widespread feeling that the growing centralization of authority in the Roman Curia is doing damage to the legitimate autonomy of the local Churches and to the inculturation of the Gospel in a truly world-wide catholicity." He went on to make a concrete proposal: "May I make bold to suggest that we need, at the beginning of the new millennium, an Ecumenical Council in order to deal directly and effectively with issues of Church Order and Government?"[16] During the Second Synod for Europe in October 1999, Cardinal Carlo Martini ended his intervention by saying, "It would surely be good and useful for the bishops of today and tomorrow, in a Church becoming ever more diverse in its languages, to repeat the experience of communion and collegiality and of the Holy Spirit which their predecessors had enjoyed at the Second Vatican Council."[17] The Indonesian bishops, in their response to the *Lineamenta* for the upcoming Episcopal Synod due in 2001, made a similar call.[18] I would like to end this note on *Ecclesia in Asia* by quoting the final section of their response:

> The evangelical mission of proclamation can be re-vitalized through a
> re-ordering of relationships between local Churches (Metropolitans and
> Suffragans; national Conferences and regional Federations) and between
> local/regional Churches and the See of Peter in Rome (a thorough over-

haul of the diplomatic corps and Roman Curia). The more appropriate forum is not a purely consultative Synod but a decision-making General Council where the agenda and secretariat would be in the hands of the bishops, as the successors of the Apostles and as the closest collaborators of the Holy See. [The Council of Constance (1414–1418) decreed that there ought to be a General Council every decade.] Would it not be splendid *to open the new millennium with a new General Council* of the Communion of Catholic Churches? In Council we would take up again the ecclesial-missionary vision of the Second Vatican Council, and we could dismantle the unnecessary centralizing power-structures that were gradually built up after the Gregorian reform at the beginning of the second millennium. The church, *semper reformanda*, would then *enter the third millennium under the inspiration of the first*: as a Communion of local/autonomous Churches, working in dynamic partnership with Rome and each other, through enhanced Metropolitan Sees, Regional Synods, and a variety of Patriarchates, both old and new. All these issues were discussed, but not decided upon, during the Second Vatican Council. Experience shows that we need to revise the structures of governance in the Church, perhaps even—as proposed by Paul VI in 1965—to draw up a comprehensive Constitution (*lex ecclesiae fundamentalis*) according to the ancient principles of collegiality, subsidiarity, and solidarity and with a clear separation of powers at each level.

APPENDIX

There are 240 footnotes. John Paul II quotes himself sixty-eight times; Paul VI, five times; Leo XIII, once. The Roman Congregation of the Doctrine of the Faith is referred to directly once, the Catechism twice, and the Roman Missal twice. The Second Vatican Council is referred to fifteen times, Augustine once, and John Chrysostom once. The Special Assembly for Asia is referred to 145 times as follows: *Lineamenta,* three times; *Instrumentum Laboris,* twice; *Nuntius,* once; *Relatio ante Disceptationem,* seven times; *Relatio post Disceptationem,* thirteen times; and the *Propositiones* 119 times.

Frequency of Recommendations Referred to in Footnotes

Six Primary References: Recommendations no. 27 (Consecrated Life) and no. 29 (Laity and Evangelization).

Five Primary References: Recommendations no. 22 (Human Rights and the Promotion of Justice and Peace) and no. 35 (Women).

Four Primary References: Recommendations no. 13 (The Church as Communion), no. 21 (Education), no. 25 (The Formation of Seminary Professors and Staff), no. 45 (Social Communications), and no. 50 (The Oriental Churches).

Three Primary References: Recommendations no. 8 (The Joy of Announcing Jesus Christ), no. 15 (The Diocese of Communion), no. 32 (Family), no. 33 (Pastoral Care of Children), no. 34 (Youth), no. 36 (Pastoral Care of Migrants), no. 38 (Tribal Peoples), no. 41 (Interreligious Dialogue), no. 44 (Human Promotion and Evangelization), no. 51 (Particular Churches in Difficult Circumstances), no. 52 (The Church in China), and no. 57 (Jerusalem).

Two Primary References: Recommendations no. 5 (Jesus Christ the Savior of All Peoples), no. 6 (Presentation of Jesus Christ), no. 7 (Problems in the Presentation of Jesus Christ in Asia), no. 11 (The Spirit of God in Creation and History), no. 12 (The Spirit of God at Work in Asia), no. 17 (The Word of God), no. 20 (Healing Ministry), no. 23 (Peacemaking), no. 28 (Missionary Societies of Apostolic Life), no. 31 (Renewal Movements), no. 39 (Option for the Marginalized), no. 43 (Inculturation), no. 48 (The Debt Crisis), no. 49 (Globalization), no. 53 (North Korea), and no. 56 (Churches in New Areas).

A Single Primary Reference: Recommendations no. 1 (Introduction), no. 3 (The Challenge of Asia), no. 14 (The Communion of Local Churches), no. 16 (The Parish), no. 18 (Biblical Formation), no. 19 (Spirituality), no. 24 (Formation of Seminarians), no. 30 (Basic Ecclesial Communities), no. 42 (Ecumenism), no. 47 (Ecology), no. 54 (Asian Saints and Martyrs), no. 55 (Embargo in Iraq), no. 58 (A Word of Gratitude), and no. 59 (The Blessed Virgin Mary).

No Primary Reference: Recommendations no. 2 (The Challenge of Asia), no. 4 (A Variety of Ecclesial Realities), no. 9 (Emphasis on God-Experience in Jesus Christ), no. 10 (The Trinitarian Plan of Salvation), no. 26 (The Priesthood Instituted within the People of God), no. 37 (Pastoral Care of Tourists), no. 40 (Proclamation), and no. 46 (Abortion).

References

Abeyasingha, Nibal (1999). "The Next Generation of Religious in Asia," *Review for Religious* 58, 6.
Curran, Michael M.S.C. (1999). "A Culture of Dialogue," *Sedos Bulletin* 31, 5.

Notes

1. The splendid citation from John Chrysostom is worth quoting in full: "Do you wish to honor the body of Christ? Then do not ignore him when he is naked. Do not pay him silken honors in the temple only then to neglect him when he goes cold and naked outside. He who said, 'This is my body' is the One who also said, 'You saw me hungry and you gave me no food.'. . . What good is it if the Eucharistic Table groans under the weight of golden chalices, when Christ is dying of hunger? Start by satisfying his hunger, and then with what remains you may adorn the altar as well." Footnote No. 203, *EA* 115. Quote from *Homilies on the Gospel of Matthew*, 50, 3–4: *PG* 58, 508–509. The Augustinian quote is brief: (The Church) "progresses on her pilgrimage amid this world's persecutions and God's consolations." Footnote No. 113, *EA* 73 (*De Civitate Dei*, XVIII 51, 2; *PL* 41, 614).
2. I refer to the first, or primary reference in each footnote. Many footnotes have additional, subsidiary references.
3. There were 168 voting participants present. Recommendation nos. 21 and 23 were accepted unanimously (on education and peacemaking respectively). Nos. 13 and 15 received 156 positive votes (The Church as Communion and The Diocese as Commun-

ion), no. 31 just 150 votes (Renewal Movements), no. 41b was accepted by 142 votes (a request for a directory on interreligious dialogue), no. 43 by 149 votes (inculturation), and no. 50 by 140 votes (the Oriental Churches). The highest number of negative votes (some 14) was against recommendation no. 43 on inculturation—it did not go far enough! The other "high" number of negatives was recommendation no. 50 on the Oriental Churches. From reactions by the bishops and patriarchs, it can be assumed that they were not satisfied that this recommendation truly represented the views expressed in their sharp interventions.

4. Other Asia-wide ecclesial bodies have also "disappeared," such as AMOR (Asia-wide Association of Religious), which received a positive endorsement in the *Lineamenta* (no. 14).

5. The Filipino interventions were published in *Philippina Sacra*. Perhaps only Indonesia has published a comprehensive "Study Guide" to the synod, translating a wide selection of the summaries from the entire range of synodal interventions, arranged thematically, with brief introductions to each theme and questions for reflection at the end of each section, a total of 386 pages in all. Outside Asia, the U.S. bishops usually publish their synodal interventions in *Origins*.

6. The ten interventions on God-experience and Asian spirituality were nos. 37 (India), 56 (India), 24 (Philippines), 88 (Germany), 121 (Vietnam), 124 (Malabar-India), 135 (Myanmar), 136 (Superior General), 139 (India), and the intervention of auditor no. 28.

7. *Instrumentum Laboris*, par. 11, p. 9.

8. *Bhinneka tunggal ika* is the official motto of Indonesia—Unity in diversity.

9. The eight recommendations not referred to in the footnotes are nos. 2 (the challenge of Asia), 4 (varied ecclesial situations), 9 (emphasis on God-experience in Jesus Christ), 10 (the Trinitarian plan of salvation), 26 (the priesthood instituted within the people of God), 37 (pastoral care of tourists), 40 (proclamation), and 46 (abortion). Nos. 2, 4, 9, 10, and 26 were very typical of the bishops' outlook. No. 40 is not quoted, but then the theme of proclamation takes up most of the exhortation with copious quotes from the pope's previous writings. The neglect to refer to the strident tune of no. 46 is fortunate; the exhortation is beautifully holistic in its approach to life.

10. A superb, duly nuanced, alternative approach is Jacques Dupuis's *Toward a Christian Theology of Religious Pluralism* (New York: Orbis, 1997).

11. Recommendation no. 55, quoting John Paul II, had called for the lifting of the embargo on Iraq. This has been very much watered down in the exhortation at the end of par. 38, p. 110.

12. The sixteen synodal interventions dealing primarily with "deep inculturation" are nos. 1 (Japan), 4 (Japan), 14 (Japan—delivered in Latin!), 25 (Philippines), 42 (India), 58 (Philippines), 64 (Indonesia), 71 (Vatican), 91 (Vietnam), 93 (Vietnam), 98 (Vietnam), 103 (Indonesia), 107 (Superior General), 145 (Philippines), 158 (Vatican), 154 (Cambodia).

13. Recommendation no. 43 sought the authority and freedom to inculturate the liturgy, including a specific request that Episcopal and Regional Bishops' Conferences have the competence to approve translations of liturgical texts in the vernacular. In the exhortation, "greater freedom" has become "work more closely with the Holy See"! (cf. par. 22, p. 65).

14. See Nibal Abeyasingha, "The Next Generation of Religious in Asia," *Review for Religious* 58/6 (1999), 621–629. Western-led democratic reform of Religious Congrega-

tions in the 1960s and 1970s has often been translated in Asia into an opportunity to incorporate local values many of which are far from democratic. The author speaks from the Sri Lankan context. Much of what he says is applicable elsewhere in Asia.

15. This is the collaborative, participative ideal behind the Asian Integrated Pastoral Approach (AsIPA) promoted by the FABC.

16. Michael Curran, "Address to the Synod for Oceania" (1999), 157–158. (Quoted from *General Bulleltin MSC,* 6/98, December 1998).

17. Carlo Martini, S.J., "Address to the Second Synod for Europe" as quoted in "Church in the World," *The Tablet* (16 October 1999). Martini listed topics for the next council such as the deepening and development of the Second Vatican Council's doctrine of the Church as communion; the lack of ordained ministers; the position of women in society and the Church; the participation of the laity in ministerial responsibilities; sexuality; marriage discipline; penitential practice; relations with the Orthodox Churches and the general need to revive ecumenical hope; the relationship between democracy and values and between civil law and the moral law.

18. The fifteen-page response is dated Jakarta, 10 August 1999, and signed by Bishop Johanes Hadiwikarta, Secretary General of the Conference.

16

Ecclesia in Asia: Challenges for Asian Christianity[*]

PETER C. PHAN

With the official promulgation of the Apostolic Exhortation *Ecclesia in Asia* by Pope John Paul II in New Delhi, India, on November 6, 1999, the Special Assembly for Asia of the Synod of Bishops, henceforth the Asian Synod for short, which had met in Rome from April 19 to May 14, 1998, in a certain sense came to an end.[1] Proclaimed as "a moment of special grace" (*EA* 3), the synod had drawn, both during its preparatory stage and in its aftermaths, both favorable and unfavorable comments, especially with regard to its *Lineamenta* and its *modus operandi*.[2] Similarly, the immediate reception of the Exhortation has been, as to be expected, mixed: it was received in some quarters with unfeigned enthusiasm; in others, with muted applause; still in others, with unalloyed disappointment.[3]

The Asian Synod in Context

As is often the case, how one reacts to the bishops' synods and the ensuing Apostolic Exhortations largely depends on the expectations one entertains of them. As is well known, the International Bishops' Synod was established by Pope Paul VI in September 1965, shortly before the close of the Second Vatican Council, as an instrument of episcopal collegiality. The synod, which the pope reserves the right to convoke, intends to foster a close collaboration between the bishops and the pope. It is, however, advisory and not deliberative. Since its foundation there have been eleven international synods (both ordinary and extraordinary)[4] and eight national or regional synods, including the five continental synods called by John Paul II's *Tertio Millennio Adveniente* to celebrate the new millennium.

Unfortunately, as Michael Fahey, S.J., a highly respected American ecclesiologist, has put it tersely, "despite high hopes for their success, results of synods have been negligible. Each new synod attracts less and less attention; the structure of their sessions has become unwieldy, they have become rituals with little practical impact on the life of the Church. In the last thirty years the institution has not been notable as a wellspring of new ideas or strategies."[5] Furthermore, because the Apostolic Exhortations that follow these continental synods (so far three have

---

[*] Peter C. Phan, "*Ecclesia in Asia:* Challenges for Asian Christianity," *EAPR* 37 (2000), 215–232.

been issued) are not the work of the synodal participants themselves (though they are supposed to incorporate the synods' "propositions") but are composed by the pope with the assistance of a post-synodal committee, they are often suspected of having filtered the results of the synods to an officially acceptable level. Moreover, being usually quite lengthy and turgid in style, they have aroused little interest, even among the clergy and theologians; and, of course, it is totally unrealistic to expect that they will be read by the laity, at least in their entirety.

These remarks are not intended to cast a cynical eye on the Asian Synod and *Ecclesia in Asia*. On the contrary, they serve as a warning that unless concrete steps are taken to put the synod's fifty-nine "propositions," which have been more or less incorporated into *Ecclesia in Asia*, into practice at the level of the local Churches, the Asian Synod will not be unlike one of the many fireworks displays celebrating the coming of the third millennium: spectacular festivals of sounds and colors but in the end, nothing more than blurred memories of the New Year's Eve extravaganzas. What steps can and should be taken by the Asian Churches to prevent their synod from joining the ranks of its predecessors, illustrious indeed, but reduced to being a convenient quarry for doctoral dissertations, bereft of real and lasting influence on the life of the Churches of Asia?[6]

In the following pages, what is being offered is neither an evaluation of the Asian Synod nor a commentary of *Ecclesia in Asia*. Rather, as an expatriate Vietnamese who has for a quarter of a century been engaged in the study and teaching of theology in the United States of America, and whose academic interest has focused on Christianity of Asia,[7] I will advance, very selectively, some reflections and proposals as to how certain teachings of the Asian Synod, as embodied in *Ecclesia in Asia*, can be implemented in Asia.[8]

The Church not *in* but *of* Asia: The Asianness of Christianity

By any standard, *Ecclesia in Asia* is John Paul II's typical theological product, with its rather forbidding length, its frequent insistence on complete orthodoxy, its abundant citation of the pope's own writings, and its emotional peroration with a prayer to Mary. Besides an introduction and a conclusion, the exhortation is composed of seven parts dealing with the following themes: the Asian context, Jesus as Savior, the Holy Spirit as Lord and Giver of Life, proclamation of Jesus in Asia (with a focus on inculturation), communion and dialogue for mission (with a focus on ecumenical and interreligious dialogue), the service of human promotion, and Christians as witnesses to the Gospel.

For an Asian reader, the inevitable question arises: has the exhortation said anything new and important for the Churches of Asia that either had not been said before by these Churches themselves or could not have been said except thanks to the work of the synod itself? To both parts of the question the answer is frankly no. Except the first section on the Asian context, most of the exhortation could have been written prior to and apart from the synod, and what the exhortation says on the other six themes has already been said, powerfully and in great detail, by the various documents of the FABC.[9]

This does not mean however that the synod and the exhortation have not rendered a valuable service. After listing the fifteen points of agreement out of the fifty-nine propositions the synod submitted, Luis Tagle acknowledges that there is nothing new in them in comparison with the teachings of the FABC, but he correctly insists that there was something genuinely new in the fact that these issues and concerns have been voiced in a synodal forum and recognized by the Church of Rome, and thereby, have been brought to the consciousness of the universal Church.[10] What was new is not what the Asian bishops said but *that* they said it and *how* they said it at the synod. What they said had been said, at length and with power and depth, for almost thirty years, ever since the founding of the FABC in 1972, in its numerous plenary assemblies and in the documents of its several institutes.[11] But at the synod, they said it again, *to the whole Church*, and with surprising *boldness* and refreshing *candor*, with what the New Testament calls *parrhēsia*.

The synod was the first official recognition that the Churches of Asia have come of age, or as a synodal participant put it, that they are not branch offices of the Roman Curia. To the universal Church the Asian bishops proclaimed, humbly but forcefully, that the Churches of Asia not only learn from but also have something to teach the Church of Rome as well as the Church universal, precisely from their experiences as Churches not simply *in* but *of* Asia. The fact that the exhortation has incorporated several elements of the Asian Synod and made them part of the papal magisterium is an eloquent witness to the value of the experiences and wisdom of the Asian Churches.

What is new, in a word, is the public recognition of the necessity and validity of the *Asianness* of the Churches of Asia. Of course, Asianness is a notoriously slippery concept, and the *Lineamenta* and the exhortation attempt to circumscribe it by listing several cultural and religious values that purportedly constitute the "Asian soul" or "being Asian": "love of silence and contemplation, simplicity, harmony, detachment, non-violence, discipline, frugal living, the thirst for learning and philosophical inquiry . . . , respect for life, compassion for all beings, closeness to nature, filial piety toward parents, elders and ancestors, and a highly developed sense of community" (*EA* 6). The exhortation also attends to the economic, social, and political contexts in which Christianity exists in Asia (*EA* 7–8). Unfortunately, when it speaks of the fact that "despite her centuries-long presence and her many apostolic endeavors, the Church in many places was still considered as foreign to Asia and indeed was often associated in people's minds with the colonial powers" (*EA* 9), it uses the past tense and fails to recognize that the foreignness of Christianity in Asia and the perception of its association with colonialism are *present* realities, and this not simply "in many places" but in *all* parts of Asia.

If the Asian Synod is to have a lasting transformative effect on the Churches of Asia, so that they may become truly *of* Asia and their association with colonialism may be removed, the most important thing, in my judgment, is that Asian Catholics take their Asianness seriously as the context of their being Christian. In practice, this means that the first and last concern for the leaders of the Asian

Churches must be not how a particular policy is conformable with canonical requirements and directives coming from Rome or elsewhere but rather how it will respond to the challenges of the Asian social, political, economic, and religious contexts and whether and how it will effectively help Christians live their faith in fidelity to the gospel and the living Christian tradition, here and now, in Asia. Determining this Asianness and making it the perspective through which the Christian faith is consistently expressed and lived should be the top priority for Asian Christianity in the post-synodal era.[12]

Those of us who live close to the ecclesiastical centers of the churches of the so-called Third World sometimes experience the sad irony of these churches trying to be "more Roman than Rome." Perhaps such a phenomenon is understandable when these churches lack the necessary resources to be on their own, especially in countries with governments hostile to Christianity, and are still, as it were, in their minority. Now that the Asian Churches have come of age, however, they should be able to move to the stage of self-government, self-support, self-propagation, and self-theologizing. As the Asian Colloquium on Ministries in the Church already put it in 1977: "The basic fact is that today in our Asian context we are in the process of re-discovering that the individual Christian can best survive, grow, and develop as a Christian person in the midst of a self-nourishing, self-governing, self-ministering, and self-propagating Christian community."[13]

To assume responsibilities in these areas, while remaining in full communion with the Church universal, demands courage, imagination, creativity, collaboration at all levels of the Church life, and above all trust in the Holy Spirit, and is much more challenging (and uncomfortable) than simply "applying" existing Church laws and traditions to the different situations of Asia. But it is only in this way that the Churches *in* Asia become truly *of* Asia. As Christian Churches, they must of course proclaim and live the Christian faith, the same *faith* handed down the ages, but not in the theological categories and with the church structures imported from without. Rather they should do so in the modalities conceived and born from within the Asian contexts. These Asian categories and structures need not of course be totally different from those of the churches elsewhere; however, whether they are identical with or different from these cannot and should not be determined beforehand and a priori but must be shaped by real experimentations in the concrete situations of each Asian country. The Churches of Asia must claim and exercise the God-given right, based on the mystery of divine incarnation (and not a concession granted by a some higher ecclesiastical authority), to find out and determine for themselves how best to proclaim and live the Christian faith in Asia. Such a task is a matter of life and death for the Church, since if the Church in Asia is not Asian, it is no Church at all.

This task of becoming *Asian* Churches is all the more urgent in light of the astounding acceptance by *Ecclesia in Asia* of a point made by the Asian Synod that "Jesus is often perceived as foreign to Asia. It is paradoxical that most Asians tend to regard Jesus—born on Asian soil—as a Western rather than an Asian figure" (*EA* 20). While ways must be found, as the exhortation urges Asian theologians to do,[14] "to present the mystery of Christ to their peoples according to their cultural patterns and ways of thinking" (*EA* 20),[15] the most effective way to present Jesus as an Asian figure is to make the Churches authentically Asian.

A New Way of Being Church

Another way of making the point I have argued for so far is to say that for the Asian Synod to have a lasting impact, the Asian Churches must, with courage and creativity, find new ways of being Church, and hence construct an alternative ecclesiology. This is a theme repeatedly emphasized by the FABC, especially in its third and fifth plenary assemblies in Bangkok, 1982 and Bandung, Indonesia, 1990 respectively. This ecclesiology, in a sort of Copernican revolution, de-centers the Church in the sense that it makes the center of the Christian life not the Church but the reign of God. Christians must be not ecclesiocentric but regnocentric. Their mission is not to expand the Church and its structures (*plantatio ecclesiae*) in order to enlarge the sphere of influence for the Church but to be a transparent sign and effective instrument of the saving presence of the reign of God, the reign of justice, peace, and love, of which the Church is a seed. As the exhortation puts it well: "Empowered by the Spirit to accomplish Christ's salvation on earth, the Church is the seed of the kingdom of God, and she looks eagerly for its final coming. Her identity and mission are inseparable from the kingdom of God. . . . The Spirit reminds the Church that she is not an end unto herself: In all that she is and all that she does, she exists to serve Christ and the salvation of the world" (*EA* 17).[16] The new way of being Church in Asia and the ecclesiology undergirding it are characterized by the following features.[17]

1. First, the Church, both at the local and universal levels, is seen primarily as "a *communion of communities*, where laity, Religious, and clergy recognize and accept each other as sisters and brothers."[18] At the heart of the mystery of the Church is the bond of communion uniting God with humanity and humans with one another, of which the Eucharist is the sign and instrument par excellence.[19]

Moreover, in this ecclesiology there is an explicit and effective recognition of the fundamental equality among all the members of the local Church as disciples of Jesus and among all the local Churches in so far as they are communities of Jesus' disciples and whose communion constitutes the universal Church. The communion (*koinonia*) that constitutes the Church, both at the local and universal levels, and from which flows the fundamental equality of all Christians, is rooted at its deepest level in the life of the Trinity in whom there is a perfect communion of equals.[20] Unless this fundamental equality of all Christians is acknowledged and put into practice through concrete policies and actions, the Church will not become a communion of communities in Asia. Living out this fundamental equality is particularly difficult in Asia, not only because the insistence on the hierarchical structure of the Church tends to obscure and minimize it but also because it goes against the class consciousness of many Asian societies.

Furthermore, this vision of Church as communion of communities and its corollary of fundamental equality are the sine qua non condition for the fulfillment of the Church's mission. Without being a communion, the Church cannot fulfill its mission, since the Church is, as intimated above, nothing more than the bond of communion between God and humanity and among humans themselves. As the exhortation puts it tersely, "communion and mission go hand in hand" (*EA* 24).

2. This pastoral "discipleship of equals" leads to the second characteristic of the new way of being Church in Asia, that is, the participatory and collaborative nature of all the ministries in the Church: "It is a *participatory* Church where the gifts that the Holy Spirit gives to all the faithful—lay, Religious, and cleric alike—are recognized and activated, so that the Church may be built up and its mission realized."[21] This participatory nature of the Church must be lived out not only in the local Church but also among all the local Churches, including the Church of Rome, of course, with due recognition of the papal primacy. In this context, it is encouraging to read in the exhortation the following affirmation: "It is in fact within the perspective of ecclesial communion that the universal authority of the Successor of Peter shines forth more clearly, not primarily as juridical power over the local Churches, but above all as a pastoral primacy at the service of the unity of faith and life of the whole people of God" (*EA* 25). A "pastoral primacy" must do everything possible to foster coresponsibility and participation of all the local Churches in the triple ministry of teaching, sanctification, and service in the Church and must be held accountable to this task so that these words do not remain at the level of pious rhetoric but are productive of concrete structures and actions.

If the Asian Synod proved that the Asian Churches do have something vital to teach the Church of Rome and the Church universal, then the "magisterium" in the Church can no longer be conceived as a one-way street from Rome to the other local Churches. Instead, there must be *mutual* learning and teaching, *mutual* encouragement and correction between the Church of Rome and the other churches, indeed among all the local Churches. Only in this way can correction be made of the widespread perception, especially in countries with the so-called national or patriotic churches, that the Christian Church in Asia is a foreign (indeed, international) organization, comparable to a multinational corporation, that must take orders from a foreign power.

In this context it may be useful to point out that a certain language to describe the relationship between the local bishop and the Bishop of Rome, traditional though it is in some ecclesiastical circles, should be avoided to obviate misunderstanding. I refer to words such as "loyalty" and "obedience" to characterize the attitude of bishops to the pope which, to Asian ears, inevitably suggest oaths of submission of vassals to their lords in a feudal system. Besides the fact that in the Church "loyalty" is owed to no one but Christ and that the bishop is not beholden to the pope for his episcopal office nor is he the pope's vicar, it is theologically much more appropriate to describe and live the relationship between the local Church and the pope in terms of collegiality and solidarity. Only in this way can the Church's teaching office and the pope's ministry of promoting unity be effectively exercised, learning from the varied and rich experiences of being Church from all corners of the globe and welcoming respectful but frank warning and correction when errors of intellectual narrowness, moral arrogance, and spiritual blindness have been committed.

3. The third characteristic of a new way of being Church in Asia is the *dialogical* spirit: "Built in the hearts of people, it is a Church that faithfully and lovingly witnesses to the Risen Lord and reaches out to people of other faiths and persuasions in a dialogue of life towards the integral liberation of all."[22] Ever since its first plenary assembly in Taipei, Taiwan, 1974, the FABC has repeatedly insisted that the primary task of the Asian Churches is the proclamation of the gospel. But it has also maintained no less frequently that the way to fulfill this task in Asia is by way of dialogue, indeed a triple dialogue, with Asian cultures, Asian religions, and the Asians themselves, especially the poor.[23] The exhortation reiterates the necessity of this triple dialogue. In the dialogue with the Asian cultures (inculturation), the exhortation highlights the areas of theology, liturgy, and the Bible (*EA* 22). In the dialogue with other religious traditions, the document emphasizes ecumenical and interreligious dialogue. It quotes approvingly the proposition 41 of the synod: "Interreligious relations are best developed in a context of openness to other believers, a willingness to listen and the desire to respect and understand others in their differences. For all this, love of others is indispensable. This should result in collaboration, harmony and mutual enrichment" (*EA* 31). In the dialogue with the poor, the exhortation affirms the necessity of the preferential love of the poor (in particular, the migrants, indigenous, and tribal people, women and children), defense of human life, health care, education, peacemaking, cancellation of foreign debts, and protection of the environment (*EA* 32–41). There is no doubt that if the Christian Church is to become truly *of* Asia, Asian Christians must be engaged, relentlessly and wholeheartedly, in this triple "dialogue of life and heart" and in this way fulfill their inalienable right and duty of proclaiming Jesus to their fellow Asians.[24]

In this context of the proclamation of the gospel and the triple dialogue with Asian cultures, religions, and the poor, it may be appropriate to raise the vexing issue of how to proclaim Christ as the Savior and as the only Savior in Asia. The exhortation affirms that "there can be no true evangelization without the explicit proclamation of Jesus as Lord" (*EA* 19) and that this proclamation "is prompted not by sectarian impulse nor the spirit of proselytism nor any sense of superiority" but "in obedience to Christ's command" (*EA* 20). Therefore, the proclamation must be done with a twofold respect: "respect for man [sic] in his quest for answers to the deepest questions of his life and respect for the action of the Spirit in man [sic]" (*EA* 20).

As to how to proclaim that Jesus is the *only* Savior, the document frankly recognizes that this proclamation is "fraught with philosophical, cultural, and theological difficulties, especially in light of the beliefs of Asia's great religions, deeply intertwined with cultural values and specific world views" (*EA* 20). This difficulty is compounded by the fact that, as has been mentioned above, Christ is perceived as foreign to Asia, as a Western rather than an Asian figure. Here the exhortation deserves praise for recommending (1) a *gradual* pedagogy in the procla-

mation that Christ is the only Savior,[25] (2) the use of narratives to complement ontological categories in this proclamation,[26] and (3) the legitimate variety of approaches to the proclamation of Jesus.[27]

This is not the place to enter the theological debate regarding exclusivism, in-
clusivism, and pluralism,[28] but in my judgment, the issue of Jesus as the only Savior, interesting though it may be in *theology*, is a red herring in preaching and
catechesis. The reason is that the immediate goal of the proclamation of the gospel is to enable a person to accept Jesus as his or her "personal Savior," to use a
favorite phrase of Pentecostal Christians, and not as the "only Savior." It is this
personal and total commitment of the catechumen to Jesus that is being promoted,
and not the rejection of *possible* ways in which God can reach *other* people, a
possibility that can no longer be denied after Vatican II. The vital question before
all else is not whether and how *other* people can be saved but how *I* can fully enter
a personal relationship with God. Once a person has found that Jesus is the way
for him or her to reach God, then out of this personal experience he or she can
bear witness to this fact to others. The strength and fervor of this witness are born
not out of the theological conviction that Jesus is the *only* Savior but out of the
deep experience that he is the *personal* Savior for me. Were I asked in my preaching questions about other religions and savior figures, I will have to recognize,
joyfully and gratefully, their various good elements and the saving presence of
God's Spirit in them, but I will testify to Jesus as *my* way to God and invite others
to try out this way for themselves. If they accept Jesus as their personal way to
God, then I will have shown that Jesus is the universal and only Savior, that is,
Savior for me as well as for others.[29]

4. The fourth and last feature of the new way of being Church in Asia is
prophecy: The Church is "a leaven of transformation in this world and serves as a
prophetic sign daring to point beyond this world to the ineffable Kingdom that is
yet fully to come."[30] As far as Asia is concerned, in being "a leaven of transformation in this world," Christianity must give up its ambition, so enthusiastically en-
dorsed in many missionary quarters at the beginning of the twentieth century, to
convert the majority of Asians to Christ.[31] The report of the demise of Asian religions was premature and vastly exaggerated. In Asia, where Christians still form
but a minuscule part of the population after four hundred years of mission, and
where non-Christian religions have recently staged a vigorous revival, the prospect of a massive conversion of Asians to the Christian faith is utterly unlikely.
Christians in Asia must come to terms with the fact that they are destined to remain for the foreseeable future a "small remnant" who must journey with adherents of other religions toward the eschatological kingdom of God.

The objective of the Church's mission of "making disciples of all nations"
(Mt 28:19) in Asia cannot therefore be adding as many members to the Church as
possible, even though baptism "in the name of the Father, and of the Son, and of
the Holy Spirit" (Mt 28:19) remains the desirable outcome of the Church's mission. Rather, the primary task of the Church is to become a credible "prophetic
sign" of the coming reign of God. This new focus of the Church's mission must be

the light guiding the ordering of its priorities and the choice of its policies, which must not aim at serving the internal interests of the Church but the proclamation of the gospel through the triple dialogue mentioned above.

One helpful way to describe this mission of the Church is, as Thomas Thangaraj has proposed, to see it as part and fulfillment of the mission of humanity itself, which is composed of three basic tasks: responsibility, solidarity, and mutuality. By responsibility Thangaraj means that humans are beings that go forth from themselves and come back to themselves in their reflexive consciousness, interpret themselves, and with a sense of accountability take responsibility for themselves and their actions. This task they must perform in solidarity with one another and mutuality for one another.[32] What the Christian mission adds to the mission of humanity from its faith perspective is to inform these three tasks with a new modality: *crucified* responsibility, *liberative* solidarity, and *eschatological* mutuality.[33]

As a consequence of this view of mission, the Churches of Asia must form not only Basic Christian Communities, which the exhortation highly recommends,[34] but also Basic Human Communities. Given the urgent need of Asian Christians to collaborate with their fellow Asians in the task of human promotion, the second kind of community is no less necessary than the first for the Church to become a credible prophetic sign of the reign of God.[35] This kind of community broadens the concerns of Christians beyond the narrow walls of their churches and puts them in constant dialogue of life and heart with followers of other religions and even non-believers.

"If the Asian Churches Do Not Discover Their Own Identity, They Will Have No Future"[36]

These prophetic words of the Asian Colloquium on Ministries in the Church held in Hong Kong on March 5, 1977, were true then and will be even truer during the post-synodal era. Since then, the FABC has been trying to develop a pastoral approach designed to implement this Asian way of being Church called "Asian Integral Pastoral Approach towards a New Way of Being Church in Asia (AsIPA)."[37] The goal is to develop "genuine Christian communities in Asia—Asian in their way of thinking, praying, living, communicating their own Christ-experience to others."[38]

The significance of the Asian Synod and *Ecclesia in Asia* lies, I have argued, not so much in what they say as in the recognition that the Churches of Asia have come of age and must continue to pursue the task of becoming *Asian*, relentlessly, courageously, creatively. Only in this way can the Christian Church fulfill its missionary vocation, which is the task of the entire Church.[39] It is only by living out a new way of being Church that Asian Christians will make true what the exhortation states as a fact: "Contemplating Jesus in his human nature, the peoples of Asia find their deepest questions answered, their hopes fulfilled, their dignity uplifted and their despair conquered" (*EA* 14).

Notes

1. For an English translation of *Ecclesia in Asia,* see the appendix below, pages 286–340, and *Origins* 29, 23 (November 18, 1999): 358–384. The document will be cited as *EA*, followed by the numbers of its paragraphs.

2. It is well known that criticisms of the *Lineamenta* were sharp, some of which came from episcopal conferences, in particular the Japanese bishops. For other evaluations, see, for instance, Chrys McVey, "The Asian Synod: What Is at Stake," *EAPR* 35, 1 (1998), 143–146; Michael Amaladoss, "Expectations from the Synod for Asia," *VJTR* 62 (1998), 144–151; G. Gisbert-Sauch, "The *Lineamenta* for the Asian Synod: Presentation and Comment," *VJTR* 61 (1997), 8–17; Paul Puthanangady, "*Lineamenta* for the Asian Synod," *Jeevadhara* XXVII, 160 (1997), 231–248; Kuncheria Pathil, "*Lineamenta* for the Asian Synod: Some Observations and Comments," *Jeevadhara* XXVII, 160 (1997), 249–259; J. Constantine Manalel, "The Jesus Movement and the Asian Renaissance: Some Random Reflections for the Asian Synod," *Jeevadhara* XXVII (1997), 133–153; Francisco Claver, "Personal Thoughts on the Asian Synod," *EAPR* 35, 2 (1998), 241–248; S. Arokiasamy, "Synod for Asia: An Ecclesial Event of Communion and Shared Witness of Faith," *VJTR* 62, 9 (1998), 666–675; Gali Bali, "Asian Synod and Concerns of the Local Church," *Jeevadhara* XXVII (1998), 297–330; John Mansford Prior, "A Tale of Two Synods: Observations on the Special Assembly for Asia," *VJTR* 62 (1998), 654–665; and Luis Antonio Tagle, "The Synod for Asia as Event," *EAPR* 35, 3 & 4 (1998), 366–378.

3. See, for instance, James H. Kroeger, "Asian Synod—Asian Pentecost. Introducing *Ecclesia in Asia*," *SEDOS* 32, 1 (2000), 8–11.

4. Complete documentation of these eleven general synods has been published by Civiltà Cattolica, Rome, under the supervision of Giovanni Caprile.

5. Michael Fahey, "The Synod of America: Reflections of a Nonparticipant," *Theological Studies* 59 (1998), 489.

6. Not that careful studies of these continental synods are of no value; on the contrary, there is a great need of objective and detailed assessments of the Apostolic Exhortations that resulted from these synods, especially by comparing them with their preceding *Instrumentum Laboris* and the "propositions" made by the synodal participants. There are indeed already some helpful studies of these synods. For the African Synod (1994), see *The African Synod: Documents, Reflections, Perspectives*, comp. and ed. Africa Faith & Justice Network under Maura Browne (Maryknoll, NY: Orbis Books, 1996); for the Synod of America (1997), see, besides the essay by Michael Fahey cited above, Paul D. Minnihan, "Encountering the American Synod," *Theological Studies* 60 (1999), 597–624.

7. For a brief explanation of the perspective from which I formulate these reflections, see Peter C. Phan, "Betwixt and Between: Doing Theology with Memory and Imagination," in *Journeys at the Margin: Toward an Autobiographical Theology in American-Asian Perspective*, ed. Peter C. Phan and Jung Young Lee (Collegeville: Liturgical Press, 1999), 113–133.

8. As is well known, the Asian Synod comprises the episcopal conferences of all the churches located in Asia, including East Asia (represented by the Federation of Asian Bishops' Conferences), Western Asia or Middle East (represented by the Council of Catholic Patriarchs of the Middle East), and Central Asia (Kazakhstan, Uzbekistan, Kyrgyzstan, Tajikistan, and Turkmenistan). In this essay, I limit my reflections to the Churches that are members of the FABC.

9. Sadly, of the exhortation's 240 notes, none refers to the documents of the FABC (except John Paul II's addresses to the FABC). Is this omission intentional? Are not the teachings of the FABC authentic magisterium? There are two references to the work of the FABC (together with the Council of Catholic Patriarchs of the Middle East) for ecclesial communion and collaboration but not to their *teachings* (nos. 3 and 26).

10. See Tagle, "The Synod for Asia as Event," 370–371.

11. For a collection of these statements, see *For All the Peoples of Asia: Federation of Asian Bishops' Conferences. Documents from 1970 to 1991*, ed. Gaudencio Rosales and C. G. Arévalo (Maryknoll, NY: Orbis Books; Quezon City, Philippines: Claretian Publications, 1992) and *For All the Peoples of Asia: Federation of Asian Bishops' Conferences. Documents from 1992 to 1996*, ed. Franz-Josef Eilers (Quezon City, Philippines: Claretian Publications, 1997). They will be cited as *For All Peoples*, vol. 1 and 2 respectively.

12. This determination of the Asian context has become the first step in the theological method adopted by the FABC.

13. *For All the Peoples*, vol. 1, 77.

14. The exhortation lists a series of images of Jesus that may be understandable to Asians: the teacher of wisdom, the healer, the liberator, the spiritual guide, the enlightened one, the compassionate friend of the poor, the good Samaritan, the good Shepherd, the obedient one (*EA* 20). For a discussion of Asian Christologies, see *Asian Faces of Jesus*, ed. R. S. Sugirtharajah (Maryknoll: Orbis Books, 1993); Peter C. Phan, "Jesus the Christ with an Asian Face," *Theological Studies* 57 (1996), 399–430; Peter C. Phan, "The Christ of Asia: An Essay on Jesus as the Eldest Son and Ancestor," *Studia Missionalia* 45 (1996): 25–55; Michel Fédou, *Regards asiatiques sur le Christ* (Paris: Desclée, 1998); and Jacques Dupuis, "Jesus with an Asian Face," *SEDOS* 31, 8/9 (1999), 211–216.

15. It is difficult to see how to reconcile this text with another text of the exhortation, which quotes Pope John Paul II's encyclical *Fides et Ratio*, 72, insisting on the necessity of appropriating and sharing the linguistic, philosophical, and cultural categories used by ecumenical councils "in the encounter with the various cultures" (*EA* 20). Are these categories (not doctrines) essential parts of divine revelation and how are they to be made into Asian "cultural patterns and ways of thinking"? For an evaluation of *Fides et Ratio*, see Peter C. Phan, "*Fides et Ratio* and Asian Philosophies: Sharing the Banquet of Truth," *Science et Esprit* 51 (1999), 333–349.

16. For a theology of the reign of God for Asia, see Peter C. Phan, "Kingdom of God: A Theological Symbol for Asians?" *Gregorianum* 79/2 (1998), 295–322.

17. In elaborating this ecclesiology, I make use of some of the FABC's statements, but the reflections on their consequences for the Church life in Asia are mine and should not be attributed to the FABC.

18. *For All Peoples*, vol. 1, 287. The exhortation unduly narrows this vision of the Church as a communion of churches by saying that in the view of the synod fathers, it applies primarily to the diocese: "The synod fathers chose to describe the diocese as a communion of communities gathered around the shepherd, where clergy, consecrated persons, and the laity are engaged in a 'dialogue of life and heart' sustained by the grace of the Holy Spirit" (*EA* 25). In fact, the FABC's vision applies to the Church both at the local and universal levels: "It [the Church] is a community not closed in on itself and its particular concerns, but *linked* with many bonds *to other communities of faith* (concretely, the parishes and dioceses around them) and to the one and universal communion, *catholica unitas*, of the holy Church of the Lord" (*For*

All the Peoples, vol. 1, 56). In other words, not only the diocese but also the Church universal are a communion of communities. The universal Church is not a church above the other dioceses and of which the local Churches are constitutive "parts" with the pope as its universal bishop. Rather, it is a communion in faith, hope, and love of all the local Churches (among which there is the Church of Rome of which the pope is the bishop), a communion in which the pope functions as the instrument of unity in collegiality and coresponsibility with other bishops. Furthermore, *EA* emphasizes the gathering of the local Church around the bishop, making him the center of unity, whereas the FABC emphasizes the basic equality of all the members of the local Church ("as brothers and sisters").

19. For an extended discussion of communion ecclesiology, see J.-M. R. Tillard, *Church of Churches: The Ecclesiology of Communion*, trans. R. C. De Peaux (Collegeville: The Liturgical Press, 1992).

20. For a theology of the Trinity as a communion and *perichoresis* of persons, see Leonardo Boff, *Trinity and Society*, trans. Paul Burns (Maryknoll: Orbis Books, 1986).

21. *For All Peoples*, vol. 1, 287. See also ibid., 56: "It [the Church] is a community of authentic *participation and co-responsibility*, where genuine sharing of gifts and responsibilities obtains, where the talents and charisms of each one are accepted and exercised in diverse ministries, and where all are schooled to the attitudes and practices of mutual listening and dialogue, common discernment of the Spirit, common witness, and collaborative action." The exhortation also recognizes this participatory character of the Church but emphasizes the fact that each person must live his or her "proper vocation" and perform his or her "proper role" (*EA* 25). There is here a concern to maintain a clear distinction of roles in ministry, whereas the FABC is concerned that all people with their varied gifts have the opportunity to participate in the ministry of the Church.

22. *For All Peoples*, vol. 1, 287–288.

23. For the intrinsic connection between the proclamation of the gospel and dialogue in its triple form, see *For All Peoples*, vol. 1, 13–16.

24. For a discussion of mission in the form of this triple dialogue, see Peter C. Phan, "Christian Mission in Contemporary Theology," *Indian Theological Studies* XXXI, 4 (1994), 297–347.

25. *EA* 20: "The presentation of Jesus Christ as the only Savior needs to follow a pedagogy that will introduce people step by step to the full appropriation of the mystery."

26. *EA* 20: "In general, narrative methods akin to Asian cultural forms are to be preferred. In fact, the proclamation of Jesus Christ can most effectively be made by narrating his story as the Gospels do. The ontological notions involved, which must always be presupposed and expressed in presenting Jesus, can be complemented by more relational, historical, and even cosmic perspectives." The question can be raised as to how "the ontological notions" can be "expressed in presenting Jesus" when Jesus is presented to billions of Asians whose world is as removed from the Hellenistic philosophical categories in which classical Christology is couched as heaven from earth. Furthermore, why should the ontological notions be those of Greek metaphysics and not those of Asian philosophies?

27. While accepting pluralism in Christology, *EA* insists that "in all evangelizing work, however, it is the complete truth of Jesus Christ that must be proclaimed. Emphasizing certain aspects of the inexhaustible mystery of Jesus is both legitimate and necessary in gradually introducing Christ to a person, but this cannot be allowed to com-

promise the integrity of the faith" (*EA* 23). The vexing question is of course how this "complete truth of Jesus Christ" is to be presented to Asians.

28. For a magisterial study of religious pluralism and the role of Christ, see Jacques Dupuis, *Toward a Christian Theology of Religious Pluralism* (Maryknoll: Orbis Books, 1997). See also *Christianity and the Wider Ecumenism*, ed. Peter C. Phan (New York: Paragon House, 1990).

29. For a discussion of the uniqueness and universality of Jesus, see Peter C. Phan, "The Claim of Uniqueness and Universality in Interreligious Dialogue," *Indian Theological Studies* XXXI, 1 (1994), 44–66.

30. *For All Peoples*, vol. 1, 288.

31. Recall the optimism of the World Mission Conference at Edinburgh in 1910, as expressed by its leader, John R. Mott, and the motto of the Student Volunteer Fellowship: "The evangelization of the world in our own generation." For considerations of the factors making such a goal no longer possible, see Thomas Thangaraj, *The Common Task: A Theology of Christian Mission* (Nashville: Abingdon Press, 1999), 16–30.

32. See Thomas Thangaraj, *The Common Task*, 49–58. For Thangaraj, the *missio humanitatis* is "an act of taking responsibility, in the mode of solidarity, shot through with a spirit of mutuality" (58).

33. See Thomas Thangaraj, *The Common Task*, 64–76.

34. *EA* accepts the synod fathers' emphasis on "the value of basic ecclesial communities as an effective way of promoting communion and participation in parishes and dioceses and as a genuine force for evangelization . . . a solid starting point for building a new society, the expression of a civilization of love" (*EA* 25).

35. On Basic Human Communities, see Aloysius Pieris, *Fire and Water: Basic Issues in Asian Buddhism and Christianity* (Maryknoll, NY: Orbis Books, 1996), 161: "What happens in the BHCs is a veritable *symbiosis* of religions. Each religion, challenged by the other religion's unique approach to the liberationist aspiration of the poor . . . discovers and renames itself in its specificity in response to the other approaches."

36. *For All Peoples*, vol. 1, 70.

37. See *For All Peoples*, vol. 2, 107–111 and 137–139.

38. *For All Peoples*, vol. 1, 70.

39. It is interesting to note that in describing the missionary task of the Church, *EA* begins with the pastors—bishops and priests—then proceeds with religious and the laity, in the descending order of importance, whereas the FABC has consistently focused on the primary role of the laity, especially women. Clearly, this variance is not merely rhetorical but indicates an important difference in ecclesiology.

17

Inculturation of Christianity into Asia: Reflections on the Asian Synod

VU KIM CHINH

The Apostolic Exhortation *Ecclesia in Asia* may be read and interpreted in many different ways. Notwithstanding such possibilities, it cannot be denied that its roots can be traced back to the *sub secreto* propositions that were submitted to the pope by the Special Assembly of the Synod of Bishops for Asia (hereinafter referred to as the "Asian Synod"). In this sense, it reflects the experience of the synod (from the Greek "syn-odos"—"walking together") of the Asian bishops as well as a long process of reflection on the part of many sections of the local churches in Asia. With many of those who took part in this process, we may say that the synod was experienced as an "event," which afforded a historic opportunity for cooperation and interaction between the See of Peter and the Asian local churches.[1]

In order to understand the exhortation fully, we should see it as the culmination of a long process: from the *Lineamenta*, through the various responses of the Asian episcopal conferences, to the *Instrumentum Laboris,* which appeared as a much-needed revision of the *Lineamenta* and, finally, to the one-month-long synod in Rome with its various documents, specifically, *Relatio ante Disceptationem, Relatio post Disceptationem*, interventions in the plenary sessions, discussions in the eleven small groups, and the promulgation of the Post-Synodal Apostolic Exhortation.

In this article, I will analyze the theme of inculturation in *Ecclesia in Asia* with its many complex perspectives. I will first explore the emergence of the theme of inculturation in the *Lineamenta*,[2] *Instrumentum Laboris*,[3] the Synod's Message,[4] and *Ecclesia in Asia*.[5] Next, I will reflect on inculturation in *Ecclesia in Asia* as a complex process, which requires a multifaceted approach from different perspectives. Lastly, I will focus on the implications of inculturation for the Vietnamese Church.

Inculturation within the Synodal Process

In view of the fact that inculturation proved to be an important issue in *Ecclesia in Asia*, I will begin by surveying the development of this issue at successive stages before and during the Asian Synod. I will begin with the *Lineamenta*, which set forth the narrow Roman curial perspective on the question of the inculturation of the Christian Gospel into the Asian milieu. This narrow view generated many critical comments from the various Asian episcopal conferences, which in turn proposed alternative perspectives worthy of a close examination.

Inculturation in the *Lineamenta*

A quick perusal of the *Lineamenta* reveals that the term "inculturation" appears only three times, unlike other terms such as "mission," "evangelization," "liberation," and "communion." In fact, one looks in vain for the term "inculturation" in Part One of the *Lineamenta* entitled "Asian Realities." The exhortation makes of course a number of positive statements on Asian realities, such as: "The religions and cultural values, e.g., love for philosophical inquiry, contemplation, simplicity, detachment, silence, nonviolence, etc., are considered by the Asian peoples as powerful assets" (no. 3) and "The Spirit of God is indeed at work in the transformation of the society in general and in particular in the people's yearning for the fullness of life" (no. 4). Nevertheless, the *Lineamenta* apparently disregards the fact that inculturation is also a significant way of evangelization in the Asian context.

Part Two of the *Lineamenta* ("Evangelization in Asia") presents a historical survey of the activities of Christian missionaries in Asia, from the Apostle Thomas who "took the sea route to south India and founded the church on the Malabar Coast around the year 50 A.D." (no. 8), to the Syrian Christians, to the Franciscan Friars in the thirteenth century, and then to the modern Christian mission in Asia (no. 10). It is in the context of this historical survey that the term "inculturation" appears for the first time, albeit on a negative tone:

> In the first place, the padroado system—the patronage of the mission by the Portuguese government and sovereign—with its rights regarding the erection of dioceses and ecclesiastical appointments, though initially well intentioned, turn out to be more a hindrance than a help for free development of the missionary efforts in various parts of Asia. The condemnation of the bold missionary effort at inculturation, adaptation and dialogue also put an end to a very promising beginning. (no. 11)

More significantly, in the judgment of the *Lineamenta*, inculturation does not seem to have played a significant enough role to warrant an in-depth review among the "lessons learned from mission history."

Furthermore, the *Lineamenta* only mentions inculturation occasionally and does not give it any sustained discussion. For example, it suggests that "ashrams have become centers of dialogue, inculturation, Asian spirituality, contemplation, God experience, sharing of spiritual experiences and connecting with followers of other religions" (no. 15). No mention of inculturation is made in Part Three of the *Lineamenta* ("God's Salvific Design in History"). In Part Four ("Jesus Christ: God's Good News of Salvation to All"), under the subheading "Jesus Christ: The Church's Gift to Asia," the *Lineamenta* warns that the "Church cannot abandon her faith in Jesus Christ for the sake of a false inculturation or irenicism, despite the fact that Asia has such a wide variety of cultures and religions" (no. 24).

As a result, it is not surprising to find in Part Five of the *Lineamenta* that inculturation appears to be incompatible with "communion," "witness" and "dialogue," notwithstanding the fact that the FABC documents have emphasized the need for "inculturation." Part Six of the *Lineamenta* ("The Church's Mission of Love and Service in Asia") may shed some light on why the *Lineamenta* takes such a cautious approach to inculturation. Among other things, this section discusses the apparent tension between "inculturation" and "mission" as follows:

> For several theoretical and historical reasons, an opinion has been expressed from some quarters in Asia during the last three decades that the age of mission is over. Now is the time for dialogue and inculturation. Radical pluralism of religion and salvation seems to become a dogma itself: At times one's culture is so absolutized that conversation is looked upon as violence done to the other. (no. 30)

The *Lineamenta* responds to this attitude by citing Pope Paul VI's encyclical, *Evangelii Nuntiandi*: "We wish to point out, above all today, that neither respect and esteem for these religions nor the complexity of the questions raised is an invitation to the church to withhold from these non-Christians the proclamation of Jesus Christ" (no. 30). According to the *Lineamenta*, true inculturation is identified with and based on the Incarnation. Accordingly, inculturation becomes a tool of mission: "Inculturation implies incarnating the Gospel in a culture, and the Gospel, in turn, evangelizes culture by purifying it from all that is sinful and dehumanizing, and by ennobling all that is good and positive in it" (no. 33). Clearly, the *Lineamenta* is not at ease with inculturation. It warns that the importance of inculturation must not be overestimated in the context of the cultures and history of Asia, because it is essential for the church to become "an intelligible sign of what She is and a more effective instrument of mission" (no. 33).

The *Lineamenta* ends with a series of questions that sought to elicit responses for the preparation of the *Instrumentum Laboris*. In line with the approach taken in the *Lineamenta*, the question on inculturation is found only in Part Four as question 10:

> Describe the extent of inculturation in the various aspects of the Church's life in your area (e.g. Christian theology, liturgy, spirituality, liturgical art, architecture, etc.) and its effects in relation to the Church's mission. What is the contribution of the efforts at inculturation in your area to the universal Church?

As it stands, question 10 alone may prompt valuable reflection on inculturation, although one may wonder why inculturation is separated from other issues such as "dialogue with other religions," "formation of agents of missionary activities," and "proclamation of the Gospel." If we read all the questions together with the main text of the *Lineamenta*, as the planning committee expected readers to do, we can see its clear theological bias against inculturation.

Inculturation in the *Instrumentum Laboris*

The *Instrumentum Laboris* is structured according to the principal topics raised in the questions of the *Lineamenta*. On the one hand, the *Instrumentum Laboris* approaches the issue of inculturation in circumspect terms. For example, in the sections entitled "Asian Realities," "Ecclesial Realities" and "Catholic Mission History," the *Instrumentum Laboris* regards inculturation as a liability: "Among these are such historically sensitive issues as colonialism, the padroado, inculturation of the Gospel, reaction to a perceived Westernization, etc." (no. 23). On the other hand, it is clear that the *Instrumentum Laboris* takes inculturation more seriously and puts it on the same level as dialogue and liberation: "Many responses insist that the Church's program of a new evangelization in Asia could receive assistance by engaging in a 'threefold dialogue'—that is, a dialogue with the poor, a dialogue with other religions of Asia, and a dialogue with Asian cultures" (no. 37).

In contrast to the *Lineamenta*, chapter 7 of the *Instrumentum Laboris* presents a longer, richer, and more positive treatment of inculturation. Here, the text highlights the interaction between faith and culture. Topics such as the transformation of cultures and the integration of Christianity are considered important for the local churches in Asia, even though this is an area where there are important differences across the continent. Thus, the process of inculturation is different for the local churches in West Asia with their apostolic foundations in comparison with the local churches in other parts of Asia, for instance, India or the Far East. The *Instrumentum Laboris* asserts that "inculturation in theology, liturgy, spirituality, art will emerge only when Christians as a community live the lifestyle of the masses, understand their ways of thinking and speak their language" (no. 50).

Inculturation becomes increasingly complex and multidimensional as the diverse and pluralistic Asian cultures evolve and incorporate new elements within the framework of increasing globalization. There are no "pure," "unadulterated" or otherwise "innocent" cultures in the "global village." Thus, a critical attitude is now crucial to inculturation, and dialogue becomes an important mediation to evangelization. To its credit, the *Instrumentum Laboris* gives a significant role to inculturation without attempting to replace it by another notion such as "incarnation." In fact, the *Instrumentum Laboris* regards "inculturation" as "the intimate transformation of authentic cultural values through their integration in Christianity in the various human cultures" (no. 50). In addition, "[i]nculturation brings about unity in diversity, in which all local churches enrich one another by their various attempts to delve deeply to the heart of the Christian mystery and to express that faith in culturally understandable ways" (no. 50).

Message of the Synod for Asia to the People of God

In their Message to the People of God, the synod fathers proclaimed that the local churches in Asia are called to acknowledge Jesus Christ as the embodiment of God's love and bring the Good News to those Asians who have not heard about Jesus Christ. According to the synod fathers, inculturation plays an important role in articulating the Good News effectively in the Asian context. In this regard, they highlight "the importance of inculturation, so that 'the church becomes a more intelligible sign of what she is and a more effective instrument of mission'" (no 5).

Inculturation in *Ecclesia in Asia*

In the Apostolic Exhortation, the theme of inculturation is developed mainly in the central paragraphs of Part Four, which are considered to be the heart of the exhortation.[6] Here, inculturation is shown to be a neuralgic issue in the question of the uniqueness and universality of Jesus as the Savior. According to the Pope, Jesus the Savior is the Gift of God to Asia from the very beginning. Yet, he has until now remained largely unknown to the Asian peoples (no. 2). It is not that Asians have no need for salvation. On the contrary, "religious systems such as Buddhism or Hinduism have a clearly soteriological character" (no. 2), and Asia has its indigenous religions, soteriologies, and saviors. The crucial issue is the identity of Jesus as the one and only Savior. As Cardinal Paul Shan explained in his inaugural address at the Asian Synod, Asians have no difficulty in seeing Jesus as a manifestation of the divine, but they find it difficult to understand him as the only Savior.[7]

The issue of Jesus Christ as "the only Savior" was raised by the Vietnamese Bishops' Conference, and it became the subject of much discussion in the Asian Synod. As George Evers points out:

> On the Christological question the Vietnamese bishops pointed out in their interventions that the language of Christian proclamation with its categorical affirmations about Jesus Christ as the unique Savior and the absolute necessity of baptism for salvation, and the demeaning way of referring to those who are not baptized and do not belong to the church as "pagan" have offended the people in Vietnam in the past.[8]

Ecclesia in Asia refers to this contentious issue by pointing out that the "effort to share the gift of faith in Jesus as the only Savior is fraught with philosophical, cultural, and theological difficulties, especially in light of the beliefs of Asia's great religions, deeply intertwined with cultural values and specific world views" (no. 20). Here inculturation emerges clearly as the central issue in so far as there is the necessity of expressing one's belief in Jesus Christ in new ways and symbols accessible to Asian minds, while remaining faithful to the Christian tradition.

It appears that *Ecclesia in Asia* is of two minds in resolving this dilemma. On the one hand, it states that foundational Christian doctrines ought to be so expressed in clear, unambiguous, and coherent terms that they are meaningful to people of different sociocultural settings. Such an exposition may add further explanations that take sociocultural and historical contexts into consideration. Thus, *Ecclesia in Asia* points out that "[t]he ontological notions involved, which must always be presupposed and expressed in presenting Jesus, can be complemented by more relational, historical, and even cosmic perspectives" (no. 20). More significantly, it states unequivocally that one must remain open to "the new and surprising ways in which the face of Jesus might be presented in Asia" (no. 20). It recalls that "the Synod Fathers stressed many times the need to evangelize in a way that appeals to the sensibilities of Asian peoples" (no. 20). It also notes that the bishops have suggested that one should speak of Jesus in ways that are intelligible to the Asian peoples, describing him as the "teacher of wisdom," the "healer," the "liberator," the "spiritual guide," the "enlightened one," the "compassionate friend of the poor," the "good Samaritan," the "Good Shepherd," and the "obedient one." In other words, *Ecclesia in Asia* acknowledges the possibility of adopting the symbolic expressions of Asia's diverse soteriologies.

On the other hand, *Ecclesia in Asia* clearly regards the foregoing approach as a pastoral strategy, to be subordinated to the need of remaining faithful to Sacred Scripture and Tradition.

Is it possible to reconcile both approaches, that is, adopting a pastoral approach with inculturation as its principal element, while at the same time defending ourselves against syncretism, relativism, indifferentism, and other risky developments? The exhortation offers a few clues. It mentions the need for a dialectical interplay between culture-transcending truths and inculturation, "mystery" and "incarnation," as well as between "the universal saving significance of the mystery of Jesus and his Church" and "rediscovering the Asian countenance of Jesus and identifying ways in which the cultures of Asia can grasp the universal saving significance of the mystery of Jesus and his Church." The document locates the "challenge of inculturation" at the level of culture itself, namely, how can the local culture be identified? As peoples and societies change over time, so too, culture changes together with them. Indeed, cultural change is not limited to Asia, but rather, it is common to any living culture. Fast-evolving, cross-fertilized cultures are characteristic of post-modernity, challenging any one-dimensional theory of inculturation. In this context, "inculturation" means a process aiming at making the Gospel alive in a given culture, a transmission of the Gospel's truth and values that bring about a renewal and transformation within the culture.[9]

Clearly, inculturation is a very complex enterprise, and it must be responsive to the challenges and opportunities posed by various cultures. In addition, inculturation can be carried out only by a local church. The Asian Synod suggested some key areas for inculturation, for instance, Christology, liturgy, translation of the Bible, biblical studies, as well as the formation of clergy, religious, and laity. In short, inculturation is a living witnessing of Christian values and Christian truth that is rooted in various cultures, such that "the people of Asia who, as Asians, wish to make the Christian faith their own, can rest assured that their hopes, expectations, anxieties and sufferings are not only embraced by Jesus, but become the very point at which the gift of faith and the power of the Spirit enter the innermost core of their lives" (no. 21).

Inculturation in Cardinal Paul Shan's Response to *Ecclesia in Asia*

This document is an interpretative summary of *Ecclesia in Asia* by Taiwanese Cardinal Paul Shan, who was the General Relator of the Asian Synod. It is particularly remarkable for its emphasis on the theme of inculturation. As Cardinal Shan explains, "The big question presently confronting us, given the religious and cultural context of Asia, is not why we should proclaim the Good News of Christ's salvation but *how*."[10] On the basis of the exhortation, Cardinal Shan proposes the following five-point framework:

(1) "An attitude of loving respect and esteem for our listeners." This entails not only respect for others as dialogue partners, but also respect for the "action of the Spirit in them."

(2) A "gradual pedagogy" that will "introduce people step by step to the full appropriation of His mystery." This is because it is often not possible to present Jesus Christ at once in his totality. Consequently, one should not be unduly anxious that many Asians find it difficult to see Jesus Christ as the only manifestation of the Divine. Rather, they should be given a chance to understand Christ fully through dialogue.[11]

(3) "Narrative methods akin to Asian cultural forms are to be preferred." Jesus was the narrator par excellence who spoke about God through parables and events that are part of daily human life. Every narrative expresses the spirit of the Gospel in new ways, thereby allowing the Gospel to respond to new circumstances.[12]

(4) "'Evocative' pedagogy, using stories, parables and symbols so characteristic of Asian methodology in teaching should be followed in the subsequent catechesis after the initial presentation."

(5) "Adaptation to the dispositions and level of maturity of those to be evangelized by fostering personal contact with them and a good understanding of their concrete life situation." This is not an option of either doctrine or pastoral concern, but rather a call for a good contextual pedagogy which responds to sociocultural challenges.

After advocating the development of "a more inculturated form of evangelization," Cardinal Shan emphasizes that the Asian local churches are always in need of inculturation. More importantly, the "Holy Spirit is the prime agent of the inculturation of the Christian faith in Asia."[13]

Inculturation as a New Pedagogy

As Cardinal Shan rightly points out, the major issue that confronts the Asian bishops is not *why* the local churches in Asia have to proclaim the Christian Gospel, but *how* best to carry out this task within the diversity and plurality of Asia's religions, cultures, and the poor. In view of this, it is clearly not possible to begin with a *tabula rasa* in the Asian continent. One cannot deny the reality that "Jesus is often perceived as foreign in Asia" because Christianity has not yet penetrated below the surface of Asian life and consciousness. In giving titles to Christ such as "guru," "teacher of wisdom," "enlightened one," "liberator," all of which are easily accessible to Asian sensibilities, the Asian bishops are attempting to clarify the fact that the Christian Gospel cannot be confined to, or monopolized by, any single human culture, even a highly esteemed culture such as the European classical culture with its long history of association with the Christian Gospel and the Church's tradition.

While it is true that the Christian Gospel is not identified with any culture, nevertheless it has no existence apart from a particular culture. In other words, the

Christian Gospel exists insofar as it is incarnated in a people's specific culture, sharing in their lives and transforming them from within, as leaven in the dough. The encounter between human cultures and the Christian Gospel is a complex dialogical process. Both culture and the Christian Gospel have something to offer to each other. They affirm each other's strengths and challenge each other's limitations, striving to help each other achieve their full potential. As a result, new cultural forms, new attitudes, as well as new ways of thinking, living and acting arise within the evangelizer and the evangelized.

On the one hand, nobody doubts the need for an inculturation of the Christian Gospel in the Asian milieu, which *Ecclesia in Asia* describes as being characterized by a "love of silence and contemplation, harmony, detachment, nonviolence, the spirit of hard work, discipline, frugal living, the thirst for learning and philosophical inquiry" (no. 6). More significantly, *Ecclesia in Asia* itself points out unequivocally that "the Church has the deepest respect for their traditions and seeks to engage in sincere dialogue with their followers. The religious values they teach await their fulfillment in Jesus Christ" (no. 6). Here, one can hear echoes of Pope John Paul II's earlier address to members of other religions in Madras on February 5, 1986, where he said, among other things:

> By dialogue, we let God be present in our midst; for as we open ourselves in dialogue to one another, we also open ourselves to God. We should use the legitimate means of human friendliness, mutual understanding, and interior persuasion. We should respect the personal and civic rights of the individual. As followers of different religions we should join together in promoting and defending common ideals in the spheres of religious liberty, human brotherhood, education, culture, social welfare and civic order.[14]

On the other hand, the capacity to bear witness presupposes an authentic understanding of the Christian Gospel and the Church's tradition. One cannot ignore the warning of *Evangelii Nuntiandi* that all cultures, as human constructs, are tainted with sinfulness and therefore are in need of purification, conversion, and transformation. In addition, all endeavors at inculturating the Christian Gospel must seek to heal "the split between Gospel and culture," as well as "to ensure a full evangelization of culture, or more correctly of cultures (*Evangelii Nuntiandi*, no. 20). At the same time, such a "religious conversion" requires an adequate transformation of the culture's worldview. It goes without saying that such transformation would also have to be carried out in a meaningful encounter with the diverse and pluralistic reality of Asia's cultures, religions, and the poor and marginalized.

Inculturation for the Vietnamese Church

The Asian Synod was also a wonderful opportunity for the leaders of the Vietnamese Church to "walk together" with their grassroots in a joint endeavor to discern the "signs of the times" in the Vietnamese context, as well as to bear witness to the Good News with a renewed vitality. It has also been a unique opportunity to communicate with a great number of other local Churches in Asia and to cooperate with them. More importantly, the Asian Synod has been an opportunity to promote inculturation in Vietnam. In fact, six out of the seven delegates of the Vietnamese Church spoke about inculturation, emphasizing the values of the Vietnamese culture that have been transmitted in Vietnamese classical writings as well as in Vietnamese folklore. The Vietnamese bishops were deeply aware of the profound cultural changes that are taking place in their country and of their own responsibility toward the generations to come.[15]

The greatest challenge facing the Vietnamese Church in its task of proclaiming the Gospel to the Vietnamese people is the fact that the Good News was first brought to Vietnam in cultural forms that were foreign to the Vietnamese ethos. The "Rites Controversy," which concerned the cult of ancestors, is an example of cultural clash with far-reaching ramifications whose impact is still being felt today.[16] It is undeniable that the dramatic conflicts in connection with the "Rites Controversy" inflicted many deep wounds. At the beginning of a new Christian millennium, the Vietnamese Church should follow the pope's example by apologizing for its past intolerance. Perhaps the Vietnamese Church could take a leaf from the Japanese Church. At the Asian Synod, Bishop Stephen Hamao from Japan spoke of "the Church and Peace." He recalled how Japan had invaded many countries in Asia and caused them untold sufferings. In his words: "We are aggressors. We must admit that the Church of Japan failed to realize and proclaim how inhuman and out of harmony with Gospel values the elements of the war were." A delegate from the Philippines reported that, at that moment, all in attendance applauded; this gesture, he added, signified that they forgave the Japanese people. Indeed, the inculturation of the Gospel must be prophetic, if it is to be authentic. A prophetic act of asking for forgiveness is difficult, but necessary in the context of Vietnam.

The Vietnamese Church must also practice inculturation as an effective way to form a new Vietnamese culture, by bearing witness to the Gospel and by removing the "structural sins" that are making havoc in Vietnam today.[17]

The Vietnamese Church can be proud of its many refugees and immigrants who are scattered all around the world, and who are bearing witness to the faith they have received in Vietnam—a faith that was severely tested through many trials and continues to grow amidst difficult circumstances. Francis Xavier Cardinal Nguyen Van Thuan, who is the most prominent figure among these Vietnamese expatriates, told the Asian Synod how he had prayed while in prison: "Lord, I cannot perform my mission as a bishop anymore." And, what was the Lord's answer? "Continue your mission in prison. Every moment live in love. That is your mission now." This testimony from the president of the Pontifical Council for Justice and Peace will no doubt inspire many people to have the courage to act likewise in their own situations, however helpless they may happen to be.[18]

Notes

1. See Orlando B. Quevedo, "Special Assembly for Asia: Pastoral Situation and Trends, Theological Issues and Expectation," *EAPR* 35 (1998), 130–140; Luis A. Tagle, "The

Synod for Asia as Event," *EAPR* 35 (1998), 366–378 (hereinafter: Tagle, "Synod as Event"); Francisco Claver, "Personal Thoughts on the Asian Synod," *EAPR* 35 (1998), 241–248; Raymond Renson, "In the Shadow of the Synod for Asia," *The Japan Mission Journal (JMJ)* 52 (1998), 75–78; Josef Neuner, "The Missionary and Pastoral Implications of the Asian Synod," in *Third Millennium* 1 (1998), 54–63 (hereinafter: Neuner, "Missionary and Pastoral Implications"); James H. Kroeger, "Rejoice, O Asian Church!" in *JMJ* 53 (1999), 256–262; John Mansford Prior, "Apostles and Martyrs: Consecrated Life at the Bishops' Synod for Asia," *Review for Religious* 58 (1999), 6–27; and James T. Bretzke, "Moral Theology out of East Asia," *Theological Studies* 61 (2000), 106–121.

2. The text of the *Lineamenta* may be found in *Origins* 26 (Jan. 23, 1997), 501–520.

3. The text of the *Instrumentum Laboris* may be found in *Origins* 27 (March 12, 1998), 634–652.

4. The text of the Synod's Message may be found in *Origins* 28 (May 28, 1998), 17–22.

5. The text of *Ecclesia in Asia* may be found in the appendix below, pages 286–340, and *Origins* 29 (Nov 18, 1999), 357–384.

6. See Josef Neuner, "*Ecclesia in Asia*: Towards a New Theology of Proclamation," *Third Millennium* 3 (2000), 110ff.

7. See Paul Cardinal Shan, "Presentation of the Post-Synodal Apostolic Exhortation" in *JMJ* 53 (1999), 266 (hereinafter: P. Shan, "Post-Synodal").

8. George Evers, "Zeugnis und Dialog: Was bringt die Bischofssynode für Asien?" *Herder-Korrespondenz* 52 (1998/4), 204: "Zu Fragen der Christologie äussern sich die vietnamesischen Bischöfe und merken an, dass die Sprache der christlichen Verkündigung in ihren kategorischen Äusserungen über den einzigen Erlöser Jesus Christus, die absolute Notwendigkeit der Taufe für das Heil und die herabsetzende Art von allen, die nicht getauft sind und nicht zur Kirche gehören, als 'Heiden' zu sprechen, die Menschen in Vietnam in der Vergangenheit verletzt habe."

9. Petro Cardinal Shirayanagi Seiichi has succinctly expressed the possibility of understanding Christ in the Japanese context: "It is not merely a case of distinguishing between what is Japanese and what is European but rather discovering how best to present Jesus' words and deeds so that they become part of Japan's culture. There is no thought of changing a nation's culture, a concept so common in colonizing days." See "Interview on *Ecclesia in Asia*," *JMJ* 54 (2000), 4.

10. See P. Shan, "Post-Synodal," 270; and Neuner, "Missionary and Pastoral Implications," 62ff.

11. See John Gnanapriagasam and Felix Wilfred (eds.), *Being Church in Asia: Theological Advisory Commission Documents (1986–92)*, vol. I (Quezon City: Claretian, 1994), esp. 7–32; and Michael Amaladoss, *Making All Things New: Mission in Dialogue* (Maryknoll: Orbis, 1990), esp. 129–208.

12. See FABC Office of Human Development, *Discovering the Face of Jesus in Asia Today. A Guide to Doing Mission in Asia*, FABC Papers, No. 84 (Hong Kong: FABC, 1999), 1–56.

13. See P. Shan, "Post-Synodal," 271.

14. J. Gnanapriagasam and F. Wilfred (eds.), *Being Church in Asia*, vol. I, 11.

15. See Nguyen Dang Truc (ed.), *Gop y chuan bi thuong hoi dong Giam Muc A chau* [Proposals for the Asian Synod of Bishops] (Reichstett: Dinh Huong, 1998).

16. See Vu Kim Chinh, "Than hoc Ban vi Hoa Vietnam" [Theology of Inculturation in Vietnam], *Dinh Huong* 22 (2000), 4–16. See also Ladislav Nemet, "Inculturation in the FABC Documents," *EAPR* 31 (1994), 77–94.

17. See Vu Kim Chinh, "Cooperation as Mutual Liberation: Background of Emerging Re-
lationship between the State and the Catholic Church in Vietnam," in *Church and
State Relations in 21st Century Asia,* ed. Beatrice Leung (Hong Kong: Centre of
Asian Studies, 1996), 175–202. See also Daniel F. Pilario, "Politics of Culture and
the Project of Inculturation," in *Jahrbuch für Kontextuelle Theologien 1999*, 172–194.
18. See Tagle, "Synod as Event," 373. See also Peter C. Phan, "Kingdom of God: A
Theological Symbol for Asians?" *Gregorianum* 79 (1998), 295–322, and Vu Kim
Chinh, *Liberation Theology: A Hermeneutical Study of Its Contextualization* [in Chi-
nese] (Taipei: Kwang Chi, 1990).

18

Of Fork and Spoon or Fingers and Chopsticks: Interreligious Dialogue in *Ecclesia in Asia**

EDMUND CHIA

Different Ways of Cooking

John Paul II was in for an exciting treat when he invited Archbishop Francis Xavier Nguyen Van Thuan to preach the Spiritual Exercises to the members of the curia in 2000. "The Lenten meditations never inspired so much interest, as this year's, from a man who spent thirteen years of his life in Vietnamese prisons" (Zenit News Agency, Rome, 21 March 2000). The Vietnamese archbishop used a combination of stories, personal testimonies, humor, biblical reflections, and theology to present the twenty-two meditations, regarded by many as "simple but very profound." One cardinal who took part in the retreat said that it "was an evangelically simple talk" and that "clearly, we must continue on that road" (ZNA, 2000). When commended on the originality of his presentation, Van Thuan said: "The content is always the same. But the way of cooking it is Asian. Because of this, in the year 2000, instead of eating with a fork, we ate with chopsticks" (ZNA, 2000).

Whether he realized it or not, in that last statement, the archbishop more or less summed up the crux of the difference between the Roman curia's vision of Christianity and that of Asia. Like Van Thuan's preaching, the content of Asia's vision of Christianity is always the same. What is different is the way in which it is expressed. In presenting the Post-Synodal Apostolic Exhortation *Ecclesia in Asia* of Pope John Paul II to the bishops of Asia, Cardinal Paul Shan pointed out that "the big question presently confronting us, given the religious and cultural context of Asia, is not why should we proclaim the Good News of Christ's Salvation but *how*" (Shan, 2000: 136). Likewise, Divine Word Missionary John Prior who was the liaison with the English-speaking press during the Synod for Asia, held in Rome from April to May 1998, had this to say: "Looking again at the 191 interventions and remembering the informal conversations during the synodical coffee breaks, I can say with absolute certainly that not a single Asian bishop

*Edmund Chia, "Of Fork and Spoon or Fingers and Chopsticks: Interreligious Dialogue in *Ecclesia in Asia*," *EAPR* 37 (2000), 243–255.

would disagree with the who of mission, with the subject of proclamation. . . . The key issue that the bishops grapple with is the *how* of mission" (Prior, 2000). In another context, Jesuit theologian Michael Amaladoss, in discussing accusations leveled against Indian theologians, had this to say: "Reflecting on the mystery of Christ from their multireligious context they are trying to say something new. But they are not being listened to, let alone understood. This may not be due to ill will. I think that one of the problems is methodology" (Amaladoss, 1999a: 327).

Thus, in reviewing *Ecclesia in Asia*, it is important to bear in mind that it is not so much the *who* or the *why* of mission that is in dispute as the *how* of mission or the methodology for theological reflection. The dispute is especially evident when one looks at how *Ecclesia in Asia* treats the subject of interreligious dialogue, which is the task of this chapter. Of course, in looking at the theme of interreligious dialogue, one also needs to look at related themes such as proclamation, evangelization, inculturation, and mission. This chapter will also look at the treatment of interreligious dialogue in *Ecclesia in Asia*, especially with reference to the context in which *Ecclesia in Asia* came into being. Moreover, the chapter will compare the theses advanced in *Ecclesia in Asia* with other theses proposed, in connection with or in response to, the release of *Ecclesia in Asia*.

What Dish Is *Ecclesia in Asia*?

To begin, let us look at what exactly *Ecclesia in Asia* is and how it has been presented to us. In the words of Cardinal Paul Shan, *Ecclesia in Asia* is "the Magna Carta for the evangelization of Asia in the Third Millennium" (Shan, 2000: 125). Shan seems to be right on target, for that is exactly what *Ecclesia in Asia* is—a manual for the evangelization of Asia. In fact, *Ecclesia in Asia* itself is explicit about its aims. No attempt is made to hide the fact that it "is a strong affirmation of the need for a new drive for evangelizing Asia and expresses a fervent hope that Asia will turn to Christ in the third millennium" (Amaladoss, 1999b: 3).

To be sure, *Ecclesia in Asia* begins by expressing this hope "that just as in the first millennium the Cross was planted on the soil of Europe, and in the second on that of the Americas and Africa, we can pray that in the Third Christian Millennium a *great harvest of faith* will be reaped in this vast and vital continent" (*EA* 1). It then continues by saying that the Synod of Bishops for Asia was actually part of a "program centered on the challenges of the new evangelization" (*EA* 2). Quoting his earlier apostolic letter, *Tertio Millennio Adveniente*, John Paul II goes on to point out specifically that "the issue of the encounter of Christianity with ancient local cultures and religions is a pressing one," and that "[t]his is a great challenge for evangelization, since religious systems such as Buddhism or Hinduism have a clearly soteriological character" (*EA* 2). He ends that section on the Background to the Special Assembly by indicating that the theme was carefully discerned "that the Synod might illustrate and explain more fully the truth that Christ is the one Mediator between God and man and the sole Redeemer of the world, to be clearly distinguished from the founders of other great religions" (*EA* 2). In the next passage the Holy Father declares that the actual celebration of the synod was an "encounter in dialogue of the Bishops and the Successor of Peter" (*EA* 3) and that through the Post-Synodal Apostolic Exhortation he wished "to share with the Church in Asia and throughout the world the fruits of the Special Assembly" (*EA* 4).

All of the above, one must bear in mind, is but from the pope's point of view. John Paul II sees the Synod for Asia as an "encounter in dialogue" and thus looks upon *Ecclesia in Asia* as the "fruits" of this encounter. In other words, *Ecclesia in Asia* is supposed to be the voice of the pope in dialogue with the voice of the bishops of Asia. Upon analyzing the document, John Prior cannot but disagree and asserts in no uncertain terms that *Ecclesia in Asia* is "a papal document." It is "the pope's response to the voice of the Asian Bishops" (Prior, 2000). Hence, it is more the voice of the pope than that of the Asian bishops. Pointing out that in *Ecclesia in Asia* John Paul II quotes himself sixty-eight times while making "not a single direct reference to any intervention by an individual bishop, nor to interventions by bishops in the name of their conferences," nor to "regional episcopal bodies such as the Federation of Asian Bishops' Conferences (FABC) or the Council of Oriental Patriarchs (CPCO)," Prior suggests that "[f]or the voice of the Asian Bishops we have to look elsewhere" (Prior, 2000). Even the *Propositiones*, quoted some 119 times, Prior suggests, cannot be regarded as the voice of the Asian bishops for there is no way to verify the "disparity between the draft proposals from the bishops' groups and the resultant recommendations." It is not surprising therefore that Amaladoss's immediate comments, shortly after the release of *Ecclesia in Asia*, are that the "exhortation is a document for Asia. It is not an Asian document. It is not the voice of Asia. The tone and style are very un-Asian" (Amaladoss, 1999b: 3). However, Prior is quick to point out that reading *Ecclesia in Asia* is "like hearing one end of a telephone conversation. It is certainly worth listening to, but so too is the voice at the other end of the line! . . . Thus, it is important not to read *Ecclesia in Asia* in isolation, but as part of an ongoing conversation" (Prior, 2000).

Spaghetti and Cheese or Rice and Curry?

Where do we turn to in order to listen to the other end of the conversation? Needless to say, it has to be none other than Asia itself. Specifically, it will be the voice of the bishops of Asia but also the voice of theologians and others who work and live in Asia. However, one is forewarned that after listening to this other end of the conversation, one might conclude that the two ends seem to be talking about radically different subjects. For the topic of evangelization in Asia continues to be understood very differently, depending on one's starting point and one's frame of reference. The theological methodology adopted makes all the difference. The telephone conversation, then, would sound as if the persons on one end were talking about spaghetti and cheese while those on the other about rice and curry. Both, of course, have in mind that they are talking about food for nourishment. The rice and curry eaters, however, have an added advantage in that they have eaten spaghetti and cheese for many generations and so can understand what the other end is saying. That, of course, could also constitute a disadvantage as some may be inclined to prepare rice and curry the same way spaghetti and cheese is prepared. The baggage of tradition can by no means be minimized (Chia, 2000b: 3).

Moreover, it was only as recently as the 1960s that rice and curry was officially recognized and allowed to be served. Even then, those who have never tasted rice and curry before may still be of the view that spaghetti and cheese is the "one and only" food for all of humanity. They do sincerely believe it to be the universal diet, the one mediator between hunger and fullness of life. And even if rice and curry is allowed, it is spaghetti and cheese that is the ordinary means of satiation. More importantly, acknowledgment of rice and curry does not in any way lessen the duty and resolve to proclaim the value of spaghetti and cheese and certainly does not thereby cancel the call to its promotion which is willed for all people.

With that in mind, let us now turn to look at the voice of Asia, beginning with the voice of Cardinal Julius Darmaatmadja, the President Delegate of the Synod for Asia, who also delivered the closing remarks at the celebration in New Delhi, soon after *Ecclesia in Asia* was proclaimed by John Paul II. In a way, his could be regarded as the first Asian response to the Post-Synodal Apostolic Exhortation. It therefore is significant. Darmaatmadja confines his response to the central theme of *Ecclesia in Asia*, namely the "new evangelization." From the perspective of *Ecclesia in Asia*, this new evangelization is essential because even "after two millennia, a major part of the human family still does not acknowledge Christ" (*EA* 29). Moreover, the pope continues, it is indeed a "mystery why the Savior of the world, born in Asia, has until now remained largely unknown to the people of the continent" (*EA* 2). Whereas, for Cardinal Darmaatmadja, the new evangelization is about the churches in Asia taking on "the face of Asia," so that it is "specifically characterizing Asia" and "at the same time becomes the more meaningful for Asian society, particularly for the poor and underprivileged" (Darmaatmadja, 1999: 888).

The cardinal also makes specific reference to the other religions of Asia. His statements, however, differ from those of *Ecclesia in Asia*, which looks at the other religions as "a great challenge to evangelization" (*EA* 2), and whose teachings and religious values "await their fulfilment in Jesus Christ" (*EA* 6). Whereas, for Darmaatmadja, the more important thing is that "the local Churches be capable of seeing the religious values and the culture they [the other religions] embody," and that they "need to be considered specifically as partners in dialogue" (1999: 888). Moreover, it is the Church which must adapt itself, bend over, change, and be open to learning from these other religions, so that "the new way the Church bears itself will enable these people to understand us better, enable them to come closer to us, but also enrich us in return in the way we live our Christian lives"(1999: 889).

In response to *Ecclesia in Asia*'s declaration that "the Church's unique contribution to the peoples of the continent is the proclamation of Jesus Christ" (*EA* 10), Darmaatmadja said emphatically that "[o]f course we are called to proclaim Jesus to the Gentiles." But then, he was quick to follow that statement by quoting *Gaudium et Spes,* which "noted that we can learn also from the world, precisely because we are faithful to Jesus; that is, we can find Jesus present in the world." Thus, the cardinal is suggesting that our Christian mission does really discover Jesus who "has always been present and working in the world, including the world of Asia," (1999: 888) rather than to proclaim him as if he hadn't been in there before.

Also, *Ecclesia in Asia* acknowledges the issue that "Jesus is often perceived as foreign to Asia . . . and that most Asians tend to regard Jesus—born on Asian soil—as a Western rather than an Asian figure" (*EA* 20). It then goes on to suggest a way to address this problem, namely by means of a "pedagogy which will introduce people step by step to the full appropriation of the mystery" (*EA* 20). Whereas, for Darmaatmadja, Jesus' perceived foreignness is on account of the Church's foreign methods of operation. Citing Propositions 3 and 5 (which, interestingly, did not appear in *Ecclesia in Asia* [at least not the aspects singled out by the cardinal]), Darmaatmadja advocated an immersion of the Church as "such immersion will help the Church define her mission to the people of Asia in an intelligible and acceptable manner" (1999: 889). Hence, the cardinal sees the Church as in need of the living water that the religions and cultures in Asia alone can give (cf. *EA* 50). Only after such a baptism will the Church be able to minister to the peoples of Asia.

In this context, the cardinal then raised the important issue of inculturation, which means rooting the Church in the local religious culture. If for *Ecclesia in Asia* inculturation is for the purpose of understanding the "various aspects of culture" so that the Church can then "begin the dialogue of salvation" where "she can offer, respectfully but with clarity and conviction, the Good News of the Redemption to all who freely wish to listen and to respond" (*EA* 21), for Darmaatmadja inculturation is aimed at allowing the Church to "grow more in Asian appearance." Indeed, he takes this to mean that the particular churches become "deeper and deeper rooted in our own cultures and in our deepest inner aspirations as peoples of Asia" (1999: 888). This is what a "new way of being Church in Asia" is all about, and the Church then is "expected to become in a concrete way a Church with and for the people in order to achieve their integral human development, culminating in the fullness of life given by Our Lord Jesus Christ" (1999: 890).

Thus, for Cardinal Darmaatmadja, such is the meaning and essence of the New Evangelization in Asia: "'Being Church in Asia' today means "participating in the mission of Christ the Savior in rendering his redemptive love and service in Asia," so that Asian men and women can more fully achieve their integral human development, and 'that they may have life, and have it abundantly' (Jn 10:10)." More specifically, the cardinal speaks about "bringing the Good News into all dimensions of human life and society and through its influence transforming humanity from within and making it anew." This, he suggests, is the new way of being Church and this also is the way "to a proper New Evangelization" (1999: 890). Against this backdrop, the cardinal ends his remarks by picking up for response the statement of John Paul II that "[t]here can be no true evangelization without the explicit proclamation of Jesus as Lord" (*EA* 19). The cardinal's response goes: "Yes, it is true that there is no authentic evangelization without announcing Jesus Christ, Savior to the whole human race. But for Asia, there will be no complete evangelization unless there is dialogue with other religions and cultures. There is no full evangelization if there is no answer to the deep yearnings of the peoples of Asia"(1999: 891).

Other Asian Dishes

If Cardinal Darmaatmadja's remarks are the first Asian response to *Ecclesia in Asia*, then the deliberations of the Seventh Plenary Assembly of the Federation of Asian Bishops' Conferences (FABC) can be regarded as the first Asian Churches' response to *Ecclesia in Asia*. Held less than two months after the New Delhi proclamation of *Ecclesia in Asia*, FABC VII did take as its theme a theme very similar to that of the Synod for Asia. It was deliberately a follow-up and indeed, the starting point for reflection during the FABC Plenary Assembly was *Ecclesia in Asia* (Chia, 1999: 892–9).[1]

Of significance is Archbishop Orlando Quevedo's opening address, meant to set the tone for the entire assembly. Drawing from statements of previous FABC Plenary Assemblies, Quevedo very clearly articulated movements which he saw as constituting an Asian vision of a renewed Church. He spoke about a movement toward a Church of the Poor and of the Young, a movement toward a local Church, a movement toward deep interiority, a movement toward an authentic community of faith, a movement toward active integral evangelization, a movement toward empowerment of the laity, and a movement toward generating and serving life. All of these speak to the need for renewal, updating, and learning on the part of the Church. Such a Church cannot evoke any fear, and hence the call of "Let no one fear the Church!" (John Paul II, 1999c) will never need to be sounded. In fact, the tone of the whole assembly, very much reflected in the Final Statement, was toward dialogue and collaboration.

Much emphasis was placed on the actual mission of love and service of a renewed Church in Asia. There was discussion on what renewal means. There was discussion on the issues and challenges in the mission. Aspects of these challenges include globalization, fundamentalism, politics, ecology, and militarization. The other religions were by no means listed as one of these challenges. There was then discussion on the process of discernment and the pastoral concerns. Among these were the concern for youth, women, the family, indigenous peoples, migrants, and refugees. The thrust of the Asian Church's response is to be in the area of formation and education. The approach suggested is that of an integrated approach. The most effective means of evangelization listed is that of witness of life.

It is interesting to compare this Seventh FABC Assembly Final Statement with that of *Ecclesia in Asia*. Both assemblies more or less touched on the same theme, namely, the Church's mission in Asia in the new millennium. Most of the bishops who took part in the Synod for Asia also took part in the FABC Plenary Assembly. Yet, the concerns and emphases that appear in the FABC statement and *Ecclesia in Asia* seem radically different. Of course, one must bear in mind that the Final Statement of the FABC Plenary Assembly is the actual voice of the bishops of Asia and not one which went through the filter of the pope, as is *Ecclesia in Asia*. Thus, in the Final Statement of FABC VII, one gets to hear the other side of the telephone line. Because the conversation topic is the same as that of the pope's, expressed in *Ecclesia in Asia*, taking the two together will help in understanding better the "encounter in dialogue."

Firstly, it must be noted that the FABC statement quotes *Ecclesia in Asia* about fifteen times, more than any other document it quotes. However, it also quotes quite lavishly from other FABC documents, which *Ecclesia in Asia* does not. In a way, then, the FABC VII statement is certainly more Asian than is *Ecclesia in Asia*, in that it is more representative of Asian views. Secondly, even as the FABC statement quotes *Ecclesia in Asia*, it does not present the Church in the superior sense as *Ecclesia in Asia* does. It certainly does not portray the other religions as waiting to be fulfilled by Christ. In fact, it asserts that "[a]s we face the needs of the twenty-first century we do so with Asian hearts, in solidarity with the poor and the marginalized, in union with all our Christian brothers and sisters— and by joining hands with all men and women of Asia of many different faiths" (FABC, 2000). It clearly operates out of a collaborative-partnership model rather than a preparation-fulfilment model. This is very typical of Asian theologies, which have gone beyond the Christocentric paradigm to the theocentric and regnocentric paradigms (Chia, 2000a).[2]

Another thing of significance is that the FABC statement does not view evangelization in terms of the spreading of "the Gospel of salvation throughout the length and breadth of the human geography of Asia" (John Paul II, 1999d). The bishops of Asia, instead, look at it as an integral activity. It involves "the whole community, every group, and every person," and has to do with "inculturation, dialogue, the Asianness of the Church, justice, the option for the poor, etc." (FABC, 2000). Thus, evangelization is an all-encompassing activity and mutually involves all other activities of the Church, including interreligious dialogue.

In this context, it must be mentioned also that the FABC VII statement has no specific section on "interreligious dialogue." In fact, a reading of the whole FABC statement will reveal that little space is given the theme of "interreligious dialogue." It only goes to show how much FABC has matured. While in the first few Plenary Assemblies (esp. in 1970, 1974, and 1978), the Final Statements had specific paragraphs on "interreligious dialogue," this Seventh Assembly, as is the case for the Sixth, is conspicuously absent on the theme. However, it notes within the statement that "[f]or thirty years, as we have tried to re-formulate our Christian identity in Asia, we have addressed different issues, one after another: evangelization, inculturation, dialogue, the Asianness of the Church, justice, the option for the poor, etc. Today, after three decades, we no longer speak of such distinct issues. We are addressing present needs that are massive and increasingly complex. These are not separate topics to be discussed, but aspects of an integrated approach to our Mission of Love and Service" (FABC, 2000). In other words, interreligious dialogue is a theme and activity to be taken for granted. It need not be spelled out, but every Christian in Asia ought to know of its import. It is to Asian Christianity much like chili is to Asian cuisine. It need not be spelled out in the recipe that chili has to be added. That is taken for granted. Asian food is by nature spicy. Even if chili is not added, there is always some on the table, alongside the salt and pepper. Likewise, from the perspectives of the bishops of Asia, interreligious dialogue is mixed into every dish in the Asian mission of love and service.

Eating What the Chef Himself Eats

Our discussions thus far have looked at the encounter in dialogue between the pope and the bishops of Asia. As suggested, the voice of the bishops of Asia was more clearly heard as we looked at the various responses, direct or otherwise, to *Ecclesia in Asia*, which in the main represents the voice of the pope. However, it is also important to point out that *Ecclesia in Asia* is but just one voice of the pope. To be sure, the voice of the Holy Father can be heard in many other contexts as well. Moreover, at times these other voices seem to contradict much of what has been discussed about his voice as expressed in *Ecclesia in Asia*. Specifically, reference is made to the numerous interreligious encounters initiated by the pope himself. In fact, about a week before delivering *Ecclesia in Asia* in New Delhi, John Paul II had assembled together more than 200 persons from all over the world for an Interreligious Assembly in Rome. Among the religious dignitaries was the Dalai Lama. The assembly was more or less a follow-up to the much-talked-about Interreligious World Day of Prayer for Peace which took place in Assisi in 1986. These were all initiatives of the Holy Father himself. To be sure, John Paul II is one pope who has done much more than all previous popes when it comes to interreligious dialogue. He has been instrumental in building bridges among the various and varied religious traditions. Practically, all of his official visits include an interreligious event. His recent visit to Egypt saw him meeting with the Grand Imam of Al-Azhar Mosque, Sayyed Tantawi. Even in New Delhi, where he came for a specifically ecclesial event, an apostolic visit to proclaim *Ecclesia in Asia*, included in the program was a meeting with representatives of the other religions. There, at New Delhi's Vigyan Bhavan or Hall of Wisdom, was a demonstration of "living dialogue wherein each participant gave witness to the strength and inspiration she or he received from their respective faiths." And it was there also that Pope John Paul II joined hands with Sankaracharya Madhavananda Saraswati, to the cheering and applause of everyone present.[3]

There is, therefore, no denying the fact that in the present pope the Catholic Church has advanced leaps and bounds in the area of interreligious dialogue. This is the witness of the pope himself. He is much concerned about the harmony and relationship between the Church and the other religions. His actions speak louder than his words. People are more likely to follow his practice than his speech. In the pope's own words, it is true that "people today put more trust in witnesses than in teachers" (*EA* 42). The Church in Asia, therefore, is hearing the pope loud and clear in this his proclamation that interreligious dialogue is essential. No clearer voice needs to be heard.

However, it would be interesting to find out how the pope actually dialogues when he encounters these peoples of other religions. It is most unlikely that he would insist to Sayyed Tantawi that the fullness of salvation comes from Christ alone and that the Church community is the ordinary means of salvation (cf. *EA* 31). It is also unlikely that the Holy Father would preach to the Dalai Lama that the peoples of Asia need Jesus Christ and his gospel and that Asia is thirsting for the living water that Jesus alone can give (cf. *EA* 50). It is probably unlikely that John Paul II will announce to Madhavananda Saraswati that the Church must be seen as the privileged place of encounter between God and humanity (cf. *EA* 24). The Church in Asia, therefore, seeks only to follow after the witness of the Holy Father. What he does, the Church in Asia will do, and what he refrains from doing, likewise, the Church in Asia will refrain from doing. In a way, the Church in Asia is more likely to trust eating that which the chef himself eats, rather than that which the chef cooks but doesn't himself eat. Thus, only if John Paul II is successful in calling to faith and baptism the Dalai Lama or Tantawi or Madhavananda Saraswati will Christians in Asia take seriously his pronouncement that this calling to faith and baptism is willed by God for all people (cf. *EA* 31).

Eating Spaghetti with Curry

Aside from his personal witness in actual encounters of interreligious dialogue, even in *Ecclesia in Asia* one finds passages of John Paul II's voice that are exceptionally pro-dialogue. Specifically, one finds that throughout *Ecclesia in Asia* there is a sincere recognition and exultation of "the goodness of the continent's peoples, cultures, and religious vitality" (*EA* 1). There is also a conscious acknowledgment of the "ancient religious traditions and civilizations, the profound philosophies and the wisdom which have made Asia what it is today" (*EA* 4). John Paul II identifies by name the various religious traditions alive in Asia and affirms that the "Church has the deepest respect for these traditions and seeks to engage in sincere dialogue with their followers" (*EA* 6). He does not fail to remind the Church in Asia that "[c]ontact, dialogue, and cooperation with the followers of other religions is a task which the Second Vatican Council bequeathed to the whole Church as a duty and a challenge" (*EA* 31). He then instructs the Church in Asia to "provide suitable models of interreligious dialogue—evangelization in dialogue and dialogue for evangelization—and suitable training for those involved" (*EA* 31). Most of all, he recounts the "memorable meeting held in Assisi, the city of Saint Francis, on 27 October 1986, between the Catholic Church and representatives of the other world religions" (*EA* 31).

Thus, one finds in the pope a man who is very much pro-dialogue, but at the same time, one who continues to make statements regarded as not in the service of dialogue. This reflects the intrapersonal tension the Holy Father goes through on account of his role as guardian of the Catholic faith and that of shepherd of the Catholic flock. As guardian his is to announce the privileged position of Christ and the Church, but, as shepherd his is to encourage greater dialogue between Catholics and persons of other religions. It is an unenviable task, but John Paul II has managed a balance. He has learnt to accept both roles as essential, necessary, and complementary. It is as if he continues to desire spaghetti and cheese but at the same time realizes that rice and curry has its value too. Thus, John Paul II is content with having spaghetti with curry, an adaptation he has had to make on account of his frequent contacts with persons who are more accustomed to rice and curry. This accounts for the fact that he is comfortable with proclaiming on the 6th of November in New Delhi Cathedral at the signing of *Ecclesia in Asia* that "Jesus Christ is the door that leads to life!" (John Paul II, 1999b) and announcing on the very next day at the New Delhi's Vigyan Bhavan to the representatives of other religions that he is but a "pilgrim of peace and a fellow-traveler on the road that leads to the complete fulfilment of the deepest human longings" (John Paul II, 1999).

The important lesson to draw from this is that John Paul II believes it is not an either-or choice, but must be a both-and option. He has been explicit in proclaiming this many times before. Dialogue does not exclude proclamation, and proclamation must always include dialogue. Both are self-involving, both are necessary, and both are integral to the evangelizing mission of the Church. On that score, the Asian bishops are very much in agreement with the pope. Theirs has always been to find means and ways to integrate the two aspects of evangelization. Theirs has always been to find more meaningful ways to be truly Christian and authentically Asian.

The preceding discussions seem to suggest it is but a matter of emphasis, on account of one's starting point and one's theological methodology. In a way, it is a matter of taste and a matter of different cooking styles. The essence of food remains constant. No matter how we eat it, with fork and spoon (as is done in the West) or with fingers (as is done in South Asia) and with chopsticks (as is done in East Asia), it is still food that we are eating.

References

Amaladoss, Michael. 1999a. "The Mystery of Christ and Other Religious: An Indian Perspective," *VJTR* 63/5, May.

Amaladoss, Michael. 1999b. *"Ecclesia in Asia* Affirms Tradition, Ignores Asian Search,"*Asia Focus: Commentary*, 26 November.

Chia, Edmund. 1999. "The 'Absence of Jesus' in the VIIth FABC Plenary Assembly," *VJTR* 63/12, December.

Chia, Edmund. 2000a. "Interreligious Dialogue in Pursuit of Fullness of Life in Asia," FABC Papers No. 92k, Seventh Plenary Assembly: Workshop Discussion Guide, Hong Kong, January.

Chia, Edmund. 2000b. "Asia's Contribution to Christianity," *Asia Focus: Commentary*, 10 March.

Darmaatmadja, Cardinal Julius. 1999. "A New Way of Being Church in Asia," *VJTR* 63/12, December.

FABC (Federation of Asian Bishops' Conferences). 2000. "A Renewed Church in Asia: A Mission of Love and Service," Final Statement of the Seventh Federation of Asian Bishops' Conferences Plenary Assembly, Samphran, Thailand, January 3–13.

John Paul II. 1999. "Meeting with Representatives of Other Religions and Other Christian Confessions," *New Delhi Vigyan Bhavan,* 7 November, No. 1.

John Paul II. 1999a. *Ecclesia in Asia*, New Delhi Cathedral, 6 November, No. 1.

John Paul II. 1999b. *Ecclesia in Asia*, New Delhi Cathedral, 6 November, No. 2.
John Paul II. 1999c. *Ecclesia in Asia*, New Delhi Cathedral, 6 November, No. 5.
John Paul II. 1999d. *Ecclesia in Asia*, New Delhi Cathedral, 6 November, No. 6.
Prior, John. 2000. "Unfinished Encounter: A Note on the Voice and Tone of *Ecclesia in Asia*," *EAPR* 37 (2000), 256–271.
Shan, Cardinal Paul. 2000. "Presentation of *Ecclesia in Asia* in New Delhi," General Relator, Synod for Asia in *Boletin Eclesiastico de Filipinas* LXXVI/ 18, January–February.
Zenit News Agency, Rome, 21 March 2000.

Notes

1. For a discussion on the less "evangelical" stance that FABC took, see Chia, 1999: 892–9.
2. For a more thorough discussion on the evolution of Asian theologies of religion, see Chia, 2000a.
3. "Editorial," *VJTR* 63/12 (Dec. 1999), 880.

Contributors

Michael Amaladoss, S.J., has held various administrative posts, including twelve years in Rome as an assistant to the Superior General, with special responsibility for Mission and Ecumenism. Since 1973 he has been professor of Systematic Theology in Vidyajyoti College of Theology, Delhi, India. He is the author of 16 books and over 260 articles. His books include: *Making All Things New: Evangelization, Dialogue and Inculturation; Life in Freedom: Liberation Theologies from Asia; Beyond Inculturation;* and *Toward Fullness: Searching for an Integral Spirituality.*

Soosai Arokiasamy, S.J., holds a doctorate in theology from the Pontifical Gregorian University, Rome. In addition to his current appointment as secretary of the Catholic Bishops' Conference of India Doctrinal Commission, he is on the faculty of Vidyajyoti College of Theology in Delhi, India. Author of many articles and essays on liberation and *dalit* theologies, ethics, and challenges facing Indian Christians, Dr. Arokiasamy has published *Dharma, Hindu and Christian According to Roberto de Nobili: Analysis of Its Meaning and Its Use in Hinduism and Christianity* (1986); *Responding to Communalism: The Task of Religions and Theology* (1991); *Social Sin: Its Challenges to Christian Life* (1991, co-edited with George V. Lobo); and *Liberation in Asia: Theological Perspectives* (1987, co-edited with G. Gispert-Sauch, S.J.).

Edmund Chia, a Christian Brother, is affiliated with the Federation of Asian Bishops' Conferences. He obtained his M.A. in religious studies from the Catholic University of America, Washington, D.C. He is the executive secretary and Interreligious Secretary of FABC's Office of Ecumenical and Interreligious Affairs. He has written extensively on interreligious dialogue. He is currently pursuing a Ph.D. in theology at Nijmegen University, The Netherlands.

James H. Kroeger, a Maryknoller, has worked in Asia, in particular the Philippines and Bangladesh, since 1970. A doctor of missiology from the Gregorian University, Rome, and author of several books, Kroeger is currently professor of Systematic Theology, Missiology, and Islamics at the Jesuit Loyola School of Theology in Manila.

Peter C. Phan, a native of Vietnam, is currently the Warren-Blanding Professor of Religion and Culture at the Catholic University of America, Washington, D.C. He holds an S.T.D. from the Pontificia Universitas Salesiana and a Ph.D. and a D.D. from the University of London. Author and editor of over 20 books and over 250 essays, he specializes in systematic theology, missiology, and interreligious dialogue.

John Mansford Prior is a Divine Word Missionary who has been working in Indonesia since 1973. Currently he is secretary of Candraditya Research Centre for the Study of Religion and Culture in Ledalaro, Indonesia. Author of many essays on the Asian Synod, he was liaison with the English-speaking press during the Synod for Asia.

Luis Antonio "Chito" Tagle, a priest from the Diocese of Imus, Philippines, completed his theological studies at the Loyola School of Theology in Manila and his doctorate at the Catholic University of America, Washington, D.C. His numerous apostolic commitments include: rector of the Tahanan ng Mabuting Pastol, pastor of the Cathedral in Imus, professor at several schools of theology, and member of the International Theological Commission. In 2001 he was made bishop of the Diocese of Imus, Philippines.

Jonathan Y. Tan, a native of Malaysia, holds a Ph.D. in religious studies from the Catholic University of America, Washington, D.C. He has published several essays on the theological method of the Federation of Asian Bishops' Conferences, liturgical inculturation in Asia, and interreligious dialogue. He is currently Assistant Professor of Minority Studies and Religion at Xavier University, Cincinnati, Ohio.

Vu Kim Chinh, S.J., of Vietnam, holds a doctorate in philosophy from the University of Innsbruck, Austria, and a doctorate in theology from Fu Jen Faculty of Theology, Fu Jen University, Taipei, Taiwan. Currently a professor of theology at the Fu Jen Faculty of Theology, Dr. Chinh has written extensively on inculturation and liberation theology.

Appendix

Post-Synodal
Apostolic Exhortation
Ecclesia In Asia
of The Holy Father
John Paul II
to the Bishops,
Priests and Deacons,
Men and Women
in the Consecrated Life
and All the Lay Faithful
on Jesus Christ the Saviour
and His Mission of Love and Service
in Asia:
". . . That They May Have Life,
and Have It Abundantly" (Jn 10:10)

INTRODUCTION

The Marvel of God's Plan in Asia

1. The Church in Asia sings the praises of the "God of salvation" (Ps 68:20) for choosing to initiate his saving plan on Asian soil, through men and women of that continent. It was in fact in Asia that God revealed and fulfilled his saving purpose from the beginning. He guided the patriarchs (cf. Gen 12) and called Moses to lead his people to freedom (cf. Ex 3:10). He spoke to his chosen people through many prophets, judges, kings and valiant women of faith. In "the fullness of time" (Gal 4:4), he sent his only-begotten Son, Jesus Christ the Saviour, who took flesh as an Asian! Exulting in the goodness of the continent's peoples, cultures, and religious vitality, and conscious at the same time of the unique gift of faith which she has received for the good of all, the Church in Asia cannot cease to proclaim: "Give thanks to the Lord for he is good, for his love endures for ever" (Ps 118:1).

Because Jesus was born, lived, died and rose from the dead in the Holy Land, that small portion of Western Asia became a land of promise and hope for all mankind. Jesus knew and loved this land. He made his own the history, the sufferings and the hopes of its people. He loved its people and embraced their Jewish traditions and heritage. God in fact had long before chosen this people and revealed himself to them in preparation for the Saviour's coming. And from this land, through the preaching of the Gospel in the power of the Holy Spirit, the Church went forth to make "disciples of all nations" (Mt 28:19). With the Church throughout the world, the Church in Asia will cross the threshold of the Third Christian Millennium marvelling at all that God has worked from those beginnings until now, and strong in the knowledge that "just as in the first millennium the Cross was planted on the soil of Europe, and in the second on that of the Americas and Africa, we can pray that in the Third Christian Millennium *a great harvest of faith* will be reaped in this vast and vital continent".[1]

Background to the Special Assembly

2. In my Apostolic Letter *Tertio Millennio Adveniente*, I set out a programme for the Church to welcome the Third Millennium of Christianity, a programme centred on the challenges of the new evangelization. An important feature of that plan was the holding of *continental Synods* so that Bishops could address the question of evangelization according to the particular situation and needs of each continent. This series of Synods, linked by the common theme of the new evangelization, has proved an important part of the Church's preparation for the Great Jubilee of the Year 2000.

In that same letter, referring to the Special Assembly for Asia of the Synod of Bishops, I noted that in that part of the world "the issue of the encounter of Christianity with ancient local cultures and religions is a pressing one. This is a great challenge for evangelization, since religious systems such as Buddhism or Hinduism have a clearly soteriological character".[2] It is indeed a mystery why the Saviour of the world, born in Asia, has until now remained largely unknown to the people of the continent. The Synod would be a providential opportunity for the Church in Asia to reflect further on this mystery and to make a renewed commitment to the mission of making Jesus Christ better known to all. Two months after the publication of *Tertio Millennio Adveniente*, speaking to the Sixth Plenary Assembly of the Federation of Asian Bishops' Conferences, in Manila, the Philippines, during the memorable Tenth World Youth Day celebrations, I reminded the Bishops: "If the Church in Asia is to fulfil its providential destiny, evangelization as the joyful, patient and progressive preaching of the saving Death and Resurrection of Jesus Christ must be your absolute priority".[3]

The positive response of the Bishops and of the particular Churches to the prospect of a Special Assembly for Asia of the Synod of Bishops was evident throughout the preparatory phase. The Bishops communicated their desires and opinions at every stage with frankness and a penetrating knowledge of the continent. They did so in full awareness of the bond of communion which they share with the universal Church. In line with the original idea of *Tertio Millennio Adveniente* and following the proposals of the Pre-Synodal Council which evaluated the views of the Bishops and the particular Churches on the Asian continent, I chose as the Synod's theme: *Jesus Christ the Saviour and his Mission of Love and Service in Asia: "That they may have Life and have it abundantly"* (Jn 10:10). Through this particular formulation of the theme, I hoped that the Synod might "illustrate and explain more fully the truth that Christ is the one Mediator between God and man and the sole Redeemer of the world, to be clearly distinguished from the founders of other great religions".[4] As we approach the Great Jubilee, the Church in Asia needs to be able to proclaim with renewed vigour: *Ecce natus est nobis Salvator mundi*, "Behold the Saviour of the World is born to us", born in Asia!

The Celebration of the Special Assembly

3. By the grace of God, the Special Assembly for Asia of the Synod of Bishops took place from 18 April to 14 May 1998 in the Vatican. It came after the Special Assemblies for Africa (1994) and America (1997), and was followed at the year's end by the Special Assembly for Oceania (1998). For almost a month, the Synod Fathers and other participants, gathered around the Successor of Peter and sharing in the gift of hierarchical communion, gave concrete voice and expression to the Church in Asia. It was indeed a moment of special grace![5] Earlier meetings of Asian Bishops had contributed to preparing the Synod and making possible an atmosphere of intense ecclesial and fraternal communion. Of particular

relevance in this respect were the past Plenary Assemblies and Seminars sponsored by the Federation of Asian Bishops' Conferences and its offices, which periodically brought together great numbers of Asian Bishops and fostered personal as well as ministerial bonds between them. I had the privilege of being able to make a visit to some of these meetings, at times presiding at the opening or closing Solemn Eucharistic Celebrations. On those occasions I was able to observe directly the *encounter in dialogue* of the particular Churches, including the Eastern Churches, in the person of their Pastors. These and other regional assemblies of Asia's Bishops served providentially as remote preparation for the Synod Assembly.

The actual celebration of the Synod itself confirmed the importance of dialogue as a *characteristic mode of the Church's life in Asia*. A sincere and honest sharing of experiences, ideas and proposals proved to be the way to a genuine meeting of spirits, a communion of minds and hearts which, in love, respects and transcends differences. Particularly moving was the encounter of the new Churches with the ancient Churches which trace their origins to the Apostles. We experienced the incomparable joy of seeing the Bishops of the particular Churches in Myanmar, Vietnam, Laos, Cambodia, Mongolia, Siberia and the new republics of Central Asia sitting beside their Brothers who had long desired to encounter them and to dialogue with them. Yet there was also a sense of sadness at the fact that Bishops from Mainland China could not be present. Their absence was a constant reminder of the heroic sacrifices and suffering which the Church continues to endure in many parts of Asia.

The encounter in dialogue of the Bishops and the Successor of Peter, entrusted with the task of strengthening his brothers (cf. Lk 22:32), was truly a confirmation in faith and mission. Day after day the Synod Hall and meeting rooms were filled with accounts of deep faith, self-sacrificing love, unwavering hope, long-suffering commitment, enduring courage and merciful forgiveness, all of which eloquently disclosed the truth of Jesus' words: "I am with you always" (Mt 28:20). The Synod was a moment of grace because it was an encounter with the Saviour who continues to be present in his Church through the power of the Holy Spirit, experienced in a fraternal dialogue of life, communion and mission.

Sharing the Fruits of the Special Assembly

4. Through this Post-Synodal Apostolic Exhortation, I wish to share with the Church in Asia and throughout the world the fruits of the Special Assembly. This document seeks to convey the wealth of that great spiritual event of communion and episcopal collegiality. The Synod was a *celebratory remembering* of the Asian roots of Christianity. The Synod Fathers remembered the first Christian community, the early Church, Jesus' little flock on this immense continent (cf. Lk 12:32). They remembered what the Church has received and heard from the beginning (cf. Rev 3:3), and, having remembered, they celebrated God's "abundant goodness" (Ps 145:7) which never fails. The Synod was also an occasion to recognize the ancient religious traditions and civilizations, the profound philosophies and the wisdom which have made Asia what it is today. Above all, the peoples of Asia themselves were remembered as the continent's true wealth and hope for the future. Throughout the Synod those of us present were witnesses of an extraordinarily fruitful meeting between the old and new cultures and civilizations of Asia, marvellous to behold in their diversity and convergence, especially when symbols, songs, dances and colours came together in harmonious accord around the one Table of the Lord in the opening and closing Eucharistic Liturgies.

This was not a celebration motivated by pride in human achievements, but one conscious of what the Almighty has done for the Church in Asia (cf. Lk 1:49). In recalling the Catholic community's humble condition, as well as the weaknesses of its members, the Synod was also *a call to conversion,* so that the Church in Asia might become ever more worthy of the graces continually being offered by God.

As well as a remembrance and a celebration, the Synod was *an ardent affirmation of faith in Jesus Christ the Saviour.* Grateful for the gift of faith, the Synod Fathers found no better way to celebrate the faith than to affirm it in its integrity, and to reflect on it in relation to the context in which it has to be proclaimed and professed in Asia today. They emphasized frequently that the faith is already being proclaimed with trust and courage on the continent, even amid great difficulties. In the name of so many millions of men and women in Asia who put their trust in no one other than the Lord, the Synod Fathers confessed: "We have believed and come to know that you are the Holy One of God" (Jn 6:69). In the face of the many painful questions posed by the suffering, violence, discrimination and poverty to which the majority of Asian peoples are subjected, they prayed: "I believe, help my unbelief" (Mk 9:24).

In 1995, I invited the Bishops of Asia gathered in Manila to "open wide to Christ the doors of Asia".[6] Taking strength from the mystery of communion with the countless and often unheralded martyrs of the faith in Asia, and confirmed in hope by the abiding presence of the Holy Spirit, the Synod Fathers courageously called all Christ's disciples in Asia to a new *commitment to mission.* During the Synod Assembly, the Bishops and participants bore witness to the character, spiritual fire and zeal which will assuredly make Asia the land of a bountiful harvest in the coming millennium.

CHAPTER I
THE ASIAN CONTEXT

Asia, the Birthplace of Jesus and of the Church

5. The Incarnation of the Son of God, which the whole Church will solemnly commemorate in the Great Jubilee of the Year 2000, took place in a definite historical and geographical context. That context exercised an important influence on the life and mission of the Redeemer as man. "In Jesus of Nazareth, God has assumed the features typical of human nature, including a person's belonging to a particular people and a particular land. . . . The physical particularity of the land and its geographical determination are inseparable from the truth of the human flesh assumed by the Word".[7] Consequently, knowledge of the world in which the Saviour "dwelt among us" (Jn 1:14) is an important key to a more precise understanding of the Eternal Father's design and of the immensity of his love for every creature: "For God so loved the world that he gave his only Son, that whoever believes in him should not perish but have eternal life" (Jn 3:16).

Likewise, the Church lives and fulfils her mission in the actual circumstances of time and place. A critical awareness of the diverse and complex realities of Asia is essential if the People of God on the continent are to respond to God's will for them in the new evangelization. The Synod Fathers insisted that the Church's mission of love and service in Asia is conditioned by two factors: on the one hand, her self-understanding as a community of disciples of Jesus Christ gathered around her Pastors, and on the other hand, the social, political, religious, cultural and economic realities of Asia.[8] The situation of Asia was examined in detail during the Synod by those who have daily contact with the extremely diversified realities of such an immense continent. The following is, in synthesis, the result of the Synod Fathers' reflections.

Religious and Cultural Realities

6. Asia is the earth's largest continent and is home to nearly two-thirds of the world's population, with China and India accounting for almost half the total population of the globe. The most striking feature of the continent is the variety of its peoples who are "heirs to ancient cultures, religions and traditions".[9] We cannot but be amazed at the sheer size of Asia's population and at the intricate mosaic of its many cultures, languages, beliefs and traditions, which comprise such a substantial part of the history and patrimony of the human family.

Asia is also the cradle of the world's major religions—Judaism, Christianity, Islam and Hinduism. It is the birthplace of many other spiritual traditions such as Buddhism, Taoism, Confucianism, Zoroastrianism, Jainism, Sikhism and Shintoism. Millions also espouse traditional or tribal religions, with varying degrees of structured ritual and formal religious teaching. The Church has the deepest respect for these traditions and seeks to engage in sincere dialogue with their followers. The religious values they teach await their fulfilment in Jesus Christ.

The people of Asia take pride in their religious and cultural values, such as love of silence and contemplation, simplicity, harmony, detachment, non-violence, the spirit of hard work, discipline, frugal living, the thirst for learning and philosophical enquiry.[10] They hold dear the values of respect for life, compassion for all beings, closeness to nature, filial piety towards parents, elders and ancestors, and a highly developed sense of community.[11] In particular, they hold the family to be a vital source of strength, a closely knit community with a powerful sense of solidarity.[12] Asian peoples are known for their spirit of religious tolerance and peaceful co-existence. Without denying the existence of bitter tensions and violent conflicts, it can still be said that Asia has often demonstrated a remarkable capacity for accommodation and a natural openness to the mutual enrichment of peoples in the midst of a plurality of religions and cultures. Moreover, despite the influence of modernization and secularization, Asian religions are showing signs of great vitality and a capacity for renewal, as seen in reform movements within the various religious groups. Many people, especially the young, experience a deep thirst for spiritual values, as the rise of new religious movements clearly demonstrates.

All of this indicates an innate spiritual insight and moral wisdom in the Asian soul, and it is the core around which a growing sense of "being Asian" is built. This "being Asian" is best discovered and affirmed not in confrontation and opposition, but in the spirit of complementarity and harmony. In this framework of complementarity and harmony, the Church can communicate the Gospel in a way which is faithful both to her own Tradition and to the Asian soul.

Economic and Social Realities

7. On the subject of economic development, situations on the Asian continent are very diverse, defying any simple classification. Some countries are highly developed, others are developing through effective economic policies, and others still find themselves in abject poverty, indeed among the poorest nations on earth. In the process of development, materialism and secularism are also gaining ground, especially in urban areas. These ideologies, which undermine traditional, social and religious values, threaten Asia's cultures with incalculable damage.

The Synod Fathers spoke of the rapid changes taking place within Asian societies and of the positive and negative aspects of these changes. Among them are the phenomenon of urbanization and the emergence of huge urban conglomerations, often with large depressed areas where organized crime, terrorism, prostitution, and the exploitation of the weaker sectors of society thrive. Migration too is a major social phenomenon, exposing millions of people to situations which are difficult economically, culturally and morally. People migrate within Asia and from Asia to other continents for many reasons, among them poverty, war and ethnic conflicts, the denial of their human rights and fundamental freedoms. The establishment of giant industrial complexes is another cause of internal and external migration, with accompanying destructive effects on family life and values. Mention was also made of the construction of nuclear power plants with an eye to cost and efficiency but with little regard for the safety of people and the integrity of the environment.

Tourism also warrants special attention. Though a legitimate industry with its own cultural and educational values, tourism has in some cases a devastating influence upon the moral and physical landscape of many Asian countries, manifested in the degradation of young women and even children through prostitution.[13] The pastoral care of migrants, as well as that of tourists, is difficult and complex, especially in Asia where basic structures for this may not exist. Pastoral planning at all levels needs to take these realities into account. In this context we should not forget the migrants from Catholic Eastern Churches who need pastoral care according to their own ecclesiastical traditions.[14]

Several Asian countries face difficulties related to population growth, which is "not merely a demographic or economic problem but especially a moral one".[15] Clearly, the question of population is closely linked to that of human promotion, but false solutions that threaten the dignity and inviolability of life abound and present a special challenge to the Church in Asia. It is perhaps appropriate at this point to recall the Church's contribution to the defence and promotion of life through health care, social development and education to benefit peoples, especially the poor. It is fitting that the Special Assembly for Asia paid tribute to the late Mother Teresa of Calcutta, "who was known all over the world for her loving and selfless care of the poorest of the poor".[16] She remains an icon of the service to life which the Church is offering in Asia, in courageous contrast to the many dark forces at work in society.

A number of Synod Fathers underlined the external influences being brought to bear on Asian cultures. New forms of behaviour are emerging as a result of over-exposure to the mass media and the kinds of literature, music and films that are proliferating on the continent. Without denying that the means of social communication can be a great force for good,[17] we cannot disregard the negative impact which they often have. Their beneficial effects can at times be outweighed by the way in which they are controlled and used by those with questionable political, economic and ideological interests. As a result, the negative aspects of the media and entertainment industries are threatening traditional values, and in particular the sacredness of marriage and the stability of the family. The effect of images of violence, hedonism, unbridled individualism and materialism "is striking at the heart of Asian cultures, at the religious character of the people, families and whole societies".[18] This is a situation which poses a great challenge to the Church and to the proclamation of her message.

The persistent reality of poverty and the exploitation of people are matters of the most urgent concern. In Asia there are millions of oppressed people who for centuries have been kept economically, culturally and politically on the margins of society.[19] Reflecting upon the situation of women in Asian societies, the Synod Fathers noted that "though the awakening of women's consciousness to their dignity and rights is one of the most significant signs of the times, the poverty and exploitation of women remains a serious problem throughout Asia".[20] Female illiteracy is much higher than that of males; and female children are more likely to be aborted or even killed after birth. There are also millions of indigenous or tribal people throughout Asia living in social, cultural and political isolation from the dominant population.[21] It was reassuring to hear the Bishops at the Synod mention that in some cases these matters are receiving greater attention at the national, regional and international levels, and that the Church is actively seeking to address this serious situation.

The Synod Fathers pointed out that this necessarily brief reflection upon the economic and social realities of Asia would be incomplete if recognition were not also given to the extensive economic growth of many Asian societies in recent decades: a new generation of skilled workers, scientists and technicians is growing daily and their great number augurs well for Asia's development. Still, not all is stable and solid in this progress, as has been made evident by the most recent and far-reaching financial crisis suffered by a number of Asian countries. The future of Asia lies in cooperation, within Asia and with the nations of other continents, but building always on what Asian peoples themselves do with a view to their own development.

Political Realities

8. The Church always needs to have an exact understanding of the political situation in the different countries where she seeks to fulfil her mission. In Asia today the political panorama is highly complex, displaying an array of ideologies ranging from democratic forms of government to theocratic ones. Military dictatorships and atheistic ideologies are very much present. Some countries recognize an official state religion that allows little or no religious freedom to minorities and the followers of other religions. Other States, though not explicitly theocratic, reduce minorities to second-class citizens with little safeguard for their fundamental human rights. In some places Christians are not allowed to practise their faith freely and proclaim Jesus Christ to others.[22] They are persecuted and denied their rightful place in society. The Synod Fathers remembered in a special way the people of China and expressed the fervent hope that all their Chinese Catholic brothers and sisters would one day be able to exercise their religion in freedom and visibly profess their full communion with the See of Peter.[23]

While appreciating the progress which many Asian countries are making under their different forms of government, the Synod Fathers also drew attention to the widespread corruption existing at various levels of both government and society.[24] Too often, people seem helpless to defend themselves against corrupt politicians, judiciary officials, administrators and bureaucrats. However, there is a growing awareness throughout Asia of people's capacity to change unjust structures. There are new demands for greater social justice, for more participation in government and economic life, for equal opportunities in education and for a just share in the resources of the nation. People are becoming increasingly conscious of their human dignity and rights and more determined to safeguard them. Long dormant ethnic, social and cultural minority groups are seeking ways to become agents of their own social advancement. The Spirit of God helps and sustains people's efforts to transform society so that the human yearning for a more abundant life may be satisfied as God wills (cf. Jn 10:10).

The Church in Asia: Past and Present

9. The history of the Church in Asia is as old as the Church herself, for it was in Asia that Jesus breathed the Holy Spirit upon his disciples and sent them to the ends of the earth to proclaim the Good News and gather communities of believers. "As the Father has sent me, even so I send you" (Jn 20:21; see also Mt 28:18–20; Mk 16:15–18; Lk 24:47; Acts 1:8). Following the Lord's command, the Apostles preached the word and founded Churches. It may help to recall some elements of this fascinating and complex history.

From Jerusalem, the Church spread to Antioch, to Rome and beyond. It reached Ethiopia in the South, Scythia in the North and India in the East, where tradition has it that Saint Thomas the Apostle went in the year 52 A.D. and founded Churches in South India. The missionary spirit of the East Syrian community in the third and fourth centuries, with its centre at Edessa, was remarkable. The ascetic communities of Syria were a major force of evangelization in Asia from the third century onwards. They provided spiritual energy for the Church, especially during times of persecution. At the end of the third century, Armenia was the first nation as a whole to embrace Christianity, and is now preparing to celebrate the 1700th anniversary of its baptism. By the end of the fifth century, the Christian message had reached the Arab kingdoms, but for many reasons, including the divisions among Christians, the message failed to take root among these peoples.

Persian merchants took the Good News to China in the fifth century. The first Christian Church was built there at the beginning of the seventh century. During the T'ang dynasty (618–907 A.D.), the Church flourished for nearly two centuries. The decline of this vibrant Church in China by the end of the First Millennium is one of the sadder chapters in the history of God's People on the continent.

In the thirteenth century the Good News was announced to the Mongols and the Turks and to the Chinese once more. But Christianity almost vanished in these regions for a number of reasons, among them the rise of Islam, geographical isolation, the absence of an appropriate adaptation to local cultures, and perhaps above all a lack of preparedness to encounter the great religions of Asia. The end of the fourteenth century saw the drastic diminution of the Church in Asia, except for the isolated community in South India. The Church in Asia had to await a new era of missionary endeavour.

The apostolic labours of Saint Francis Xavier, the founding of the Congregation of *Propaganda Fide* by Pope Gregory XV, and the directives for missionaries to respect and appreciate local cultures all contributed to achieving more positive results in the course of the sixteenth and seventeenth centuries. Again in the nineteenth century there was a revival of missionary activity. Various religious congregations dedicated themselves wholeheartedly to this task. *Propaganda Fide* was reorganized. Greater emphasis was placed upon building up the local Churches. Educational and charitable works went hand in hand with the preaching of the Gospel. Consequently, the Good News continued to reach more people, especially among the poor and the underprivileged, but also here and there among the social and intellectual elite. New attempts were made to inculturate the Good News, although they proved in no way sufficient. Despite her centuries-long presence and her many apostolic endeavours, the Church in many places was still considered as foreign to Asia, and indeed was often associated in people's minds with the colonial powers.

This was the situation on the eve of the Second Vatican Council; but thanks to the impetus provided by the Council, a new understanding of mission dawned and with it a great hope. The universality of God's plan of salvation, the missionary nature of the Church and the responsibility of everyone in the Church for this task, so strongly reaffirmed in the Council's Decree on the Church's Missionary Activity *Ad Gentes*, became the framework of a new commitment. During the Special Assembly, the Synod Fathers testified to the recent growth of the ecclesial community among many different peoples in various parts of the continent, and they appealed for further missionary efforts in the years to come, especially as new possibilities for the proclamation of the Gospel emerge in the Siberian region and the Central Asian countries which have recently gained their independence, such as Kazakhstan, Uzbekistan, Kyrgyzstan, Tajikistan and Turkmenistan.[25]

A survey of the Catholic communities in Asia shows a splendid variety by reason of their origin and historical development, and the diverse spiritual and liturgical traditions of the various Rites. Yet all are united in proclaiming the Good News of Jesus Christ, through Christian witness, works of charity and human solidarity. While some particular Churches carry out their mission in peace and freedom, others find themselves in situations of violence and conflict, or feel threatened by other groups, for religious or other reasons. In the vastly diversified cultural world of Asia, the Church faces multiple philosophical, theological and pastoral challenges. Her task is made more difficult by the fact of her being a minority, with the only exception the Philippines, where Catholics are in the majority.

Whatever the circumstances, the Church in Asia finds herself among peoples who display an intense yearning for God. The Church knows that this yearning can only be fully satisfied by Jesus Christ, the Good News of God for all the nations. The Synod Fathers were very keen that this Post-Synodal Apostolic Exhortation should focus attention on this yearning and encourage the Church in Asia to proclaim with vigour in word and deed that *Jesus Christ is the Saviour.*

The Spirit of God, always at work in the history of the Church in Asia, continues to guide her. The many positive elements found in the local Churches, frequently highlighted in the Synod, strengthen our expectation of a "new springtime of Christian life".[26] One solid cause of hope is the increasing number of better trained, enthusiastic and Spirit-filled lay people, who are more and more aware of their specific vocation within the ecclesial community. Among them the lay catechists deserve special recognition and praise.[27] The apostolic and charismatic movements too are a gift of the Spirit, bringing new life and vigour to the formation of lay men and women, families and the young.[28] Associations and ecclesial movements devoted to the promotion of human dignity and justice make accessible and tangible the universality of the evangelical message of our adoption as children of God (cf. Rom 8:15–16).

At the same time, there are Churches in very difficult circumstances, "experiencing intense trials in the practice of their faith".[29] The Synod Fathers were moved by reports of the heroic witness, unshaken perseverance and steady growth of the Catholic Church in China, by the efforts of the Church in South Korea to offer assistance to the people of North Korea, the humble steadfastness of the Catholic community in Vietnam, the isolation of Christians in such places as Laos and Myanmar, the difficult co-existence with the majority in some predominantly Islamic states.[30] The Synod paid special attention to the situation of the Church in the Holy Land and in the Holy City of Jerusalem, "the heart of Christianity",[31] a city dear to all the children of Abraham. The Synod Fathers expressed the belief that the peace of the region, and even the world, depends in large measure on the peace and reconciliation which have eluded Jerusalem for so long.[32]

I cannot bring to an end this brief survey of the situation of the Church in Asia, though far from complete, without mentioning the Saints and Martyrs of Asia, both those who have been recognized and those known only to God, whose example is a source of "spiritual richness and a great means of evangelization".[33] They speak silently but most powerfully of the importance of holiness of life and readiness to offer one's life for the Gospel. They are the teachers and the protectors, the glory of the Church in Asia in her work of evangelization. With the whole Church I pray to the Lord to send many more committed labourers to reap the harvest of souls which I see as ready and plentiful (cf. Mt 9:37–38). At this moment, I call to mind what I wrote in *Redemptoris Missio*: "God is opening before the Church the horizons of a humanity more fully prepared for the sowing of the Gospel".[34] This vision of a new and promising horizon I see being fulfilled in Asia, where Jesus was born and where Christianity began.

CHAPTER II
JESUS THE SAVIOUR: A GIFT TO ASIA

The Gift of Faith

10. As the Synod discussion of the complex realities of Asia unfolded, it became increasingly obvious to all that the Church's unique contribution to the peoples of the continent is the proclamation of Jesus Christ, true God and true man, the one and only Saviour for all peoples.[35] What distinguishes the Church from other religious communities is her faith in Jesus Christ; and she cannot keep this precious light of faith under a bushel (cf. Mt 5:15), for her mission is to share that light with everyone. "[The Church] wants to offer the new life she has found in Jesus Christ to all the peoples of Asia as they search for the fullness of life, so that they can have the same fellowship with the Father and his Son Jesus Christ in the power of the Spirit".[36] This faith in Jesus Christ is what inspires the Church's evangelizing work in Asia, often carried out in difficult and even dangerous circumstances. The Synod Fathers noted that proclaiming Jesus as the only Saviour can present particular difficulties in their cultures, given that many Asian religions teach divine self-manifestations as mediating salvation. Far from discouraging the Synod Fathers, the challenges facing their evangelizing efforts were an even greater incentive in striving to transmit "the faith that the Church in Asia has inherited from the Apostles and holds with the Church of all generations and places".[37] Indeed they expressed the conviction that "the heart of the Church in Asia will be restless until the whole of Asia finds its rest in the peace of Christ, the Risen Lord".[38]

The Church's faith in Jesus is a gift received and a gift to be shared; it is the greatest gift which the Church can offer to Asia. Sharing the truth of Jesus Christ with others is the solemn duty of all who have received the gift of faith. In my Encyclical Letter *Redemptoris Missio*, I wrote that "the Church, and every individual Christian within her, may not keep hidden or monopolize this newness and richness which has been received from God's bounty in order to be communicated to all mankind".[39] In the same Letter I wrote: "Those who are incorporated in the Catholic Church ought to sense their privilege and for that very reason their greater obligation of *bearing witness to the faith and to the Christian life* as a service to their brothers and sisters and as a fitting response to God".[40]

Deeply convinced of this, the Synod Fathers were equally conscious of their personal responsibility to grasp through study, prayer and reflection the timeless truth of Jesus in order to bring its power and vitality to bear on the present and future challenges of evangelization in Asia.

Jesus Christ, the God-Man Who Saves

11. The Scriptures attest that Jesus lived an authentically human life. The Jesus whom we proclaim as the only Saviour walked the earth as the God-Man in full possession of a human nature. He was like us in all things except sin. Born of a Virgin Mother in humble surroundings at Bethlehem, he was as helpless as any other infant, and even suffered the fate of a refugee fleeing the wrath of a ruthless leader (cf. Mt 2:13–15). He was subject to human parents who did not always understand his ways, but in whom he trusted and whom he lovingly obeyed (cf. Lk 2:41–52). Constantly at prayer, he was in intimate relationship with God whom he addressed as *Abba*, "Father", to the dismay of his listeners (cf. Jn 8:34–59).

He was close to the poor, the forgotten and the lowly, declaring that they were truly blessed, for God was with them. He ate with sinners, assuring them that at the Father's table there was a place for them when they turned from their sinful ways and came back to him. Touching the unclean and allowing them to touch him, he let them know the nearness of God. He wept for a dead friend, he restored a dead son to his widowed mother, he welcomed children, and he washed the feet of his disciples. Divine compassion had never been so immediately accessible.

The sick, the lame, the blind, the deaf and the dumb all experienced healing and forgiveness at his touch. As his closest companions and co-workers he chose an unusual group in which fishermen mixed with tax collectors, Zealots with people untrained in the Law, and women also. A new family was being created under the Father's all-embracing and surprising love. Jesus preached simply, using examples from everyday life to speak of God's love and his Kingdom; and the people recognized that he spoke with authority.

Yet he was accused of being a blasphemer, a violator of the sacred Law, a public nuisance to be eliminated. After a trial based on false testimony (cf. Mk 14:56), he was sentenced to die as a criminal on the Cross and, forsaken and humiliated, he seemed a failure. He was hastily buried in a borrowed tomb. But on the third day after this death, and despite the vigilance of the guards, the tomb was found empty! Jesus, risen from the dead, then appeared to his disciples before returning to the Father from whom he had come.

With all Christians, we believe that this particular life, in one sense so ordinary and simple, in another sense so utterly wondrous and shrouded in mystery, ushered into human history the Kingdom of God and "brought its power to bear upon every facet of human life and society beset by sin and death".[41] Through his words and actions, especially in his suffering, death and resurrection, Jesus fulfilled the will of his Father to reconcile all humanity to himself, after original sin had created a rupture in the relationship between the Creator and his creation. On the Cross, he took upon himself the sins of the world—past, present and future. Saint Paul reminds us that we were dead as a result of our sins and his death has brought us to life again: "God made [us] alive together with him, having forgiven us all our trespasses, having cancelled the bond which stood against us with its legal demands; this he set aside, nailing it to the cross" (Col 2:13–14). In this way, salvation was sealed once and for all. Jesus is our Saviour in the fullest sense of the word because his words and works, especially his resurrection from the dead, have revealed him to be the Son of God, the pre-existent Word, who reigns for ever as Lord and Messiah.

The Person and Mission of the Son of God

12. The "scandal" of Christianity is the belief that the all-holy, all-powerful and all-knowing God took upon himself our human nature and endured suffering and death to win salvation for all people (cf. 1 Cor 1:23). The faith we have received declares that Jesus Christ revealed and accomplished the Father's plan of saving the world and the whole of humanity because of "*who he is*" and "*what he does because of who he is*". "*Who he is*" and "*what he does*" acquire their full meaning only when set within the mystery of the Triune God. It has been a constant concern of my Pontificate to remind the faithful of the communion of life of the Blessed Trinity and the unity of the three Persons in the plan of creation and redemption. My Encyclical Letters *Redemptor Hominis*, *Dives in Misericordia* and *Dominum et Vivificantem* are reflections on the Son, the Father and the Holy Spirit respectively and on their roles in the divine plan of salvation. We cannot however isolate or separate one Person from the others, since each is revealed only within the communion of life and action of the Trinity. The saving action of Jesus has its origin in the communion of the Godhead, and opens the way for all who believe in him to enter into intimate communion with the Trinity and with one another in the Trinity.

"He who has seen me has seen the Father", Jesus claims (Jn 14:9). In Jesus Christ alone dwells the fullness of God in bodily form (cf. Col 2:9), establishing him as the unique and absolute saving Word of God (cf. Heb 1:1–4). As the Father's definitive Word, Jesus makes God and his saving will known in the fullest way possible. "No one comes to the Father but by me", Jesus says (Jn 14:6). He is "the Way, and the Truth, and the Life" (Jn 14:6), because, as he himself says, "the Father who dwells in me does his works" (Jn 14:10). Only in the person of Jesus does God's word of salvation appear in all its fullness, ushering in the final age (cf. Heb 1:1–2). Thus, in the first days of the Church, Peter could proclaim: "There is salvation in no one else, for there is no other name under heaven given among men by which we must be saved" (Acts 4:12).

The mission of the Saviour reached its culmination in the Paschal Mystery. On the Cross, when "he stretched out his arms between heaven and earth in the everlasting sign of [the Father's] covenant",[42] Jesus uttered his final appeal to the Father to forgive the sins of humanity: "Father, forgive them; for they know not what they do" (Lk 23:34). Jesus destroyed sin by the power of his love for his Father and for all mankind. He took upon himself the wounds inflicted on humanity by sin, and he offered release through conversion. The first fruits of this are evident in the repentant thief hanging beside him on another cross (cf. Lk 23:43). His last utterance was the cry of the faithful Son: "Father, into your hands I commit my spirit" (Lk 23:46). In this supreme expression of love he entrusted his whole life and mission into the hands of the Father who had sent him. Thus he handed over to the Father the whole of creation and all humanity, to be accepted finally by him in compassionate love.

Everything that the Son is and has accomplished is accepted by the Father, who then offers this gift to the world in the act of raising Jesus from the dead and setting him at his right hand, where sin and death have power no more. Through Jesus' Paschal Sacrifice *the Father irrevocably offers reconciliation and fullness of life to the world*. This extraordinary gift could only come through the beloved Son, who alone was capable of fully responding to the Father's love, rejected by sin. In Jesus Christ, through the power of the Holy Spirit, we come to know that God is not distant, above and apart from man, but is very near, indeed united to every person and all humanity in all of life's situations. This is the message which Christianity offers to the world, and it is a source of incomparable comfort and hope for all believers.

Jesus Christ: the Truth of Humanity

13. How does the humanity of Jesus and the ineffable mystery of the Incarnation of the Son of the Father shed light on the human condition? The Incarnate Son of God not only revealed completely the Father and his plan of salvation; he also "fully reveals man to himself".[43] His words and actions, and above all his Death and Resurrection, reveal the depths of what it means to be human. Through Jesus, man can finally know the truth of himself. Jesus' perfectly human life, devoted wholly to the love and service of the Father and of man, reveals that the vocation of every human being is to receive love and give love in return. In Jesus we marvel at the inexhaustible capacity of the human heart to love God and man, even when this entails great suffering. Above all, it is on the Cross that Jesus breaks the power of the self-destructive resistance to love which sin inflicts upon us. On his part, the Father responds by raising Jesus as the first-born of all those predestined to be conformed to the image of his Son (cf. Rom 8:29). At that moment, Jesus became once and for all both the revelation and the accomplishment of a humanity re-created and renewed according to the plan of God. In Jesus then, we discover the greatness and dignity of each person in the heart of God who created man in his own image (cf. Gen 1:26), and we find the origin of the new creation which we have become through his grace.

The Second Vatican Council taught that "by his Incarnation, he, the Son of God, in a certain way united himself with each individual".[44] In this profound insight the Synod Fathers saw the ultimate source of hope and strength for the people of Asia in their struggles and uncertainties. When men and women respond with a living faith to God's offer of love, his presence brings love and peace, transforming the human heart from within. In *Redemptor Hominis* I wrote that "the redemption of the world—this tremendous mystery of love in which creation is renewed—is, at its deepest root, the fullness of justice in a human Heart—the Heart of the First-born Son—in order that it may become justice in the hearts of many human beings, predestined from eternity in the First-born Son to be children of God and called to grace, called to love".[45]

Thus, the mission of Jesus not only restored communion between God and humanity; it also established a new communion between human beings alienated from one another because of sin. Beyond all divisions, Jesus makes it possible for people to live as brothers and sisters, recognizing a single Father who is in heaven (cf. Mt 23:9). In him, a new harmony has emerged, in which "there is neither Jew nor Greek, . . . neither slave nor free, . . . neither male nor female, for you are all one in Christ Jesus" (Gal 3:28). Jesus is our peace, "who has made us both one, and has broken down the dividing wall of hostility" (Eph 2:14). In all that he said and did, Jesus was the Father's voice, hands and arms, gathering all God's children into one family of love. He prayed that his disciples might live in communion just as he is in communion with the Father (cf. Jn 17:11). Among his last words we hear him say: "As the Father has loved me, so have I loved you; abide in my love. . . . This is my commandment, that you love one another as I have loved you" (Jn 15:9, 12). Sent by the God of communion and being truly God and truly man, Jesus established communion between heaven and earth in his very person. It is our faith that "in him all the fullness of God was pleased to dwell, and through him to reconcile to himself all things, whether on earth or in heaven, making peace by the blood of his Cross" (Col 1:19–20). Salvation can be found in the person of the Son of God made man and the mission entrusted to him alone as the Son, a mission of service and love for the life of all. Together with the Church throughout the world, the Church in Asia proclaims the truth of faith: "There is one God, and there is one mediator between God and men, the man Christ Jesus who gave himself as a ransom for all" (1 Tim 2:5–6).

The Uniqueness and Universality of Salvation in Jesus

14. The Synod Fathers recalled that the pre-existent Word, the eternally begotten Son of God, "was already present in creation, in history and in every human yearning for good".[46] Through the Word, present to the cosmos even before the Incarnation, the world came to be (cf. Jn 1:1–4, 10; Col 1:15–20). But as the incarnate Word who lived, died and rose from the dead, Jesus Christ is now proclaimed as the fulfilment of all creation, of all history, and of all human yearning for fullness of life.[47] Risen from the dead, Jesus Christ "is present to all and to the whole of creation in a new and mysterious way".[48] In him, "authentic values of all religious and cultural traditions, such as mercy and submission to the will of God, compassion and rectitude, non-violence and righteousness, filial piety and harmony with creation find their fullness and realization".[49] From the first moment of time to its end, Jesus is the one universal Mediator. Even for those who do not explicitly profess faith in him as the Saviour, salvation comes as a grace from Jesus Christ through the communication of the Holy Spirit.

We believe that Jesus Christ, true God and true man, is the one Saviour because he alone—the Son—accomplished the Father's universal plan of salvation. As the definitive manifestation of the mystery of the Father's love for all, Jesus is indeed unique, and "it is precisely this uniqueness of Christ which gives him an absolute and universal significance, whereby, while belonging to history, he remains history's centre and goal".[50]

No individual, no nation, no culture is impervious to the appeal of Jesus who speaks from the very heart of the human condition. "It is his life that speaks, his humanity, his fidelity to the truth, his all-embracing love. Furthermore, his death on the Cross speaks—that is to say the inscrutable depth of his suffering and abandonment".[51] Contemplating Jesus in his human nature, the peoples of Asia find their deepest questions answered, their hopes fulfilled, their dignity uplifted and their despair conquered. Jesus is the Good News for the men and women of every time and place in their search for the meaning of existence and for the truth of their own humanity.

CHAPTER III
THE HOLY SPIRIT: LORD AND GIVER OF LIFE

The Spirit of God in Creation and History

15. If it is true that the saving significance of Jesus can be understood only in the context of his revelation of the Trinity's plan of salvation, then it follows that the Holy Spirit is an absolutely vital part of the mystery of Jesus and of the salvation which he brings. The Synod Fathers made frequent references to the role of the Holy Spirit in the history of salvation, noting that a false separation between the Redeemer and the Holy Spirit would jeopardize the truth of Jesus as the one Saviour of all.

In Christian Tradition, the Holy Spirit has always been associated with life and the giving of life. The Nicene-Constantinopolitan Creed calls the Holy Spirit "the Lord, the Giver of Life". It is not surprising, therefore, that many interpretations of the creation account in Genesis have seen the Holy Spirit in the mighty wind that swept over the waters (cf. Gen 1:2). The Holy Spirit is present from the first moment of creation, the first manifestation of the love of the Triune God, and is always present in the world as its life-giving force.[52] Since creation is the beginning of history, the Spirit is in a certain sense a hidden power at work in history, guiding it in the ways of truth and goodness.

The revelation of the person of the Holy Spirit, the mutual love of the Father and the Son, is proper to the New Testament. In Christian thought he is seen as the wellspring of life for all creatures. Creation is God's free communication of love, a communication which, out of nothing, brings everything into being. There is nothing created that is not filled with the ceaseless exchange of love that marks the innermost life of the Trinity, filled that is with the Holy Spirit: "the Spirit of the Lord has filled the world" (Wis 1:7). The presence of the Spirit in creation generates order, harmony and interdependence in all that exists.

Created in the image of God, human beings become the dwelling-place of the Spirit in a new way when they are raised to the dignity of divine adoption (cf. Gal 4:5). Reborn in Baptism, they experience the presence and power of the Spirit, not just as the Author of Life but as the One who purifies and saves, producing fruits of "love, joy, peace, patience, kindness, goodness, faithfulness, gentleness, self-control" (Gal 5:22–23). These fruits of the Spirit are the sign that "God's love has been poured into our hearts through the Holy Spirit who has been given to us" (Rom 5:5). When accepted in freedom, this love makes men and women visible instruments of the unseen Spirit's ceaseless activity. It is above all this new capacity to give and receive love which testifies to the interior presence and power of the Holy Spirit. As a consequence of the transformation and re-creation which he produces in people's hearts and minds, the Spirit influences human societies and cultures.[53] "Indeed, the Spirit is at the origin of the noble ideals and undertakings which benefit humanity on its journey through history. 'The Spirit of God with marvellous foresight directs the course of the ages and renews the face of the earth'".[54]

Following the lead of the Second Vatican Council, the Synod Fathers drew attention to the multiple and diversified action of the Holy Spirit who continually sows the seeds of truth among all peoples, their religions, cultures and philosophies.[55] This means that these religions, cultures and philosophies are capable of helping people, individually and collectively, to work against evil and to serve life and everything that is good. The forces of death isolate people, societies and religious communities from one another, and generate the suspicion and rivalry that lead to conflict. The Holy Spirit, by contrast, sustains people in their search for mutual understanding and acceptance. The Synod was therefore right to see the Spirit of God as the prime agent of the Church's dialogue with all peoples, cultures and religions.

The Holy Spirit and the Incarnation of the Word

16. Under the Spirit's guidance, the history of salvation unfolds on the stage of the world, indeed of the cosmos, according to the Father's eternal plan. That plan, initiated by the Spirit at the very beginning of creation, is revealed in the Old Testament, is brought to fulfilment through the grace of Jesus Christ, and is carried on in the new creation by the same Spirit until the Lord comes again in glory at the end of time.[56] The Incarnation of the Son of God is the supreme work of the Holy Spirit: "The conception and birth of Jesus Christ are in fact the greatest work accomplished by the Holy Spirit in the history of creation and salvation: the supreme grace—'the grace of union', source of every other grace".[57] The Incarnation is the event in which God gathers into a new and definitive union with himself not only man but the whole of creation and all of history.[58]

Having been conceived in the womb of the Virgin Mary by the Spirit's power (cf. Lk 1:35; Mt 1:20), Jesus of Nazareth, the Messiah and only Saviour, was filled with the Holy Spirit. The Spirit descended upon him at his baptism (cf. Mk 1:10) and led him into the wilderness to be strengthened before his public ministry (cf. Mk 1:12; Lk 4:1; Mt 4:1). In the synagogue at Nazareth he began his prophetic ministry by applying to himself Isaiah's vision of the Spirit's anointing which leads to the preaching of good news to the poor, freedom to captives and a time acceptable to the Lord (cf. Lk 4:18–19). By the power of the Spirit, Jesus healed the sick and cast out demons as a sign that the Kingdom of God had come (cf. Mt 12:28). After rising from the dead, he imparted to the disciples the Holy Spirit whom he had promised to pour out on the Church when he returned to the Father (cf. Jn 20:22–23).

All of this shows how Jesus' saving mission bears the unmistakable mark of the Spirit's presence: life, *new life*. Between the *sending of the Son* from the Father and the *sending of the Spirit* from the Father and the Son, there is a close and vital link.[59] The action of the Spirit in creation and human history acquires an altogether new significance in his action in the life and mission of Jesus. The "seeds of the Word" sown by the Spirit prepare the whole of creation, history and man for full maturity in Christ.[60]

The Synod Fathers expressed concern about the tendency to separate the activity of the Holy Spirit from that of Jesus the Saviour. Responding to their concern, I repeat here what I wrote in *Redemptoris Missio*: "[The Spirit] is . . . not an alternative to Christ, nor does he fill a sort of void which is sometimes suggested as existing between Christ and the Logos. Whatever the Spirit brings about in human hearts and in the history of peoples, in cultures and religions serves as a preparation for the Gospel and can only be understood in reference to Christ, the Word who took flesh by the power of the Spirit 'so that as perfectly human he would save all human beings and sum up all things'".[61]

The universal presence of the Holy Spirit therefore cannot serve as an excuse for a failure to proclaim Jesus Christ explicitly as the one and only Saviour. On the contrary, the universal presence of the Holy Spirit is inseparable from universal salvation in Jesus. The presence of the Spirit in creation and history points to Jesus Christ in whom creation and history are redeemed and fulfilled. The presence and action of the Spirit both before the Incarnation and in the climactic moment of Pentecost point always to Jesus and to the salvation he brings. So too the Holy Spirit's universal presence can never be separated from his activity within the Body of Christ, the Church.[62]

The Holy Spirit and the Body of Christ

17. The Holy Spirit preserves unfailingly the bond of communion between Jesus and his Church. Dwelling in her as in a temple (cf. 1 Cor 3:16), the Spirit guides the Church, first of all, to the fullness of truth about Jesus. Then, it is the Spirit who empowers the Church to continue Jesus' mission, in the first place by witnessing to Jesus himself, thus fulfilling what he had promised before his death and resurrection, that he would send the Spirit to his disciples *so that they might bear witness to him* (cf. Jn 15:26–27). The work of the Spirit in the Church is also to testify that believers are the adopted children of God destined to inherit salvation, the promised fullness of communion with the Father (cf. Rom 8:15–17). Endowing the Church with different charisms and gifts, the Spirit makes the Church grow in communion as one body made up of many different parts (cf. 1 Cor 12:4; Eph 4:11–16). The Spirit gathers into unity all kinds of people, with their different customs, resources and talents, making the Church a sign of the communion of all humanity under the headship of Christ.[63] The Spirit shapes the Church as a community of witnesses who, through his power, bear testimony to Jesus the Saviour (cf. Acts 1:8). In this sense, the Holy Spirit is the prime agent of evangelization. From this the Synod Fathers could conclude that, just as the earthly ministry of Jesus was accomplished in the power of the Holy Spirit, "the same Spirit has been given to the Church by the Father and the Son at Pentecost to bring to completion Jesus' mission of love and service in Asia".[64]

The Father's plan for the salvation of man does not end with the death and resurrection of Jesus. By the gift of Christ's Spirit, the fruits of his saving mission are offered through the Church to all peoples of all times through the proclamation of the Gospel and loving service of the human family. As the Second Vatican Council observed, "the Church is driven by the Holy Spirit to do her part for the full realization of the plan of God, who has constituted Christ as the source of salvation for the whole world".[65] Empowered by the Spirit to accomplish Christ's salvation on earth, the Church is the seed of the Kingdom of God and she looks eagerly for its final coming. Her identity and mission are inseparable from the Kingdom of God which Jesus announced and inaugurated in all that he said and did, above all in his death and resurrection. The Spirit reminds the Church that she is not an end unto herself: in all that she is and all that she does, she exists to serve Christ and the salvation of the world. In the present economy of salvation the workings of the Holy Spirit in creation, in history and in the Church are all part of the one eternal design of the Trinity over all that is.

The Holy Spirit and the Church's Mission in Asia

18. The Spirit who moved upon Asia in the time of the patriarchs and prophets, and still more powerfully in the time of Jesus Christ and the early Church, moves now among Asian Christians, strengthening the witness of their faith among the peoples, cultures and religions of the continent. Just as the great dialogue of love between God and man was prepared for by the Spirit and accomplished on Asian soil in the mystery of Christ, so the dialogue between the Saviour and the peoples of the continent continues today by the power of the same Holy Spirit at work in the Church. In this process, Bishops, priests, religious and lay men and women all have an essential role to play, remembering the words of Jesus, which

are both a promise and a mandate: "You shall receive power when the Holy Spirit has come upon you; and you shall be my witnesses in Jerusalem and in all Judea and Samaria and to the end of the earth" (Acts 1:8).

The Church is convinced that deep within the people, cultures and religions of Asia there is a thirst for "living water" (cf. Jn 4:10–15), a thirst which the Spirit himself has created and which Jesus the Saviour alone can fully satisfy. The Church looks to the Holy Spirit to continue to prepare the peoples of Asia for the saving dialogue with the Saviour of all. Led by the Spirit in her mission of service and love, the Church can offer an encounter between Jesus Christ and the peoples of Asia as they search for the fullness of life. In that encounter alone is to be found the living water which springs up to eternal life, namely, the knowledge of the one true God and Jesus Christ whom he has sent (cf. Jn 17:3).

The Church well knows that she can accomplish her mission only in obedience to the promptings of the Holy Spirit. Committed to being a genuine sign and instrument of the Spirit's action in the complex realities of Asia, she must discern, in all the diverse circumstances of the continent, the Spirit's call to witness to Jesus the Saviour in new and effective ways. The full truth of Jesus and the salvation he has won is always a gift, never the result of human effort. "It is the Spirit himself bearing witness with our spirit that we are children of God, and if children, then heirs, heirs of God and fellow heirs with Christ" (Rom 8:16–17). Therefore the Church ceaselessly cries out, "Come, Holy Spirit! Fill the hearts of your faithful and enkindle in them the fire of your love!" This is the fire which Jesus casts upon the earth. The Church in Asia shares his zeal that this fire be re-kindled now (cf. Lk 12:49). With this ardent desire, the Synod Fathers sought to discern the principal areas of mission for the Church in Asia as she crosses the threshold of the new millennium.

CHAPTER IV
JESUS THE SAVIOUR: PROCLAIMING THE GIFT

The Primacy of Proclamation

19. On the eve of the Third Millennium, the voice of the Risen Christ echoes anew in the heart of every Christian: "All authority in heaven and on earth has been given to me. Go, therefore, and make disciples of all nations, baptizing them in the name of the Father and of the Son and of the Holy Spirit, teaching them to observe all that I have commanded you; and lo, I am with you always, to the close of the age" (Mt 28:18–20). Certain of the unfailing help of Jesus himself and the presence and power of his Spirit, the Apostles set out immediately after Pentecost to fulfil this command: "they went forth and preached everywhere, while the Lord worked with them" (Mk 16:20). What they announced can be summed up in the words of Saint Paul: "For what we preach is not ourselves, but Jesus Christ as Lord, with ourselves as your servants for Jesus' sake" (2 Cor 4:5). Blessed with the gift of faith, the Church, after two thousand years, continues to go out to meet the peoples of the world in order to share with them the Good News of Jesus Christ. She is a community aflame with missionary zeal to make Jesus known, loved and followed.

There can be no true evangelization without the explicit proclamation of Jesus as Lord. The Second Vatican Council and the Magisterium since then, responding to a certain confusion about the true nature of the Church's mission, have repeatedly stressed the primacy of the proclamation of Jesus Christ in all evangelizing work. Thus Pope Paul VI explicitly wrote that "there is no true evangelization if the name, the teaching, the life, the promises, the Kingdom and the mystery of Jesus of Nazareth, the Son of God, are not proclaimed".[66] This is what generations of Christians have done down the centuries. With understandable pride the Synod Fathers recalled that "many Christian communities in Asia have preserved their faith down the centuries against great odds and have clung to this spiritual heritage with heroic perseverance. For them to share this immense treasure is a matter of great joy and urgency".[67]

At the same time the participants in the Special Assembly testified over and over again to the need for a renewed commitment to the proclamation of Jesus Christ precisely on the continent which saw the beginning of that proclamation two thousand years ago. The words of the Apostle Paul become still more pointed, given the many people on that continent who have never encountered the person of Jesus in any clear and conscious way: "Everyone who calls upon the name of the Lord will be saved. But how are they to call upon him in whom they have not believed? And how are they to believe in him of whom they have never heard? And how are they to hear without a preacher?" (Rom 10:13–14). The great question now facing the Church in Asia is *how* to share with our Asian brothers and sisters what we treasure as the gift containing all gifts, namely, the Good News of Jesus Christ.

Proclaiming Jesus Christ in Asia

20. The Church in Asia is all the more eager for the task of proclamation knowing that "through the working of the Spirit, there already exists in individuals and peoples an expectation, even if an unconscious one, of knowing the truth about God, about man, and about how we are to be set free from sin and death".[68] This insistence on proclamation is prompted not by sectarian impulse nor the spirit of proselytism nor any sense of superiority. The Church evangelizes in obedience to Christ's command, in the knowledge that every person has the right to hear the Good News of the God who reveals and gives himself in Christ.[69] To bear witness to Jesus Christ is the supreme service which the Church can offer to the peoples of Asia, for it responds to their profound longing for the Absolute, and it unveils the truths and values which will ensure their integral human development.

Deeply aware of the complexity of so many different situations in Asia, and "speaking the truth in love" (Eph 4:15), the Church proclaims the Good News with loving respect and esteem for her listeners. Proclamation which respects the rights of consciences does not violate freedom, since faith always demands a free response on the part of the individual.[70] Respect, however, does not eliminate the need for the explicit proclamation of the Gospel in its fullness. Especially in the context of the rich array of cultures and religions in Asia it must be pointed out that "neither respect and esteem for these religions nor the complexity of the questions raised are an invitation to the Church to withhold from these non-Christians the proclamation of Jesus Christ".[71] While visiting India in 1986, I stated clearly that "the Church's approach to other religions is one of genuine respect. . . . This respect is twofold: respect for man in his quest for answers to the deepest questions of his life, and respect for the action of the Spirit in man".[72] Indeed, the Synod Fathers readily recognized the Spirit's action in Asian societies, cultures and religions, through which the Father prepares the hearts of Asian peoples for the fullness of life in Christ.[73]

Yet even during the consultations before the Synod many Asian Bishops referred to *difficulties in proclaiming Jesus as the only Saviour*. During the Assembly, the situation was described in this way: "Some of the followers of the great religions of Asia have no problem in accepting Jesus as a manifestation of the Divine or the Absolute, or as an 'enlightened one'. But it is difficult for them to see Him as the only manifestation of the Divine".[74] In fact, the effort to share the gift of faith in Jesus as the only Saviour is fraught with philosophical, cultural and theological difficulties, especially in light of the beliefs of Asia's great religions, deeply intertwined with cultural values and specific world views.

In the opinion of the Synod Fathers, the difficulty is compounded by the fact that Jesus is often perceived as foreign to Asia. It is paradoxical that most Asians tend to regard Jesus—born on Asian soil—as a Western rather than an Asian figure. It was inevitable that the proclamation of the Gospel by Western missionaries would be influenced by the cultures from which they came. The Synod Fathers recognized this as an unavoidable fact in the history of evangelization. At the same time they took advantage of the occasion "to express in a very special way their gratitude to all the missionaries, men and women, religious and lay, foreign and local, who brought the message of Jesus Christ and the gift of faith. A special word of gratitude again must be expressed to all the particular Churches which have sent and still send missionaries to Asia".[75]

Evangelizers can take heart from the experience of Saint Paul who engaged in dialogue with the philosophical, cultural and religious values of his listeners (cf. Acts 14:13–17; 17:22–31). Even the Ecumenical Councils of the Church which formulated doctrines binding on the Church had to use the linguistic, philosophical and cultural resources available to them. Thus these resources become a shared possession of the whole Church, capable of expressing her Christological doctrine in an appropriate and universal way. They are part of the heritage of faith which must be appropriated and shared again and again in the encounter with the various cultures.[76] Thus the task of proclaiming Jesus in a way which enables the peoples of Asia to identify with him, while remaining faithful both to the Church's theological doctrine and to their own Asian origins is a paramount challenge.

The presentation of Jesus Christ as the only Saviour needs to follow a *pedagogy* which will introduce people step by step to the full appropriation of the mystery. Clearly, the initial evangelization of non-Christians and the continuing proclamation of Jesus to believers will have to be different in their approach. In initial proclamation, for example, "the presentation of Jesus Christ could come as the fulfilment of the yearnings expressed in the mythologies and folklore of the Asian peoples".[77] In general, narrative methods akin to Asian cultural forms are to be preferred. In fact, the proclamation of Jesus Christ can most effectively be made by narrating his story, as the Gospels do. The ontological notions involved, which must always be presupposed and expressed in presenting Jesus, can be complemented by more relational, historical and even cosmic perspectives. The Church, the Synod Fathers noted, must be open to the new and surprising ways in which the face of Jesus might be presented in Asia.[78]

The Synod recommended that subsequent catechesis should follow "an evocative pedagogy, using stories, parables and symbols so characteristic of Asian methodology in teaching".[79] The ministry of Jesus himself shows clearly the value of personal contact, which requires the evangelizer to take the situation of the listener to heart, so as to offer a proclamation adapted to the listener's level of maturity, and in an appropriate form and language. In this perspective, the Synod Fathers stressed many times the need to evangelize in a way that appeals to the sensibilities of Asian peoples, and they suggested images of Jesus which would be intelligible to Asian minds and cultures and, at the same time, faithful to Sacred Scripture and Tradition. Among them were "Jesus Christ as the Teacher of Wisdom, the Healer, the Liberator, the Spiritual Guide, the Enlightened One, the Compassionate Friend of the Poor, the Good Samaritan, the Good Shepherd, the Obedient One".[80] Jesus could be presented as the Incarnate Wisdom of God whose grace brings to fruition the "seeds" of divine Wisdom already present in the lives, religions and peoples of Asia.[81] In the midst of so much suffering among Asian peoples, he might best be proclaimed as the Saviour "who can provide meaning to those undergoing unexplainable pain and suffering".[82]

The faith which the Church offers as a gift to her Asian sons and daughters cannot be confined within the limits of understanding and expression of any single human culture, for it transcends these limits and indeed challenges all cultures to rise to new heights of understanding and expression. Yet at the same time the Synod Fathers were well aware of the pressing need of the local Churches in Asia to present the mystery of Christ to their peoples according to their cultural patterns and ways of thinking. They pointed out that such an inculturation of the faith on their continent involves rediscovering the Asian countenance of Jesus and identifying ways in which the cultures of Asia can grasp the universal saving significance of the mystery of Jesus and his Church.[83] The penetrating insight into peoples and their cultures, exemplified in such men as Giovanni da Montecorvino, Matteo Ricci and Roberto de Nobili, to mention only a few, needs to be emulated at the present time.

The Challenge of Inculturation

21. Culture is the vital space within which the human person comes face to face with the Gospel. Just as a culture is the result of the life and activity of a human group, so the persons belonging to that group are shaped to a large extent by the culture in which they live. As persons and societies change, so too does the culture change with them. As a culture is transformed, so too are persons and societies transformed by it. From this perspective, it becomes clearer why evangelization and inculturation are naturally and intimately related to each other. The Gospel and evangelization are certainly not identical with culture; they are independent of it. Yet the Kingdom of God comes to people who are profoundly linked to a culture, and the building of the Kingdom cannot avoid borrowing elements from human cultures. Thus Paul VI called the split between the Gospel and culture the drama of our time, with a profound impact upon both evangelization and culture.[84]

In the process of encountering the world's different cultures, the Church not only transmits her truths and values and renews cultures from within, but she also takes from the various cultures the positive elements already found in them. This is the obligatory path for evangelizers in presenting the Christian faith and making it part of a people's cultural heritage. Conversely, the various cultures, when refined and renewed in the light of the Gospel, can become true expressions of the one Christian faith. "Through inculturation the Church, for her part, becomes a more intelligible sign of what she is, and a more effective instrument of mission".[85] This engagement with cultures has always been part of the Church's pilgrimage through history. But it has a special urgency today in the multi-ethnic, multi-religious and multi-cultural situation of Asia, where Christianity is still too often seen as foreign.

It is good to remember at this point what was said repeatedly during the Synod: that the Holy Spirit is the prime agent of the inculturation of the Christian faith in Asia.[86] The same Holy Spirit who leads us into the whole truth makes possible a fruitful dialogue with the cultural and religious values of different peoples, among whom he is present in some measure, giving men and women with a sincere heart the strength to overcome evil and the deceit of the Evil One, and indeed offering everyone the possibility of sharing in the Paschal Mystery in a manner known to God.[87] The Spirit's presence ensures that the dialogue unfolds in truth, honesty, humility and respect.[88] "In offering to others the Good News of the Redemption, the Church strives to understand their culture. She seeks to know the minds and hearts of her hearers, their values and customs, their problems and difficulties, their hopes and dreams. Once she knows and understands these various aspects of culture, then she can begin the dialogue of salvation; she can offer, respectfully but with clarity and conviction, the Good News of the Redemption to all who freely wish to listen and to respond".[89] Therefore the people of Asia who, as Asians, wish to make the Christian faith their own, can rest assured that their hopes, expectations, anxieties and sufferings are not only embraced by Jesus, but become the very point at which the gift of faith and the power of the Spirit enter the innermost core of their lives.

It is the task of the Pastors, in virtue of their charism, to guide this dialogue with discernment. Likewise, experts in sacred and secular disciplines have important roles to play in the process of inculturation. *But the process must involve the entire People of God*, since the life of the Church as a whole must show forth the faith which is being proclaimed and appropriated. To ensure that this is done soundly, the Synod Fathers identified certain areas for particular attention—theological reflection, liturgy, the formation of priests and religious, catechesis and spirituality.[90]

Key Areas of Inculturation

22. The Synod expressed encouragement to *theologians* in their delicate work of developing an inculturated theology, especially in the area of Christology.[91] They noted that "this theologizing is to be carried out with courage, in faithfulness to the Scriptures and to the Church's Tradition, in sincere adherence to the Magisterium and with an awareness of pastoral realities".[92] I too urge theologians to work in a spirit of union with the Pastors and the people, who—in union with one another and never separated from one another—"reflect the authentic sensus fidei which must never be lost sight of".[93] Theological work must always be guided by respect for the sensibilities of Christians, so that by a gradual growth into inculturated forms of expressing the faith people are neither confused nor scandalized. In every case inculturation must be guided by compatibility with the Gospel and communion with the faith of the universal Church, in full compliance with the Church's Tradition and with a view to strengthening people's faith.[94] The test of true inculturation is whether people become more committed to their Christian faith because they perceive it more clearly with the eyes of their own culture.

The *Liturgy* is the source and summit of all Christian life and mission.[95] It is a decisive means of evangelization, especially in Asia, where the followers of different religions are so drawn to worship, religious festivals and popular devotions.[96] The liturgy of the Oriental Churches has for the most part been successfully inculturated through centuries of interaction with the surrounding culture, but the more recently established Churches need to ensure that the liturgy becomes an ever greater source of nourishment for their peoples through a wise and effective use of elements drawn from the local cultures. Yet liturgical inculturation requires more than a focus upon traditional cultural values, symbols and rituals. There is also a need to take account of the shifts in consciousness and attitudes caused by the emerging secularist and consumer cultures which are affecting the Asian sense of worship and prayer. Nor can the specific needs of the poor, migrants, refugees, youth and women be overlooked in any genuine liturgical inculturation in Asia.

The national and regional Bishops' Conferences need to work more closely with the Congregation for Divine Worship and the Discipline of the Sacraments in the search for effective ways of fostering appropriate forms of worship in the Asian context.[97] Such cooperation is essential because the Sacred Liturgy expresses and celebrates the one faith professed by all and, being the heritage of the whole Church, cannot be determined by local Churches in isolation from the universal Church.

The Synod Fathers stressed particularly the importance of the biblical word in passing on the message of salvation to the peoples of Asia, where the transmitted word is so important in preserving and communicating religious experience.[98] It follows that an effective biblical apostolate needs to be developed in order to ensure that the sacred text may be more widely diffused and more intensively and prayerfully used among the members of the Church in Asia. The Synod Fathers urged that it be made the basis for all missionary proclamation, catechesis, preaching and styles of spirituality.[99] Efforts to translate the Bible into local languages need to be encouraged and supported. Biblical formation should be considered an important means of educating people in the faith and equipping them for the task of proclamation. Pastorally oriented courses on the Bible, with due emphasis on applying its teachings to the complex realities of Asian life, ought to be incorporated into formation programmes for the clergy, for consecrated persons and for the laity.[100] The Sacred Scriptures should also be made known among the followers of other religions; the word of God has an inherent power to touch the hearts of people, for through the Scriptures the Holy Spirit reveals God's plan of salvation for the world. Moreover, the narrative style found in many books of the Bible has an affinity with the religious texts typical of Asia.[101]

Another key aspect of inculturation upon which the future of the process in large part depends is *the formation of evangelizers*. In the past, formation often followed the style, methods and programmes imported from the West, and while appreciating the service rendered by that mode of formation, the Synod Fathers recognized as a positive development the efforts made in recent times to adapt the formation of evangelizers to the cultural contexts of Asia. As well as a solid grounding in biblical and patristic studies, seminarians should acquire a detailed and firm grasp of the Church's theological and philosophical patrimony, as I urged in my Encyclical Letter *Fides et Ratio*.[102] On the basis of this preparation, they will then benefit from contact with Asian philosophical and religious traditions.[103] The Synod Fathers also encouraged seminary professors and staff to seek a profound understanding of the elements of spirituality and prayer akin to the Asian soul, and to involve themselves more deeply in the Asian peoples' search for a fuller life.[104] To this end, emphasis was placed on the need to ensure the proper formation of seminary staff.[105] The Synod also expressed concern for the formation of men and women in the consecrated life, making it clear that the spirituality and lifestyle of consecrated persons needs to be sensitive to the religious and cultural heritage of the people among whom they live and whom they serve, always presupposing the necessary discernment of what conforms to the Gospel and what does not.[106] Moreover, since the inculturation of the Gospel involves the entire People of God, the role of the laity is of paramount importance. It is they above all who are called to transform society, in collaboration with the Bishops, clergy and religious, by infusing the "mind of Christ" into the mentality, customs, laws and structures of the secular world in which they live.[107] A wider inculturation of the Gospel at every level of society in Asia will depend greatly on the appropriate formation which the local Churches succeed in giving to the laity.

Christian Life as Proclamation

23. The more the Christian community is rooted in the experience of God which flows from a living faith, the more credibly it will be able to proclaim to others the fulfilment of God's Kingdom in Jesus Christ. This will result from faithfully listening to the word of God, from prayer and contemplation, from celebrating the mystery of Jesus in the sacraments, above all in the Eucharist, and from giving example of true communion of life and integrity of love. The heart of the particular Church must be set on the contemplation of Jesus Christ, God-made-Man, and strive constantly for a more intimate union with him whose mission she continues. *Mission is contemplative action and active contemplation.* Therefore, a missionary who has no deep experience of God in prayer and contemplation will have little spiritual influence or missionary success. This is an insight drawn from my own priestly ministry and, as I have written elsewhere, my contact with representatives of the non-Christian spiritual traditions, particularly those of Asia, has confirmed me in the view that the future of mission depends to a great extent on contemplation.[108] In Asia, home to great religions where individuals and entire peoples are thirsting for the divine, the Church is called to be a praying Church, deeply spiritual even as she engages in immediate

human and social concerns. All Christians need a true missionary spirituality of prayer and contemplation.

A genuinely religious person readily wins respect and a following in Asia. Prayer, fasting and various forms of asceticism are held in high regard. Renunciation, detachment, humility, simplicity and silence are considered great values by the followers of all religions. Lest prayer be divorced from human promotion, the Synod Fathers insisted that "the work of justice, charity and compassion is interrelated with a genuine life of prayer and contemplation, and indeed it is this same spirituality that will be the wellspring of all our evangelizing work".[109] Fully convinced of the importance of authentic witnesses in the evangelization of Asia, the Synod Fathers stated: "The Good News of Jesus Christ can only be proclaimed by those who are taken up and inspired by the love of the Father for his children, manifested in the person of Jesus Christ. This proclamation is a mission needing holy men and women who will make the Saviour known and loved through their lives. A fire can only be lit by something that is itself on fire. So, too, successful proclamation in Asia of the Good News of salvation can only take place if Bishops, clergy, those in the consecrated life and the laity are themselves on fire with the love of Christ and burning with zeal to make him known more widely, loved more deeply and followed more closely".[110] Christians who speak of Christ must embody in their lives the message that they proclaim.

In this regard, however, a particular circumstance in the Asian context demands attention. The Church realizes that *the silent witness of life* still remains the only way of proclaiming God's Kingdom in many places in Asia where explicit proclamation is forbidden and religious freedom is denied or systematically restricted. The Church consciously lives this type of witness, seeing it as the "taking up of her cross" (cf. Lk 9:23), all the while calling upon and urging governments to recognize religious freedom as a fundamental human right. The words of the Second Vatican Council are worth repeating here: "the human person has a right to religious freedom. Such freedom consists in this, that all should have such immunity from coercion by individuals, or by social groups, or by any human power, that no one should be forced to act against his conscience in religious matters, nor prevented from acting according to his conscience, whether in private or in public, whether alone or in association with others, within due limits".[111] In some Asian countries, this statement still has to be acknowledged and put into effect.

Clearly, then, the proclamation of Jesus Christ in Asia presents many complex aspects, both in content and in method. The Synod Fathers were keenly aware of the legitimate variety of approaches to the proclamation of Jesus, provided that the faith itself is respected in all its integrity in the process of appropriating and sharing it. The Synod noted that "evangelization today is a reality that is both rich and dynamic. It has various aspects and elements: witness, dialogue, proclamation, catechesis, conversion, baptism, insertion into the ecclesial community, the implantation of the Church, inculturation and integral human promotion. Some of these elements proceed together, while some others are successive steps or phases of the entire process of evangelization".[112] In all evangelizing work, however, it is the complete truth of Jesus Christ which must be proclaimed. Emphasizing certain aspects of the inexhaustible mystery of Jesus is both legitimate and necessary in gradually introducing Christ to a person, but this cannot be allowed to compromise the integrity of the faith. In the end, a person's acceptance of the faith must be grounded on a sure understanding of the person of Jesus Christ, as presented by the Church in every time and place, the Lord of all who is "the same yesterday, today and for ever" (Heb 13:8).

CHAPTER V
COMMUNION AND DIALOGUE FOR MISSION

Communion and Mission Go Hand in Hand

24. In accordance with the Father's eternal design, the Church, foreshadowed from the world's beginning, prepared for in the old Covenant, instituted by Christ Jesus and made present to the world by the Holy Spirit on the day of Pentecost, "progresses on her pilgrimage amid this world's persecutions and God's consolations",[113] as she strives towards her perfection in the glory of heaven. Since God desires "that the whole human race may become one People of God, form one Body of Christ, and be built up into one temple of the Holy Spirit",[114] the Church is in the world "the visible plan of God's love for humanity, the sacrament of salvation".[115] The Church cannot therefore be understood merely as a social organization or agency of human welfare. Despite having sinful men and women in her midst, the Church must be seen as the privileged place of encounter between God and man, in which God chooses to reveal the mystery of his inner life and carry out his plan of salvation for the world.

The mystery of God's loving design is made present and active in the community of the men and women who have been buried with Christ by baptism into death, so that as Christ was raised from the dead by the glory of the Father, they might walk in newness of life (cf. Rom 6:4). At the heart of the mystery of the Church is the bond of communion which unites Christ the Bridegroom to all the baptized. Through this living and life-giving communion, "Christians no longer belong to themselves but are the Lord's very own".[116] United to the Son in the Spirit's bond of love, Christians are united to the Father, and from this communion flows the communion which Christians share with one another through Christ in the Holy Spirit.[117] The Church's first purpose then is to be the sacrament of *the inner union of the human person with God*, and, because people's communion with one another is rooted in that union with God, the Church is also the sacrament of *the unity of the human race*.[118] In her this unity is already begun; and at the same time she is the "sign and instrument" of the full realization of the unity yet to come.[119]

It is an essential demand of life in Christ that whoever enters into communion with the Lord is expected to bear fruit: "He who abides in me, and I in him, he it is that bears much fruit" (Jn 15:5). So true is this that the person who does not bear fruit does not remain in communion: "Each branch of mine that bears no fruit [my Father] takes away" (Jn 15:2). Communion with Jesus, which gives rise to the communion of Christians among themselves, is the indispensable condition for bearing fruit; and communion with others, which is the gift of Christ and his Spirit, is the most magnificent fruit that the branches can give. In this sense, communion and mission are inseparably connected. They interpenetrate and mutually imply each other, so that "communion represents both the source and fruit of mission: communion gives rise to mission and mission is accomplished in communion".[120]

Using the theology of communion, the Second Vatican Council could describe the Church as the pilgrim People of God to whom all peoples are in some way related.[121] On this basis the Synod Fathers stressed the mysterious link between the Church and the followers of other Asian religions, noting that they are "related to [the Church] in varying degrees and ways".[122] In the midst of so many different peoples, cultures and religions "the life of the Church as communion assumes greater importance".[123] In effect, the Church's service of unity has a specific relevance in Asia where there are so many tensions, divisions and conflicts, caused by ethnic, social, cultural, linguistic, economic and religious differences. It is in this context that the local Churches in Asia, in communion with the Successor of Peter, need to foster greater communion of mind and heart through close cooperation among themselves. Vital also to their evangelizing mission are their relations with other Christian Churches and ecclesial communities, and with the followers of other religions.[124] The Synod therefore renewed the commitment of the Church in Asia to the task of improving both ecumenical relations and interreligious dialogue, recognizing that building unity, working for reconciliation, forging bonds of solidarity, promoting dialogue among religions and cultures, eradicating prejudices and engendering trust among peoples are all essential to the Church's evangelizing mission on the continent. All this demands of the Catholic community a sincere examination of conscience, the courage to seek reconciliation and a renewed commitment to dialogue. At the threshold of the Third Millennium it is clear that the Church's ability to evangelize requires that she strive earnestly to serve the cause of unity in all its dimensions. Communion and mission go hand in hand.

Communion within the Church

25. Gathered around the Successor of Peter, praying and working together, the Bishops of the Special Assembly for Asia personified as it were the communion of the Church in all the rich diversity of the particular Churches over which they preside in charity. My own presence at the Synod's General Sessions was both a welcome opportunity to share the joys and hopes, the difficulties and anxieties of the Bishops, and an intense and deeply-felt exercise of my own ministry. It is in fact within the perspective of ecclesial communion that the universal authority of the Successor of Peter shines forth more clearly, not primarily as juridical power over the local Churches, but above all as a pastoral primacy at the service of the unity of faith and life of the whole People of God. Fully aware that "the Petrine office has a unique ministry in guaranteeing and promoting the unity of the Church",[125] the Synod Fathers acknowledged the service which the Dicasteries of the Roman Curia and the Holy See's Diplomatic Service render to the local Churches, in the spirit of communion and collegiality.[126] An essential feature of this service is the respect and sensitivity which these close co-workers of the Successor of Peter show towards the legitimate diversity of the local Churches and the variety of cultures and peoples with which they are in contact.

Each particular Church must be grounded in the witness of ecclesial communion which constitutes its very nature as Church. The Synod Fathers chose to describe the Diocese as *a communion of communities* gathered around the Shepherd, where clergy, consecrated persons and the laity are engaged in a "dialogue of life and heart" sustained by the grace of the Holy Spirit.[127] It is primarily in the Diocese that the vision of a communion of communities can be actualized in the midst of the complex social, political, religious, cultural and economic realities of Asia. Ecclesial communion implies that each local Church should become what the Synod Fathers called a "participatory Church", a Church, that is, in which all live their proper vocation and perform their proper role. In order to build up the "communion for mission" and the "mission of communion", every member's unique charism needs to be acknowledged, developed and effectively utilized.[128] In particular there is a need to foster greater involvement of the laity and consecrated men and women in pastoral planning and decision-making, through such participatory structures as Pastoral Councils and Parish Assemblies.[129]

In every Diocese, *the parish* remains the ordinary place where the faithful gather to grow in faith, to live the mystery of ecclesial communion and to take part in the Church's mission. Therefore, the Synod Fathers urged Pastors to devise new and effective ways of shepherding the faithful, so that everyone, especially the poor, will feel truly a part of the parish and of God's People as a whole. Pastoral planning with the lay faithful should be a normal feature of all parishes.[130] The Synod singled out young people in particular as those for whom "the parish should provide greater opportunity for fellowship and communion . . . by means of organized youth apostolates and youth clubs".[131] No one should be excluded *a priori* from sharing fully in the life and mission of the parish because of their social, economic, political, cultural or educational background. Just as each follower of Christ has a gift to offer the community, so the community should show a willingness to receive and benefit from the gift of each one.

In this context, and drawing on their pastoral experience, the Synod Fathers underlined the value of *basic ecclesial communities* as an effective way of promoting communion and participation in parishes and Dioceses, and as a genuine force for evangelization.[132] These small groups help the faithful to live as believing, praying and loving communities like the early Christians (cf. Acts 2:44–47; 4:32–35). They aim to help their members to live the Gospel in a spirit of fraternal love and service, and are therefore a solid starting point for building a new society, the expression of *a civilization of love*. With the Synod, I encourage the Church in Asia, where possible, to consider these basic communities as a positive feature of the Church's evangelizing activity. At the same time they will only be truly effective if—as Pope Paul VI wrote—they live in union with the particular and the universal Church, in heartfelt communion with the Church's Pastors and the Magisterium, with a commitment to missionary outreach and without yielding to isolationism or ideological exploitation.[133] The presence of these small communities does not do away with the established institutions and structures, which remain necessary for the Church to fulfil her mission.

The Synod also recognized the role of *renewal movements* in building communion, in providing opportunities for a more intimate experience of God through faith and the sacraments, and in fostering conversion of life.[134] It is the responsibility of Pastors to guide, accompany and encourage these groups so that they may be well integrated into the life and mission of the parish and Diocese. Those involved in associations and movements should offer their support to the local Church and not present themselves as alternatives to Diocesan structures and parish life. Communion grows stronger when the local leaders of these movements work together with the Pastors in a spirit of charity for the good of all (cf. 1 Cor 1:13).

Solidarity among the Churches

26. This communion *ad intra* contributes to *solidarity among the particular Churches themselves*. Attention to local needs is legitimate and indispensable, but communion requires that the particular Churches remain open to one another and collaborate with one another, so that in their diversity they may preserve and clearly manifest the bond of communion with the universal Church. Communion calls for mutual understanding and a coordinated approach to mission, without prejudice to the autonomy and rights of the Churches according to their respective theological, liturgical and spiritual traditions. History however shows how divisions have often wounded the communion of the Churches in Asia. Down the centuries, relations between particular Churches of different ecclesiastical jurisdictions, liturgical traditions and missionary styles have sometimes been tense and difficult. The Bishops present at the Synod acknowledged that even today within and among the particular Churches in Asia there are sometimes unfortunate divisions, often connected with ritual, linguistic, ethnic, caste and ideological differences. Some wounds have been partially healed, but there is not yet full healing. Recognizing that wherever communion is weakened the Church's witness and missionary work suffer, the Fathers proposed concrete steps to strengthen relations between the particular Churches in Asia. As well as the necessary spiritual expressions of support and encouragement, they suggested a more equitable distribution of priests, more effective financial solidarity, cultural and theological exchanges, and increased opportunities for partnership between Dioceses.[135]

Regional and continental associations of Bishops, notably the Council of Catholic Patriarchs of the Middle East and the Federation of Asian Bishops' Conferences have helped to
foster union among the local Churches and have provided venues for cooperation in resolving pastoral problems. Similarly, there are many centres of theology, spirituality and
pastoral activity across Asia which foster communion and practical cooperation.[136] It must
be the concern of all to see these promising initiatives develop further for the good of both
the Church and society in Asia.

The Catholic Eastern Churches

27. The situation of *the Catholic Eastern Churches*, principally of the Middle East and India, merits special attention. From Apostolic times they have been the custodians of a precious spiritual, liturgical and theological heritage. Their traditions and rites, born of a deep
inculturation of the faith in the soil of many Asian countries, deserve the greatest respect.
With the Synod Fathers, I call upon everyone to recognize the legitimate customs and the
legitimate freedom of these Churches in disciplinary and liturgical matters, as stipulated by
the Code of Canons of the Eastern Churches.[137] Following the teaching of the Second Vatican Council, there is an urgent need to overcome the fears and misunderstandings which
appear at times between the Catholic Eastern Churches and the Latin Church, and among
those Churches themselves, especially with regard to the pastoral care of their people, also
outside their own territories.[138] As children of the one Church, reborn into the newness of
life in Christ, believers are called to undertake all things in a spirit of common purpose,
trust and unfailing charity. Conflicts must not be allowed to create division, but must instead be handled in a spirit of truth and respect, since no good can come except from
love.[139]

These venerable Churches are directly involved in ecumenical dialogue with their sister
Orthodox Churches, and the Synod Fathers urged them to pursue this path.[140] They have
also had valuable experiences in interreligious dialogue, especially with Islam. This can be
helpful to other Churches in Asia and elsewhere. It is clear that the Catholic Eastern
Churches possess a great wealth of tradition and experience which can greatly benefit the
whole Church.

Sharing Hopes and Sufferings

28. The Synod Fathers were also aware of the need for effective communion and cooperation with the local Churches present in the ex-Soviet territories of Asia, which are rebuild-
ing in the trying circumstances inherited from a difficult period of history. The Church accompanies them in prayer, sharing their sufferings and their new-found hopes. I encourage
the whole Church to lend moral, spiritual and material support, and much needed ordained
and non-ordained personnel to help these communities in the task of sharing with the peoples of these lands the love of God revealed in Jesus Christ.[141]

In many parts of Asia, our brothers and sisters continue to live their faith in the midst of restrictions or even the total denial of freedom. For these *suffering members of the Church*,
the Synod Fathers expressed special concern and solicitude. With the Bishops of Asia, I
urge our brothers and sisters of these Churches in difficult circumstances to join their sufferings to those of the crucified Lord, for we and they know that the Cross alone, when
borne in faith and love, is the path to resurrection and new life for humanity. I encourage
the various national Episcopal Conferences in Asia to establish an office to help these
Churches; and I pledge the Holy See's continued closeness to and concern for all those
who are suffering persecution for their faith in Christ.[142] I appeal to governments and the
leaders of nations to adopt and implement policies that guarantee religious freedom for all
their citizens.

On many occasions the Synod Fathers turned their thoughts to the Catholic Church in Mainland China and prayed that the day may soon come when our beloved Chinese brothers and sisters will be completely free to practise their faith in full communion with the See of Peter and the universal Church. To you, dear Chinese brothers and sisters, I make this fervent exhortation: never allow hardship and sorrow to diminish your devotion to Christ and your commitment to your great nation.[143] The Synod also expressed a cordial sense of solidarity with the Catholic Church in Korea, and supported "the efforts of Catholics to give assistance to the people of North Korea who are deprived of the minimal means of survival, and to bring reconciliation among two countries of one people, one language and one cultural heritage".[144]

Likewise, the Synod's thoughts frequently returned to the Church in Jerusalem, which has a special place in the hearts of all Christians. Indeed, the words of the Prophet Isaiah find an echo in the hearts of millions of believers throughout the world, for whom Jerusalem occupies a unique and cherished position: "Rejoice with Jerusalem, and be glad for her, all you who love her . . . that you may drink deeply with delight from the abundance of her glory" (66:10–11). Jerusalem, the city of reconciliation of men with God and among themselves, has so often been a place of conflict and division. The Synod Fathers called upon the particular Churches to stand in solidarity with the Church in Jerusalem by sharing her sorrows, by praying for her and cooperating with her in serving peace, justice and reconciliation between the two peoples and the three religions present in the Holy City.[145] I renew the appeal which I have often made to political and religious leaders and to all people of good will to search for ways to ensure the peace and integrity of Jerusalem. As I have already written, it is my own fervent wish to go there on a religious pilgrimage, like my predecessor Pope Paul VI, to pray in the Holy City where Jesus Christ lived, died and rose again and to visit the place from which, in the power of the Holy Spirit, the Apostles went forth to proclaim the Gospel of Jesus Christ to the world.[146]

A Mission of Dialogue

29. The common theme of the various "continental" Synods which have helped to prepare the Church for the Great Jubilee of the Year 2000 is that of the *new evangelization.* A new era of proclamation of the Gospel is essential not only because, after two millennia, a major part of the human family still does not acknowledge Christ, but also because the situation in which the Church and the world find themselves at the threshold of the new millennium is particularly challenging for religious belief and the moral truths which spring from it. There is a tendency almost everywhere to build progress and prosperity without reference to God, and to reduce the religious dimension of the human person to the private sphere. Society, separated from the most basic truth about man, namely his relationship to the Creator and to the redemption brought about by Christ in the Holy Spirit, can only stray further and further from the true sources of life, love and happiness. This violent century which is fast coming to a close bears terrifying witness to what can happen when truth and goodness are abandoned in favour of the lust for power and self-aggrandizement. The new evangelization, as a call to conversion, grace and wisdom, is the only genuine hope for a better world and a brighter future. The question is not whether the Church has something essential to say to the men and women of our time, but how she can say it clearly and convincingly!

At the time of the Second Vatican Council, my predecessor Pope Paul VI declared, in his Encyclical Letter *Ecclesiam Suam,* that the question of the relationship between the Church and the modern world was one of the most important concerns of our time. He wrote that "its existence and its urgency are such as to create a burden on our soul, a stimulus, a vocation".[147] Since the Council the Church has consistently shown that she wants to pursue that relationship in a spirit of dialogue. The desire for dialogue, however, is not simply a strategy for peaceful coexistence among peoples; it is an essential part of the Church's mission because it has its origin in the Father's loving dialogue of salvation with humanity through the Son in the power of the Holy Spirit. The Church can accomplish her mission only in a way that corresponds to the way in which God acted in Jesus Christ: he became man, shared our human life and spoke in a human language to communicate his saving message. The dialogue which the Church proposes is grounded in the logic of the Incarnation. Therefore, nothing but fervent and unselfish solidarity prompts the Church's dialogue with the men and women of Asia who seek the truth in love.

As the sacrament of the unity of all mankind, the Church cannot but enter into dialogue with all peoples, in every time and place. Responding to the mission she has received, she ventures forth to meet the peoples of the world, conscious of being a "little flock" within the vast throng of humanity (cf. Lk 12:32), but also of being leaven in the dough of the world (cf. Mt 13:33). Her efforts to engage in dialogue are directed in the first place to those who share her belief in Jesus Christ the Lord and Saviour. It extends beyond the Christian world to the followers of every other religious tradition, on the basis of the religious yearnings found in every human heart. Ecumenical dialogue and interreligious dialogue constitute a veritable vocation for the Church.

Ecumenical Dialogue

30. Ecumenical dialogue is a challenge and a call to conversion for the whole Church, especially for the Church in Asia where people expect from Christians a clearer sign of unity. For all peoples to come together in the grace of God, communion needs to be restored among those who in faith have accepted Jesus Christ as Lord. Jesus himself prayed and does not cease to call for the visible unity of his disciples, so that the world may believe that the Father has sent him (cf. Jn 17:21).[148] But the Lord's will that his Church be one awaits a complete and courageous response from his disciples.

In Asia, precisely where the number of Christians is proportionately small, division makes missionary work still more difficult. The Synod Fathers acknowledged that "the scandal of a divided Christianity is a great obstacle for evangelization in Asia".[149] In fact, the division among Christians is seen as a counter-witness to Jesus Christ by many in Asia who are searching for harmony and unity through their own religions and cultures. Therefore the Catholic Church in Asia feels especially impelled to work for unity with other Christians, realizing that the search for full communion demands from everyone charity, discernment, courage and hope. "In order to be authentic and bear fruit, ecumenism requires certain fundamental dispositions on the part of the Catholic faithful: in the first place, charity that shows itself in goodness and a lively desire to cooperate wherever possible with the faithful of other Churches and Ecclesial Communities; secondly, fidelity towards the Catholic Church, without however ignoring or denying the shortcomings manifested by some of her members; thirdly, a spirit of discernment in order to appreciate all that is good and worthy of praise. Finally, a sincere desire for purification and renewal is also needed".[150]

While recognizing the difficulties still existing in the relationships between Christians, which involve not only prejudices inherited from the past but also judgments rooted in profound convictions which involve conscience,[151] the Synod Fathers also pointed to signs of improved relations among some Christian Churches and Ecclesial Communities in Asia. Catholic and Orthodox Christians, for example, often recognize a cultural unity with one another, a sense of sharing important elements of a common ecclesial tradition. This forms a solid basis for a continuing fruitful ecumenical dialogue into the next millennium, which, we must hope and pray, will ultimately bring an end to the divisions of the millennium that is now coming to a close.

On the practical level, the Synod proposed that the national Episcopal Conferences in Asia invite other Christian Churches to join in a process of prayer and consultation in order to explore the possibilities of new ecumenical structures and associations to promote Christian unity. The Synod's suggestion that the Week of Prayer for Christian Unity be celebrated more fruitfully is also helpful. Bishops are encouraged to set up and oversee ecumenical centres of prayer and dialogue; and adequate formation for ecumenical dialogue needs to be included in the curriculum of seminaries, houses of formation and educational institutions.

Interreligious Dialogue

31. In my Apostolic Letter *Tertio Millennio Adveniente* I indicated that the advent of a new millennium offers a great opportunity for interreligious dialogue and for meetings with the leaders of the great world religions.[152] Contact, dialogue and cooperation with the followers of other religions is a task which the Second Vatican Council bequeathed to the whole Church as a duty and a challenge. The principles of this search for a positive relationship with other religious traditions are set out in the Council's Declaration *Nostra Aetate*, promulgated on 28 October 1965, the Magna Carta of interreligious dialogue for our times. From the Christian point of view, interreligious dialogue is more than a way of fostering mutual knowledge and enrichment; it is a part of the Church's evangelizing mission, an expression of the mission *ad gentes*.[153] Christians bring to interreligious dialogue the firm belief that the fullness of salvation comes from Christ alone and that the Church community to which they belong is the *ordinary means* of salvation.[154] Here I repeat what I wrote to the Fifth Plenary Assembly of the Federation of Asian Bishops' Conferences: "Although the Church gladly acknowledges whatever is true and holy in the religious traditions of Buddhism, Hinduism and Islam as a reflection of that truth which enlightens all people, this does not lessen her duty and resolve to proclaim without failing Jesus Christ who is 'the way and the truth and the life'... The fact that the followers of other religions can receive God's grace and be saved by Christ apart from the ordinary means which he has established does not thereby cancel the call to faith and baptism which God wills for all people".[155]

In the process of dialogue, as I have already written in my Encyclical Letter *Redemptoris Missio*, "there must be no abandonment of principles nor false irenicism, but instead a witness given and received for mutual advancement on the road of religious inquiry and experience, and at the same time for the elimination of prejudice, intolerance and misunderstandings".[156] Only those with a mature and convinced Christian faith are qualified to engage in genuine interreligious dialogue. "Only Christians who are deeply immersed in the mystery of Christ and who are happy in their faith community can without undue risk and with hope of positive fruit engage in interreligious dialogue".[157] It is therefore important for the Church in Asia to provide suitable models of interreligious dialogue—evangelization in dialogue and dialogue for evangelization—and suitable training for those involved.

Having stressed the need in interreligious dialogue for firm faith in Christ, the Synod Fathers went on to speak of the need for *a dialogue of life and heart*. The followers of Christ must have the gentle and humble heart of their Master, never proud, never condescending, as they meet their partners in dialogue (cf. Mt 11:29). "Interreligious relations are best developed in a context of openness to other believers, a willingness to listen and the desire to respect and understand others in their differences. For all this, love of others is indispensable. This should result in collaboration, harmony and mutual enrichment".[158]

To guide those engaged in the process, the Synod suggested that a directory on interreligious dialogue be drawn up.[159] As the Church explores new ways of encountering other religions, I mention some forms of dialogue already taking place with good results, including scholarly exchanges between experts in the various religious traditions or representatives of those traditions, common action for integral human development and the defence of human and religious values.[160] I repeat how important it is to revitalize prayer and contemplation in the process of dialogue. Men and women in the consecrated life can contribute very significantly to interreligious dialogue by witnessing to the vitality of the great Christian traditions of asceticism and mysticism.[161]

The memorable meeting held in Assisi, the city of Saint Francis, on 27 October 1986, between the Catholic Church and representatives of the other world religions shows that religious men and women, without abandoning their own traditions, can still commit themselves to praying and working for peace and the good of humanity.[162] The Church must continue to strive to preserve and foster at all levels this spirit of encounter and cooperation between religions.

Communion and dialogue are two essential aspects of the Church's mission, which have their infinitely transcendent exemplar in the mystery of the Trinity, from whom all mission comes and to whom it must be directed. One of the great "birthday" gifts which the members of the Church, and especially her Pastors, can offer the Lord of History on the two thousandth anniversary of his Incarnation is a strengthening of the spirit of *unity and communion* at every level of ecclesial life, a renewed "holy pride" in the Church's continuing fidelity to what has been handed down, and a new confidence in the unchanging grace and mission which sends her out among the peoples of the world to witness to God's saving love and mercy. Only if the People of God recognize the gift that is theirs in Christ will they be able to communicate that gift to others through *proclamation* and *dialogue*.

CHAPTER VI
THE SERVICE OF HUMAN PROMOTION

The Social Doctrine of the Church

32. In the service of the human family, the Church reaches out to all men and women without distinction, striving to build with them a civilization of love, founded upon the universal values of peace, justice, solidarity and freedom, which find their fulfilment in Christ. As the Second Vatican Council said so memorably: "The joys and the hopes, the griefs and the anxieties of the people of this age, especially those who are poor or in any way afflicted, these too are the joys and hopes, the griefs and anxieties of the followers of Christ. Indeed, nothing genuinely human fails to raise an echo in their hearts".[163] The Church in Asia then, with its multitude of poor and oppressed people, is called to live a communion of life which shows itself particularly in loving service to the poor and defenceless.

If in recent times the Church's Magisterium has insisted more and more upon the need to promote the authentic and integral development of the human person,[164] this is in response to the real situation of the world's peoples, as well as to an increased consciousness that not just the actions of individuals but also structures of social, political and economic life are often inimical to human well-being. The imbalances entrenched in the increasing gap between those who benefit from the world's growing capacity to produce wealth and those who are left at the margin of progress call for a radical change of both mentality and structures *in favour of the human person*. The great *moral challenge* facing nations and the international community in relation to development is to have *the courage of a new solidarity*, capable of taking imaginative and effective steps to overcome both dehumanizing underdevelopment and the "overdevelopment" which tends to reduce the person to an economic unit in an ever more oppressive consumer network. In seeking to bring about this change, "the Church does not have technical solutions to offer", but "offers her first contribution to the solution of the urgent problem of development when she proclaims the truth about Christ, about herself and about man, applying this truth to a concrete situation".[165] After all, human development is never a merely technical or economic question; it is fundamentally *a human and moral question.*

The social doctrine of the Church, which proposes a set of principles for reflection, criteria for judgement and directives for action,[166] is addressed in the first place to the members of the Church. It is essential that the faithful engaged in human promotion should have a firm grasp of this precious body of teaching and make it an integral part of their evangelizing mission. The Synod Fathers therefore stressed the importance of offering the faithful—in all educational activities, and especially in seminaries and houses of formation—a solid training in the social doctrine of the Church.[167] Christian leaders in the Church and society, and especially lay men and women with responsibilities in public life, need to be well formed in this teaching so that they can inspire and vivify civil society and its structures with the leaven of the Gospel.[168] The social doctrine of the Church will not only alert these Christian leaders to their duty, but will also give them guidelines for action in favour of human development, and will free them from false notions of the human person and human activity.

The Dignity of the Human Person

33. Human beings, not wealth or technology, are the prime agents and destination of development. Therefore, the kind of development that the Church promotes reaches far beyond questions of economy and technology. It begins and ends with the integrity of the human person created in the image of God and endowed with a God-given dignity and inalienable human rights. The various international declarations on human rights and the many initiatives which these have inspired are a sign of growing attention on a worldwide level to the dignity of the human person. Unfortunately, these declarations are often violated in practice. Fifty years after the solemn proclamation of the Universal Declaration of Human Rights, many people are still subjected to the most degrading forms of exploitation and manipulation, which make them veritable slaves to those who are more powerful, to an ideology, economic power, oppressive political systems, scientific technocracy or the intrusiveness of the mass media.[169]

The Synod Fathers were well aware of the persistent violations of human rights in many parts of the world, and particularly in Asia, where "teeming millions are suffering from discrimination, exploitation, poverty and marginalization".[170] They expressed the need for all God's people in Asia to come to a clear awareness of the inescapable and unrenounceable challenge involved in the defence of human rights and the promotion of justice and peace.

Preferential Love of the Poor

34. In seeking to promote human dignity, the Church shows a preferential love of the poor and the voiceless, because the Lord has identified himself with them in a special way (cf. Mt 25:40). This love excludes no one, but simply embodies a priority of service to which the whole Christian tradition bears witness. "This love of preference for the poor, and the decisions which it inspires in us, cannot but embrace the immense multitudes of the hungry, the needy, the homeless, those without medical care and, above all, those without hope of a better future. It is impossible not to take account of the existence of these realities. To

ignore them would mean becoming like the 'rich man' who pretended not to know the beggar Lazarus lying at his gate (cf. Lk 16:19–31)".[171] This is especially so with regard to Asia, a continent of plentiful resources and great civilizations, but where some of the poorest nations on earth are to be found, and where more than half the population suffers deprivation, poverty and exploitation.[172] The poor of Asia and of the world will always find their best reason for hope in the Gospel command to love one another as Christ has loved us (cf. Jn 13:34); and the Church in Asia cannot but strive earnestly to fulfil that command towards the poor, in word and in deed.

Solidarity with the poor becomes more credible if Christians themselves live simply, following the example of Jesus. Simplicity of life, deep faith and unfeigned love for all, especially the poor and the outcast, are luminous signs of the Gospel in action. The Synod Fathers called on Asian Catholics to adopt a lifestyle consonant with the teachings of the Gospel, so that they may better serve the Church's mission and so that the Church herself may become a Church of the poor and for the poor.[173]

In her love for the poor of Asia, the Church concerns herself especially with migrants, with indigenous and tribal peoples, with women and with children, since they are often the victims of the worst forms of exploitation. In addition, untold numbers of people suffer discrimination because of their culture, colour, race, caste, economic status, or because of their way of thinking. They include those who are victimized on the basis of their conversion to Christianity.[174] I join the Synod Fathers in appealing to all nations to recognize the right to freedom of conscience and religion and the other basic human rights.[175]

At the present time Asia is experiencing an unprecedented flow of refugees, asylum seekers, immigrants and overseas workers. In the countries to which they come, these people often find themselves friendless, culturally estranged, linguistically disadvantaged and economically vulnerable. They need support and care in order to preserve their human dignity and their cultural and religious heritage.[176] Despite limited resources, the Church in Asia generously seeks to be a welcoming home to the weary and heavy-burdened, knowing that in the Heart of Jesus, where no one is a stranger, they will find rest (cf. Mt 11:28–29).

In almost every Asian country, there are large aboriginal populations, some of them on the lowest economic rung. The Synod repeatedly noted that indigenous or tribal people often feel drawn to the person of Jesus Christ and to the Church as a community of love and service.[177] Herein lies an immense field of action in education and health care, as well as in promoting social participation. The Catholic community needs to intensify pastoral work among these people, attending to their concerns and to the questions of justice which affect their lives. This implies an attitude of deep respect for their traditional religion and its values; it implies as well the need to help them to help themselves, so that they can work to improve their situation and become the evangelizers of their own culture and society.[178]

No one can remain indifferent to the suffering of the countless children in Asia who fall victim to intolerable exploitation and violence, not just as the result of the evil perpetrated by individuals but often as a direct consequence of corrupt social structures. The Synod Fathers identified child labour, paedophilia and the drug culture as the social evils which affect children most directly, and they saw clearly that these ills are compounded by others like poverty and ill-conceived programmes of national development.[179] The Church must do all she can to overcome such evils, to act on behalf of those most exploited, and to seek to guide the little ones to the love of Jesus, for to such belongs the Kingdom of God (cf. Lk 18:16).[180]

The Synod voiced special concern for women, whose situation remains a serious problem in Asia, where discrimination and violence against women is often found in the home, in the workplace and even within the legal system. Illiteracy is most widespread among women, and many are treated simply as commodities in prostitution, tourism and the entertainment industry.[181] In their fight against all forms of injustice and discrimination, women should find an ally in the Christian community, and for this reason the Synod proposed that where possible the local Churches in Asia should promote human rights activities on behalf of women. The aim must be to bring about a change of attitude through a proper understanding of the role of men and women in the family, in society and in the Church, through greater awareness of the original complementarity between men and women, and through clearer appreciation of the importance of the feminine dimension in all things human. The contributions of women have all too often been undervalued or ignored, and this has resulted in a spiritual impoverishment of humanity. The Church in Asia would more visibly and effectively uphold women's dignity and freedom by encouraging their role in the Church's life, including her intellectual life, and by opening to them ever greater opportunities to be present and active in the Church's mission of love and service.[182]

The Gospel of Life

35. The service of human development begins with the service of life itself. Life is a great gift entrusted to us by God: he entrusts it to us as a project and a responsibility. We are therefore guardians of life, not its proprietors. We receive the gift freely and, in gratitude, we must never cease to respect and defend it, from its beginning to its natural conclusion. From the moment of conception, human life involves God's creative action and remains forever in a special bond with the Creator, who is life's source and its sole end. There is no true progress, no true civil society, no true human promotion without respect for human life, especially the life of those who have no voice of their own with which to defend themselves. The life of every person, whether of the child in the womb, or of someone who is sick, handicapped or elderly, is a gift for all.

The Synod Fathers wholeheartedly reaffirmed the teaching of the Second Vatican Council and the subsequent Magisterium, including my Encyclical Letter *Evangelium Vitae,* on the sanctity of human life. I join them here in calling upon the faithful in their countries, where the demographic question is often used as an argument for the need to introduce abortion and artificial population control programmes, to resist "the culture of death".[183] They can show their fidelity to God and their commitment to true human promotion by supporting and participating in programmes which defend the life of those who are powerless to defend themselves.

Health Care

36. Following in the steps of Jesus Christ who had compassion for all and cured "all kinds of disease and illness" (Mt 9:35), the Church in Asia is committed to becoming still more involved in the care of the sick, since this is a vital part of her mission of offering the saving grace of Christ to the whole person. Like the Good Samaritan of the parable (cf. Lk 10:29–37), the Church wants to care for the sick and disabled in concrete ways,[184] especially where people are deprived of elementary medical care as a result of poverty and marginalization.

On numerous occasions during my visits to the Church in different parts of the world I have been deeply moved by the extraordinary Christian witness borne by religious and consecrated persons, doctors, nurses and other health care workers, especially those working with the handicapped, or in the field of terminal care, or contending with the spread of new diseases such as AIDS. Increasingly, Christian health care workers are called to be generous and self-giving in tending the victims of drug addiction and AIDS, who are often despised and abandoned by society.[185] Many Catholic medical institutions in Asia are facing pressures from public health care policies not based on Christian principles, and many of them are burdened by ever increasing financial difficulties. In spite of these problems, it is the exemplary self-giving love and dedicated professionalism of those involved that make these facilities an admirable and appreciated service to the community, and a particularly visible and effective sign of God's unfailing love. These health care workers must be encouraged and supported in the good that they do. Their continuing commitment and effectiveness is the best way to ensure that Christian values and ethics enter deeply into the health care systems of the continent and transform them from within.[186]

Education

37. Throughout Asia, the Church's involvement in education is extensive and highly visible, and is therefore a key element of her presence among the peoples of the continent. In many countries, Catholic schools play an important role in evangelization, inculturating the faith, teaching the ways of openness and respect, and fostering interreligious understanding. The Church's schools often provide the only educational opportunities for girls, tribal minorities, the rural poor and less privileged children. The Synod Fathers were convinced of the need to extend and develop the apostolate of education in Asia, with an eye in particular to the disadvantaged, so that all may be helped to take their rightful place as full citizens in society.[187] As the Synod Fathers noted, this will mean that the system of Catholic education must become still more clearly directed towards human promotion, providing an environment where students receive not only the formal elements of schooling but, more broadly, an integral human formation based upon the teachings of Christ.[188] Catholic schools should continue to be places where the faith can be freely proposed and received. In the same way, Catholic universities, in addition to pursuing the academic excellence for which they are already well known, must retain a clear Christian identity in order to be a Christian leaven in Asian societies.[189]

Peacemaking

38. At the end of the twentieth century the world is still threatened by forces which generate conflicts and wars, and Asia is certainly not exempt from these. Among these forces are intolerance and marginalization of all kinds—social, cultural, political, and even religious. Day by day fresh violence is inflicted upon individuals and entire peoples, and the culture of death takes hold in the unjustifiable recourse to violence to resolve tensions. Given the appalling situation of conflict in so many parts of the world, the Church is called to be deeply involved in international and interreligious efforts to bring about peace, justice and reconciliation. She continues to insist on the negotiated and non-military resolution of conflicts, and she looks to the day when nations will abandon war as a way of vindicating claims or a means of resolving differences. She is convinced that war creates more problems than it ever solves, that dialogue is the only just and noble path to agreement and reconciliation, and that the patient and wise art of peacemaking is especially blessed by God.

Especially troubling in Asia is the continual race to acquire weapons of mass destruction, an immoral and wasteful expenditure in national budgets, which in some cases cannot even satisfy people's basic needs. The Synod Fathers also spoke of the vast number of landmines in Asia, which have maimed or killed hundreds of thousands of innocent people, while despoiling fertile land which could otherwise be used for food production.[190] It is the responsibility of all, especially of those who govern nations, to work more energetically for disarmament. The Synod called for a stop to the manufacture, sale and use of nuclear, chemical and biological arms and urged those who have set landmines to assist in the work of rehabilitation and restoration.[191] Above all the Synod Fathers prayed to God, who knows the depths of every human conscience, to put sentiments of peace in the hearts of those tempted to follow the ways of violence so that the biblical vision will become a reality: "they shall beat their swords into ploughshares, and their spears into pruning hooks; nation shall not lift up sword against nation, neither shall they learn war any more" (Is 2:4).

The Synod heard many testimonies concerning the sufferings of the people of Iraq, and about the fact that many Iraqis, especially children, have died because of the lack of medicines and other basic commodities deriving from the continuing embargo. With the Synod Fathers, I wish to express once again my solidarity with the Iraqi people, and I am particularly close in prayer and hope to the sons and daughters of the Church in that country. The Synod prayed that God will enlighten the minds and hearts of all those who bear responsibility for bringing about a just solution to the crisis, in order that an already sorely tried people may be spared further suffering and sorrow.[192]

Globalization

39. Considering the question of human promotion in Asia, the Synod Fathers recognized the importance of the process of economic globalization. While acknowledging its many positive effects, they pointed out that globalization has also worked to the detriment of the poor,[193] tending to push poorer countries to the margin of international economic and political relations. Many Asian nations are unable to hold their own in a global market economy. And perhaps more significantly, there is also the aspect of a *cultural* globalization, made possible by the modern communications media, which is quickly drawing Asian societies into a global consumer culture that is both secularist and materialistic. The result is an eroding of traditional family and social values which until now had sustained peoples and societies. All of this makes it clear that *the ethical and moral aspects of globalization* need to be more directly addressed by the leaders of nations and by organizations concerned with human promotion.

The Church insists upon the need for "globalization without marginalization".[194] With the Synod Fathers, I call upon the particular Churches everywhere, and especially those in the Western countries, to work to ensure that the Church's social doctrine has its due impact upon the formulation of ethical and juridical norms for regulating the world's free markets and for the means of social communication. Catholic leaders and professionals should urge governments and financial and trade institutions to recognize and respect such norms.[195]

Foreign Debt

40. Furthermore, in her search for justice in a world marred by social and economic inequalities, the Church cannot ignore the heavy burden of debt incurred by many developing nations in Asia, with its consequent impact upon their present and future. In many cases, these countries are forced to cut down spending on the necessities of life such as food, health, housing and education, in order to service their debts to international monetary agencies and banks. This means that many people are trapped in living conditions which are an affront to human dignity. While aware of the technical complexities of this matter, the Synod recognized that this issue tests the capacity of peoples, societies and governments to value the human person and the lives of millions of human beings more highly than financial and material gain.[196]

The approach of the Great Jubilee of the Year 2000 is an opportune time for the Episcopal Conferences of the world, especially of the wealthier nations, to encourage international monetary agencies and banks to explore ways of easing the international debt situation.

Among the more obvious are a renegotiation of debts, with either substantial reduction or outright cancellation, as also business ventures and investments to assist the economies of the poorer countries.[197] At the same time the Synod Fathers also addressed the debtor countries. They emphasized the need to develop a sense of national responsibility, reminding them of the importance of sound economic planning, transparency and good management, and invited them to wage a resolute campaign against corruption.[198] They called upon the Christians of Asia to condemn all forms of corruption and the misappropriation of public funds by those holding political power.[199] The citizens of debtor countries have too often been victims of waste and inefficiency at home, before falling victim to the international debt crisis.

The Environment

41. When concern for economic and technological progress is not accompanied by concern for the balance of the ecosystem, our earth is inevitably exposed to serious environmental damage, with consequent harm to human beings. Blatant disrespect for the environment will continue as long as the earth and its potential are seen merely as objects of immediate use and consumption, to be manipulated by an unbridled desire for profit.[200] It is the duty of Christians and of all who look to God as the Creator to protect the environment by restoring a sense of reverence for the whole of God's creation. It is the Creator's will that man should treat nature not as a ruthless exploiter but as an intelligent and responsible administrator.[201] The Synod Fathers pleaded in a special way for greater responsibility on the part of the leaders of nations, legislators, business people and all who are directly involved in the management of the earth's resources.[202] They underlined the need to educate people, especially the young, in environmental responsibility, training them in the stewardship over creation which God has entrusted to humanity. The protection of the environment is not only a *technical* question; it is also and above all an *ethical* issue. All have a moral duty to care for the environment, not only for their own good but also for the good of future generations.

In conclusion, it is worth remembering that in calling on Christians to work and sacrifice themselves in the service of human development the Synod Fathers were drawing upon some of the core insights of biblical and ecclesial tradition. Ancient Israel insisted passionately upon the unbreakable bond between worship of God and care for the weak, represented typically in Scripture as "the widow, the stranger and orphan" (cf. Ex 22:21–22; Dt 10:18; 27:19), who in the societies of the time were most vulnerable to the threat of injustice. Time and again in the Prophets we hear the cry for justice, for the right ordering of human society, without which there can be no true worship of God (cf. Is 1:10–17; Am 5:21–24). In the appeal of the Synod Fathers we thus hear an echo of the Prophets filled with the Spirit of God, who wants "mercy not sacrifice" (Hos 6:6). Jesus made these words his own (cf. Mt 9:13), and the same is true of the Saints in every time and place. Consider the words of Saint John Chrysostom: "Do you wish to honour the body of Christ? Then do not ignore him when he is naked. Do not pay him silken honours in the temple only then to neglect him when he goes cold and naked outside. He who said; 'This is my body' is the One who also said, 'You saw me hungry and you gave me no food'. . . . What good is it if the Eucharistic Table groans under the weight of golden chalices, when Christ is dying of hunger? Start by satisfying his hunger, and then with what remains you may adorn the altar as well!".[203] In the Synod's appeal for human development and for justice in human affairs, we hear a voice which is both old and new. It is old because it rises from the depths of our Christian tradition, which looks to that profound harmony which the Creator intends; it is new because it speaks to the immediate situation of countless people in Asia today.

CHAPTER VII
WITNESSES TO THE GOSPEL

A Witnessing Church

42. The Second Vatican Council taught clearly that the entire Church is missionary, and that the work of evangelization is the duty of the whole People of God.[204] Since the whole People of God is sent forth to preach the Gospel, evangelization is never an individual and isolated act; it is always an ecclesial task which has to be carried out in communion with the whole community of faith. The mission is one and indivisible, having one origin and one final purpose; but within it there are different responsibilities and different kinds of activity.[205] In every case it is clear that there can be no true proclamation of the Gospel unless Christians also offer the witness of lives in harmony with the message they preach: "The first form of witness is the very life of the missionary, of the Christian family, and of the ecclesial community, which reveal a new way of living... Everyone in the Church, striving to imitate the Divine Master, can and must bear this kind of witness; in many cases it is the only possible way of being a missionary".[206] Genuine Christian witness is needed especially now, because "people today put more trust in witnesses than in teachers, in experience than in teaching, and in life and action than in theories".[207] This is certainly true in the Asian context, where people are more persuaded by holiness of life than by intellectual argument. The experience of faith and of the gifts of the Holy Spirit thus becomes the basis of all missionary work, in towns or villages, in schools or hospitals, among the handicapped, migrants or tribal peoples, or in the pursuit of justice and human rights. Every situation is an opportunity for Christians to show forth the power which the truth of Christ has become in their lives. Therefore, inspired by the many missionaries who bore heroic witness to God's love among the peoples of the continent in the past, the Church in Asia strives now to witness with no less zeal to Jesus Christ and his Gospel. Christian mission demands no less.

Conscious of the Church's essentially missionary character and looking to a new outpouring of the dynamism of the Holy Spirit as the Church enters the new millennium, the Synod Fathers asked that this Post-Synodal Apostolic Exhortation should offer some directives and guidelines to those working in the vast field of evangelization in Asia.

Pastors

43. It is the Holy Spirit who enables the Church to accomplish the mission entrusted to her by Christ. Before sending out his disciples as his witnesses, Jesus gave them the Holy Spirit (cf. Jn 20:22), who worked through them and stirred the hearts of those who heard them (cf. Acts 2:37). The same is true of those whom he sends out now. At one level, all the baptized, by the very grace of the Sacrament, are deputed to take part in continuing the saving mission of Christ, and they are capable of this task precisely because God's love has been poured into their hearts through the Holy Spirit which has been given to them (Rom 5:5). But on another level this common mission is accomplished through a variety of specific functions and charisms in the Church. The principal responsibility for the Church's mission has been entrusted by Christ to the Apostles and their successors. By virtue of episcopal ordination and hierarchical communion with the Head of the Episcopal College, Bishops receive the mandate and authority to teach, govern and sanctify the People of God. By the will of Christ himself, within the College of Bishops, the Successor of Peter—the rock upon which the Church is built (cf. Mt 16:18)—exercises a special ministry of unity. Bishops therefore are to fulfil their ministry in union with the Successor of Peter, the guarantor of the truth of their teaching and of their full communion in the Church.

Associated with the Bishops in the work of proclaiming the Gospel, priests are called upon at ordination to be shepherds of the flock, preachers of the good news of salvation and ministers of the sacraments. To serve the Church as Christ intends, Bishops and priests need a solid and continuing formation, which should provide opportunities for human, spiritual and pastoral renewal, as well as courses on theology, spirituality and the human sciences.[208] People in Asia need to see the clergy not just as charity workers and institutional administrators but as men whose minds and hearts are set on the deep things of the Spirit (cf. Rom 8:5). The reverence which Asian peoples have for those in authority needs to be matched by a clear moral uprightness on the part of those with ministerial responsibilities in the Church. By their life of prayer, zealous service and exemplary conduct, the clergy witness powerfully to the Gospel in the communities which they shepherd in the name of Christ. It is my fervent prayer that the ordained ministers of the Churches in Asia will live and work in a spirit of communion and cooperation with the Bishops and all the faithful, bearing witness to the love which Jesus declared to be the true mark of his disciples (cf. Jn 13:35).

I particularly wish to underline the Synod's concern for the preparation of those who will staff and teach in seminaries and theological faculties.[209] After a thorough training in the sacred sciences and related subjects, they should receive a specific formation focused on priestly spirituality, the art of spiritual direction, and other aspects of the difficult and delicate task that awaits them in the education of future priests. This is an apostolate second to none for the Church's well-being and vitality.

The Consecrated Life and Missionary Societies

44. In the Post-Synodal Apostolic Exhortation *Vita Consecrata,* I emphasized the intimate connection between the consecrated life and mission. Under its three aspects of *confessio Trinitatis*, *signum fraternitatis* and *servitium caritatis*, the consecrated life shows forth God's love in the world by its specific witness to the saving mission which Jesus accomplished by his total consecration to the Father. Recognizing that all action in the Church has its support in prayer and communion with God, the Church in Asia looks with profound respect and appreciation to the contemplative religious communities as a special source of strength and inspiration. Following the recommendations of the Synod Fathers, I strongly encourage the establishment of monastic and contemplative communities wherever possible. In this way, as the Second Vatican Council reminds us, the work of building up the earthly city can have its foundation in the Lord and can tend towards him, lest those who build labour in vain.[210]

The search for God, a life of fraternal communion, and service to others are the three chief characteristics of the consecrated life which can offer an appealing Christian testimony to the peoples of Asia today. The Special Assembly for Asia urged those in the consecrated life to be witnesses to the universal call to holiness and inspiring examples to Christians and non-Christians alike of self-giving love for everyone, especially the least of their brothers and sisters. In a world in which the sense of God's presence is often diminished, consecrated persons need to bear convincing prophetic witness to the primacy of God and to eternal life. Living in community, they attest to the values of Christian fraternity and to the transforming power of the Good News.[211] All who have embraced the consecrated life are called to become leaders in the search for God, a search which has always stirred the human heart and which is particularly visible in Asia's many forms of spirituality and asceticism.[212] In the numerous religious traditions of Asia, men and women dedicated to the contemplative and ascetical life enjoy great respect, and their witness has an especially persuasive power. Their lives lived in community, in peaceful and silent testimony, can inspire people to work for greater harmony in society. No less is expected of consecrated men and women in the Christian tradition. Their silent example of poverty and abnegation, of purity and sincerity, of self-sacrifice in obedience, can become an eloquent witness capable of touching all people of good will and leading to a fruitful dialogue with surrounding cultures and religions, and with the poor and the defenceless. This makes the consecrated life a privileged means of effective evangelization.[213]

The Synod Fathers recognized the vital role played by religious orders and congregations, missionary institutes and societies of apostolic life in the evangelization of Asia in past centuries. For this magnificent contribution, the Synod expressed to them the Church's gratitude and urged them not to waver in their missionary commitment.[214] I join the Synod Fathers in calling on those in the consecrated life to renew their zeal to proclaim the saving truth of Christ. All are to have appropriate formation and training, which should be Christ-centred and faithful to their founding charism, with emphasis on personal sanctity and witness; their spirituality and lifestyle should be sensitive to the religious heritage of the people among whom they live and whom they serve.[215] While maintaining respect for their specific charism, they should integrate themselves into the pastoral plan of the Diocese in which they work. The local Churches, for their part, need to foster awareness of the ideal of the religious and consecrated life, and promote such vocations. This requires that each Diocese should devise a pastoral programme for vocations, including the assignment of priests and religious to full-time work among the young to help them hear and discern the call of God.[216]

In the context of the communion of the universal Church, I cannot fail to urge the Church in Asia to send forth missionaries, even though she herself needs labourers in the vineyard. I am glad to see that in several Asian countries missionary institutes of apostolic life have recently been founded in recognition of the Church's missionary character and of the responsibility of the particular Churches in Asia to preach the Gospel to the whole world.[217] The Synod Fathers recommended "the establishment within each local Church of Asia, where such do not exist, of missionary societies of apostolic life, characterized by their special commitment to the mission *ad gentes, ad exteros* and *ad vitam*".[218] Such an initiative is sure to bear abundant fruit not only in the Churches which receive the missionaries but also in the Churches which send them.

The Laity

45. As the Second Vatican Council clearly indicated, the vocation of lay people sets them firmly in the world to perform the most varied tasks, and it is here that they are called to spread the Gospel of Jesus Christ.[219] By the grace and call of Baptism and Confirmation, all lay people are missionaries; and the arena of their missionary work is the vast and complex worlds of politics, economics, industry, education, the media, science, technology, the arts and sport. In many Asian countries, lay people are already serving as true missionaries, reaching out to fellow Asians who might never have contact with clergy and religious.[220] To them I express the thanks of the whole Church, and I encourage all lay people to assume their proper role in the life and mission of the People of God, as witnesses to Christ wherever they may find themselves.

It is the task of the Pastors to ensure that the laity are formed as evangelizers able to face the challenges of the contemporary world, not just with worldly wisdom and efficiency, but with hearts renewed and strengthened by the truth of Christ.[221] Witnessing to the Gospel in every area of life in society, the lay faithful can play a unique role in rooting out injustice and oppression, and for this too they must be adequately formed. To this end, I join the Synod Fathers in proposing the establishment at the diocesan or national level of lay formation centres to prepare the laity for their missionary work as witnesses to Christ in Asia today.[222]

The Synod Fathers were most concerned that the Church should be a participatory Church in which no one feels excluded, and they judged the wider participation of women in the life and mission of the Church in Asia to be an especially pressing need. "Woman has a quite special aptitude in passing on the faith, so much so that Jesus himself appealed to it in the work of evangelization. That is what happened to the Samaritan woman whom Jesus met at Jacob's well: he chose her for the first expansion of the new faith in non-Jewish territory".[223] To enhance their service in the Church, there should be greater opportunities for women to take courses in theology and other fields of study; and men in seminaries and houses of formation need to be trained to regard women as co-workers in the apostolate.[224] Women should be more effectively involved in pastoral programmes, in diocesan and parish pastoral councils, and in diocesan synods. Their abilities and services should be fully appreciated in health care, in education, in preparing the faithful for the sacraments, in building community and in peacemaking. As the Synod Fathers noted, the presence of women in the Church's mission of love and service contributes greatly to bringing the compassionate Jesus, the healer and reconciler, to Asian people, especially the poor and marginalized.[225]

The Family

46. The family is the normal place where the young grow to personal and social maturity. It is also the bearer of the heritage of humanity itself, because through the family life is passed on from generation to generation. The family occupies a very important place in Asian cultures; and, as the Synod Fathers noted, family values like filial respect, love and care for the aged and the sick, love of children and harmony are held in high esteem in all Asian cultures and religious traditions.

Seen through Christian eyes, the family is "the domestic Church" (*ecclesia domestica*).[226] The Christian family, like the Church as a whole, should be a place where the truth of the Gospel is the rule of life and the gift which the family members bring to the wider community. The family is not simply the object of the Church's pastoral care; it is also one of the Church's most effective agents of evangelization. Christian families are today called to witness to the Gospel in difficult times and circumstances, when the family itself is threatened by an array of forces.[227] To be an agent of evangelization in such a time, the Christian family needs to be genuinely "the domestic Church", humbly and lovingly living out the Christian vocation.

As the Synod Fathers pointed out, this means that the family should be active in parish life, partaking of the sacraments, especially the Holy Eucharist and the Sacrament of Penance, and being involved in service to others. It also means that parents should strive to make the moments when the family naturally comes together an opportunity for prayer, for Bible reading and reflection, for appropriate rituals presided over by the parents and for healthy recreation. This will help the Christian family to become a hearth of evangelization, where each member experiences God's love and communicates it to others.[228] The Synod Fathers also acknowledged that children have a role in evangelization, both in their family and in the wider community.[229] Convinced that "the future of the world and of the Church passes through the family",[230] I once again propose for study and implementation what I wrote on the theme of the family in the Apostolic Exhortation *Familiaris Consortio*, following the Fifth Ordinary General Assembly of the Synod of Bishops in 1980.

Young People

47. The Synod Fathers were particularly sensitive to the theme of youth in the Church. The many complex problems which young people now face in the changing world of Asia impel the Church to remind the young of their responsibility for the future of society and the

Church, and to encourage and support them at every step to ensure that they are ready to accept that responsibility. To them the Church offers the truth of the Gospel as a joyful and liberating mystery to be known, lived and shared, with conviction and courage.

If young people are to be effective agents of mission, the Church needs to offer them suitable pastoral care.[231] In agreement with the Synod Fathers, I recommend that, where possible, every diocese in Asia should appoint youth chaplains or directors to promote the spiritual formation and apostolate of young people. Catholic schools and parishes have a vital role in providing all-round formation for the young, by seeking to lead them in the way of true discipleship and developing in them the human qualities that mission requires. Organized youth apostolates and youth clubs can provide the experience of Christian friendship which is so important for the young. The parish, and associations and movements, can help young people to cope better with social pressures by offering them not only a more mature growth in the Christian life but also help in the form of career guidance, vocational training and youth counselling.

The Christian formation of young people in Asia should recognize that they are not only the object of the Church's pastoral care but also "agents and co-workers in the Church's mission in her various apostolic works of love and service".[232] In parishes and dioceses, young men and women should therefore be invited to take part in the organization of activities which concern them. Their freshness and enthusiasm, their spirit of solidarity and hope can make them peacemakers in a divided world; and, on this score, it is encouraging to see young people involved in exchange programmes between the particular Churches and countries in Asia and elsewhere fostering interreligious and intercultural dialogue.

Social Communication

48. In an era of globalization, "the means of social communication have become so important as to be for many the chief means of information and education, of guidance and inspiration in their behaviour as individuals, families and within society at large. In particular, the younger generation is growing up in a world conditioned by the mass media".[233] The world is seeing the emergence of a new culture that "originates not just from whatever content is eventually expressed, but from the very fact that there exist new ways of communicating, with new languages, new techniques and a new psychology".[234] The exceptional role played by the means of social communication in shaping the world, its cultures and ways of thinking has led to rapid and far-reaching changes in Asian societies.

Inevitably, the Church's evangelizing mission too is deeply affected by the impact of the mass media. Since the mass media have an ever increasing influence even in remote areas of Asia, they can assist greatly in the proclamation of the Gospel to every corner of the continent. However, "it is not enough to use the media simply to spread the Christian message and the Church's authentic teaching. It is necessary to integrate that message into the 'new culture' created by modern communications".[235] To this end, the Church needs to explore ways of thoroughly integrating the mass media into her pastoral planning and activity, so that by their effective use the Gospel's power can reach out still further to individuals and entire peoples, and infuse Asian cultures with the values of the Kingdom.

I echo the Synod Fathers' commendation of *Radio Veritas Asia,* the only continent-wide radio station for the Church in Asia, for its almost thirty years of evangelization through broadcasting. Efforts must be made to strengthen this excellent instrument of mission, through appropriate language programming, personnel and financial help from Episcopal Conferences and Dioceses in Asia.[236] In addition to radio, Catholic publications and news agencies can help to disseminate information and offer continuing religious education and formation throughout the continent. In places where Christians are a minority, these can be an important means of sustaining and nurturing a sense of Catholic identity and of spreading knowledge of Catholic moral principles.[237]

I take up the recommendations of the Synod Fathers on the point of evangelization through social communications, the "areopagus of the modern age", in the hope that it may serve human promotion and the spreading of the truth of Christ and the teaching of the Church.[238] It would help if each Diocese would establish, where possible, a communications and media office. Media education, including the critical evaluation of media output, needs to be an increasing part of the formation of priests, seminarians, religious, catechists, lay professionals, students in Catholic schools and parish communities. Given the wide influence and extraordinary impact of the mass media, Catholics need to work with the members of other Churches and Ecclesial Communities, and with the followers of other religions to ensure a place for spiritual and moral values in the media. With the Synod Fathers, I encourage the development of pastoral plans for communications at the national and diocesan levels, following the indications of the Pastoral Instruction *Aetatis Novae*, with appropriate attention to the circumstances prevailing in Asia.

The Martyrs

49. However important programmes of formation and strategies for evangelization may be, in the end *it is martyrdom which reveals to the world the very essence of the Christian message.* The word itself, "martyr", means witness, and those who have shed their blood for Christ have borne the ultimate witness to the true value of the Gospel. In the Bull of Indiction of the Great Jubilee of the Year 2000, *Incarnationis Mysterium,* I stressed the vital importance of remembering the martyrs: "From the psychological point of view, martyrdom is the most eloquent proof of the truth of the faith, for faith can give a human face even to the most violent of deaths and show its beauty even in the midst of the most atrocious persecutions".[239] Through the ages, Asia has given the Church and the world a great host of these heroes of the faith, and from the heart of Asia there rises the great song of praise: *Te martyrum candidatus laudat exercitus.* This is the song of those who died for Christ on Asian soil in the first centuries of the Church, and it is also the joyful cry of men and women of more recent times like Saint Paul Miki and his companions, Saint Lorenzo Ruiz and his companions, Saint Andrew Dung Lac and his companions, Saint Andrew Kim Taegon and his companions. May the great host of Asian martyrs, old and new, never cease to teach the Church in Asia what it means to bear witness to the Lamb in whose blood they have washed their shining robes (cf. Rev 7:14)! May they stand as indomitable witnesses to the truth that Christians are called always and everywhere to proclaim nothing other than *the power of the Lord's Cross!* And may the blood of Asia's martyrs be now as always the seed of new life for the Church in every corner of the continent!

CONCLUSION

Gratitude and Encouragement

50. At the end of this Post-Synodal Apostolic Exhortation which, seeking to discern the Spirit's word to the Churches in Asia (cf. Rev 1:11), has endeavoured to set forth the fruits of the Special Assembly for Asia of the Synod of Bishops, I wish to express the Church's gratitude to all of you, dear Asian brothers and sisters, who have contributed in any way to the success of this important ecclesial event. First and foremost, we again praise God for the wealth of cultures, languages, traditions and religious sensibilities of this great continent. Blessed be God for the peoples of Asia, so rich in their diversity yet one in their yearning for peace and fullness of life. Especially now, in the immediate vicinity of the 2000th anniversary of the Birth of Jesus Christ, we thank God for choosing Asia as the earthly dwelling place of his incarnate Son, the Saviour of the world.

I cannot fail to express my appreciation to the Bishops of Asia for their deep love of Jesus Christ, the Church and the peoples of Asia, and for their testimony of communion and generous dedication to the task of evangelization. I am grateful to all those who form the great family of the Church in Asia: the clergy, the men and women religious and other consecrated persons, the missionaries, the laity, families, the young, indigenous peoples, workers, the poor and afflicted. Deep in my heart there is a special place for those in Asia who are persecuted for their faith in Christ. They are the hidden pillars of the Church, to whom Jesus himself speaks words of comfort: "You are blessed in the Kingdom of heaven" (cf. Mt 5:10).

The words of Jesus reassure the Church in Asia: "Fear not, little flock, for it is your Father's good pleasure to give you the Kingdom" (Lk 12:32). Those who believe in Christ are still a small minority in this vast and most populous continent. Yet far from being a timid minority, they are lively in faith, full of the hope and vitality which only love can bring. In their humble and courageous way, they have influenced the cultures and societies of Asia, especially the lives of the poor and the helpless, many of whom do not share the Catholic faith. They are an example to Christians everywhere to be eager to share the treasure of the Good News "in season and out of season" (2 Tim 4:2). They find strength in the wondrous power of the Holy Spirit who, despite the generally small numbers of the Church in Asia, ensures that the Church's presence is like the yeast which mixes with the flour in a quiet and hidden way till it is all leavened (cf. Mt 13:33).

The peoples of Asia need Jesus Christ and his Gospel. Asia is thirsting for the living water that Jesus alone can give (cf. Jn 4:10–15). The disciples of Christ in Asia must therefore be unstinting in their efforts to fulfil the mission they have received from the Lord, who has promised to be with them to the end of the age (cf. Mt 28:20). Trusting in the Lord who will not fail those whom he has called, the Church in Asia joyfully makes her pilgrim way into the Third Millennium. Her only joy is that which comes from sharing with the multitude of Asia's peoples the immense gift which she herself has received—the love of Jesus the Saviour. Her one ambition is to continue his mission of service and love, so that all Asians "may have life and have it abundantly" (Jn 10:10).

Prayer to the Mother of Christ

51. Faced with such a challenging mission, we turn to Mary, for whom, as the Synod Fathers said, Asian Christians have a great love and affection, revering her as their own Mother and the Mother of Christ.[240] Throughout Asia there are hundreds of Marian sanctuaries and shrines where not only the Catholic faithful gather, but also believers of other religions too.

To Mary, model of all disciples and bright Star of Evangelization, I entrust the Church in Asia at the threshold of the Third Millennium of the Christian era, trusting absolutely that hers is an ear that always listens, hers a heart that always welcomes, and hers a prayer that never fails:

O Holy Mary, Daughter of the Most High God,
Virgin Mother of the Saviour and Mother of us all,
look tenderly upon the Church of your Son
planted on Asian soil.
Be her guide and model
as she continues your Son's mission
of love and service in Asia.

You fully and freely accepted the Father's call
to be the Mother of God;
teach us to empty our hearts
of all that is not of God,
that we too may be filled
with the Holy Spirit from on high.
You pondered the mysteries of God's will
in the silence of your heart;
help us on our journey
to discern the signs of God's powerful hand.
You went quickly to visit Elizabeth
and help in her days of waiting;
obtain for us the same spirit of zeal and service
in our evangelizing task.
You sang the praises of the Lord;
lead us in joyful proclamation of faith
in Christ our Saviour.
You had compassion on the needy
and spoke to your Son on their behalf;
teach us never to fear
to speak of the world to Jesus
and of Jesus to the world.
You stood at the foot of the Cross
as your Son breathed his last;
be with us as we seek to be one
in spirit and service with all who suffer.
You prayed with the disciples in the Upper Room;
help us to wait upon the Spirit
and to go wherever he leads us.

Protect the Church from all the powers
that threaten her.
Help her to be a true image
of the Most Holy Trinity.
Pray that through the Church's love and service
all the peoples of Asia may come
to know your Son
Jesus Christ, the only Saviour of the world,
and so taste the joy of life in all its fullness.
O Mary, Mother of the New Creation
and Mother of Asia,
pray for us, your children, now and always!

Given at New Delhi, in India, on the sixth day of November in the year 1999, the twenty-second of my Pontificate.

JOHN PAUL II

INDEX

Introduction

Chapter I
The Asian Context

Asia, the Birthplace of Jesus and of the Church [5]
Religious and Cultural Realities [6]
Economic and Social Realities [7]
Political Realities [8]
The Church in Asia: Past and Present [9]

Chapter II
Jesus the Saviour: A Gift to Asia

The Gift of Faith [10]
Jesus Christ, the God-Man Who Saves [11]
The Person and Mission of the Son of God [12]
Jesus Christ: the Truth of Humanity [13]
The Uniqueness and Universality of Salvation in Jesus [14]

Chapter III
The Holy Spirit: Lord and Giver of Life

The Spirit of God in Creation and History [15]
The Holy Spirit and the Incarnation of the Word [16]
The Holy Spirit and the Body of Christ [17]
The Holy Spirit and the Church's Mission in Asia [18]

Chapter IV
Jesus the Saviour: Proclaiming the Gift

The Primacy of Proclamation [19]
Proclaiming Jesus Christ in Asia [20]
The Challenge of Inculturation [21]
Key Areas of Inculturation [22]
Christian Life as Proclamation [23]

Chapter V
Communion and Dialogue for Mission

Communion and Mission Go Hand in Hand [24]
Communion within the Church [25]
Solidarity among the Churches [26]
The Catholic Eastern Churches [27]
Sharing Hopes and Sufferings [28]
A Mission of Dialogue [29]
Ecumenical Dialogue [30]
Interreligious Dialogue [31]

Chapter VI
The Service of Human Promotion

The Social Doctrine of the Church [32]
The Dignity of the Human Person [33]
Preferential Love of the Poor [34]
The Gospel of Life [35]
Health Care [36]
Education [37]

Notes

(1) John Paul II, Address to the Sixth Plenary Assembly of the Federation of Asian Bishops' Conferences (FABC), Manila (15 January 1995), 11: *Insegnamenti* XVIII, 1 (1995), 159.

(2) Apostolic Letter *Tertio Millennio Adveniente* (10 November 1994), 38: *AAS* 87 (1995), 30.

(3) No. 11: *Insegnamenti* XVIII, 1 (1995), 159.

(4) John Paul II, Apostolic Letter *Tertio Millennio Adveniente* (10 November 1994), 38: *AAS* 87 (1995), 30.

(5) Cf. Special Assembly for Asia of the Synod of Bishops, *Nuntius (Final Message)*, 2.

(6) Address to the Sixth Plenary Assembly of the Federation of Asian Bishops' Conferences (FABC), Manila (15 January 1995), 10: *Insegnamenti* XVIII, 1 (1995), 159.

(7) John Paul II, *Letter Concerning Pilgrimage to the Places Linked to the History of Salvation* (29 June 1999), 3: *L'Osservatore Romano* (30 June–1 July 1999), 8.

(8) Cf. *Propositio* 3.

(9) *Propositio* 1.

(10) Cf. Special Assembly for Asia of the Synod of Bishops, *Lineamenta,* 3.

(11) Cf. *ibid.*

(12) Cf. *Propositio* 32.

(13) Cf. Special Assembly for Asia of the Synod of Bishops, *Instrumentum Laboris*, 9.

(14) Cf. *Propositiones* 36 and 50.

(15) *Propositio* 44.

(16) *Propositio* 27.

(17) Cf. *Propositio* 45.

(18) Special Assembly for Asia of the Synod of Bishops, *Instrumentum Laboris*, 9.

(19) Cf. *Propositio* 39.

(20) *Propositio* 35.

(21) Cf. *Propositio* 38.

(22) Cf. *Propositio* 22.

(23) Cf. *Propositio* 52.

(24) Cf. Special Assembly for Asia of the Synod of Bishops, *Lineamenta*, 6.

(25) Cf. *Propositio* 56.

(26) John Paul II, Apostolic Letter *Tertio Millennio Adveniente* (10 November 1994), 18: *AAS* 87 (1995), 16.

(27) Cf. *Propositio* 29.

(28) Cf. *Propositiones* 29 and 31.

(29) *Propositio* 51.

(30) Cf. *Propositiones* 51, 52 and 53.

(31) *Propositio* 57.

(32) Cf. *ibid.*

(33) *Propositio* 54.

(34) No. 3: *AAS* 83 (1991), 252.

(35) Cf. *Propositio* 5.

(36) Special Assembly for Asia of the Synod of Bishops, *Relatio ante disceptationem*: *L'Osservatore Romano* (22 April 1998), 5.

(37) Special Assembly for Asia of the Synod of Bishops, *Relatio post disceptationem*, 3.

(38) *Propositio* 8.

(39) No. 11: *AAS* 83 (1991), 260.

(40) *Ibid.*

(41) Special Assembly for Asia of the Synod of Bishops, *Relatio post disceptationem*, 3.

(42) *Roman Missal*: Eucharistic Prayer I for Masses of Reconciliation.

(43) John Paul II, Encyclical Letter *Redemptor Hominis* (4 March 1979), 10: *AAS* 71 (1979), 274.

(44) Pastoral Constitution on the Church in the Modern World *Gaudium et Spes*, 22.

(45) No. 9: *AAS* 71 (1979), 272f.

(46) Special Assembly for Asia of the Synod of Bishops, *Relatio post disceptationem*, 3.

(47) Cf. *ibid.*

(48) *Ibid.*

(49) *Propositio* 5.

(50) John Paul II, Encyclical Letter *Redemptoris Missio* (7 December 1990), 6: *AAS* 83 (1991), 255.

(51) John Paul II, Encyclical Letter *Redemptor Hominis* (4 March 1979), 7: *AAS* 71 (1979), 269.

(52) Cf. John Paul II, Encyclical Letter *Dominum et Vivificantem* (18 May 1986), 54: *AAS* 78 (1986), 875.

(53) Cf. *ibid.*, 59: *loc. cit.*, 885.

(54) John Paul II, Encyclical Letter *Redemptoris Missio* (7 December 1990), 28: *AAS* 83 (1991), 274; cf. Second Vatican Ecumenical Council, Pastoral Constitution on the Church in the Modern World *Gaudium et Spes*, 26.

(55) Cf. *Propositio* 11; Second Vatican Ecumenical Council, Decree on the Missionary Activity of the Church *Ad Gentes*, 4 and 15; Dogmatic Constitution on the Church *Lumen Gentium*, 17; Pastoral Constitution on the Church in the Modern World *Gaudium et Spes*, 11, 22 and 38; John Paul II, Encyclical Letter *Redemptoris Missio* (7 December 1990), 28: *AAS* 83 (1991), 273f.

(56) Cf. Special Assembly for Asia of the Synod of Bishops, *Relatio ante disceptationem*: *L'Osservatore Romano* (22 April 1998), 5.

(57) John Paul II, Encyclical Letter *Dominum et Vivificantem,* (18 May 1986), 50: *AAS* 78 (1986), 870; cf. Saint Thomas Aquinas, *Summa Theologiae*, III, 2, 10–12; 6, 6; 7, 13.

(58) Cf. John Paul II, Encyclical Letter *Dominum et Vivificantem* (18 May 1986), 50: *AAS* 78 (1986), 870.

(59) Cf. *ibid.*, 24: *loc. cit.*, 832.

(60) Cf. John Paul II, Encyclical Letter *Redemptoris Missio* (7 December 1990), 28: *AAS* 83 (1991), 274.

(61) No. 29: *AAS* 83 (1991), 275; cf. Second Vatican Ecumenical Council, Pastoral Constitution on the Church in the Modern World *Gaudium et Spes*, 45.

(62) Cf. John Paul II, Encyclical Letter *Redemptoris Missio* (7 December 1990), 29: *AAS* 83 (1991), 275.

(63) Cf. Second Vatican Ecumenical Council, Dogmatic Constitution on the Church *Lumen Gentium*, 13.

(64) *Propositio* 12.

(65) Dogmatic Constitution on the Church *Lumen Gentium*, 17.

(66) Apostolic Exhortation *Evangelii Nuntiandi* (8 December 1975), 22: *AAS* 68 (1976), 20.

(67) *Propositio* 8.

(68) John Paul II, Encyclical Letter *Redemptoris Missio* (7 December 1990), 45: *AAS* 83 (1991), 292.

(69) Cf. *ibid.*, 46: *loc. cit.*, 292f.

(70) Cf. Second Vatican Ecumenical Council, Declaration on Religious Freedom *Dignitatis Humanae*, 3–4; John Paul II, Encyclical Letter *Redemptoris Missio* (7 December 1990), 39: *AAS* 83 (1991), 287; *Propositio* 40.

(71) Paul VI, Apostolic Exhortation *Evangelii Nuntiandi* (8 December 1975), 53: *AAS* 68 (1976), 41f.

(72) Address to Representatives of Non-Christians Religions, Madras (5 February 1986), 2: *AAS* 78 (1986), 767.

(73) Cf. *Propositiones* 11 and 12; John Paul II, Encyclical Letter *Redemptoris Missio* (7 December 1990), 28: *AAS* 83 (1991), 273f.

(74) Special Assembly for Asia of the Synod of Bishops, *Relatio ante disceptationem*: *L'Osservatore Romano* (22 April 1998), 5.

(75) *Propositio* 58.

(76) Cf. *John Paul II, Encyclical Letter Fides et Ratio* (14 September 1998), 72: *AAS* 91 (1999), 61.

(77) Special Assembly for Asia of the Synod of Bishops, *Relatio post disceptationem,* 15.

(78) Cf. *ibid.*

(79) *Ibid.*

(80) *Propositio* 6.

(81) Cf. Special Assembly for Asia of the Synod of Bishops, *Relatio post disceptationem,* 6.

(82) *Ibid.*

(83) Cf. Special Assembly for Asia of the Synod of Bishops, *Relatio ante disceptationem*: *L'Osservatore Romano* (22 April 1998), 5.

(84) Cf. Apostolic Exhortation *Evangelii Nuntiandi* (8 December 1975), 20: *AAS* 68 (1976), 18f.

(85) John Paul II, Encyclical Letter *Redemptoris Missio* (7 December 1990), 52: *AAS* 83 (1991), 300.

(86) Cf. Special Assembly for Asia of the Synod of Bishops, *Relatio post disceptationem,* 9.

(87) Cf. Second Vatican Ecumenical Council, Pastoral Constitution on the Church in the Modern World *Gaudium et Spes*, 22; John Paul II, Encyclical Letter *Redemptoris Missio* (7 December 1990), 28: *AAS* 83 (1991), 273f.

(88) Cf. John Paul II, Encyclical Letter *Redemptoris Missio* (7 December 1990), 56: *AAS* 83 (1991), 304.

(89) John Paul II, Homily at the Mass for the Catholics of West Bengal, Calcutta (4 February 1986), 3: *Insegnamenti* IX, 1 (1986), 314.

(90) Cf. *Propositio* 43.

(91) Cf. *Propositio* 7.

(92) *Ibid.*

(93) John Paul II, Encyclical Letter *Redemptoris Missio* (7 December 1990), 54: *AAS* 83 (1991), 302.

(94) Cf. *ibid.: loc. cit.,* 301.

(95) Cf. Second Vatican Ecumenical Council, Constitution on the Sacred Liturgy *Sacrosanctum Concilium*, 10; Special Assembly for Asia of the Synod of Bishops, *Relatio post disceptationem,* 14.

(96) Cf. Special Assembly for Asia of the Synod of Bishops, *Relatio post disceptationem,* 14; *Propositio* 43.

(97) Cf. *Propositio* 43.

(98) Cf. Special Assembly for Asia of the Synod of Bishops, *Relatio post disceptationem,* 13.

(99) Cf. *Propositio* 17.

(100) Cf. *Propositio* 18.

(101) Cf. *Propositio* 17.

(102) Nos. 60; 62; 105: *AAS* 91 (1999), 52f.; 54; 85f.

(103) Cf. *Propositio* 24.

(104) Cf. *Propositio* 25.

(105) Cf. *ibid.*

(106) Cf. *Propositio* 27.

(107) Cf. *Propositio* 29.

(108) Cf. Encyclical Letter *Redemptoris Missio* (7 December 1990), 91: *AAS* 83 (1991), 338.

(109) *Propositio* 19.

(110) *Propositio* 8.

(111) Declaration on Religious Freedom *Dignitatis Humanae*, 2.

(112) *Propositio* 6.

(113) Saint Augustine, *De Civitate Dei*, XVIII, 51, 2: *PL* 41, 614; cf. Second Vatican Ecumenical Council, Dogmatic Constitution on the Church *Lumen Gentium*, 8.

(114) Second Vatican Ecumenical Council, Decree on the Missionary Activity of the Church *Ad Gentes*, 7; cf. Dogmatic Constitution on the Church *Lumen Gentium*, 17.

(115) Paul VI, Address to the College of Cardinals (22 June 1973): *AAS* 65 (1973), 391.

(116) John Paul II, Post-Synodal Apostolic Exhortation *Christifideles Laici* (30 December 1988), 18: *AAS* 81 (1989), 421.

(117) Cf. *ibid.*; Second Vatican Ecumenical Council, Dogmatic Constitution on the Church *Lumen Gentium*, 4.

(118) Cf. *Catechism of the Catholic Church*, 775.

(119) Cf. *ibid.*

(120) John Paul II, Post-Synodal Apostolic Exhortation *Christifideles Laici* (30 December 1988), 32: *AAS* 81 (1989), 451f.

(121) Cf. Dogmatic Constitution on the Church *Lumen Gentium*, 16.

(122) *Propositio* 13.

(123) *Ibid.*

(124) Cf. Special Assembly for Asia of the Synod of Bishops, *Relatio ante disceptationem*: *L'Osservatore Romano* (22 April 1998), 6.

(125) *Propositio* 13; cf. Second Vatican Ecumenical Council, Dogmatic Constitution on the Church *Lumen Gentium*, 22.

(126) Cf. *Propositio* 13.

(127) Cf. *Propositio* 15; Congregation for the Doctrine of the Faith, Letter to the Bishops of the Catholic Church on Some Aspects of the Church Understood as Communion *Communionis Notio* (28 May 1992), 3–10: *AAS* 85 (1993), 839–844.

(128) Cf. *Propositio* 15.

(129) Cf. *ibid.*

(130) Cf. *Propositio* 16.

(131) *Propositio* 34.

(132) Cf. *Propositio* 30; cf. John Paul II, Encyclical Letter *Redemptoris Missio* (7 December 1990), 51: *AAS* 83 (1991), 298.

(133) Cf. Apostolic Exhortation *Evangelii Nuntiandi* (8 December 1975), 58: *AAS* 68 (1976), 46–49; John Paul II, Encyclical Letter *Redemptoris Missio*, 51: *AAS* 83 (1991), 299.

(134) Cf. *Propositio* 31.

(135) Cf. *Propositio* 14.

(136) Cf. Special Assembly for Asia of the Synod of Bishops, *Relatio ante disceptationem*: *L'Osservatore Romano* (22 April 1998), 6.

(137) Cf. *Propositio* 50.

(138) Cf. *Propositiones* 36 and 50.

(139) Cf. John Paul II, Address to the Synod of Bishops of the Syro-Malabar Church (8 January 1996), 6: *AAS* 88 (1996), 41.

(140) Cf. *Propositio* 50.

(141) Cf. *Propositio* 56.

(142) Cf. *Propositio* 51.

(143) Cf. *Propositio* 52.

(144) *Propositio* 53.

(145) Cf. *Propositio* 57.

(146) Cf. *Letter Concerning Pilgrimage to the Places Linked to the History of Salvation* (29 June 1999), 7: *L'Osservatore Romano* (30 June–1 July 1999), 9.

(147) *AAS* 56 (1964), 613.

(148) Cf. *Propositio* 42.

(149) *Ibid.*

(150) John Paul II, Address at the General Audience (26 July 1995), 4: *Insegnamenti* XVIII, 2 (1995), 138.

(151) Cf. John Paul II, Address at the General Audience (20 January 1982), 2: *Insegnamenti* V, 1 (1982), 162.

(152) Cf. No. 53: *AAS* 87 (1995), 37.

(153) Cf. John Paul II, Encyclical Letter *Redemptoris Missio* (7 December 1990), 55: *AAS* 83 (1991), 302.

(154) Cf. *ibid.*: *loc. cit.*, 304.

(155) No. 4: *AAS* 83 (1991), 101f.

(156) No. 56: *AAS* 83 (1991), 304.

(157) *Propositio* 41.

(158) *Ibid.*

(159) Cf. *ibid.*

(160) Cf. John Paul II, Encyclical Letter *Redemptoris Missio* (7 December 1990), 57: *AAS* 83 (1991), 305.

(161) Cf. John Paul II, Post-Synodal Apostolic Exhortation *Vita Consecrata* (25 March, 1996), 8: *AAS* 88 (1996), 383.

(162) Cf. John Paul II, Encyclical Letter *Sollicitudo Rei Socialis* (30 December 1987), 47: *AAS* 80 (1988), 582.

(163) Pastoral Constitution on the Church in the Modern World *Gaudium et Spes*, 1.

(164) In many ways the point of departure was the Encyclical Letter *Rerum Novarum* of Pope Leo XIII (15 May 1891) which ushered in a series of solemn Church statements on various aspects of the social question. Among these was the Encyclical Letter *Populorum Progressio* (26 March 1967) which Pope Paul VI issued in response to the teachings of the Second Vatican Council and a changed world situation. To commemorate the twentieth anniversary of that Encyclical, I released the Encyclical Letter *Sollicitudo Rei Socialis* (30 December 1987) in which, following the earlier Magisterium, I invited all the faithful to see themselves as called to a mission of service which necessarily includes the promotion of integral human development.

(165) John Paul II, Encyclical Letter *Sollicitudo Rei Socialis* (30 December 1987), 41: *AAS* 80 (1988), 570f.

(166) Cf. Congregation for the Doctrine of the Faith, Instruction on Christian Freedom and Liberation *Libertatis Conscientia* (22 March 1986), 72: *AAS* 79 (1987), 586.

(167) Cf. *Propositio* 22.

(168) Cf. *Propositio* 21.

(169) Cf. John Paul II, Post-Synodal Apostolic Exhortation *Christifideles Laici* (30 December 1988), 5: *AAS* 81 (1989), 400–402; Encyclical Letter *Evangelium Vitae* (25 March 1995), 18: *AAS* 87 (1995), 419f.

(170) *Propositio* 22; cf. *Propositio* 39.

(171) John Paul II, Encyclical Letter *Sollicitudo Rei Socialis* (30 December 1987), 42: *AAS* 80 (1988), 573; cf. Congregation for the Doctrine of the Faith, Instruction on Christian Freedom and Liberation *Libertatis Conscientia* (22 March 1986), 68: *AAS* 79 (1987), 583.

(172) Cf. *Propositio* 44.

(173) Cf. *ibid.*

(174) Cf. *Propositio* 39.

(175) Cf. *Propositio* 22.

(176) Cf. *Propositio* 36.

(177) Cf. *Propositio* 38.

(178) Cf. *ibid.*

(179) Cf. *Propositio* 33.

(180) Cf. *ibid.*

(181) Cf. *Propositio* 35.

(182) Cf. *ibid.*

(183) *Propositio* 32.

(184) Cf. John Paul II, Apostolic Letter *Salvifici Doloris* (11 February 1984), 28–29: *AAS* 76 (1984), 242–244.

(185) Cf. *Propositio* 20.

(186) Cf. *ibid.*

(187) Cf. *Propositio* 21.

(188) Cf. *ibid.*

(189) Cf. *ibid.*

(190) Cf. *Propositio* 23.

(191) Cf. *ibid.*

(192) Cf. *Propositio* 55.

(193) Cf. *Propositio* 49.

(194) John Paul II, *Message for the World Day of Peace* (1 January 1998), 3: *AAS* 90 (1998), 50.

(195) Cf. *Propositio* 49.

(196) Cf. *Propositio* 48.

(197) Cf. *ibid.*; John Paul II, Apostolic Letter *Tertio Millennio Adveniente* (10 November 1994), 51: *AAS* 87 (1995), 36.

(198) Cf. *Propositio* 48.

(199) Cf. *Propositio* 22; John Paul II, Encyclical Letter *Sollicitudo Rei Socialis* (30 December 1987), 44: *AAS* 80 (1988), 576f.

(200) Cf. John Paul II, Encyclical Letter *Redemptor Hominis* (4 March 1979), 15: *AAS* 71 (1979), 287.

(201) Cf. *ibid.*

(202) Cf. *Propositio* 47.

(203) *Homilies on the Gospel of Matthew,* 50, 3–4: *PG* 58, 508–509.

(204) Cf. Decree on the Church's Missionary Activity *Ad Gentes*, 2 and 35.

(205) Cf. John Paul II, Encyclical Letter *Redemptoris Missio* (7 December 1990), 31: *AAS* 83 (1991), 277.

(206) *Ibid.* 42: *loc. cit.*, 289.

(207) *Ibid.*

(208) Cf. *Propositio* 25.

(209) Cf. *ibid.*

(210) Cf. Dogmatic Constitution on the Church *Lumen Gentium*, 46.

(211) Cf. *Propositio* 27.

(212) Cf. John Paul II, Post-Synodal Apostolic Exhortation *Vita Consecrata* (25 March 1996), 103: *AAS* 88 (1996), 479.

(213) Cf. Paul VI, Apostolic Exhortation *Evangelii Nuntiandi* (8 December 1975), 69: *AAS* 68 (1976), 59.

(214) Cf. *Propositio* 27.

(215) Cf. *ibid.*

(216) Cf. *ibid.*

(217) Cf. *Propositio* 28.

(218) *Ibid.*

(219) Cf. Dogmatic Constitution on the Church *Lumen Gentium*, 31.

(220) Cf. *Propositio* 29.

(221) Cf. *ibid.*

(222) Cf. *ibid.*

(223) John Paul II, Address at the General Audience (13 July 1994), 4: *Insegnamenti* XVII, 2 (1994), 40.

(224) Cf. *Propositio* 35.

(225) Cf. *ibid.*

(226) Second Vatican Ecumenical Council, Dogmatic Constitution on the Church *Lumen Gentium*, 11.

(227) Cf. Special Assembly for Asia of the Synod of Bishops, *Relatio ante disceptationem*: *L'Osservatore Romano* (22 April 1998), 6.

(228) Cf. *Propositio* 32.

(229) Cf. *Propositio* 33.

(230) John Paul II, Address to the Confederation of Family Advisory Bureaus of Christian Inspiration (29 November 1980), 4: *Insegnamenti* III, 2 (1980), 1454.

(231) Cf. *Propositio* 34.

(232) *Ibid.*

(233) John Paul II, Encyclical Letter *Redemptoris Missio* (7 December 1990), 37: *AAS* 83 (1991), 285.

(234) *Ibid.*

(235) *Ibid.*

(236) Cf. *Propositio* 45.

(237) Cf. *ibid.*

(238) Cf. *ibid.*

(239) No. 13: *AAS* 91 (1999), 142.

(240) Cf. *Propositio* 59.

Index